P9-AGT-056

iPhone® Game Development

iPhone® Game Development

Chris Craft and Jamey McElveen

WILEY

Wiley Publishing, Inc.

JUDITH ZAFFIRINI LIBRARY

iPhone® Game Development

Published by
Wiley Publishing, Inc.
10475 Crosspoint Boulevard
Indianapolis, IN 46256
www.wiley.com

Copyright © 2010 by Wiley Publishing, Inc., Indianapolis, Indiana

Published by Wiley Publishing, Inc., Indianapolis, Indiana

Published simultaneously in Canada

ISBN: 978-0-470-49666-4

Manufactured in the United States of America

10 9 8 7 6 5 4 3 2 1

No part of this publication may be reproduced, stored in a retrieval system or transmitted in any form or by any means, electronic, mechanical, photocopying, recording, scanning or otherwise, except as permitted under Sections 107 or 108 of the 1976 United States Copyright Act, without either the prior written permission of the Publisher, or authorization through payment of the appropriate per-copy fee to the Copyright Clearance Center, 222 Rosewood Drive, Danvers, MA 01923, (978) 750-8400, fax (978) 646-8600. Requests to the Publisher for permission should be addressed to the Permissions Department, John Wiley & Sons, Inc., 111 River Street, Hoboken, NJ 07030, 201-748-6011, fax 201-748-6008, or online at http://www.wiley.com/go/permissions.

LIMIT OF LIABILITY/DISCLAIMER OF WARRANTY: THE PUBLISHER AND THE AUTHORS MAKE NO REPRESENTATIONS OR WARRANTIES WITH RESPECT TO THE ACCURACY OR COMPLETENESS OF THE CONTENTS OF THIS WORK AND SPECIFICALLY DISCLAIM ALL WARRANTIES, INCLUDING WITHOUT LIMITATION WARRANTIES OF FITNESS FOR A PARTICULAR PURPOSE. NO WARRANTY MAY BE CREATED OR EXTENDED BY SALES OR PROMOTIONAL MATERIALS. THE ADVICE AND STRATEGIES CONTAINED HEREIN MAY NOT BE SUITABLE FOR EVERY SITUATION. THIS WORK IS SOLD WITH THE UNDERSTANDING THAT THE PUBLISHER IS NOT ENGAGED IN RENDERING LEGAL, ACCOUNTING, OR OTHER PROFESSIONAL SERVICES. IF PROFESSIONAL ASSISTANCE IS REQUIRED, THE SERVICES OF A COMPETENT PROFESSIONAL PERSON SHOULD BE SOUGHT. NEITHER THE PUBLISHER NOR THE AUTHORS SHALL BE LIABLE FOR DAMAGES ARISING HEREFROM. THE FACT THAT AN ORGANIZATION OR WEBSITE IS REFERRED TO IN THIS WORK AS A CITATION AND/OR A POTENTIAL SOURCE OF FURTHER INFORMATION DOES NOT MEAN THAT THE AUTHORS OR THE PUBLISHER ENDORSES THE INFORMATION THE ORGANIZATION OR WEBSITE MAY PROVIDE OR RECOMMENDATIONS IT MAY MAKE. FURTHER, READERS SHOULD BE AWARE THAT INTERNET WEBSITES LISTED IN THIS WORK MAY HAVE CHANGED OR DISAPPEARED BETWEEN WHEN THIS WORK WAS WRITTEN AND WHEN IT IS READ.

QA
76.8
.I64
C73
2010

For general information on our other products and services or to obtain technical support, please contact our Customer Care Department within the U.S. at (877) 762-2974, outside the U.S. at (317) 572-3993 or fax (317) 572-4002.

Library of Congress Control Number: 2009936818

Trademarks: Wiley, the Wiley logo, and related trade dress are trademarks or registered trademarks of John Wiley & Sons, Inc. and/or its affiliates, in the United States and other countries, and may not be used without written permission. iPhone is a registered trademark of Apple, Inc. All other trademarks are the property of their respective owners. Wiley Publishing, Inc., is not associated with any product or vendor mentioned in this book.

Wiley also publishes its books in a variety of electronic formats. Some content that appears in print may not be available in electronic books.

MAR 2 4 2010

*This book is dedicated to the two most important women
in my life: Mom, without your many sacrifices,
nothing would have been possible;
and Kathy, the love of my life, your love and patience strengthens me.*
—Chris

*To my wife and kids, who made this possible,
I thank God for all of you.*
—Jamey

About the Authors

Chris Craft is a software developer focusing primarily on device application development. He is a frequent CodeProject.com article author. Chris currently serves as a senior software architect for ACS Technologies Group, Inc., where he concentrates on his passion: mobile development. He previously was a senior developer for Taylor Data Systems, where he worked on sales force automation, field service, inventory, and data collection mobile applications. In the technical community, Chris is cofounder of a local developer user group and is also a member of Revolution Church. He has recently become engaged to Kathy Gulledge of Florence, South Carolina.

Jamey McElveen has been a game development enthusiast since 1995. He began coding games back in the days of DOS. With the release of the iPhone SDK he was one of the developers in the original gold rush to the App Store. Jamey works in Florence, South Carolina, as lead software architect at ACS Technologies Group, Inc. He is passionate about software and its role in Christianity and the field of Ministry. Jamey obtained his degree in Computer Engineering from Clemson University. He lives with his wife, Connie, and three boys, Jake, Slater, and Seth, in Timmonsville, South Carolina.

Chris and Jamey are the founders of the popular iPhone development site, http://appsamuck. com. They released their first training example the first day the NDA was lifted from the 2.0 SDK: 10/1/2008. They continued the series every day for 31 days until 10/31/2008.

Credits

Acquisitions Editor
Aaron Black

Executive Editor
Jody Lefevere

Project Editor
Lynn Northrup

Technical Editor
Jesse David Hollington

Editorial Director
Robyn Siesky

Editorial Manager
Cricket Krengel

Business Manager
Amy Knies

Senior Marketing Manager
Sandy Smith

Vice President and Executive Group Publisher
Richard Swadley

Vice President and Executive Publisher
Barry Pruett

Project Coordinator
Kristie Rees

Graphics and Production Specialists
Andrea Hornberger
Jennifer Mayberry

Proofreading
Laura L. Bowman

Indexing
BIM Indexing & Proofreading Services

Media Development Project Manager
Laura Moss

Media Development Assistant Project Manager
Jenny Swisher

Media Development Associate Producer
Doug Kuhn

Contents

Part II: Creating Simple iPhone Applications 61

Part III: Shall We Play a Game? 149

Acknowledgments

Several people played an important role in the making of this book and we would like to acknowledge them here.

Most importantly, we would like to thank our Almighty God for the ability to learn, share, and many more reasons too numerous to count.

We would like to thank ACS Technologies Group, Inc., and its staff for their support and encouragement during this endeavor.

We would like to thank Wiley Publishing for having faith in two new authors with a passion for iPhone development. We would like to thank our acquisitions editor, Aaron Black, and our technical reviewer, Jesse David Hollington. We would like to thank our project editor, Lynn Northrup, for having the patience to initiate two new authors.

We would like to thank our reviewers, Page Brooks, Josh Hamrick, Alfonso Acevedo, Dayton Pruet, and Thorben C. Primke, for their insight and valued perspective.

Jamey McElveen would like to thank his wife, Connie, for her love, support, and encouragement during this endeavor. He would like to thank his boys, Jake, Slater, and Seth, for their understanding and extra efforts to help their dad out when he needed it. Jamey would also like to thank his mom, dad, and the rest of his family and friends for all their support and encouragement during this project. Finally, he would like to thank his friend and co-author, Chris, for encouraging him to take on this project in the first place and helping to push through the long hours together.

Chris Craft would like to thank his fiancée, Kathy, for her love, support, and encouragement. He would like to thank his mom, brother, and close friend, Shawn Morris, for their support and encouragement during this project.

Introduction

It was liberating to the computer industry when computers finally became small enough to take home and set up on a desk. As the technology has gotten smaller and more portable, it has continued to grow in power. The device and the components also became less expensive as the years and months passed. Soon all the components were consolidated into one device and we began using notebook computers that we could use in our laps.

In 1993, Apple had a vision for mobile computing that they first implemented in their device, the Newton Message Pad. This was a device that allowed you to do simple day-to-day tasks in the palm of your hand. Although it was not a successful venture for Apple at the time, we believe this was a pivotal milestone for the modern PDA. Others entered the PDA market, cell phones became the norm, and Apple introduced the iPod. In 2007, Apple took the best from all these mobile innovations and wrapped them together in the device you know today as the iPhone.

In summer 2008 Apple began allowing developers to write custom applications for the iPhone and sell them in their hugely successful App Store. We are realizing that these technologies that Apple has cleverly combined will synergize if leveraged with the right application. As we move forward with the iPhone we see the potential for applications that can connect people in ways we may not have considered until now.

iPhone Game Development is about releasing the potential to use this small but powerful device to host games that are fun, engaging, and just as powerful as the device they run on. Use the material in this book to help you bring your creations to life. We aim to help you explore beyond just porting your favorite games to a new platform and see the iPhone for its potential to connect and share experiences with other players.

How This Book Is Organized

If you are new to iPhone development, we suggest reading Part I to help you get started. The first steps in iPhone development can be some of the toughest ones, and they can be make-or-break points for many developers. The instructions in Part I can help new developers overcome these obstacles. If you are not new to iPhone development, feel free to skip ahead to Part II to begin learning game development.

iPhone Game Development is organized into five main parts:

Part I: Beginning iPhone Programming

This part of the book helps developers who may be new to iPhone development get started. There is much more to developing applications for the iPhone than just syntax and compiling. The chapters in this part keep you pointed in the right direction.

Part II: Creating Simple iPhone Applications

This part of the book gets you started creating basic games for the iPhone. If you are not new to iPhone development but you are new to iPhone game development, this is where you will want to begin. Many profitable games are still being sold today that use only the basic technologies discussed in these chapters.

Part III: Shall We Play a Game?

In this part we up the ante a little. The technologies introduced in this section help you move your creations to the next level. Even if you already have a successful game, you can use techniques discussed in these chapters to improve your game with Facebook integration, peer-to-peer connectivity, or global networking. These additions can lead to the holy grail of game sales: viral marketing.

Part IV: Advanced Technical and Business Programming Concepts

The chapters in this part cover advanced techniques you may want to pursue later. We have included a chapter on grasping advanced programming topics to serve as a catalyst for beginning to learn advanced techniques that you may wish to include in your game. The chapter on understanding the business of software helps you understand what to expect on the App Store and how to use strategies that other developers have used to get better results. We also discuss cost-effective ways to generate more sales and make your applications even more successful.

Part V: Appendixes

Check this part of the book for a list of useful links, books, and other helpful resources; a look at our 31 days of iPhone applications from http://appsamuck.com; and a glossary for concise definitions of terms that are helpful for you to know as you get started in iPhone game development.

Icons Used in This Book

To make this book as usable as possible, icons in the margins alert you to special or important information. Look for the following:

CAUTION
The Caution icon offers important information about a procedure to which you should pay particular attention.

CROSS-REFERENCE
The Cross-Reference icon refers you to a related topic elsewhere in the book. Because you may not read this book straight through from cover to cover, you can use cross-references to quickly find the information you need.

NOTE
The Note icon alerts you to a special point or supplementary information about a feature or task that may be helpful.

TIP
The Tip icon marks a tip that saves you time and helps you work more efficiently.

To further assist you in reading and learning the material in this book, the following conventions are used throughout:

New words or phrases that may require definition and explanation appear in *italics*. Text that carries emphasis and single characters that may be easy to lose in the text also appear in *italics*.

Menu commands are indicated in chronological order by using command arrows: File ⇨ Open.

Beginning iPhone Programming

Getting Started

If you are new to iPhone development or you are considering it, you may feel like it is a daunting prospect. We wish we could say it's a piece of cake, but the truth is, there's a little more to it. However, with a little guidance and encouragement, you will soon see your creations up and running on your device.

We cannot mention this enough about iPhone development: The best part is the reward. As a developer, nothing is more gratifying than to see your applications take life. It's even more satisfying to see your creations take life on the screen of the iPhone. Applications can really come alive when they respond to Multi-Touch, an accelerometer, and a compass.

Appreciating the History of Mobile Devices

Apple has had the vision for a powerful mobile device like the iPhone for many years. In August 1993, Apple announced the Newton Message Pad, a device that marked Apple's entry into the market of personal digital assistants (Figure 1.1).

The Apple Newton was not the success Apple hoped for—perhaps it was ahead of its time, and the market was just not ready for such an innovative idea. There is much speculation to why the Apple Newton failed, but after its fall, the market remained quiet for a few years. In March 1996, U.S. Robotics entered the marketplace. Taking design cues from the Apple Newton, they introduced the Pilot 1000 (or Palm Pilot). This time the market was ready, and the Palm Pilot became the first successful PDA. In the years that followed, more and more PDAs were introduced: Pocket PC, Handspring, and Compaq iPaq, to name a few. At the same time, mobile phones were becoming more affordable and commonplace. To help bridge this journey, devices like Palm, iPaq, and the Blackberry began to integrate with these mobile phones creating the "smart phone" device space.

In 2001 Apple announced the iPod, which was an almost-instant success (Figure 1.2).

In This Chapter

Appreciating the history of mobile devices

Introducing the iPhone SDK

Introducing the iPhone Developer Program

Un-boxing your iPhone developer tools

Testing applications on your device

Figure 1.1

Possibly the first personal digital assistant (PDA): the Newton Message Pad

Figure 1.2

The first iPod was introduced in 2001.

It is not surprising that Apple seized the opportunity and ingeniously combined the PDA, iPod, and mobile phone into one brilliant device, and in 2007, the iPhone was born (Figure 1.3).

Figure 1.3

The iPhone took the market
by storm when it was
introduced in 2007.

The iPhone was not the first device to combine the elements of PDA, media player, and phone. Blackberry and Windows mobile devices with these capabilities were being sold long before the iPhone. So why is the iPhone considered to be new and revolutionary? We believe it can be attributed to the unique and powerful design and user interface. In a nutshell, Apple got it right, marketing and designing the iPhone with the day-to-day user, not the businessperson or those just interested in business tools, in mind. You do not have to be a tech-savvy user to embrace the iPhone. In fact, the original iPhone lacked a lot of features found in other devices; however, it includes all the critical features that the average consumer cares about, and it arranges these features in a brilliant user interface.

Introducing the iPhone SDK

While thinking of the needs and desires of a day-to-day user, Apple realized that it needed to include variety. Apple had created a device that could, of course, browse the Web, check e-mail, and play music. However, this was just the tip of the iceberg. The device was also powerful enough to host many applications, including games. At first, developers were restricted to developing applications that were strictly browser-based. Applications in this space leveraged HTML, JavaScript, and Web-Kit. These applications were actually surprisingly good; however, the tides turned when Apple released the 2.0 OS and the iPhone SDK. To leverage the iPhone to its fullest capability and create the maximum amount of variety, Apple released the iPhone SDK in 2008. Developers flocked to the gates and began creating the first entries into the massive collection of native applications we see on the App Store today. The iPhone SDK is your opportunity to add to this variety of applications available for the iPhone.

The SDK itself is broken into four major layers:

- **Cocoa Touch.** Contains the tools necessary to create rich event-driven user interfaces without diving into the details of the lower levels.
- **Media.** When stock user interfaces are not enough, you can use the media layer to create the best multimedia experience available on a mobile device today.
- **Core Services.** This layer grants you access to iPhone OS services such as file access, data types, Bonjour services, network sockets, and more.
- **Core OS.** At the lowest layer of access in the group, you can manage the memory system, create threads, access the file system, connect to the network, and more. Leverage this layer in situations where the other layers do not meet your needs.

Introducing the iPhone Developer Program

Because you bought this book, we know you are interested in developing game applications for the iPhone. If you are not familiar with the iPhone Developer Program, then it's time to get acquainted.

Joining the iPhone Developer Program gives you access to the technical resources in the iPhone Development Center. This includes getting access to the SDK, developer tools, getting-started videos, documentation, sample code, and more. Once you have joined, you'll have access to the tools necessary for developing, debugging, and distributing your applications for the iPhone and iPod touch.

TIP

If you are curious about iPhone development but not ready to spend the money, you can sign up for free as a registered iPhone developer. As a registered iPhone developer you will have access to documentation and videos. If you have an intel-based Mac at your disposal, you can download and install the iPhone SDK, which includes the Xcode IDE, iPhone Simulator, and a suite of additional tools. With these tools you can try your hand at developing applications and running them in the Simulator. Register at `http://developer.apple.com/iphone/program/start/register/`.

The cost of getting started

To get started in iPhone development, you are going to have some unavoidable expenses. You will need to sign up for the iPhone Developer Program, which costs $99 at the time of this writing. You will want to implement your native iPhone applications using Xcode, which will only run on a Mac, so if you do not have a Mac to develop on, you will need to get one. If you do need to purchase a Mac, consider signing up for an Apple Developer Connection Membership at `http://developer.apple.com/products`. This gives you access to many resources and developer discounts. At the time of this writing, the standard membership costs $499; however, if you use the membership discount to purchase a MacBook Pro, it more than pays for itself. If you are just looking to spend as little as possible, you can get a Mac mini for around $599, depending on where you buy it.

Finally, if you don't already have one, you'll need to get an iPhone or an iPod touch to test your applications on. The iPhone SDK does come with a Simulator; however, it is just that—a simulator, not an emulator. To get a true and accurate experience, you must deploy your application to a physical device. With a new mobile plan and a two-year contract, you can purchase an iPhone 3G for $99. The iPhone 3GS will cost at least $199 with a two-year contract. Alternatively, you can purchase an iPod touch for around $220.

Decide what to buy based on the needs of your application. Most game application needs will be met by the iPod touch, especially the second generation, which now includes speakers. Look at the features you want to include in your application and make sure the device you are looking to buy supports those features. For instance, if you need a camera, you need the iPhone because the iPod touch has no camera. If you need a compass, currently the iPhone 3GS is the only device that has one.

TIP

Sometimes it's better to develop for a lower-end device like the iPod touch. This ensures that your application will reach the broadest audience.

Signing up to be an iPhone Developer

If you are serious about developing games, we recommend that you go ahead and spend the money necessary to join the iPhone Developer Program. The cost is $99 for the Standard program. This is the program you need to sign up for in order to publish your applications on the App Store. Start by browsing to `http://developer.apple.com/iphone/program/` and click the Enroll Now button. Continue through the steps, making sure to select the Standard program.

The Standard iPhone Developer Program is currently the only choice that allows you to publish applications to the App Store. With this program you get all the tools you need to develop applications for the iPhone. Most importantly, it includes your pass to publish and sell your creations on the App Store.

The other option is the Enterprise program, which costs $299. This is not an enhanced version of the Standard program; rather, it is designed to allow large companies to create and distribute in-house applications within an organization without going through the App Store. This is probably not what anyone would want for game development.

Once you have signed up for the program, you will need to provide personal and banking information before you can submit paid applications to the App Store. Before doing this you will need to decide if you would like to set up an Individual or Company account. In your situation, this answer may be clear, but if not, you need to choose carefully. With a Company account you can add team members who will be able to log in to the iPhone Developer Program Portal and gain access to the SDK and other related development tools. If others are working on your projects with you, a Company account is definitely the better way to go. If you choose an Individual account, all of these tools can only be accessed by one person.

We are not going to advise you one way or the other, but consider your intent and decide carefully.

CAUTION

It is possible to convert an Individual account to a Company account; however, there is a drawback. During the conversion process, Apple will temporarily disable your Developer account and pull your apps from the App Store while your account is in transition, which can take several days. Also note that you currently cannot convert from a Company account to an Individual account.

Un-Boxing Your iPhone Developer Tools

After joining the iPhone Developer Program, you will have access to a wealth of tools and resources. Here are some of the things you'll find when you crack open your new toolbox (Figure 1.4):

Figure 1.4

Home sweet home: Welcome to the iPhone Dev Center home page.

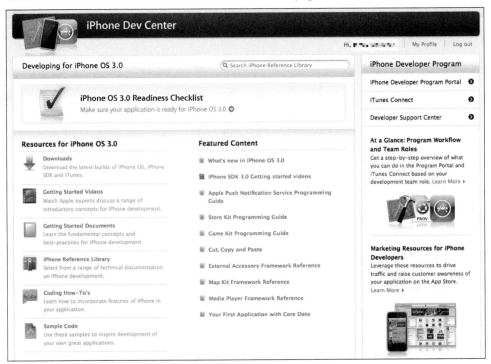

- **Full Access to the iPhone Dev Center.** This includes access to documentation and resources you will need when developing applications for new and existing features of the iPhone OS: `http://developer.apple.com/iphone/`.

- **iPhone Developer Program Portal.** Here you will be guided through the steps needed to test applications on your iPhone and iPod touch. You'll also find the tools and resources necessary to prepare your applications for distribution: `http://developer.apple.com/iphone/manage/overview/`.

- **iTunes Connect.** This site provides you with a growing collection of tools you will need in order to upload and manage your applications in the iTunes App Store: `https://itunesconnect.apple.com/`.

- **iPhone Developer Support Center.** Here you will find detailed information about using the features listed in the previous bullets. You'll also find information about participating in discussion forums, obtaining technical support, reporting bugs, and more: `http://developer.apple.com/support/iphone/`.

iPhone Dev Center

When you first sign up for the program, the iPhone Dev Center is one of the first places you will want to visit. Here you can review the documentation, download example programs, and watch all the technical videos. The videos are a great place to start. You can download them all to your iPod or iPhone and watch them any time. Next time you go to the gym you can "get your learn on" while you are on the treadmill.

When a beta OS is on the horizon, the iPhone Dev Center will be divided according to version, with sections for the public and beta versions of the OS. Beta versions of the OS and SDK are sometimes released early to paid members of the iPhone Developer Program. In each section you should find version-specific information and resources. If you are looking at the public/release version of the OS, you probably won't be able to download the OS itself or iTunes there. If iTunes is not there, you can download the latest version of iTunes directly from Apple. If the OS is not there, you can install the publically available OS from the current version of iTunes. Also keep in mind that an application developed on a beta SDK won't be accepted on the App Store until the beta is in general release.

In the iPhone Dev Center you have access to the following resources:

- **Downloads.** Gives you access to the latest iPhone OS, iPhone SDK, and iTunes.

- **Getting Started Videos.** Watch the experts as they guide you through the basic concepts you need to get started.

- **Getting Started Documentation.** Teach yourself the fundamentals and best practices recommended by Apple.

- **iPhone Reference Library.** Find detailed instructions on every concept and library in the frameworks.

- **Coding How-To's.** Find more guidance and instruction on integrating new and existing features into your applications. This is a great first place to look when trying something new.

- **Sample Code.** One of our personal favorites. Download, compile, and execute sample code that was written by the experts. Download it all and pick it apart line by line. (Of course, we love examples, which is why we created `http://AppsAmuck.com`.)

● **Apple Developer Forums.** When all else fails and you are stuck or question your implementation, this is where you want to go. You can discuss your issues and questions with peers and Apple engineers.

iPhone Developer Program Portal

When you are ready to install your application on your iPhone or iPod touch, you can find detailed information and the resources that you need in the iPhone Developer Program Portal. Preparing your device for development requires that you install a Provisioning Profile and a Development Certificate before you can install applications on it. The iPhone Developer Program Portal is where you need to go to create Development Certificates, create Provisioning Profiles, register Device IDs, and do everything else you need to do to distribute your application (Figure 1.5).

Figure 1.5

The iPhone Developer Program Portal provides all the tools and resources you will need for tasks like distributing your application.

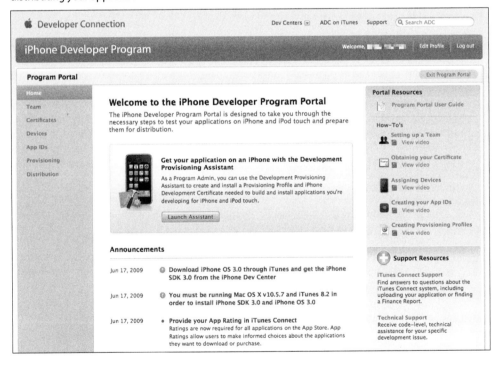

The tools and resources found in the iPhone Developer Program Portal enable you to accomplish the following:

- **Test Applications on Devices.** Before you can install an application on your development device, you must have a Development Certificate, Device ID, App ID, and Provisioning Profile. These requirements can be created and downloaded, or registered here.

- **App Store Distribution.** When preparing an application for the App Store, you will need a Distribution Certificate, App ID, and Provisioning Profile.

- **Ad Hoc Distribution.** This type of distribution allows you to share your application with testers and other developers remotely. You will need to get their Device ID and send them the application's Provisioning Profile. Once they have this, they can install your application from iTunes. For Ad Hoc distribution, you need a Distribution Certificate, Device ID, App ID, and Provisioning Profile (Figure 1.6).

Figure 1.6

The iPhone Developer Program Portal contains tools and information that carry you through the steps necessary to publish your application to the App Store or share your application through Ad Hoc distribution.

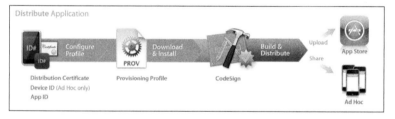

- **In App Purchase.** This feature allows you to charge for application add-ons, optional features, or additional content. You will need to visit the App IDs section of the iPhone Developer Program Portal to enable this feature for your application.

- **Apple Push Notification Service.** This service allows you to push events in the form of alerts, sounds, and tags to your application even when it is not running. Because this process requires you to communicate with the Apple Push Notification server, you will need to come here to activate this feature for your application. You will need to visit the App IDs section of the iPhone Developer Program Portal to create and download a Push SSL Certificate.

This list should help you decide which features of the iPhone Developer Program Portal you will need, depending on what you are trying to accomplish. When you visit the site, you will have the following options to choose from:

- **Home.** This is a general dashboard to the portal. The Portal Resources section is where you will find a collection of videos that we recommend watching. There are links to Support Resources and a feed where you can read Apple's latest developer announcements. The Development Provisioning Assistant is a new addition and a great tool for getting started (Figure 1.7).

Figure 1.7

Get a jump-start by using the Development Provisioning Assistant.

- **Team.** This option is divided into the following sections:
  - **Manage:** If you join the iPhone Developer Program as a Company, this is where you will manage your list of team members. If you join as an Individual, you will be the only person on your team.
  - **Tech Support:** Incidents grant you code level assistance from Apple engineers. The Standard program includes two such incidences for the year.
  - **Agreements:** Here you can revisit the list of agreements you or your company has accepted.
  - **Contact Info:** Here you can review the contact information you or your company submitted when you signed up for the program.
- **Certificates.** In this section of the portal, you can request iPhone Development and Distribution Certificates. This option is divided into the following sections:
  - **Development:** This sub-section allows you to create and download Development Certificates. iPhone applications must be signed by a valid certificate before they can be installed on an iPhone or iPod touch.
  - **Distribution:** This sub-section allows you to create the certificate you will use to sign your application in preparation for submission to the App Store. This certificate is needed to associate a developer or company with the applications they submit.
  - **History:** Here you can view a list of all development and distribution certificates you have created in the past.
- **Devices.** This option is divided into the following sections:
  - **Manage:** You will be allowed to install your applications on up to 100 devices for testing purposes. This sub-section is where you will manage this list of registered devices. Be aware that any devices you remove from your list still count against your 100-device limit. However, you can reset the total count of your Registered Devices List for the upcoming membership year. You can only do this once per membership year. Be sure to leave open slots for new devices that may come out during the year.
  - **History:** Here you can view a list of all the devices you have added and removed in the past.

- **App IDs.** You need to generate App IDs to identify your applications. This allows your application to associate with a certificate, connect to Apple Push Notification servers, communicate with external hardware, and share keychain data between applications.

  An App ID begins with a unique 10-character Bundle Seed ID that is generated by Apple. The ID ends with a Bundle Identifier that is entered by you. It is recommended that you use reverse-domain-style strings for your Bundle Identifier; for example, **1234567890.com.yourdomain.YourAppName**.

  If you need to share the same keychain between applications, you will need to create a single App ID for all of these applications by appending a trailing asterisk as a wildcard character to the end of the App ID; for example, **1234567890.com.yourdomain***.

- **Provisioning.** Provisioning Profiles are necessary to tie devices to an authorized iPhone Development Team. Development and Ad Hoc Provisioning Profiles combine an App ID, a certificate, and a list of Device IDs. A Distribution Provisioning Profile combines only an App ID and a certificate, because it can be installed on any device from the App Store.

  - **Development:** Use this option to manage your list of Development Provisioning Profiles.

  - **Distribution:** Use this option to manage your list of Distribution and Ad Hoc Provisioning Profiles.

  - **History:** Here you can view a list of all the Provisioning Profile activity that has taken place in the past.

iTunes Connect

iTunes Connect is where you upload your applications and start cashing in! Here you will find tools to help manage your applications on the App Store. The following options are available (Figure 1.8):

- **Sales/Trend Reports.** Go here to see how many times your applications have been downloaded. This is the first place you are going to want to go the morning after your application is published on the App Store. The reports here are for monitoring trends only and should not be used for firm financial purposes.

- **Contracts, Tax, & Banking Information.** This is where you manage your iTunes contracts and agreements. You have a different contract for free applications and paid applications. You need to provide contact, bank, and tax information in order to complete the contract that enables you to publish paid applications.

- **Financial Reports.** Download or view your monthly financial reports here. There is a separate report for each currency/territory your application has been sold in. Apple withholds payment until you accumulate more than $250 USD (or equivalent) in a given currency/territory.

- **Manage Users.** In this option you can create and manage iTunes Connect and In App Purchase test user accounts.

Figure 1.8

iTunes Connect is your vehicle for managing and publishing your applications in the iTunes App Store.

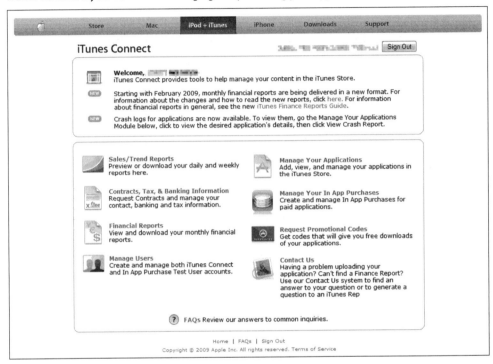

● **Manage Your Applications.** This is where you manage the applications you have submitted to the App Store. There are several pieces of information you need to provide when you publish an application. Have this information and the files handy before you begin or you will spend a lot of time running back and forth:

- Name, description, and device type
- Primary and secondary categories
- Copyright
- Version number
- SKU number
- Application URL
- Support URL
- Support e-mail address

- Demo account—full access login credentials (if applicable)
- Rating information
- Application binary
- Large 512 x 512 icon (used in iTunes)
- Primary screen shot
- Additional screen shots (optional, up to four)
- Availability date
- Price tier ($0.99–$999.99)
- Supported languages

- **Manage Your In App Purchases.** Manage the price and availability of add-ons to your applications here. The types of In App Purchases allowed are Consumables, Subscriptions, and Non-Consumables. Consumables and Subscriptions require users to pay for the In App Purchase each time it is downloaded. With Non-Consumables, users only pay for the In App Purchase once. Once set, the In App Purchase type cannot be changed.

- **Request Promotional Codes.** You are allotted 50 promotional codes for each version of your application. These non-commercial codes can be used in the U.S. iTunes Store to allow users to download review or promotional versions of your application for free. This is the option you need to use to request these codes.

- **Contact Us.** If you are having any problems using iTunes Connect, you can use this option to search for an answer or to submit a question to an iTunes representative.

iPhone Developer Support Center

The iPhone Developer Support Center provides you with answers to questions about all areas of the program. This includes support resources for the following:

- Program enrollment
- Account management
- iPhone Dev Center
- Discussion forums
- iPhone Developer Program Portal
- App submission
- iTunes Connect support
- Tech support
- University program
- Bug reporting

Testing Applications on Your Device

One of the biggest benefits of being in the iPhone Developer Program is the ability to test your creations on physical devices. If you are like us, this is also one of the first things that you'll want to try to do. Unfortunately, it's not as easy as just plugging the device into your Mac and clicking Run. If you could do this, you could potentially install your application on any device that you plug into the Mac—and that is exactly what Apple does *not* want you to do. If this were possible it would be easy to circumvent the App Store entirely. Apple has put a series of checks and balances in place to ensure that only developers can install software on their registered devices easily. The following steps illustrate what you need to do to install an application on your iPhone or iPod touch (Figure 1.9):

Figure 1.9

Installing and testing your applications on your iPhone and iPod touch

1. Generate and install a Development Certificate.

2. Register iPhone and iPod touch Device IDs.

3. Create an App ID to identify your application.

4. Generate and install a Development Provisioning Profile.

5. Configure the Code Signing Identity of your application.

6. Build and test your application on your development device.

Let's look at each of these steps in more detail.

Generate and install a Development Certificate

Certificates are electronic documents that associate your digital identity with your iPhone Developer Program account. iPhone Development Certificates can only be used for application development and are set to expire after a limited amount of time. Apple can also revoke your Development Certificate before it expires. In short, you need the certificate to deploy and test applications on your device, but Apple has ensured that it can prevent developers from abusing this privilege.

There are two steps to generating the certificate. First, you have to use the keychain tool on your Mac to create a certificate request. Next, you upload your certificate request in the iPhone Developer Program Portal, where the certificate is generated. Once this is done you can download and install the certificate.

To generate a certificate request, follow these steps:

1. On your Mac, launch the application Keychain Access.

2. From the application menu, choose Keychain Access ⇨ Preferences. From here, set Online Certificate Status Protocol (OSCP) and Certificate Revocation List (CRL) to Off.

3. Choose Keychain Access ⇨ Certificate Assistant ⇨ Request a Certificate From a Certificate Authority (Figure 1.10).

Figure 1.10

Using Keychain Access to request a certificate from a certificate authority to begin the process of generating your certificate

CAUTION

Make sure you are choosing Request a Certificate From a Certificate Authority and not Request a Certificate From a Certificate Authority with <Private Key>. If you happen to have a private key selected in Keychain Access when executing this action, the certificate request generated will not be accepted by the iPhone Developer Program Portal.

4. Enter your e-mail address in the User Email Address field. Be sure that the e-mail address you enter here matches the e-mail address that you used when you registered as an iPhone Developer.

5. Enter a name in the Common Name field. Likewise, the name you enter here should match the name you used when you registered as an iPhone Developer.

6. Leave the CA (Certificate Authority) Email Address field blank.

7. Click the Saved to disk radio button and click in the Let me specify key pair information check box (Figure 1.11). Click Continue.

8. In the popup menu, specify a filename and click Save. For the Key Pair Information settings, choose 2048 bits for the Key Size and RSA for the Algorithm (Figure 1.12). Click Continue.

9. The Certificate Assistant creates your CSR file. By default the CSR will be saved to your desktop with the name you specified in Step 8.

Figure 1.11

When specifying your certificate information for your certificate request, make sure that the e-mail address you enter matches the e-mail address that you used when you registered as an iPhone Developer.

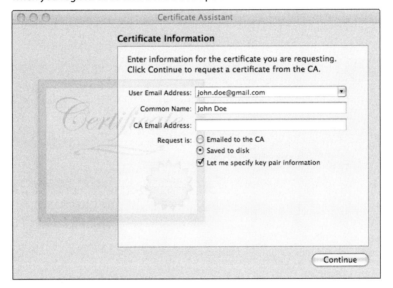

Using the iTunes Developer Program Portal to generate your Development Certificate

Follow these steps to generate and install your Development Certificate:

1. Log in to the iPhone Developer Program Portal and choose Certificates ➪ Development ➪ Add Certificate.

2. In the Open File dialog box, click Choose file and select the CSR you created using Keychain Access.

3. After submission, a Team Administrator will need to click Approve to approve the certificate request if you are using a Company account. If you are the Team Administrator, it is your job to click Approve.

Figure 1.12

When asked to specify key pair information, make sure you choose 2048 bits
for the Key Size and RSA for the Algorithm.

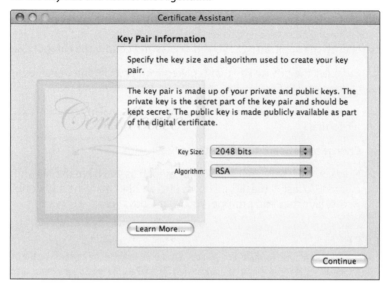

4. After approval, the status of the certificate changes to Pending Issuance; if successful,
   it then changes to Issued. After the status has changed to Issued, click the Download
   button next to the certificate name and download your iPhone Development
   Certificate to your local machine.

5. On the same Web page, you will see the following link near the bottom of the grid: If
   you do not have the WWDR intermediate certificate installed, click here to download
   now. Click the link to download the WWDR certificate.

6. On your local machine, double-click the WWDR intermediate certificate. The Keychain
   Access application will launch and install the certificate.

7. Double-click the iPhone Development Certificate file that you downloaded in Step 4
   and install it the same way.

Exporting your private key

It is important that you save your private key in case you need to develop on multiple computers or you need to reinstall your OS. If you neglect to do this, you will not be able to sign your
binaries in Xcode and test your applications. The Keychain Access application creates a private
key for you on your login keychain. This key is tied to your user account and cannot be reproduced. You will need to import this private key onto all systems that you develop and test on. If

you are using a Company account, individual team members will go through this process independently and create a personal Development Certificate for themselves. It is not necessary to copy the private key to development computers for other team members.

To export your private key and certificate, follow these steps:

1. Launch the application Keychain Access and choose the category Keys.

2. Ctrl+click the private key that is paired with your iPhone Development Certificate you created earlier. Click on Export <Name> from the menu.

3. Save the file in a secure location using the Personal Information Exchange (.p12) file format.

4. Choose a password to secure the .p12 file with.

5. Now you can share your private key as long as you have this file and the password you created. To install the file, just copy it to another machine and double-click it. Keychain Access launches and prompts you for the password.

NOTE

Your private key is never sent to Apple. Private keys can only be found in the keychain on the machine that generated the CSR. It's important that you export your private key for safekeeping and so you can use it on other machines.

Register iPhone and iPod touch Device IDs

Apple wants to know which devices you are using to develop on before you install applications on them for testing. Every iPhone and iPod touch has a Unique Device ID (UDID) that uniquely identifies that device. Registering your device is as simple as inputting your Device IDs on the iPhone Developer Program Portal site. Here are the steps to do this:

1. Locate and record your Device ID. The easiest way to do this is to plug in your device and open Xcode. From the Xcode menu, choose Window ➪ Organizer. You will see your Device ID immediately to the right of the label Identifier (Figure 1.13).

Figure 1.13

Locating your Device ID in the Xcode Organizer window

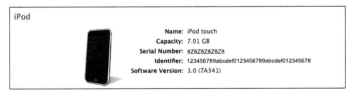

TIP

Even though it looks like a label, you can select the Device ID (Identifier) in Organizer and copy it.

2. Go back to the iPhone Developer Portal and choose Program Portal ⇨ Devices ⇨ Manage.

3. On the Manage tab, click the Add Device button.

4. On the Add Devices screen (Figure 1.14), enter the Device ID you copied from Organizer and a Device Name to help you identify the device you are registering.

Figure 1.14

Use the Add Devices screen to register the devices you wish to use for development.

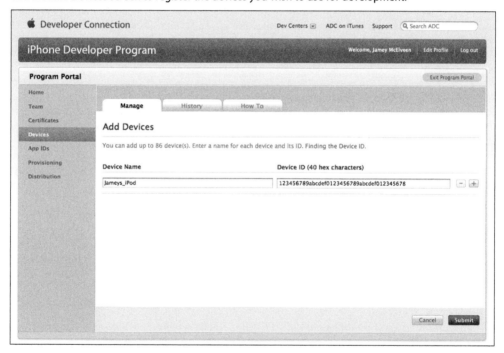

Users can also determine their Device ID by clicking on the Serial Number field in the iTunes Summary screen. When displayed, the Device ID can be copied to the clipboard by choosing Edit ⇨ Copy from the iTunes menu. This can be particularly useful when assigning Device IDs for beta testers who may not have the SDK installed.

Create an App ID to identify your application

App IDs are necessary to tie applications into the provisioning process. In addition, they allow your applications to use Apple Push Notification and to connect with external hardware and accessories. App IDs are also necessary when you need to share keychain data between your applications. To create an App ID, follow these steps:

1. Return to the iPhone Developer Portal and choose Program Portal ⇨ App IDs ⇨ Manage.

2. On the Manage tab, click the Add ID button.

3. On the Create App ID screen (Figure 1.15), enter an App ID Name and an App ID. We recommend using a wildcard unless you need to use the Apple Push Notification service. To create an App ID with a wildcard, it should be of the format **com.yourdomain***. A wildcard App ID can be used on all of your applications. If you do not use a wildcard, your App ID should follow the format **com.yourdomain.YourAppName**.

Figure 1.15

Use the Create App ID screen to create an App ID for your application or applications.

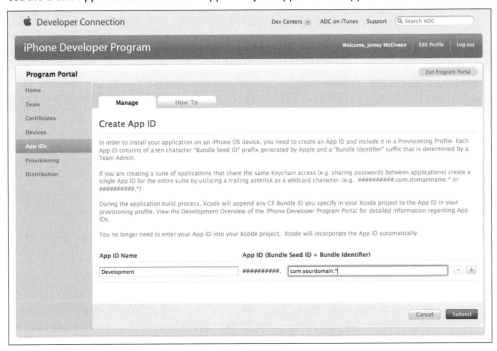

4. Finally, click Submit to save the App ID.

Generate and install a Development Provisioning Profile

Now that you have a Development Certificate and you have registered your device, you need to create a Development Provisioning Profile to associate with your iPhone Developer Account, Development Certificate, application, and device. Follow these steps to generate and install the Provisioning Profile:

1. Return to the iPhone Developer Portal and choose Program Portal ➪ Provisioning ➪ Manage.

2. On the Manage tab, click the Add Profile button.

3. On the Create iPhone Development Provisioning Profile screen (Figure 1.16), fill in all the field values, making sure you select a certificate, App ID, and at least one device.

Figure 1.16

Use the Create iPhone Development Provisioning Profile screen to register the devices you wish to use for development.

4. Click Submit to save. This returns you to the list of Development Provisioning Profiles. Find the profile you just created and click Download in the Actions column. Save the downloaded profile to your desktop.

5. Back on your machine, find the file you just downloaded and drag the file onto your Xcode icon.

6. Plug in your device and open Xcode. In Organizer, choose Devices ➪ <Your Device Name> ➪ Summary. In the Provisioning section of the Summary tab, you should see your new Provisioning Profile in the list indicating that it was installed on the device, as shown in Figure 1.17.

Figure 1.17

You can use Xcode Organizer to confirm that your iPhone Development Provisioning Profile has been installed on your device.

Configure the Code Signing Identity of your application

Finally, you need to associate your Development Certificate with your application and assign your App ID. Once this is done, you are ready to test your application on your device.

Here are the steps you need to follow to get started testing your application on your device:

1. Launch Xcode and open your project.

2. In the Xcode Project Window, the top-left pull-down control in the toolbar is the Overview popup menu. Click this pull-down menu and change the setting to #.# Device | Debug. To do this, choose Active SDK ⇨ iPhone Device #.# (Figure 1.18). (The current SDK version number is represented by #.#; version 3.0 is selected in the figure.)

3. In the Xcode Project Window, choose Groups & Files ⇨ Targets and click your project target. Next, click the Info icon on the toolbar.

4. Once inside the Info window, click the Build pane. Make sure that, in the settings list, Code Signing ⇨ Code Signing Identity is expanded, and then click on the Any iPhone OS Device popup menu in the Value column. Choose the iPhone Development Provisioning Profile and Certificate pair that you created earlier (Figure 1.19).

Figure 1.18

Changing the Active SDK setting to build for a physical device.

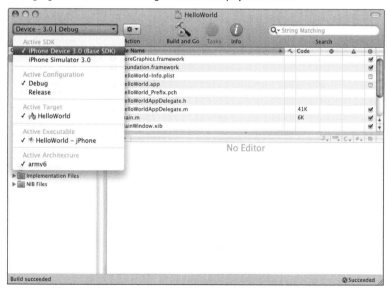

Figure 1.19

Configuring the Code Signing Identity of your application

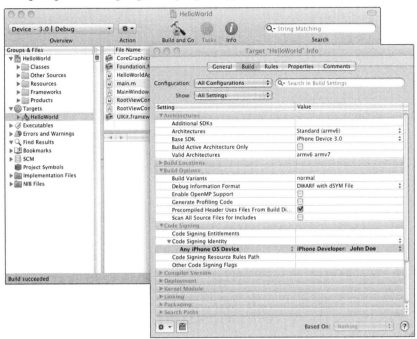

5. Click on the Properties pane of the Info window. From there, input the Bundle Identifier you defined when you created your App ID. In our example we entered **1234567890.com.yourdomain*** as an example. For this example you will want to enter **com.yourdomain.HelloWorld** as the identifier leaving off the Bundle Seed ID portion and replacing the wildcard asterisk character with your application name (Figure 1.20).

If you did not use a wildcard, you will need to use the full Bundle Identifier and only leave off the Bundle Seed ID. In our previous example we used the App ID **1234567890.com.yourdomain.YourAppName**. In this case you would want to input **com.yourdomain.YourAppName**.

Figure 1.20

Setting the target Identifier with the Bundle Identifier from your App ID

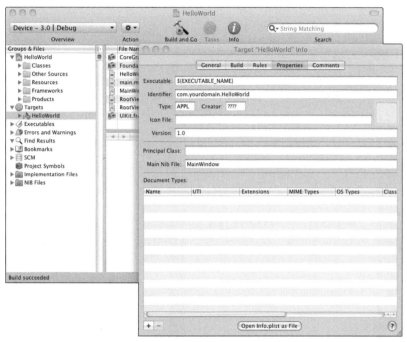

Build and test your application on your development device

After completing all of the previous steps, you are ready to build and test on your iPhone or iPod touch. At this point all you need to do is plug in your device and click Build and Go. You should see your application load up and start running after a few seconds (Figure 1.21). In this environment you can run and debug just as you would have in the Simulator. Breakpoints, watches, and console output work the same way.

Figure 1.21

Follow the steps in this chapter, and you'll soon see your first application running on your iPhone or iPod touch.

Summary

In this chapter you learned a little about the history of mobile devices. It has been a long road with successes and failures that have paved the way to where we are today. Most notable is that Apple started this journey with the Apple Newton, which ended in failure. However, despite setbacks, Apple has kept the vision alive, setting the bar with the iPhone. As a result, you can enjoy the benefits of developing games for this beautifully designed device.

Next, you took a first look at the iPhone SDK and what it has to offer. You gained an understanding of what steps you will need to take to get started as an iPhone developer, including how deep you will need to dip into your pocket for cash. You took a tour of the iPhone SDK and the iPhone Developer Program, and you learned about all the tools from the iPhone SDK you can expect to leverage as a developer. You also got a peek at the resources and benefits offered to you as a member of the iPhone Developer Program.

Finally, you learned how to utilize your new set of tools and deploy applications to your iPhone and iPod touch for testing. You walked through all of these steps in detail, since this is one of the more difficult tasks and causes developers to stumble when they are getting started. You will find this walk-through most beneficial, especially if you are new to the Mac world, as many iPhone developers are. This guide will help you find your way through a process that can feel alien to first-time visitors.

Creating Your First App: Hello World

Now that you have had an introduction to the iPhone SDK, it's time to get your hands dirty. In the grand programming tradition, we are going to assist you through writing the Hello World application for the iPhone. If you follow the steps in this chapter, you will get to see your first application happily running in the palm of your hand.

But before you start coding, you need to be sure that your development environment is set up correctly. This is similar to a pilot performing a preflight check of the plane before takeoff. Things can go wrong in the air, but you will minimize them if you confirm everything is correct before you leave the ground.

You will need to download and install all the necessary iPhone SDK tools. Following this you will then download and run one of the example applications provided in the iPhone SDK tutorials. The example will verify your environment and whet your appetite. Finally, you will be ready to write your first application from scratch, and as a bonus you will become oriented with the tools and processes that will become your friends as you move forward.

Setting Up Your Environment

As we've mentioned, it's important to make sure that your development environment is up and running before you begin writing code. If this is the first time you have installed the iPhone SDK, you should have no problems. If you have tried to install it before, you may need to follow a few more steps to ensure that you get started properly. Once you get the SDK installed, you will need to be sure everything you need is installed properly. The best way to test things out is to fire off some code and watch it run. We know you want to get started, but when you start trying to track down errors, you will find it frustrating to pinpoint the issue if your environment or setup is contributing to the problems you are experiencing.

Getting the iPhone SDK

This section will guide you through the process of downloading and installing the tools you will need in order to develop applications for the iPhone. The tools you need can be found at iPhone Dev Center, so start by going to `http://developer.apple.com/iphone/`.

Registering for the tools

If this is your first time visiting iPhone Dev Center, you will need to register to be able to download the iPhone SDK. Once at iPhone Dev Center, look in the right column right below the login button and you will see a Not a Registered iPhone Developer? section. Click the Start Now link. You will be guided through a simple wizard, and shortly you will have a valid Apple ID with which to log in. This process is free and painless, but it does not allow you to publish your applications to the App Store or even install and test on your device. In order to do these things you will need to apply for the iPhone Developer Program. The Developer Program membership is $99 as of this writing. Once you're a member of the program you can create and debug applications on your device. You will also have a license to distribute your creations on the App Store. To get started in the iPhone Developer Program, go to `http://developer.apple.com/iphone/program/` and click Learn More for the next page, where you can click Apply Now to get started. Unfortunately, this is not an instant process and it may take several weeks for your application to get approved. However, you can continue to develop on the iPhone Simulator with a large amount of success until you are approved.

CROSS-REFERENCE

Learn more about the iPhone Developer Program in Chapter 1.

Downloading the tools

Once you have your Apple ID you can begin downloading the tools. If you are waiting on approval for the iPhone Developer Program, you can still download the SDK and get started. Tune your browser back to the iPhone Dev Center, `http://developer.apple.com/iphone/`, and log in with your Apple ID. Scroll down to the iPhone OS 3.0 Downloads section. Once there, your screen should look similar to Figure 2.1.

Figure 2.1

The Downloads section of the iPhone Dev Center is where you go to download the iPhone SDK.

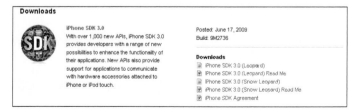

This section changes its form from time to time depending on which version of the OS is currently available. If a version of the OS is available to download that is not currently published for public use, you will have an option to download the latest usually non-released beta version of the iPhone SDK for it or the one that is currently available to consumers. We like to stick with the version that is available to consumers.

It is still safe to download the latest version because you can select the OS version you would like to build for. However, unless you have an extra device that has the current OS installed on it for testing purposes, you may feel more confident sticking with the currently distributed OS. Also be aware that Apple has forced developers to test their applications on upcoming new OS releases. For example, before iPhone OS 3.0 came out there was a period when apps had to work on both iPhone OS 2.0 and iPhone OS 3.0.

On the iPhone Dev Center page, scroll down to the Downloads section (Figure 2.1) to find the following links:

- **iPhone SDK.** This is the download link for the iPhone SDK. It includes iPhone SDK frameworks, Xcode, Interface Builder, iPhone Simulator, and more.
- **iPhone SDK Read Me.** This PDF tells you what is in the latest and greatest SDK, how to install or uninstall it, and more.
- **iPhone SDK Agreement.** This PDF is your SDK license agreement. Make sure you read through the agreement and familiarize yourself with any special restrictions that may affect your project efforts. It is a good idea to read this agreement again after you scope out your project to make sure you are in compliance with your agreement.

If you are a registered developer, at times you will have access to pre-release beta versions of the iPhone OS. Down the road you may find it useful to begin developing for a beta OS if you are expecting an extended development cycle. If a beta OS is available, from the iPhone Dev Center page select the beta OS version and you will find these additional links (Figure 2.2):

- **iPhone OS.** This is the download link for the iPhone OS beta. Once downloaded you can drag this package onto your Xcode icon to install.
- **iPhone OS Pre-Install Advisory.** This PDF contains some important information about setting up your environment and device for development purposes. It is very important to follow the advice of this document before you begin. Some of the steps highlighted within can help prevent you from damaging your iPhone or iPod touch.

TIP
If you do not have a link to a beta version of the iPhone OS anymore, chances are it has been released and you can install directly from iTunes.

Figure 2.2

The Downloads section of the iPhone Dev Center contains beta versions of the iPhone OS if available and if you are a registered developer.

Installing the iPhone SDK

Now you are ready to install the iPhone SDK. The SDK is a pretty hefty download. Version 2.2.1 was 1.7GB and version 3.1 was 2.4GB, so, depending on your connection speed, be prepared to wait.

Installing the iPhone SDK is a fairly straightforward process if you are installing the SDK for the first time. However, it is still nice to have this process broken down for you if you are taking your first steps in the Mac environment. This section will guide you through this process.

In order to install the iPhone SDK, you will need to:

1. Download the iPhone SDK if you have not done so already.

2. Locate the downloaded SDK, and double-click to mount the DMG file.

3. From the mounted DMG file folder, double-click the installer.

4. Follow the on-screen instructions given to you by the installer.

That's all there is to installing the iPhone SDK. You now have the tools you need to start writing iPhone games. Take a few minutes to open your new toolbox and discover all the tools inside the iPhone SDK.

N O T E

If you are experiencing strange compile and runtime errors that leave you frustrated, you may want to uninstall the SDK completely and start over. Sometimes starting over with a clean plate can clear up these issues.

Uninstalling previous versions of the iPhone SDK

If you run into some issues you feel could be occurring because you installed one version of the SDK on top of another, we recommend that you take time to uninstall the SDK and then reinstall it. You can find the latest uninstall procedure in the iPhone SDK Read Me file, or follow these steps:

1. If you would like to uninstall Xcode developer tools on the boot volume, along with the <Xcode> directory, from a Terminal window use this command:

```
$ sudo <Xcode>/Library/uninstall-devtools --mode=all
```

2. If you would like to remove the underlying developer content on the boot volume but leave the <Xcode> directory and supporting files untouched, from a Terminal window use this command:

```
$ sudo <Xcode>/Library/uninstall-devtools --mode=systemsupport
```

3. If you would like to remove just the UNIX development support on the boot volume but leave the <Xcode> directory and supporting files untouched, from a Terminal window use this command:

```
$ sudo <Xcode>/Library/uninstall-devtools --mode=unixdev
```

4. If you would like to uninstall just the <Xcode> directory, you can simply drag it to the trash, or from a Terminal window use this command:

```
$ sudo <Xcode>/Library/uninstall-devtools --mode=xcodedir
```

Unless you are experienced, we recommend that you uninstall using the first option. By default the <Xcode> folder is installed in \Developer\Library. To run this uninstall command from the default location, follow these steps:

1. Open a terminal window.

2. Type **cd /** and press Enter.

3. Type **sudo Developer/Library/uninstall-devtools --mode=all** and press Enter.

NOTE

During installation and when running the uninstall command, you will be prompted for a password. Don't worry; this is your Mac OS protecting you. You will need to supply the administrative password that was used when setting up for your Mac.

Test-Driving the SDK

Now that you have installed your environment, it's time to run one of the samples from the iPhone Sample Code library. This tests your setup and makes sure your environment is in good health. We understand you are eager to get started, but you don't want to spend hours chasing a bug in your app only to find out there was a problem with your environment setup. Here is what you need to do to test your environment with one of Apple's Code Samples.

Getting a sample app to try out

Go back to iPhone Dev Center (`http://developer.apple.com/iphone/`) and scroll down to the Sample Code link under the Resources for iPhone section, as shown in Figure 2.3. From there click the Sample Code link to navigate to a full listing of Apple's sample applications.

Figure 2.3

There are many useful resources in the Resources for iPhone section of iPhone Dev Center, including many examples in the Sample Code section

Resources for iPhone OS 3.0	Featured Content
Downloads — Download the latest builds of iPhone OS, iPhone SDK, and iTunes.	▪ What's new in iPhone OS 3.0
Getting Started Videos — Watch Apple experts discuss a range of introductory concepts for iPhone development.	▪ iPhone SDK 3.0 Getting started videos
Getting Started Documents — Learn the fundamental concepts and best-practices for iPhone development.	▪ Apple Push Notification Service Programming Guide
iPhone Reference Library — Select from a range of technical documentation on iPhone development.	▪ Store Kit Programming Guide
Coding How-To's — Learn how to incorporate features of iPhone in your application.	▪ Game Kit Programming Guide
Sample Code — Use these samples to inspire development of your own great applications.	▪ Cut, Copy and Paste
Apple Developer Forums Beta — Discuss iPhone development with other developers and Apple engineers.	▪ External Accessory Framework Reference
	▪ Map Kit Framework Reference
	▪ Media Player Framework Reference
	▪ Your First Application with Core Data

You will now be on the Sample Code page, which lists all available iPhone Dev Center sample applications (see Figure 2.4).

Figure 2.4

You will find a plethora of example applications in the iPhone Dev Center's Sample Code library.

Sample Code

Details: ⦿ On ◯ Off ▸ Set Filters (64 of 64 documents)

Title	Topic	Subtopic ▲	Framework	Date
Reflection — This sample shows how to implement a "reflection" special effect on a given UIImageView.	Graphics & Animation	2D Drawing	UIKit	2009-04-29 Content Update iPhone OS 3.0
QuartzDemo — Demonstrates many of the Quartz2D APIs made available by the CoreGraphics framework.	Graphics & Animation	2D Drawing	Core Graphics	2009-05-21 Content Update iPhone OS 3.0
GLSprite — Shows how to create an OpenGL texture from image data in a Core Graphics bitmap context.	Graphics & Animation	3D Drawing	OpenGL ES	2008-07-02 Minor Change
GLPaint — Demonstrates how to support single finger painting using OpenGL ES.	Graphics & Animation	3D Drawing	OpenGL ES	2008-07-02 Minor Change
GLGravity — Demonstrates how to use the UIAccelerometer class in combination with OpenGL ES rendering.	Graphics & Animation	3D Drawing	OpenGL ES	2008-07-03 Content Update
ViewTransitions — Demonstrates how to perform transitions between two views using built-in Core Animation transitions.	Graphics & Animation	Animation	Quartz Core	2009-05-21 Content Update iPhone OS 3.0
oalTouch — iPhone example to play a single audio source using OpenAL	Audio & Video	Audio	Audio Toolbox	2009-04-21 Minor Change
avTouch — avTouch is a sample project for playing an audio file using the AVFoundation framework.	Audio & Video	Audio	AV Foundation	2009-04-29 Minor Change
aurioTouch — iPhone example to monitor audio input and play it out (duplex audio I/O)	Audio & Video	Audio	Audio Unit	2009-07-07 Content Update
SysSound — Demonstrates how to play short sounds and invoke vibration.	Audio & Video	Audio	Audio Toolbox	2008-09-24 First Version
SpeakHere — Demonstrates iPhone recording and playback using the Audio Toolbox framework.	Audio & Video	Audio	Audio Toolbox	2009-06-17 Minor Change

Scroll down to the GLPaint example and click on it. This example takes advantage of the touch-screen and the accelerometer. When the page loads, you should be presented with a screen similar to Figure 2.5. Click on the Download Sample Code link.

Wait for the sample to finish downloading, then open it. Finder will unzip the GLPaint.zip archive and you will see the GLPaint folder in your download folder.

Now you should move the GLPaint folder to a new location if you do not want to keep it in the download folder. Open the GLPaint folder and double-click GLPaint.xcodeproj. You should now see the main Xcode window open with the GLPaint project open, as shown in Figure 2.6.

TIP

If you have not already docked Xcode on your Dock, now is a good time to do so. Click Keep in Dock from the Dock icon option menu.

Figure 2.5

On the GLPaint download page, you can download the full example or take a quick peek at the code files using the View Source Code dropdown box.

Figure 2.6

The GLPaint example project after it has been opened in Xcode

Running the sample in the iPhone Simulator

Now you will finally get to experience an iPhone application in action! From the GLPaint project toolbar, click Build and Go and the example will launch in the iPhone Simulator. If everything has been installed properly, you should see the GLPaint application up and running, as shown in Figure 2.7.

Figure 2.7

The GLPaint example running in the iPhone Simulator.
Starting with the iPhone SDK 3.0, you have an option to "shake" the iPhone Simulator.

Play around with the example and the iPhone Simulator to start familiarizing yourself with the tools. You can rotate the device and use your mouse to draw on the screen as you would if you were touching the device. There is even an option to rotate the device under the iPhone Simulator Hardware menu. The screen on the iPhone Simulator is screaming "SHAKE ME!". At the time of writing, 3.0 did not include support for the accelerometer in the iPhone Simulator, so you may not be "shaking" anything until you install this example on your device.

N O T E
A new feature of the iPhone SDK 3.0 allows you perform a "shake gesture" in the iPhone Simulator. Unfortunately, this is not the same as accelerometer support in the iPhone Simulator and will not work in the GLPaint example yet. Shake is a new gesture that joins a family of gestures, including swipe and pinch. To perform the shake gesture in the iPhone Simulator, go to the menu bar and choose Hardware ⇨ Shake Gesture.

Running the sample on your iPhone or iPod touch

If that did not get you a little stoked, then this next exercise will. You are going to run this same application on your iPhone or iPod touch. The first thing you will need to do is plug your device into your Mac. If you have Xcode open, you can open Organizer to confirm that it has been detected. To open Organizer, choose Window ⇨ Organizer from the Xcode menu (Figure 2.8). If your device has been detected, you will see your device name in the left pane with a green dot beside it.

While in Organizer you should go ahead and install the Provisioning Profile on your device. In Chapter 1 we talked about creating Provisioning Profiles; now it's time to use them. Download the Provisioning Profile that you created for your device. Once the download has completed, drag the Provisioning Profile onto the Xcode icon on your Dock. Head back into Organizer and make sure your Provisioning Profile has been added to your device in the Provisioning section. If not, click the + (plus) button and click the file you just downloaded.

Now that your device has a Provisioning Profile installed, you can deploy, execute, and debug the sample directly on your device. Even though you have installed the Provisioning Profile on your device for development, you also need to tell your application about the Provisioning Profile. This pairing allows you to test applications on your device while also ensuring that you cannot freely distribute your app without going through the App Store. This may seem like a pain, but today distributing through the App Store has major advantages.

Figure 2.8

Organizer is your tool for installing Provisioning Profiles on your development devices, installing the beta version of the iPhone OS, and more.

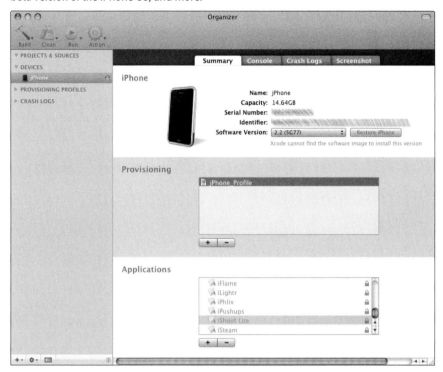

Now you are ready to walk through the steps necessary to run the example on your device:

1. Launch Xcode if you have not already done so.

2. Set the Overview pull-down menu to the version of the SDK that you wish to test against, as shown in Figure 2.9.

3. Choose Groups & Files ⇨ Resources and add a new file.

4. From the New File dialog box, choose iPhone OS ⇨ Code Signing ⇨ Entitlements (Figure 2.10) and click Next.

Figure 2.9

Selecting the Active SDK that you will be using for your project

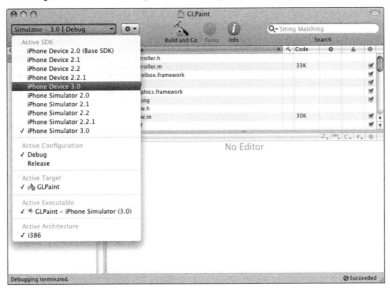

Figure 2.10

Choosing the Code Signing Entitlements template from the New File dialog box

5. You will now be in the New File dialog box. In the File Name edit box, change the name from untitled.plist to **Entitlement.plist** and click Finish (see Figure 2.11).

Figure 2.11

Specifying a name for the Entitlements file you are creating

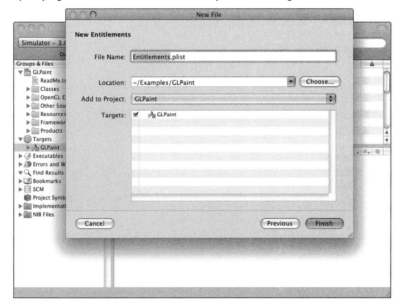

6. Select the newly created Entitlements.plist and make sure the property get-task-allow is checked off (Figure 2.12).

Figure 2.12

Configuring Code Signing Entitlements

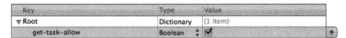

7. Choose Groups & Files ⇨ Targets ⇨ GLPaint.

8. Click the Information icon in the toolbar.

9. If not previously selected, you will need to click on the Build tab.

10. Select your Provisioning Profile under Code Signing ⇨ Code Signing Identity ⇨ Any iPhone OS Device (Figure 2.13).

Figure 2.13

Setting the Provisioning Profile here can be a stumbling block for new developers.

11. For the property Code Signing ⇨ Code Signing Entitlements, type **Entitlements.plist** (Figure 2.14).

12. Click OK and then click Build and Go, and you should see your application up and running on your iPhone or iPod touch.

Figure 2.14

Assigning the Entitlements.plist that you just created for your application

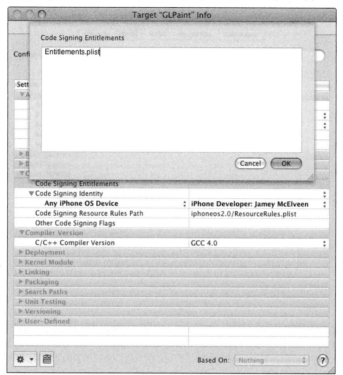

Programming: Hello World

Tradition dictates that the first program we explore creating should be the well-known Hello World application. At its simplest, Hello World is a computer program that simply displays the text "Hello World." Considered a classic of computer science, Hello World is the first application many new developers write when learning a new programming language. There are a few reasons for this. Hello World is simple enough for beginning programmers to fully understand what the application will do. And since the application does just one simple thing, you only have to learn how to do that one thing to see results. A more advanced application would require you to have a more advanced understanding before you would be prepared to create it.

Defining your goals

One thing that really sets iPhone developers apart from other developers is the expectation placed on them to always raise the bar with everything they create. This is a part of the iPhone's fit and finish that Apple has been able to create. Everything has to both look great and work great. So why should it be any different when it comes to creating your first iPhone application, Hello World? An iPhone application is expected to stand out when judged against other non-iPhone applications. Today's iPhone owners want to be surprised and delighted by any and all iPhone applications they try. And you don't want to let them down!

Before you tackle how to create a Hello World application of your very own, review Apple's Hello World sample from the iPhone Dev Center at `http://developer.apple.com/ iphone/library/samplecode/HelloWorld_iPhone/index.html`. Apple describes their Hello World as "Say hello with style. See how you can transform the mundane into the memorable with graphical flair." As you can see in Figure 2.15, Apple has done a pretty good job of taking the mundane Hello World application and making it a first-class citizen that seems perfectly at home on the iPhone.

How did they do it? Some might say they did it with style. Every detail has to be just right, and nothing can be left to chance. Although the minimum requirement for a Hello World application is to simply display the text "Hello World," this app goes so much further. Everything about the application looks and feels good, even the application icon. There are professionally published applications on many desktops right now that have only the same dull default icon.

We see planet Earth at the center of the screen, from a fascinating vantage point of someone perhaps standing on the moon. Functionality is not sacrificed for the sake of form, either, because not only does the application display "Hello, World!" but it takes any input the user provides and displays it as the output. It just happens to default to "Hello, World!" Once again, the app does more than the bare minimum required.

TIP

While the Hello World application may not appear to do much, it does accomplish one important task: You can use it to validate that the compiler, development environment, and run-time environment are all correctly installed and working as expected.

Examining your options

Take a step back and decide how you can raise the bar for your remake of the classic Hello World application. There are two areas to focus on: form and function. It's usually a good idea to think of a lot of ideas first, and then decide on the best ones to actually do.

Figure 2.15

iPhone SDK Hello World sample

Form and function are important with many things. Think about how they apply to cars, for example. People expect their cars to function properly, but they also want them to look great. What's the difference between a low-end car and a high-end car? Usually you will find great quality in how the high-end car runs, works, and looks. And along with this increase in quality you will find an increase in profit to the manufacturer. Keep this in mind when you are deciding how much time and money to invest in your future iPhone applications.

Here are some ideas to consider for making the Hello World app even better:

- Have an animated Earth graphic that revolves.
- Have the Earth graphic zoom in from far away to up close.
- Get the user's location programmatically from his device. Then center the Earth graphic on this location, and finally zoom out to space to see the full Earth graphic.
- Have the Earth graphic respond to user touch, allowing rotation and zooming options.
- Have the Earth graphic respond back by displaying the user name from the device database.
- Have the device play a Hello World audio recording.
- Display the Hello World text first in one language and then in others over time.
- Have the Hello World text scroll across the screen in a large, banner-size font.
- Start from a star field perspective and zoom in on the Earth graphic when the user touches the screen.
- Have an animated star field background behind the Earth graphic to show motion effect.
- Have an animated moon graphic, or at least a full-sphere moon graphic similar to the Earth image.

All of these ideas are great, but of course, you cannot do every one of them. Since this is the first application you will create, don't make it your most challenging. Instead, focus on a single feature that will give you the most return for your investment of time and effort. Here is the idea that will be the most exciting for end users to experience, and easy for new developers to program: Display the Hello World text first in one language and then in others over time. You will learn to make the foundation for this application in the sections ahead. From there you should be in a position to experiment and try some of the ideas listed above on your own.

Xcode

Now you are ready to create a Hello World app of your very own. Open Xcode and choose File ⇨ New Project. Under iPhone OS, choose Application, and then choose the Utility Application template (Figure 2.16). Save the New Project as HelloWorldEx.

Xcode now generates all the base code files required for your HelloWorldEx utility project (Figure 2.17). Specifically, Xcode creates a Main View, a Flipside View, and all the navigation controls and plumbing you need to move between these two views. You will use the Main View for all of the core functionality of the application, and save the flipside view for an About Us screen.

The iPhone's screen resolution is 320 pixels wide by 480 pixels tall. You will make your Hello World application run full-screen so that you can take advantage of every pixel of screen space. But first you will add all of your application's graphic assets to the application project. You can either create your own or use the ones included in the book's sample code. The first file is called *starfield.png* and is a nice image of stars in space. This will be used as your background image. On top of this you will place the *earth.png* file, an image of the Earth. This is the main graphic of the application, and will be placed in the center of the screen.

Figure 2.16

Xcode New Project dialog box

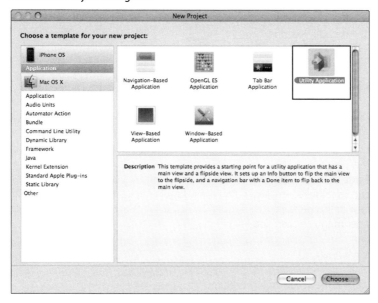

Figure 2.17

Hello World opened inside of the Xcode Project Explorer

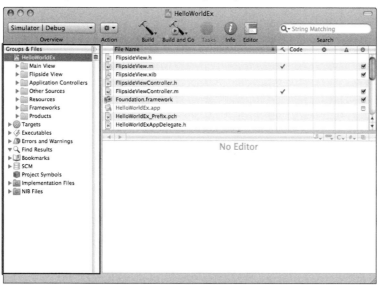

On the left-hand side of the Xcode Project Explorer you will see a Groups & Files list. Double-click on the Resources folder to expand it and choose Project ➪ Add to Project. Find the files *starfield.png* and *earth.png*, click on them, and click Add. Be sure to check the Copy items into destination group's folder (if needed) check box on the next dialog box. The rest of the settings can remain on their default settings.

TIP

Using separate image files for the Earth and stars images allows you to keep the application flexible enough to make future changes. For example, someday you might decide to make the star field image scroll horizontally across the screen behind the Earth image, or replace the static image of the Earth with a series of images you could play as an animation of the Earth revolving.

Interface Builder

On the left-hand side of the Xcode Project Explorer you will see a Groups & Files list. Double-click on the Resources folder to expand it and then double-click on the `MainView.xib` file to open the Main View in Interface Builder (Figure 2.18). Click in the Main View window, and from the Interface Builder menu choose Tools ➪ Library (Figure 2.19).

Figure 2.18

MainView.xib selected in the Xcode Project Explorer

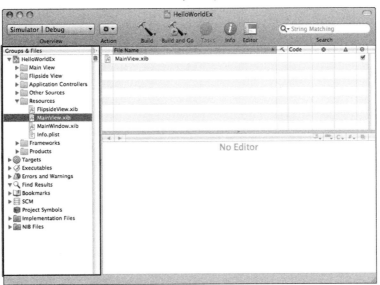

From the Library window click the Image View item and drag it over to the Main View window. If you do not see the Image View item, be sure that you have Objects selected, and that you are in the following section: Library ⇨ Cocoa Touch Plugin ⇨ Data Views. It will expand itself, and you will be able to fill the entire Main View window with it. You will use this Image View, or UIImageView as it is also known, to hold your star field image.

Figure 2.19

Interface Builder with Main View loaded

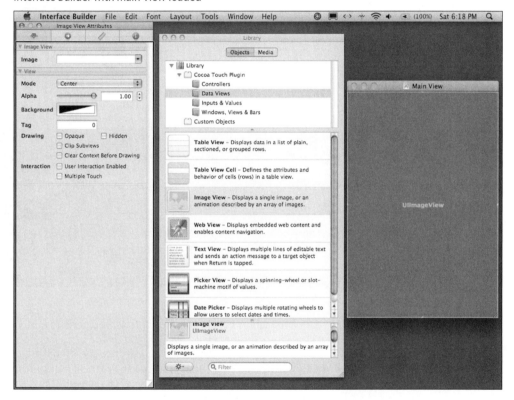

Choose Tools ⇨ Inspector. The Inspector window has a toolbar at the top with four buttons: Image View Attributes, Image View Connections, Image View Size, and Image View Identity. Click the first button, Image View Attributes. You should see a pull-down menu labeled Image, under the section named Image View (Figure 2.19). Set the Image to *starfield.png*. Repeat this process to add another UIImageView to hold the Earth image. This time set the Image to *earth. png*. Once you have done this your Main View should match the one shown in Figure 2.20.

Figure 2.20

Adding an Image View using the Inspector

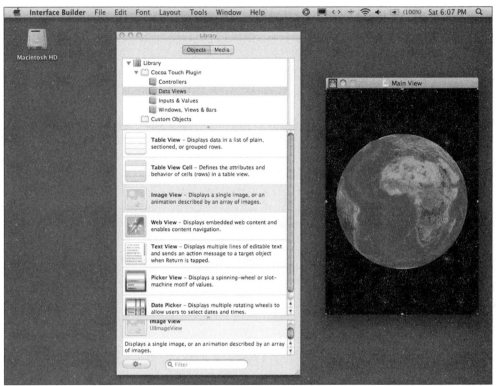

Now that you have added your application's basic graphic controls, you need to add a label to the Main View to be able to show the user the "Hello, World!" text. In the Library window, under Objects, choose Library ⇨ Cocoa Touch Plugin ⇨ Inputs & Values. Click and drag the Label control on to the Main View window under the Earth image. As you move the label control down the screen, Xcode shows a grid line marking the bottom border of the screen. This is a great place to anchor the label control. On the left and right of the label control you will see control size handles that can be grabbed with the mouse and used to resize the control's width. Grab the label control's right handle and drag it toward the right edge of the screen until Xcode displays the right-edge border grid line. Do the same for the label control's left handle and the left-edge border grid line.

Make sure that this label control is still selected in the Main View window and choose Tools ⇨ Inspector. Be sure the first item, Text Field Attributes, is chosen in the Inspector window's top toolbar. The top-most item shown should now be the Text field. Set this text to "Hello, World!" and then click the center Alignment option. Your Main View window should now look very similar to the one in Figure 2.21.

Figure 2.21

Editing Label Attributes using the Inspector

Now you need to wire up your controls. This allows you to respond to any events that occur to your application's controls and to change any of your controls' attributes at run-time. Since in this version of the application both the Earth and stars images will remain static at run-time, you can leave both of these UIImageViews as they are. However, in order to update the label's text at run-time, you will need to take the following steps. Open the Inspector window, if you do not already have it open. Select the label control and click on the Identity tab at the top of the Inspector window.

Notice that the Inspector window is dynamic and updates to match which control you have selected at any given time. Click on the Main View window's title bar and the Inspector's title should change to Main View Identity. You should find a Class Outlets section that lists Outlets and Types. Click the add class outlet button (the small plus sign), add a new outlet named hello-WorldLabel, and set its Type to UILabel.

Now the Main View class has an outlet named helloWorldLabel that can accept a UILabel control. But what if you had multiple UILabel controls on your form? How would the Main View class know which UILabel it should use for the helloWorldLabel outlet? Actually, right now it doesn't, even with only one UILabel. Basically you have a box that a UILabel control can fit into, and now you need to assign a UILabel control to it. To do this, right-click the label control and choose New Referencing Outlet. Click the little circle on the left of New Referencing Outlet and drag it to the title bar of the Main View's window. You should now see helloWorldLabel and Main View listed in the displayed menu, as shown in Figure 2.22.

Figure 2.22

Adding a label outlet to a Main View

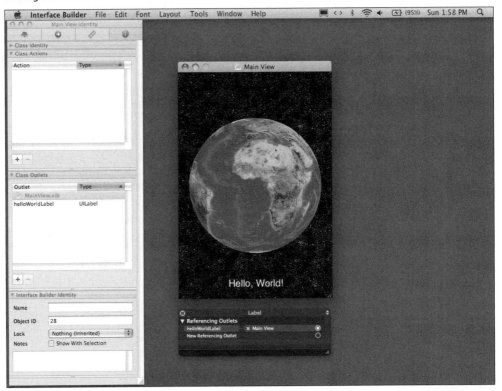

Generating code

Interface Builder generates the matching classes and code that you will need in Xcode for the user interface you have created thus far. On the Interface Builder, choose File ⇨ Write Class Files. A Save dialog box should appear and you should see Save As: MainView selected, as shown in Figure 2.23. If not, make sure you have the Main View window selected in Interface Builder and try again. Once you have the correct settings in the Save dialog box, click the Save button.

Figure 2.23

Save dialog box

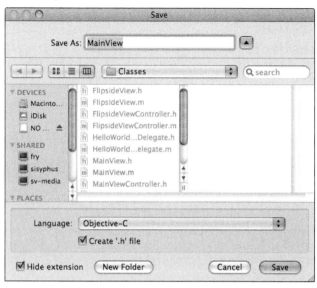

You are asked if you want to replace the existing files with the new files Interface Builder has generated (Figure 2.24). You can safely click Replace, since you do not have any code you have hand-written at this point. If you did have existing code of your own, you could click Merge to merge the two code sets. For the most part, Xcode can merge code safely, but it can be a little too advanced for new developers first starting out, so it is best to avoid this option for now. (The third option, Cancel, is available in case you decide you are not ready to generate code.)

Figure 2.24

Replace or Merge prompt

A lot of the heavy lifting is done now. You have all of your graphics and text controls placed and ready. If you like, you can click the Build and Go button in the main toolbar of the Xcode Project

Explorer, or simply press ⌘+R. Either option will cause Xcode to launch your Hello World application in the iPhone Simulator.

Coding the application

You're not quite done. You still need to write a little code to make the real magic happen. Go back into Xcode and choose Groups & Files ➪ HelloWorldEx ➪ Main View ➪ MainView.m. Type the following code to make your `MainView.m` match the following listing:

```
#import "MainView.h"
@implementation MainView
-(void)awakeFromNib {
   helloWorldLabel.text = "Hello, World!";
}
@end
```

The `awakeFromNib` method is an event that is by design automatically called when a view is first being loaded. You can try changing the `helloWorldLabel` text and then use Build and Go to see the results in the iPhone Simulator. Even better, you can write some code to do it for you. We are going to use an `NSTimer` object to update the `helloWorldLabel` every three seconds. Update your `MainView.m` file to look like the following:

```
#import "MainView.h"
@implementation MainView
static int timerCount = 0;
- (void)awakeFromNib {
   helloWorldLabel.text = "Hello, World!";
   [NSTimer scheduledTimerWithTimeInterval(3.0) target:self
   selector:@selector(onTimer)
      userInfo: nil repeats:YES];
}
   - (void)onTimer {
      timerCount++;

         switch (timerCount % 5) {
         case 0:
         // say "Hello, World!" in English
         helloWorldLabel.text = @"Hello, World!";
         break;
         case 1:
         // say "Hello, World!" in French
         helloWorldLabel.text = @"Bonjour, monde!";
         break;
         case 2:
         // say "Hello, World!" in Spanish
         helloWorldLabel.text = @"Hola, Mundo!";
         break;
         case 3:
```

```
        // say "Hello, World!" in German
        helloWorldLabel.text = @"Hallo, Welt!";
        break;
    case 4:
        // say "Hello, World!" in Italian
        helloWorldLabel.text = @"Ciao, Mondo!";
        break;
    }
}
@end
```

You now have a fairly functional application. Go ahead and give it a try by clicking Build and Go. What's left? You need to remove the iPhone Status Bar at the top of the screen. You need to add content to your Flipside View—it will make a great About Us screen when you're done. And you need to give your application a custom icon.

To remove the Status Bar from the top of the screen, add one line of code to the beginning of your `awakeFromNib` function:

```
[[UIApplication sharedApplication] setStatusBarHidden:YES animated:NO];
```

About Us screen

Next, you will add the Flipside View content. From the Xcode Project Explorer, choose Groups & Files ⇨ HelloWorldEx ⇨ Resources ⇨ FlipsideView.xib. Double-click on `FlipsideView.xib` to open it in Interface Builder, and you should see a blank canvas ready to hold your ideas. We have a lot of options for what we could do with this screen and how we could do it. But to keep things simple starting out, we are going to add a full-screen graphic to this form. This is an easy but powerful way to present to the application user almost anything we want.

You can either use the *aboutus.png* from the sample code or create one of your own. We will add this graphic to the screen in the same manner as the *starfield.png* and the *earth.png* files. Under Groups & Files in Xcode, find the Resources folder under HelloWorldEx. Right-click on the Resources folder and choose Add ⇨ Existing Files.

Now locate the *aboutus.png* image you will use and choose Add. Check the Copy items into destination group's folder (if needed) check box and keep everything else on their default settings. Set Reference Type to Default, set Text Encoding to Unicode (UTF-8), and make sure the option Recursively create groups for any added folders is selected. When you're done, click the Add button.

From inside Interface Builder, choose Tools ⇨ Library. As you did earlier in the chapter, click on an Image View and drag it onto the Flipside View form. You can find the Image View control under Objects ⇨ Library ⇨ Cocoa Touch Plugin ⇨ Data Views. After you have placed the UIImageView control on the form, make sure it fills the entire screen and choose Tools ⇨ Inspector. On the first tab, Image View Attributes, set the Image field to your chosen *aboutus.png* file. Your Flipside View form should now look similar to the one in Figure 2.25.

Click Build and Go in Xcode to see the application as it now stands. To get to the About Us screen, click the small info icon in the bottom-right corner of the screen. We do have a little touching up left to do on the About Us screen. By default the Flipside View's title text is set to the application's project name, which is HelloWorldEx in our case. This is not the most user-friendly message we could give, so we should go ahead and change it now.

Going back to Xcode, one way to update the text is to choose Edit ⇨ Find in Project, and search for the text HelloWorldEx. Xcode should find one occurrence of HelloWorldEx that is located in the `RootViewController.m` file. You can double-click the filename in the search results to open the file directly. Or you can locate the file inside the Xcode Project Explorer's Groups & Files list under HelloWorldEx ⇨ Application Controllers ⇨ RootViewController.m. Once you find the HelloWorldEx text, change it to **Hello World**. Feel free to give the application another spin to see the corrected text at run-time.

Figure 2.25

The About Us screen

Application icon

Finally, you need to add a custom icon to your application and set the application name to finish it off. Again, you can use either the *icon.png* file we provided or one of your own. Use Xcode to add your selected *icon.png* to the Resources folder as you did with previous images. Once you have done this, in Xcode choose Groups & Files ⇨ Targets ⇨ HelloWorldEx. Right-click on HelloWorldEx and choose Get Info. You should see the following tabs at the top of the form: General, Build, Rules, Properties, and Comments. Click on the Properties tab and set the Icon File field to *icon.png*. Click on the General tab and set the Name field to Hello World. Click Save, and then click Build and Go to see your finished application. Your application icon should now look like the one in Figure 2.26.

Figure 2.26

The application icon for Hello World on the iPhone Simulator

Summary

Now that you have completed your first application, we can officially welcome you to the exciting world of iPhone programming! We have only begun to scratch the surface of all of the possibilities that are open to you. By now you have the skills you need to begin exploring many of those possibilities. You are ready to create your own iPhone applications from scratch. You have the knowledge to display text and graphics. And you know how to make the application respond to timers repeatedly. It's time for you to begin thinking of ideas for your next iPhone application; to take what you know and push it a little further.

You have covered a lot of material in this chapter. Now you should take a moment and review the most important topics. First you learned about setting up your environment. This included information on registering, downloading, and installing the iPhone SDK. Then you learned how to run an iPhone SDK sample application both in the iPhone Simulator and on a real device. After learning how to run a sample application, you then learned how to program a new application on your own. You should now understand the process of defining your goals, examining your options, and coding the application. And by now you should be familiar with the basic tools of Xcode, including the Xcode Project Explorer, Interface Builder, and the Library and Inspector tools. Finally, you should have an understanding of the different kinds of files Xcode uses to make your application, especially code and image files. There is still a lot more to learn, but you should feel that you could write a simple iPhone application on your own now. And we highly encourage you to do so, because that way you will learn even more.

Creating Simple iPhone Applications

Constructing Puzzle Apps

Now that you've gotten your feet wet, we are going to examine our first game. The games developed in this chapter can be found on the App Store and the source code downloaded from our Web site, `http://appsamuck.com`. Puzzle apps can be the least complex type of game to build, so they are a great place to start. However, do not underestimate the popularity of your app just because it is easy to build. A good puzzle app can have a longer life span than just about any other type of game. Puzzle apps can be fun, challenging, and addictive. Just think for a minute how many platforms you have seen Tetris ported to. Tetris has a staying power like no other application. Even in its simplest form, Tetris is still a fun game to play to pass the time.

In this chapter we'll review some of the classic examples of puzzle games, and hopefully they will inspire you to invent the next great puzzle app for the iPhone.

Reviewing Famous Examples

Successful games all share a few key features: They need to be easy to learn, increasingly challenging, and downright addictive. It is fairly straightforward to code a game that is easy to learn or one that challenges the players. However, creating a game that is fun and addictive is not so black and white. To accomplish this you have to mix the ingredients in such a way that they synergize into an exciting and addictive game.

As we've mentioned, Tetris is one of the most celebrated puzzle applications ever written. It is difficult to find any gaming platform that it is not available on. Tetris meets our requirements of being easy to learn and increasingly challenging. Most importantly, Tetris is addictive!

What are some other puzzle applications we can think of? Here are a few that come to mind. All meet the requirements of being easy to learn, increasingly challenging, and addictive:

- **Minesweeper.** `http://en.wikipedia.org/wiki/Minesweeper_(computer_game)`

- **Bomberman.** http://en.wikipedia.org/wiki/Bomberman
- **The Incredible Machine.** http://en.wikipedia.org/wiki/The_Incredible_Machine
- **Sudoku.** http://en.wikipedia.org/wiki/Sudoku
- **Luxor.** http://en.wikipedia.org/wiki/Luxor_(computer_game)
- **Pipe Dream.** http://en.wikipedia.org/wiki/Pipe_Dream_(video_game)
- **Portal.** http://en.wikipedia.org/wiki/Portal_(video_game)
- **Bejeweled.** http://en.wikipedia.org/wiki/Bejeweled
- **Lemmings.** http://en.wikipedia.org/wiki/Lemmings_(video_game)

You've probably played at least one game in this list. You may even have them on your iPhone now. If so, identify the attributes that make the game fun and exciting for you. Now with these elements in mind, dig deep and try to develop an idea that will keep a player occupied time and time again. If you look at the list, the most addictive element about these games is the fact that they become increasingly challenging the longer you play them.

Here are three techniques you can use to present challenges, which we'll discuss in detail in the next section:

- **Create time pressure.** When solving the puzzle, make sure gamers have only a limited amount of time to complete the task.
- **Limit number of turns.** Some puzzle games are turn- or step-based applications. You can limit the number of turns allowed to gamers or base their score on how few moves they can complete the level in.
- **Limit space.** If you allow blocks to fill up all the space at the top of the screen, the game ends. Tetris is a perfect example of this.

The best bonus concerning puzzle games is they can be easy to develop. Most of them have a very small code base compared to other game types that can take so long to pull together that they become a full-fledged production. However, do not let this trap you into taking the easy way out. You still need to spend plenty of time polishing up the menus and screens to get noticed when you get to the App Store.

So, what can you learn from the previous examples and other puzzles that will help ensure that your game is successful? Make sure your puzzle game . . .

- Is user friendly and easy to learn.
- Makes a good first impression and has an attractive overall appearance.
- Engages the gamer in an increasingly challenging series of stages or levels.
- Is addictive enough to keep the gamer coming back and telling his friends about the game.

CROSS-REFERENCE
See Chapter 8 for an in-depth discussion on turn-based games.

Understanding Game Design: Presenting Challenges

It is a fact that the human mind likes challenges. Very early in our lives we are presented with learning challenges. When we were toddlers we liked to play with learning toys. You have probably seen the shape-sorter cubes that toddlers play with, such as the one shown in Figure 3.1. The cube has different-shaped holes in it and it comes with matching plastic or wooden shapes that will only fit into the matching hole. At this age most children cannot talk much, yet they love to be challenged.

Figure 3.1

A shape-sorter learning toy

Preschool children like to play games that require them to recognize patterns, match similar items, or follow a mechanical process. As we age we continue to crave challenges. This drive compels us to stick with a challenge until we can defeat it. Infusing these challenges into your design is what creating puzzle games is all about.

Earlier in the chapter we mentioned the three different ways puzzle games can present challenges. Let's look at each of these ways in more detail.

Create time pressure

It is always beneficial to analyze a system that is not software based to help understand a concept before committing it to code. With applying this concept to games, browse through the board game section of your local toy store. Here you can find a bounty of rich examples. For time-sensitive games, take a look at the game Perfection.

Perfection requires the player to locate and fit odd-shaped pegs into their matching holes before the timer runs out. Does this remind you of the sorter cube we just looked at? With just a little imagination you should be able to conceive how you could apply this concept in code.

TIP

When brainstorming ideas, grab a pen and paper and jot them down so you don't forget them. You may find yourself writing some of your best ideas on napkins or in the Notes app on the iPhone.

Time pressure adds an element of anxiety to a video game. Adding time pressure may lure players into making rash decisions that they would otherwise have reasoned through with ease. This pressure also opens up possibilities for increasing the difficulty level as players progress. You can start players off with an ample amount of time to complete the puzzle, then your game can become greedier with the time allotted as players progress through your levels.

Limit number of turns

Most turn-based games limit the user to exactly one turn. This gives the user only one decision or move on each turn to change the course of the game. This limitation often leads to users memorizing and employing move patterns to be successful at the game. Consider the game of chess, shown in Figure 3.2.

Figure 3.2

The classic board game of chess

The best chess players can think several moves ahead even though they are limited to making one move at a time. The creators of chess probably never envisioned that the game would become such a fertile ground for challenge and competitiveness. Chess has transcended beyond a simple board game that holds a player's attention for one or two turns into a culture of players with their own unique styles and strategies.

Okay, we understand that trying to build a game that is as good as chess would be setting a high standard; however, it really showcases the potential for a great turn-based game. Think in terms of progression and goals. If you are playing a game that limits turns, like in chess, that generally means there is another player with his own goals and agenda. You take a turn, then the other player takes a turn, and this continues until one of the players achieves his goal.

When creating a turn-based game, consider the following tips:

- **Craft a clear and simple goal.** The goal should be enticing and the reward should deliver a certain degree of excitement.

- **Carve a clear and easy path to the goal.** When you first start the game, the first few levels should be easy. Achieving the goal should be more instructional than challenging. Use this as a starting point, or you can even make this the first level to help orient the player to your game.

- **Introduce obstacles.** Now that the player can see the goal, throw in a few roadblocks. This can even be controlled by the other player. Player 1 overcomes an obstacle on his turn, and then player 2 introduces a new obstacle on her turn.

- **Add escalation elements.** No matter how great your game is, players will get tired if it drags out too long. If the game lasts too long, consider giving more power to the players on each sequential turn. This adds pressure on each turn for the player to try and end the match. You see this in a lot of sports with tiebreakers, sudden death, and so on.

An excellent example of a puzzle game that utilizes some of these tips is Trism, which is played on a board of triangular prisms called trisms (Figure 3.3). The game is played by sliding the trisms in six different directions to match colors. The game starts at an easy level and progresses in difficulty. The game becomes even more interesting and difficult as obstacles such as bombs and locks are introduced.

Check out Trism for yourself by browsing to `http:/itunes.com/apps/trism` on your iPhone or on a computer with iTunes installed.

 CROSS-REFERENCE

The link `http:/itunes.com/apps/trism` is an iTunes Deep Link. See Chapter 10 for more about iTunes Deep Links.

Your game should not be so easy that players always know what the best move is to make on their next turn. If that is the case, you will want to consider making some changes to make the game more challenging. If users approach your game with calculation and strategy, you have crafted a good turn-based game.

Figure 3.3

Trism is one of the first and most famous iPhone puzzle games.

Courtesy of Steve Demeter

Limit space

A good puzzle game can present challenges by requiring the player to navigate in a limited space. These types of challenges work really well on the iPhone because your screen real estate is limited to begin with. Instead of trying to work around this limitation, you will find you can compile games that leverage this limitation.

Here again, we can look at Tetris as a classic example of a challenge that is enhanced by making space a limiting factor. In Tetris, as the blocks pile to the top of the screen, the play area becomes very cramped and it becomes increasingly challenging to position the blocks without taking up even more space.

Consider some of the same key points when presenting challenges by limiting space:

- **Craft a clear and simple goal.** You could provide the player with a target or exit, or you could have a puzzle that is only solved when all the pieces are oriented properly.

- **Carve a clear and easy path to the goal.** Again, start with a simple, achievable goal. On early levels space may not even be a factor. However, it should be apparent that less space presents a challenge, which can actually add more enjoyment to the game.

- **Introduce obstacles.** As the play progresses, you can start closing in the walls. Some of the same puzzles that players breezed through earlier become more difficult as the available space vanishes.

You have looked at three examples of presenting challenges, but by no means are these the only three. If you can invent a new way to present challenges, your game will stand out because it will be fresh and unique.

Embracing Multi-Touch

Multi-Touch is one of the many exciting features of the iPhone. You have probably played around with touchscreens before, but something about the experience created by the iPhone is new and unique. When your applications embrace Multi-Touch, you are delivering the experience iPhone owners have come to love (and expect).

When envisioning your game, try to think beyond buttons and joysticks and think in terms of interaction with your virtual environment. This is a bit more challenging than buttons because the interaction is no longer so cut and dry. The iPhone does not have a big red button to fire missiles. The relationship between input and response becomes fuzzier. This is a good thing! Input is now a rich and flexible world for you to leverage.

Leveraging a new style of input

Your goal should be to design a puzzle app with a user interface that delivers a more immersive experience than is possible with joysticks and keyboards. Multi-Touch opens the door to a new level of interaction that would be cumbersome otherwise. Think about dealing with keyboard input on joystick-based games. How many times have you had to enter your initials or name in a game where you had to scroll through the alphabet to select each character? The iPhone simply scrolls a virtual keyboard on the screen, allowing you to quickly enter the characters with minimal keystrokes. The AmuckSlider game we discuss later in this chapter greatly benefits from Multi-Touch (Figure 3.4).

In a real slider puzzle game, you physically slide the tiles from where they are to an adjacent empty cell (Figure 3.5). To truly embrace Multi-Touch, you need to create a virtual experience as close to the physical sensation as possible. AmuckSlider accomplishes this by requiring players to mimic the same physical gestures that they would use on a real puzzle.

Figure 3.4

AmuckSlider in action

Figure 3.5

A traditional sliding
puzzle game

Learning the technology

The examples on the Apple development portal are great! If you have not done so already, we highly recommend that you peruse the plethora of example apps available there. At the time of this writing you could find an example there called MoveMe (`http://developer.apple.com/iphone/library/samplecode/MoveMe/`), which is a great introduction to Multi-Touch. This simple application has a placard on the screen that you can grab and drag with your finger (Figure 3.6). When you release the placard, it springs back to the center and wobbles a little.

Figure 3.6

The MoveMe example from iPhone Dev Center is an excellent example to get you started with Multi-Touch.

Let's examine the code that makes this work. In order to begin capturing touch input, you will need to implement one or more of the following events in your `UIView`:

```
- (void)touchesBegan:(NSSet *)touches withEvent:(UIEvent *)event;
- (void)touchesMoved:(NSSet *)touches withEvent:(UIEvent *)event;
- (void)touchesEnded:(NSSet *)touches withEvent:(UIEvent *)event;
- (void)touchesCancelled:(NSSet *)touches withEvent:(UIEvent *)event;
```

Responding to touchesBegan

If you run the example, you will notice that when you touch the placard it grows a little and then you can drag it. This first response is captured in the `touchesBegan` event:

```
- (void)touchesBegan:(NSSet *)touches withEvent:(UIEvent *)event {
    UITouch *touch = [touches anyObject];
    if ([touch view] != placardView) {
        ...
        return;
    }
    CGPoint touchPoint = [touch locationInView:self];
    [self animateFirstTouchAtPoint:touchPoint];
}
```

Notice that you do not have a single touch parameter but an `NSSet` of touches. The first thing this example does is distill this down to one touch within the line:

```
UITouch *touch = [touches anyObject];
```

Now a check is performed to see if the view that is responsible for reporting the touch is the placard; if it is not, the method exits before any animations are started:

```
- (void)touchesBegan:(NSSet *)touches withEvent:(UIEvent *)event {
    UITouch *touch = [touches anyObject];
    if ([touch view] != placardView) {
        ...
        return;
    }
    CGPoint touchPoint = [touch locationInView:self];
    [self animateFirstTouchAtPoint:touchPoint];
}
```

Next, `locationInView` is used to convert the position of the touch into a new position that is relative to the Main View:

```
CGPoint touchPoint = [touch locationInView:self];
```

Finally, an animation is performed and you see the button grow on the screen:

```
[self animateFirstTouchAtPoint:touchPoint];
```

Responding to touchesMoved

As you drag your finger on the screen, you experience the placard sliding across the screen. This behavior is achieved by responding to the `touchesMoved` event:

```
- (void)touchesMoved:(NSSet *)touches withEvent:(UIEvent *)event {
   UITouch *touch = [touches anyObject];
   if ([touch view] == placardView) {
      CGPoint location = [touch locationInView:self];
      placardView.center = location;
      return;
   }
}
```

Most of the setup code in `touchesMoved` is the same as in `touchesBegan`. All you need to do is reset the center of the placard to the center of the touch:

```
placardView.center = location;
```

Responding to touchesEnded

When you remove your finger from the screen, you see the placard spring back to the center of the screen. This behavior is achieved by responding to the `touchesEnded` event:

```
- (void)touchesEnded:(NSSet *)touches withEvent:(UIEvent *)event {
   UITouch *touch = [touches anyObject];
   if ([touch view] == placardView) {
      self.userInteractionEnabled = NO;
      [self animatePlacardViewToCenter];
      return;
   }
}
```

Most of the setup code in `touchesEnded` is the same as in `touchesBegan`. After the common setup is complete, you will want to turn off any user interaction until the placard returns to its original location. This is accomplished with the following line:

```
self.userInteractionEnabled = NO;
```

Now that interaction is disabled, you can begin the animation. In our example this is accomplished by a call to the instance method `animatePlacardViewToCenter`:

```
[self animatePlacardViewToCenter];
```

It is important that you restore user interaction when the animation is complete. It is not shown here, but when the animation is complete, user interaction is restored. You can accomplish this by setting the value of the property `userInteractionEnabled` to YES, as shown below:

```
self.userInteractionEnabled = YES;
```

Responding to touchesCancelled

The `touchesCancelled` event is fired when the touch sequence is cancelled by a system event, such as an incoming phone call. You should respond to this event, but your goal should be to clean up and get out as quickly as possible:

```
- (void)touchesCancelled:(NSSet *)touches withEvent:(UIEvent *)event {
    placardView.center = self.center;
    placardView.transform = CGAffineTransformIdentity;
}
```

Notice that we are simply setting the placard back to its original state with no glitz or animations. The player will probably not even see this happen, so keep it short and sweet.

Envisioning Animations

Like Multi-Touch, animations add an element of excitement and immersion to a player's overall gaming experience. Animations are not new to gamers; in fact, we would argue that in today's gaming market, this is a minimal expectation. However, high-quality games with smooth animations were not generally seen on a hand-held phone. This is yet another quality of the iPhone that sets it apart from other mobile devices.

Luckily for you, Apple did not stop with making high-quality animations possible. High-quality animations are easy to achieve without having to code every frame of the process. Let's revisit the previous example but this time focus on animations.

Earlier you saw the code for the method `touchesBegan`. In `touchesBegan` you will see a call to the method `animateFirstTouchAtPoint`. This method is responsible for the animation you see when you first touch the placard. Here's a look at the source to this method:

```
- (void)animateFirstTouchAtPoint:(CGPoint)touchPoint {
    NSValue *touchPointValue = [[NSValue valueWithCGPoint:touchPoint] retain];
    [UIView beginAnimations:nil context:touchPointValue];
    [UIView setAnimationDuration:0.15];
    CGAffineTransform transform =
        CGAffineTransformMakeScale(1.2, 1.2);
    [UIView setAnimationDidStopSelector:
        @selector(growAnimationDidStop:finished:context:)];
    placardView.transform = transform;
    [UIView commitAnimations];
}
```

The previous block of code is the complete `animateFirstTouchAtPoint` method. In this method you will see that the first line sets the `touchPointValue` by converting the parameter `touchPoint` to an `NSValue`. The `touchPointValue` is passed as the context parameter of the call to `beginAnimations:context:`. Ultimately, the context parameter will be passed the method `growAnimationDidStop`, which is assigned as the selector parameter of the method `setAnimationDidStopSelector:`. Now the `growAnimationDidStop` method will be called when the animation stops and `touchPointValue` will be passed in as the context parameter.

The following code is a further breakdown of the animation steps. First, you will set up the animation by calling these methods:

```
[UIView beginAnimations:nil context:touchPointValue];
[UIView setAnimationDuration:0.15];
[UIView setAnimationDidStopSelector:
    @selector(growAnimationDidStop:finished:context:)];
```

The first line above begins the animation and passes in the context. The second line tells the animation how long it should last. The third line assigns a selector to be called when the animation is finished.

Now you are ready to tell the view how to animate:

```
CGAffineTransform transform = CGAffineTransformMakeScale(1.2, 1.2);
placardView.transform = transform;
```

In the previous section of code, a call to `CGAffineTransformMakeScale` is made to create a transform. The transform will scale the placard up by 20 percent:

```
[UIView commitAnimations];
```

Finally, the previous line of code is responsible for committing the animation. This is all you have to do! When you call `commitAnimations`, the animation engine calculates how many frames are necessary and plays them one by one until the specified transform has been performed. In this example, once this is complete, the message `growAnimationDidStop` is sent.

Programming: AmuckSlider

Now we are going to review our first game with you. We have used Multi-Touch and animations to create the simple puzzle application that we call AmuckSlider. With each of the applications in this book, we will guide you through some design and analysis before you get started reviewing the code.

Defining your goals

Before beginning any project, you need to define its goals. In AmuckSlider we want to create a simple but entertaining puzzle game reminiscent of the classic puzzle slider games that were played before we had video games. Here are our goals for AmuckSlider:

- The game should feel similar to classic slider games so that it's easy to learn to play.
- The game should try to introduce elements that you can only experience in an electronic device.
- The game should increase in difficulty as you play.
- The game should include some features to facilitate viral sales.

NOTE

Viral sales are a good thing—we are not talking about creating a virus! *Viral marketing* and *viral advertising* are buzz-terms that refer to marketing through word of mouth or social networking. Any time you have a player's attention, you should be thinking about how to make it easy for him to tell a friend about your game.

Examining your options

Our options will be constrained by the goals we have chosen. We must also filter our options based on the capabilities of the iPhone SDK.

Let's examine our first goal: "The game should feel similar to classic slider games so that the game play is easy to learn." This goal has Multi-Touch written all over it. When playing a classic slider game, you generally hold the game in one hand and use a finger to slide the tiles with the other. This is exactly the experience we want to try and achieve with the Multi-Touch interface.

Our second goal is "The game should try to introduce elements that you can only experience in an electronic device." This takes a little creativity. Instead of just having a plain old slider app, we wanted to add some spice. After considering this awhile, we decided that instead of having a scrambled picture, we would put arrows on the tiles. The arrows should point in the direction of their home or the correct location they need to be in in order for the puzzle to be solved. This provides a slightly different challenge than a classic slider puzzle and hopefully enough difference to set AmuckSlider apart from the other slider puzzles already available on the App Store.

Our third goal is "The game should increase in difficulty as you play." We can accomplish this by increasing the number of tiles as you progress in the game. Another option is to increase the number of tiles you have to get in the correct position in order to solve the puzzle. Since we are not using a picture, we can limit the number of tiles that the player has to get in the right location in order to solve the puzzle. The best option is to combine the two and increase the difficulty a little on each level.

Our final goal is "The game should include some viral aspect to help increase sales." Two options immediately come to mind:

- Have a high-score system that allows players to view and upload their high score to a high-score server, and then to send an e-mail to their friends bragging about their score.

- Allow players to e-mail their high score to a friend, and in the e-mail include a link that encourages them to get the game and beat their friend's score.

For AmuckSlider, we chose the second option. This option does not require a high-score server and we do not have to invest in an online service to accomplish this goal. If the game does extremely well, we may want to consider the first option in an update.

Coding the application

Now it's time to get started reviewing the code in the application. We know how we want to build the code, and we have reviewed some of skills necessary to make it happen. Each of the game projects in this book can be very detailed, so in order to prevent the important details from getting lost, we will focus on explaining the important areas.

We recommend that you download the code for this example from `http://appsamuck.com/gamedevbook/amuckslider` and peruse the source as you read the book. Download the "Before Polish" version of the source code.

Creating the project

For this project we have chosen to use the Utility Application template. This template has a small information icon in the bottom-right corner (Figure 3.7). When you click this icon the screen flips, revealing an information screen (Figure 3.8).

NOTE

You can include information about yourself or your company and advertise other games and products you may have on the info screen.

Figure 3.7
Click the small "i" info icon to bring up the info screen.

You can use the info screen to do the following:

- Show some information and a description for the game.
- Show the player's current high score (in our case, the highest level that has been completed).
- Provide a button that, when clicked, allows players to brag to their friends about their high score.
- Tell people about this book and show them how to get it.
- Tell people about other games in this book.

Figure 3.8

After the info icon is clicked, the info screen is displayed.

Hopefully you have already downloaded the code from `http://appsamuck.com` and are ready to follow through. If you have been using Xcode and developing for the iPhone, you already know how to create new projects. However, if you have not, we'll take a moment at the beginning of the application to walk you through the steps of creating a project and a new class for some of the shorter, less involved items. As we progress to larger items, we'll assume you are following along and just cover the relevant material and methods.

Here are the steps you need to follow to create a utility app the same way we started AmuckSlider. Launch Xcode and choose File ⇨ New Project. From the New Project dialog box, click Application under iPhone OS on the left and then click Utility Application (see Figure 3.9).

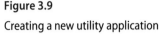

Figure 3.9

Creating a new utility application

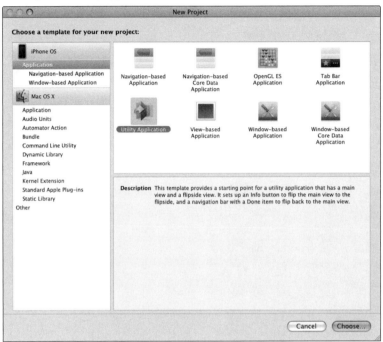

You will be prompted to name your project. We named ours **AmuckSlider**, but choose whatever name you like. When the project is created, several files are created for you. To get started, let's go ahead and complete our Info View.

Putting info in the Info View

You will find the source you will want to modify for the Info View in the files FlipsideView Controller.h and FlipsideViewController.m. Most of the information in this screen is static, but two elements are not. First, we need the high score to change to reflect the player's current best score. Second, we need a button that sends a message to the controller whenever it is clicked so we can send an e-mail to a friend bragging about our score. Start by opening up FlipsideViewController.h. You will need an IBOutlet to reference the highScore Label, and you will need an IBAction to respond to your button click. When you open FlipsideViewController.h, you see the following code:

```
#import <UIKit/UIKit.h>
@interface FlipsideView : UIView {
}
@end
```

Add a label and action to the code so that it looks like this (additions are in bold):

```
#import <UIKit/UIKit.h>
@interface FlipsideView : UIView {
    IBOutlet UILabel *highScoreLabel;
}
@property (nonatomic, retain) UILabel *highScoreLabel;
IBAction onEmailButtonClick;
@end
```

Now we need to make some completer changes to `FlipsideViewController.m`. When you open this file it will look like this:

```
#import "FlipsideViewController.h"
@implementation FlipsideViewController
- (void)viewDidLoad {
  [super viewDidLoad];
  self.view.backgroundColor = [UIColor
  viewFlipsideBackgroundColor];
}
- (void)didReceiveMemoryWarning {
  [super didReceiveMemoryWarning];
}
- (void)dealloc {
  [super dealloc];
}
@end
```

Again, add code for a label and action so that it looks like Listing 3.1.

CROSS-REFERENCE

To download all of the code listings in this chapter, go to `www.wileydevreference.com` and click the Downloads link.

Listing 3.1

The Complete Implementation for the FlipsideViewController Class

```
#import "FlipsideViewController.h"
@synthesize highScoreLabel;
@implementation FlipsideViewController
- (void)viewDidLoad {
  [super viewDidLoad];
  NSString* highScore = [Helper getUserValueForKey:
     @"highscore" withDefault:@"0"];
  highScoreLabel.text = [NSString stringWithFormat:
```

continued

Listing 3.1   *(continued)*

```
    @"High Score: %@", highScore];
    self.view.backgroundColor = [UIColor viewFlipsideBackgroundColor];
}
- (void)onEmailButtonClick {
  NSString* highScore = [Helper getUserValueForKey:
      @"highscore" withDefault:@"0"];
  NSString *emailBody = [NSString stringWithFormat:
      @"Do you think you can beat my high score at AmuckSlider?
        My current high score is:%@", highScore];
  [Helper sendEmailWithSubject:@"Beat this score!" withBody:emailBody];
}
- (void)didReceiveMemoryWarning {
  [super didReceiveMemoryWarning];
}
- (void)dealloc {
  [highScoreLabel release];
  [super dealloc];
}
@end
```

You probably noticed that `sendEmailWithSubject` and `getUserValueForKey` are method calls from the static class `Helper`. As you know, it's best to encapsulate code that you will be using time and time again. The full listings for the methods `sendEmailWithSubject` and `getUserValueForKey` are right here:

```
+ (void)sendEmailWithSubject:(NSString*)aSubject withBody:(NSString*)aBody{
    NSString *urlString = [NSString stringWithFormat:
        @"mailto:?subject=%@&body=%@", aSubject, aBody];
    urlString = [urlString stringByReplacingOccurrencesOfString:
        @" " withString:@"%20"];
    NSURL* mailURL = [NSURL URLWithString: urlString];
    [[UIApplication sharedApplication] openURL: mailURL];
}
+ (NSString*)getUserValueForKey:(NSString*)aKey
    withDefault:(NSString*)aDefaultValue {
    NSString *result = [[NSUserDefaults standardUserDefaults]
        stringForKey: aKey];
    if (result == nil || [result isEqualToString:@""]) {
       return aDefaultValue;
    }
    return result;
}
```

Managing level data

We want our game to have several different levels to keep players' interest, and we need to store data for each of our levels. In addition, we want our game to have different degrees of challenge, such as easy, medium, and hard. Since this is a puzzle game and you have to be clever to figure out the patterns, we have decided to make the degree of challenge a literal degree. The levels of difficulty are Bachelors for easy, Masters for medium, and Doctorate for hard. We have eight levels for each degree, for a total of 24 levels.

We need to set up some interfaces to define this model. The ultimate goal is to create an easy way for us to get level data and to separate that concern from the rest of the system. In order to host the class model, we've created a new pair of files, Game.h and Game.m. In these files we have defined a few interfaces and enumerations to fulfill our requirements.

The whole purpose of the Game class is to implement the following methods:

```
+ (Difficulty)getBestDifficulty;
+ (int)getBestLevelForDifficulty:(Difficulty)aDifficulty;
+ (int)getCurrentLevelIndex;
+ (void)setCurrentLevelIndex;
+ (Level*)getLevelAtLevelIndex:(int)aLevelIndex;
```

These methods will help us easily access information necessary to the game system. Here is a short description of what these methods do:

- **getBestDifficulty:** Initially, a player can only play at the Bachelors level; he must earn the right to play at the Masters and Doctorate levels. This method indicates at which level a player is allowed to play.

- **getBestLevelForDifficulty:** A player must start at level one and complete it before he is allowed to progress to level two, and so on. This method indicates the level a player is allowed to play next for the difficulty specified.

- **getCurrentLevelIndex:** This method returns the player to the level he last played on startup without needing to go to the menu. This is convenient for returning to the game after being interrupted by a phone call, for example.

- **setCurrentLevelIndex:** This method allows you to set the current level index. Call this method to record when a player beats a level so the next level will be unlocked.

- **getLevelAtLevelIndex:** This method returns data necessary to describe a given level. A level is defined by its grid size, tile size, and tile data. The tile data defines the location in grid coordinates where the tile currently resides. It defines the index of where the tile should be. Finally, it defines a type: an empty, blank, or arrow tile.

Examining the Game class in detail

The Game class is responsible for defining these methods. The class interface is listed here:

```
@interface Game : NSObject {
   Level *levels[24];
}
+ (Difficulty)getBestDifficulty;
+ (int)getBestLevelForDifficulty:(Difficulty)aDifficulty;
+ (int)getCurrentLevelIndex;
+ (void)setCurrentLevelIndex;
+ (Level*)getLevelAtLevelIndex:(int)aLevelIndex;
@end
```

Let's look at each of these items in more detail. First, we define a field array of `Level`:

```
Level *levels[24];
```

Since we know there will be exactly 24 levels, we can go ahead and create an array to reference each one. This makes the call to `getLevelAtLevelIndex` easy; all we need to do is return the level for the specified index, like so:

```
+ (Level*)getLevelAtLevelIndex:(int)aLevelIndex {
  return [Game getInstance].levels[aLevelIndex];
}
```

Notice that we called `[Game getInstance]` to get an instance of the `Game` class. The array of levels is populated here when the `Game` class is constructed. Later in this section we will show you the method that populates the array.

The methods `getCurrentLevelIndex` and `setCurrentLevelIndex` enable us to keep track of the last level the player was on. This way, when he comes back to the game, the last level he has not completed can be automatically loaded. This index is a number between 0 and 24 to make it easier to load levels and reference the levels array:

```
+ (int)getCurrentLevelIndex {
  return [[Helper getUserValueForKey:@"currentlevel"
    withDefault:@"0"] intValue];
}
+ (void)setCurrentLevelIndex:(int)aLevelIndex {
  int bestIndex = [[Helper getUserValueForKey:@"currentlevel"
    withDefault:@"0"] intValue];
  if (bestIndex < aLevelIndex)
    [Helper setUserValue:[NSString stringWithFormat:@"%d", aLevelIndex]
    forKey:@"bestlevel"];
  [Helper setUserValue:[NSString stringWithFormat:@"%d", aLevelIndex]
    forKey:@"currentlevel"];
}
```

We use our `Helper` class again to get and set values by their key names. Notice that we do not use a private field; we just go ahead and write and read directly to the user settings. This keeps us from having to decide when to save the value, and you can rest assured the value will be what you set it to even if the game is interrupted by a phone call. We also set the best level index when we write the current level index. This is good practice because it helps us keep data logic out of the Game View later.

Now we'll look at the methods `getBestDifficulty` and `getBestLevelFor Difficulty`. These methods prevent users from having to perform data logic in the Menu View (covered later in this chapter):

```
+ (Difficulty)getBestDifficulty {
    int bestIndex = [[Helper getUserValueForKey:@"currentlevel"
        withDefault:@"0"] intValue];
    return (Difficulty)floor(bestIndex / 3);
}
+ (int)getBestLevelForDifficulty:(Difficulty)aDifficulty {
    int bestIndex = [[Helper getUserValueForKey:@"currentlevel"
        withDefault:@"0"] intValue];
    int offset = [self getBestDifficulty] * 8;
    return bestIndex - offset;
}
```

These methods give us a way to find the best level the player has completed. The player is presented with levels in the menus as Bachelors levels 1-8, Masters levels 1-8, and so on. This means that Masters level 1 is actually level index 8, and Bachelors level 1 is actually level index 0. By providing these methods, we ensure that we always calculate levels the same way.

Examining supporting Game classes and more

There are a handful of other classes and a couple of enums that are used to help support the Game class. Now you are going to get a closer look at these supporting items.

As you have seen earlier, the Game class ultimately exposes tile data, and on each tile you encounter a tile type. For the enum `TileType`, there are three different types of tiles:

- **Empty** is used if the tile is the blank puzzle. There should only be one empty tile per puzzle.

- **Blank** is used if the tile is active but does not have an arrow. Blank tiles can be moved around, but they are not part of the solution. Early levels should have many blank tiles.

- **Arrow** is used to define a tile with an arrow on it; these tiles have to be in the correct location to solve the puzzle.

The following code defines these types for us:

```
typedef enum {
    empty,
    blank,
    arrow
} TileType;
```

The `Tile` itself is very simple; it is just a `struct` used to hold the data elements for the tile. You may have noticed that we mentioned a tile index, but it is not present here. The index is the same index used to store the item in its collection. Therefore, to keep from creating redundant data, we do not store that information again here.

Here is the definition you will see in the code for the `Tile`:

```
typedef struct {
    int location;
    TileType tileType;
} Tile;
```

CAUTION

Duplication of data can lead to mistakes and confusion. In this case we chose not to store the index because we can just use the index we used to pull an item out of the tile array. If we were to store the index in the struct, we would have to be extremely careful to always update or set this index when necessary. By choosing not to store it again, we eliminate this concern.

Now that you have seen tiles, you can understand how they can be used to construct a level. Levels contain a collection of tiles, among other parameters. One of these other parameters is difficulty. We discussed difficulty earlier and decided to create three different levels. Here is the listing for the enum `Difficulty`:

```
typedef enum {
    bachelors,
    masters,
    doctorate
} Difficulty;
```

Like the `Tile`, the `Level` is just a simple struct used to hold the data elements for the level. Here is what the definition looks like:

```
typedef struct {
    Difficulty difficulty;
    int tileSize;
    int gridSize;
    Tile tiles[16];
} Level;
```

That's it for type definitions, but we have left out an important piece. Where does the data come from? This is really up to you. We have chosen to use a static array to store all of the level data. When the game instance is initialized, we rip through the static array and load our collections, tiles, and levels. As you can imagine, this is very straightforward. However, if you are interested in the details, please download the source if you have not already and take a look. You can download the code from `http://appsamuck.com/gamedevbook/amuckslider`.

Building the Menu View

Now we need to erect a menu so the user can start the game, select a difficulty level, and all those good things. In puzzle games, it is at times best to lock the player out of advanced levels at first and have them build up to them. If you fail to do this, many players will rush to the difficult levels first and quickly get bored with the game. There is just something about the way we are programmed—if we are challenged to defeat levels in sequence, we are always lured by the temptation to attempt just one more level. So in the spirit of keeping the challenge high, we have chosen to require the player to defeat the levels in sequence the first time through. Once a challenge has been beaten, a player can go back and replay a previous level.

You could take this idea a step further by allowing the player to achieve badges for accomplishing specific items. A badge system keeps players coming back to replay existing levels after they get good at the game. For example, the second time through the game would challenge the player to try and finish faster or with fewer moves. You could award an "Ace" badge if the player beats a level with minimal moves or award a "Speedster" badge if he beats the level in record time. But before any of this is possible, we must begin by setting up a menu system.

Follow these steps to create the Menu View by adding a new view controller and view XIB:

1. Under Groups & Files, choose the root project node. In our case it is the topmost node named AmuckSlider.

2. From the menu choose Project ⇨ New Group. Name the new group **Menu View**.

3. From the menu choose File ⇨ New File to launch the New File dialog box.

4. From the New File dialog box, choose iPhone OS ⇨ Cocoa Touch Classes ⇨ UIViewController subclass.

5. Name the class **MenuViewController.m**. Make sure the check box Also create MenuViewController.h is checked, then click Finish.

6. Choose the group Resources.

7. Again, choose File ⇨ New File to launch the New File dialog box.

8. This time, in the New File dialog box, choose iPhone OS ⇨ User Interfaces ⇨ View XIB. Name it **MenuView.xib**.

TIP

If you are creating a new class and an XIB to match, you will need to recompile the app before you can connect `IBActions` and `UIOutlets` to controls in Interface Builder.

Now let's add some controls to the view. Double-click the `MenuView.xib` file to open the menu user interface in Interface Builder. If you have downloaded the code and are following along, you should see a screen that looks like the one shown in Figure 3.10.

Figure 3.10

Menu View in Interface Builder

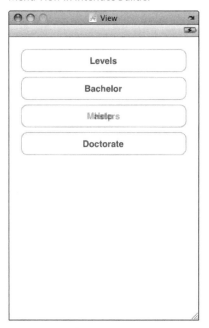

Notice in the previous figure that the third button is blurry. That's because the text from two different buttons is overlapping. This is not a problem, because we manage which button is shown at run-time in the class `MenuViewController`. When you click New Game from the Game View, you are presented with a menu that has the buttons Levels and Help on it (Figure 3.11).

Figure 3.11

First page of the menu screen

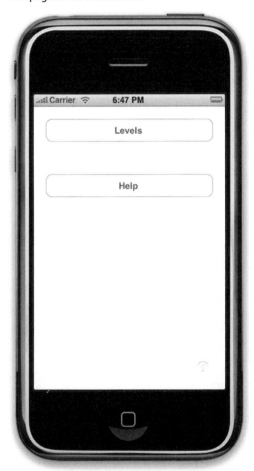

When you click Levels, you are presented with the three levels of difficulty: Bachelor, Masters, and Doctorate (Figure 3.12).

Figure 3.12

Choosing the level of difficulty from the menu screen

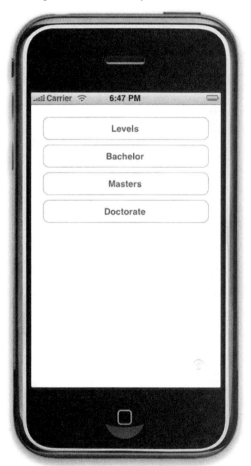

After choosing the difficulty, you will be presented with levels One through Eight (Figure 3.13). Finally, you can click the Help button to display a list of instructions.

Notice that this is not a very attractive set of screens. We will come back later and polish up the menu. You will find that if you spend time polishing as you go along you will get caught up in the details too early in the process. If you do this you can lose your focus on the big picture and have trouble getting reoriented at each stage of the process.

Another problem with polishing too early is that if you have to rethink or change anything, you will have to throw away work and time that you cannot recoup. Take it from us: Get the app working and functional, then come back and polish it up. You will save time and find the polishing process fun and rewarding.

Figure 3.13

Choosing the level from the menu screen

Now open the file `MenuViewController.h` and you will see the following:

```
@protocol MenuViewDelegate <NSObject>
@optional
    -(void)loadLevel:(int)levelIndex;
@end
@interface MenuViewController : UIViewController {
    Difficulty difficulty;
    int level;
    id <MenuViewDelegate>delegate;
    UIButton *levelNumberButton[8];
    IBOutlet UIButton *levelButton;
```

```
        IBOutlet UIButton *helpButton;
        IBOutlet UIButton *bachelorsButton;
        IBOutlet UIButton *doctorateButton;
        IBOutlet UIButton *mastersButton;
    }
    @property (nonatomic, retain) id /*<UIAlertViewDelegate>*/
        delegate;
    - (IBAction)onLevelClick;
    - (IBAction)onHelpClick;
    - (IBAction)onBachelorsClick;
    - (IBAction)onDoctorateClick;
    - (IBAction)onMastersClick;
    - (void)showRoot:(bool)aHidden;
    - (void)showDifficulty:(bool)aHidden;
    - (void)showLevels:(bool)aHidden;
    @end
```

We have used two styles of building a user interface on this controller in order to give you a little variety. The buttons defined with `IBOutlet UIButton *`... are connected at design time using Interface Builder. When connecting with Interface Builder, you will need to connect the `IBOutlet` and the `IBAction` using the same method described in the Hello World example from Chapter 2. The other style used is to create the buttons at run-time when the `MenuView Controller` class is instantiated. After these buttons are created, they are stored in this array:

```
    UIButton *levelNumberButton[8];
```

In the example code file `MainViewController.m` you will find the method `initLevel-NumberButtons` (Listing 3.2). This method creates the buttons that are stored in the array.

Listing 3.2

The Method initLevelNumberButtons Positions the Level Buttons on the Screen

```
- (void)initLevelNumberButtons {
  int btnTopOffset = 65;
  int btnHeight = 37;
  int btnWidth = 137;
  int btnTopMargin = 9;
  int btnEvenLeft = 20;
  int btnOddLeft = 164;
  for (int i=0; i<8; i++) {
    int btnRow = i/2;
    int btnLeft = i%2 == 0 ? btnEvenLeft : btnOddLeft;
    int btnTop = ((btnHeight + btnTopMargin) * btnRow) + btnTopOffset;
    CGRect buttonFrame = CGRectMake(btnLeft, btnTop, btnWidth, btnHeight);
```

```
    levelNumberButton[i] = [UIButton buttonWithType: UIButtonTypeRoundedRect];
    levelNumberButton[i].frame = buttonFrame;
    levelNumberButton[i].hidden = true;
    levelNumberButton[i].tag = i+1;
    [levelNumberButton [i] addTarget:self action:
        @selector(onLevelNumberButtonClick:)
        forControlEvents:UIControlEventTouchUpInside];
    [levelNumberButton [i] setTitle:buttonNames[i]
        forState:UIControlStateNormal];
    [self.view addSubview: levelNumberButton [i]];
  }
}
```

Take notice of the following line from above:

```
[levelNumberButton [i] addTarget:self action:
    @selector(onLevelNumberButtonClick:)
    forControlEvents:UIControlEventTouchUpInside];
```

This line attaches the selector onLevelNumberClick to the button's TouchUpInside event. All eight buttons are assigned to the same method. However, we are using the tag property of the button to distinguish which button was clicked. This is what the onLevelNumber-ButtonClick method looks like:

```
- (void)onLevelNumberButtonClick:(id)sender {
    UIButton *btn = (UIButton*)sender;
    int levelIndex = (int)btn.tag;
    [self selectLevel:levelIndex];
}
```

Since we have all the buttons on the same view at the same time, it is simple to just hide and show the appropriate buttons by changing the button's "hidden" property. This gives the player the feeling that he is paging through options while keeping all of the view logic in one class.

Once the player has made a selection, we need to report his choice back to the main Game View. This is where the protocol that you saw at the top of MenuViewController.h comes into play:

```
@protocol MenuViewDelegate <NSObject>
@optional
    - (void)loadLevel:(int)levelIndex;
@end
```

This protocol defines an interface that the implementing classes can define to receive messages from. In this case, the `MainViewController` implements the method `loadLevel` as defined by the protocol. The `selectLevel` method in `MenuViewController` calls the `loadLevel` of the delegate, which sends the message to the implementing class instance referenced by the delegate:

```
- (void)selectLevel:(int)levelIndex {
    [delegate loadLevel:levelIndex-1];
}
```

Polishing the Menu View

We recommend that you completely finish the game logic before polishing up the Game View. However, since we are guiding you through a complete example, let's take a break from discussing implementation and look at how our screens are going to look after we polish them up. In this example we are going to add a better background image and a little animation to spice it up a bit. You will be amazed how a few simple changes can add interest. Go back to the AmuckSlider source link (`http://appsamuck.com/gamedevbook/amuckslider`) and this time download the "After Polish" version of the source code.

To polish up the menus, we will add a background image to the Menu View. You can do this in Interface Builder without touching this code. For each of the buttons we will add a background image to add a little spice there, too. This is a little more complicated because you need to tell the button how to treat the edges of the background image. You will see that a background image has been assigned to each button similar to the line below:

```
UIImage *buttonBackground = [[UIImage imageNamed:@"menuButtonBack
    ground.png"]
    stretchableImageWithLeftCapWidth:12.0 topCapHeight:12.0 ];
[levelButton setBackgroundImage:buttonBackground
    forState:UIControlStateNormal];
```

The trick to this is creating the `UIImage` with the `imageNamed:stretchableImageWith`
`LeftCapWidth:topCapHeight:` signature. Figures 3.14, 3.15, and 3.16 show what the finished product looks like.

Figure 3.14

Polished first page of the menu screen

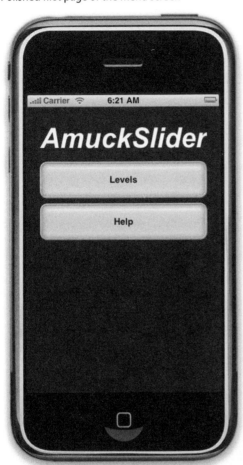

Figure 3.15

Choosing the level of difficulty from the polished menu screen

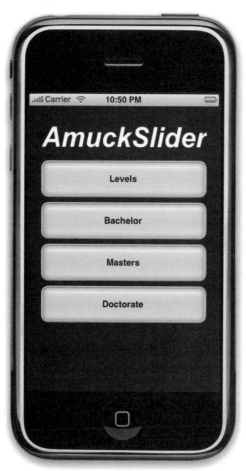

Figure 3.16

Choosing the level from the polished menu screen

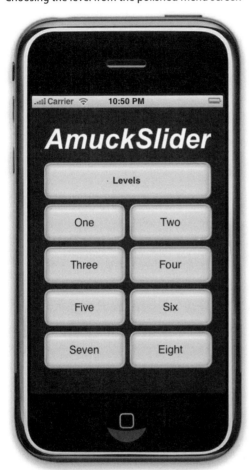

We could leave it alone now because it looks good, but let's add just a bit more excitement. When a button in clicked, add a little animation to the process to make the click feel more inter-active. Figure 3.17 shows the animation midway through its progress, but you really need to run the app to get the full effect.

Figure 3.17

Button animation still from the polished menu screen

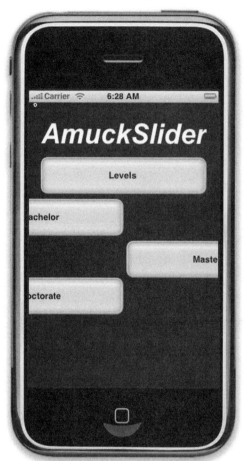

For one final touch as part of polishing the menu, you can add a default.png image to your project. When you launch your app, the iPhone OS displays this image while the player is waiting for the app to load. Apple asks that you do not use this image as a splash screen. Apple prefers that you use an image that looks like the first page your player will see. The best way to do this is to take a screen shot of your root menu screen and save it in your project with the name default.png. If you have never taken a screen shot before, it's easy. Hold down the Home button and then click the on/off button located at the top of your device. You should see the screen flash, and then you will find the screen shot in the Camera Roll of the Photos app.

Once you have a screen shot you can add it to your app as a resource with the name Default.png.

Apple recommends that you use an image that looks like the first page users will see. However, this may make the app feel unresponsive to users during initial startup, because they will see a screen where they expect to be able to tap buttons yet they cannot because they are looking at an image instead of a UI. We have found placing the text "loading. . ." in the center of the screen helps players understand what to expect.

Programming the Game View

Now that we have some content on the info screen, a way to persist and retrieve game data, and a menu, it's time to build the Game View. For simplicity we will place most of the game logic for AmuckSlider in the class `MainViewController` and a little view logic in the class `TileView`. In more complicated examples you will want to take time to break up your concerns into relevant classes.

TIP

Notice the pattern of having a `View` and a `ViewController`. As a general rule, try to place your game or business logic in the `ViewController`. Game logic would be collision detection, processing user input, calculating moves, and so on. Likewise, try to place all of your view logic in the `View` classes. View logic can include animations, setting backgrounds, colors, and things of this nature.

Go ahead and review the classes `MainViewController` and `TileView` from the unpolished version of the source code. (Again, this source can be found at http://appsamuck. com/gamedevbook/amuckslider.) Now we will review all the key pieces of game and view logic found in these files. When you are done you will understand what makes AmuckSlider tick.

Reviewing the TileView class

The `TileView` class wraps up all the view logic necessary to give our tiles the desired appearance and behavior for our requirements. We decided that a tile could be blank or contain an arrow. When a `TileView` is created, an arrow `UIImageView` is added as a subview:

```
UIImage *arrowImage = [UIImage imageNamed:@"arrowImage.png"];
UIImageView *imageView = [[UIImageView alloc] initWithImage:arrowImage];
// make the arrow image half the size of the TileView so that when it is
// rotated it will not wander outside the bounds of the tile.
imageView.frame = CGRectMake(aSize/4, aSize/4, aSize/2, aSize/2);
[imageView release];
[imageView setHidden:true];
[self addSubview:imageView];
self.arrowView = imageView;
[self updateArrowPoint];
```

This code can be found in the initialization method `initWithIndex`. The last line above calls out to `updateArrowPoint`. The method rotates the arrow image so that it points in the direction of its home location, or hides the arrow if the tile is in the home location. Also note that if the tile is not an arrow, this code makes sure the arrow image is never shown:

```
- (void)updateArrowPoint {
    // if this tile in not an arrow never show it
    if (tileType != arrow) return;
    [self updateArrowPointToIndex:self.index fromIndex:self.location];
}
- (void)updateArrowPointToIndex:(int)toIndex fromIndex:(int)fromIndex {
    // if the tile is in its home location then hide the arrow
    if (toIndex == fromIndex){
        [self.arrowView setHidden:true];
        return;
    }
    [self.arrowView setHidden:false];
    // calculate the angle
    float angle = [self getArrowDirectionToIndex:toIndex fromIndex:fromIndex];
    CATransform3D rotationTransform = CATransform3DIdentity;
    rotationTransform = CATransform3DRotate(rotationTransform, angle, 0.0, 0.0,
        1.0);
     self.arrowView.layer.transform = rotationTransform;
}
```

The angle for the arrow is calculated in `getArrowDirectionToIndex`. We need to know what angle to point the arrow in. The "to" and "from" positions are calculations in grid coordinates. From there we have the information to calculate the rise and run. Finally, we use the `atan2()` function to derive the angle:

```
- (float)getArrowDirectionToIndex:(int)toIndex fromIndex:(int)fromIndex {
    CGFloat toX = toIndex % dimension;
    CGFloat toY = toIndex / dimension;
    CGFloat fromX = fromIndex % dimension;
    CGFloat fromY = fromIndex / dimension;
    double rise = toY - fromY;
    double run = toX - fromX;
    float angle = atan2(rise, run);
    return angle;
}
```

One last thing to take notice of: `TileView` defines three helper methods that calculate where to place a tile based on an index or location. This is needed because we frequently reference tiles based on their index in the tile array:

```
+ (CGRect)getRectForLocation:(int)aLocation withDimension:(int)aDimension
        withSize:(int)aSize{
    int x = [TileView getXForLocation:aLocation withDimension:aDimension];
    int y = [TileView getYForLocation:aLocation withDimension:aDimension];
    return CGRectMake(x*aSize+x, y*aSize+y, aSize, aSize);
}
+ (int)getXForLocation:(int)aLocation withDimension:(int)aDimension {
    return aLocation % aDimension;
}
+ (int)getYForLocation:(int)aLocation withDimension:(int)aDimension {
    return aLocation / aDimension;
}
```

Understanding the magic behind the MainViewController

The MainViewController or Game View is where the rest of the game logic resides. Here you will find the code that initializes the collection of tiles and positions them in the grid. The MainViewController receives touch events and translates these gestures into the expected behavior of the tiles.

In MainViewController.h you will find a concise definition for the MainView Controller class. Here is a listing of the MainViewController interface:

```
@interface MainViewController : UIViewController <MenuViewDelegate> {
    int currentLevelIndex;
    Level currentLevel;
    int emptyTile;
    TileView *tiles[100];
    MenuViewController *menuViewController;
}
-(void)loadLevel:(int)levelIndex;
@end
```

In the previous code segment, pay attention to the following items of interest:

- **<MenuViewDelegate>** is defined in MenuViewController.h. As you see above, MainViewController implements this protocol. This allows us to receive the message loadLevel: whenever the MenuView is closed.

- **currentLevelIndex** keeps track of the integer value of the current level the player is on.

- **currentLevel** is assigned to the active level structure.

- **emptyTile** contains the location index of where the empty tile currently resides.

- **tiles[25]** is the collection of pointers to the MainViewControllers tiles. Not all the tile pointers are used depending on the difficulty of the currently active level.

- **menuViewController** provides a reference for the active instance of our menu that we discussed earlier.

Initializing the display

In the initialization method `initWithNibName` we fill all the tile pointers with `nil`. Shortly you will see iterations that perform a `nil` check on this array. This step gives us confidence that the value will be correct when this happens. Next, we load the initial value `currentLevelIndex` using the `Game` class discussed earlier (Listing 3.3).

Listing 3.3

Code Used to Initialize the Display and Load Current Level

```objc
- (id)initWithNibName:(NSString *)nibNameOrNil bundle:(NSBundle *)nibBundleOrNil
{
    if (self = [super initWithNibName:nibNameOrNil bundle:nibBundleOrNil]){
        for (int i=0; i<25; i++) tiles[i]=nil;
        currentLevelIndex =[Game getCurrentLevelIndex];
    }
    return self;
}
-(void)loadLevel:(int)levelIndex {
    currentLevelIndex = levelIndex;
    [Game setCurrentLevelIndex:levelIndex];
    [menuViewController.view removeFromSuperview];
    [self clearTiles];
    currentLevel = [Game getLevelAtLevelIndex:levelIndex];
    for (int i=0 ; i<(currentLevel.gridSize*currentLevel.gridSize)-1; i++) {
        Tile tile = currentLevel.tiles[i]; //[currentLevel getTileAtIndex:i];
        TileView *tileView = [[TileView alloc] initWithIndex:i
            atLocation:tile.location withSize:currentLevel.tileSize
            withDimension:currentLevel.gridSize withType:tile.tileType];
        tiles[i] = tileView;
        [self.view addSubview:tiles[i]];
    }
    emptyTile = currentLevel.gridSize*currentLevel.gridSize-1;
}
- (void)viewDidLoad {
    [super viewDidLoad];
    menuViewController = [[MenuViewController alloc] initWithNibName:
        @"MenuView" bundle:nil];
    menuViewController.delegate = self;
    [self.view addSubview:menuViewController.view];
}
```

Responding to touches

`touchesMoved` is a key method of the `MainViewController`. As discussed earlier in the example we reviewed, this event is fired whenever one or more touch gestures have moved.

When this happens we locate the tile (if any) that the touch is inside of. If the tile can be moved, we allow it to move as the location of the touch moves. We determine if the tile can be moved by checking to see if it is adjacent to the empty tile. Finally, we restrict the movement of the tile in order to keep it inside an allowed region. This region is calculated by union of the original location rectangle of the tile in motion with the rectangle of the empty tile (Listing 3.4).

Listing 3.4

Code Used to Move a Tile from Its Current Tile to an Empty Cell

```
- (void)touchesMoved:(NSSet *)touches withEvent:(UIEvent *)event {
    UITouch *touch = [touches anyObject];
    for (int i=0 ; i<(currentLevel.gridSize*currentLevel.gridSize)-1; i++) {
        if ([touch view] ==tiles[i]) {
            if ([self tileCanMoveToIndexFromIndex:tiles[i].location]) {
                CGPoint location = [touch locationInView:self.view];
                CGFloat maxX, minX, minY, maxY;
                CGRect movingTileRect = [TileView
                    getRectForLocation:tiles[i].location
                    withDimension:currentLevel.gridSize
                    withSize:currentLevel.tileSize];
                CGRect emptyTileRect = [TileView getRectForLocation:emptyTile
                    withDimension:currentLevel.gridSize
                    withSize:currentLevel.tileSize];
                CGRect slideRect = CGRectUnion(movingTileRect, emptyTileRect);
                CGFloat centerPadding = (currentLevel.tileSize) / 2;
                minX = slideRect.origin.x + centerPadding;
                minY = slideRect.origin.y + centerPadding;
                maxX = slideRect.origin.x + slideRect.size.width - centerPadding;
                maxY = slideRect.origin.y + slideRect.size.height - centerPadding;
                if (location.x > maxX)
                    location.x = maxX;
                if (location.y > maxY)
                    location.y = maxY;
                if (location.y < minY)
                    location.y = minY;
                if (location.x < minX)
                    location.x = minX;
                tiles[i].center = location;
                return;
            }
        }
    }
}
```

Once again, as discussed in the earlier example, the `touchesEnded` event fires whenever a player lifts his finger off the glass at the conclusion of a touch gesture. When this happens we check to see if the touch is inside of any of our tiles that can move as we did in the previous listing. If the touch is in a legal tile, we check to see if the center of the tile that the touch is inside of is contained in the original tile location or in the empty tile location. We then animate the tile to the appropriate location and update the location property of the tile and the `emptyTile` field of the `MainViewController`. This ensures that the tile is always in a legal location and gives the player the feeling that it snaps into place:

```
- (void) touchesEnded: (NSSet *) touches withEvent: (UIEvent *) event {
    UITouch *touch = [touches anyObject];
    for (int i=0 ; i<(currentLevel.gridSize*currentLevel.gridSize)-1; i++) {
        if ([touch view] == tiles[i]) {
            if ([self tileCanMoveToIndexFromIndex:tiles[i].location]) {
                int oldLocation = tiles[i].location;
                int newLocation = emptyTile;
                // only move to the new location if the center of the moving tile is
                // inside the empty tile
                CGRect emptyTileRect = [TileView getRectForLocation:emptyTile
                    withDimension:currentLevel.gridSize
                    withSize:currentLevel.tileSize];
                if (CGRectContainsPoint(emptyTileRect, tiles[i].center)) {
                    [self moveTile:tiles[i] toLocation:newLocation];
                    emptyTile = oldLocation;
                }
                else {
                    [self moveTile:tiles[i] toLocation:oldLocation];
                }
            }
            break;
        }
    }
    [self testDidWin];
}
```

After reviewing these two methods that handle touch, play around with the example on the iPhone. We believe you will find that this treatment of the touch events creates a realistic experience for players.

Reviewing the utility methods

The `moveTile` method is used to snap a tile into place. First, it begins the animation. Next, we set the location of the tile. By setting the location index of the tile view, we will internally update its frame. Finally, we commit the animation. This produces our nice little effect of snapping the tile into place:

```
- (void) moveTile: (TileView*) tileView toLocation: (int) aLocation {
    [UIView beginAnimations:nil context:nil];
    [UIView setAnimationDuration:0.25];
    tileView.location = aLocation;
    [UIView commitAnimations];
    [tileView updateArrowPoint];
}
```

You will see the method `tileCanMoveToIndexFromIndex` used a lot. As expected, this method returns true if a tile can make a legal move from its current index to the empty tile index. This is calculated by checking to see if the tile in question is adjacent to the empty tile:

```
- (bool)tileCanMoveToIndexFromIndex:(int)index {
    int fromX = [TileView getXForLocation:index
        withDimension:currentLevel.gridSize];
    int fromY = [TileView getYForLocation:index
        withDimension:currentLevel.gridSize];
    int toX = [TileView getXForLocation:emptyTile
        withDimension:currentLevel.gridSize];
    int toY = [TileView getYForLocation:emptyTile
        withDimension:currentLevel.gridSize];
    if (fromX == toX && (fromY+1 == toY || fromY-1 == toY) )
        return true;
    if (fromY == toY && (fromX+1 == toX || fromX-1 == toX) )
        return true;
    return false;
}
```

The method `tilesInCorrectLocation` checks to see if all arrow tiles are currently seated in their correct location. We can determine this by comparing the tile's index to the tile's location. If this is the case for every arrow tile, this method returns true:

```
- (bool)tilesInCorrectLocation {
    for (int i=0 ; i<(currentLevel.gridSize*currentLevel.gridSize)-1; i++) {
        TileView *tileView = tiles[i];
        if (tileView.tileType == arrow && tileView.location != i)
            return false;
    }
    return true;
}
```

The last method we will review in this example is `testDidWin`. This method is called at the completion of each move (look at the earlier method `touchesEnded`). If the method `tilesInCorrectLocation` returns true, we know that the player has completed the level.

If we pass this condition, we see an alert view that proclaims the player's success. Finally, we call `loadLevel` to automatically load the next level in the sequence. When the player dismisses the alert, he can begin playing the next level:

```
- (void)testDidWin {
    if (![self tilesInCorrectLocation]) return;
    NSString *message = [NSString stringWithFormat:
        @"You have just completed level %d on to the next level",
        currentLevelIndex+1];
    UIAlertView *alertView = [[UIAlertView alloc] initWithTitle:
        @"Level Complete!" message:message delegate:nil cancelButtonTitle:
        @"OK" otherButtonTitles:nil];
    [alertView show];
```

```
    [alertView release];
    [Helper setUserValue:[NSString stringWithFormat:
       @"%d", currentLevelIndex] forKey:@"currentlevel"];
    currentLevelIndex++;
    [self loadLevel:currentLevelIndex];
}
```

Now you have been over all of the important details of how this application works. This is a simple puzzle app, but it illustrates how easy it can be to bring ideas to life on the iPhone. Most everything else you will find in the source is just the standard scaffolding necessary in all the applications you will build. Here is what the AmuckSlider looks like before any polishing (Figure 3.18).

Figure 3.18

AmuckSlider Game View before polishing

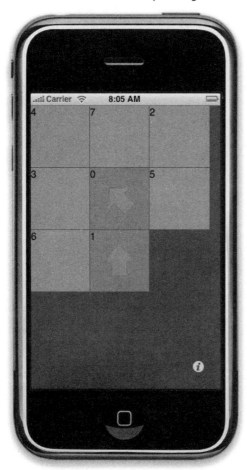

TIP

Try to prevent your code from nesting too deep. Change your logic so that you exit instead of nesting if-statements. You will thank yourself because the code will be much easier to maintain.

Polishing the Game View

So far you have been looking at the source from the unpolished version of this application. Now let's look at ways we can add excitement to the user's experience in the Game View just like we did for the Menu View. Like the Menu View, it does not take much to make the screen look a lot snazzier. Simply adding a few images and animations will do the trick. After a little image treatment you'll see how much more interesting the game board can be.

Here are the things we added to accomplish a better look:

- A background image to the whole Game View
- A semi-opaque background image to each tile
- A much more interesting arrow image
- A glass effect in front of the arrow
- A green glow image that is visible when a tile is seated in its correct location

We also added a few animations to make the game more interesting:

- The arrow spins to its correct location instead of snapping at the end of each turn.
- The arrow fades out as the green glow fades in when the tile is in the correct location.
- A puff effect shoots out from around a tile when it pops into the correct location.
- When a level is completed, the puff effect replays for each arrow tile.

That is about it for polish. You will need to add an application icon before you are ready to publish an application to the App Store. For this application we have chosen to show a small two-by-two grid version of the AmuckSlider game board. You need two images to submit a game: One needs to be 57 x 57 pixels (Figure 3.19) and the other should be 512 x 512 pixels (Figure 3.20).

Figure 3.19

Small 57 x 57 icon used for AmuckSlider

Figure 3.20

Large 512 x 512 icon used by AmuckSlider

CAUTION

Apple suggests that the large icon should not be a stretched version of the small one. The large icon is displayed in iTunes and will not have the quality you will want to attract buyers if it is stretched and dithered. Also, there is a good chance your app will be rejected if you try to submit a stretched image.

Figures 3.21 and 3.22 show the images we used for AmuckSlider.

Figure 3.21

iPhone Home screen with AmuckSlider installed

Figure 3.22

AmuckSlider Game View after several rounds of polishing

Analyzing Business Aspects

You have planned, implemented, and polished—now it's time to reap some rewards. When its doors first opened, simply publishing an application to the App Store meant good sales. Now that the newness has worn off, the App Store is saturated with applications. A new strategy is needed. By analyzing the business aspect, you can learn how to use apps to your advantage.

Puzzle apps are generally less involved and thus less costly to write than other types of applications. Most puzzle apps are pattern driven. You generally only have to set up the engine and plug in several levels as simple data files. This will help you release many updates by simply adding levels. Be careful to keep this in mind when deciding on how to process your logic to make sure you can make small adjustments to the code or even allow the player to download new content.

Since puzzle apps are easy to create, they tend to dominate the market. Your game really needs to have something to set it apart and to excel in this arena. When building AmuckSlider, we looked at all the other slider apps that we could find on the App Store and made it a requirement to add something different and compelling that would hopefully attract users to ours instead of to other slider apps. We came up with using arrows instead of a sliced-up picture of numbers on each tile.

As we mentioned earlier in this chapter, puzzle apps need to be addictive. We have chosen to lock levels to require and entice players to continue on to the next level until they complete the game. We also noticed that slider apps can be pretty tough. Puzzle apps are generally better if they start easy and increase in difficulty. To help make the game easier to start with, AmuckSlider does not require players to get all the tiles in the right location in the beginning levels. Also, we start with a 3 x 3 grid and increase to a 5 x 5 grid as players gain skills and increase their difficulty.

Obviously, we hope AmuckSlider will be a runaway success simply by putting it on the App Store. However, we will be sorely disappointed if we just depend on that for marketing. If we make the mark and build an app that is addictive, then word of mouth will be our best sales tool. Just as the App Store has made applications easy to buy, you should focus on making your apps easy to sell. What do we mean by this? Remember the little e-mail bragging we added on the info page? This type of feature makes it easy to tell a friend about the game and at the same time challenge them to beat your score. Facebook is another great way to brag about your app.

CROSS-REFERENCE

See Chapter 6 for more on how you can display your game achievements as a Facebook status.

Summary

Puzzle apps are a great place to get started programming for the iPhone. They can be very simple and easy to build, yet still be some of the most addictive games you will find. A great puzzle app can keep your players interested much longer than any other type of game. For this reason your application will have a much longer shelf life than other games you spent more time developing.

In this chapter you reviewed some existing popular puzzle games such as Tetris and Trism. You learned how to add elements of strategy to your game by limiting time, number of turns, and space. You reviewed how animations could be used to make the game more compelling and interesting. You used Multi-Touch to see how to give your game a more realistic feel and how to make it truly become a game designed for the iPhone.

We hope this chapter has helped you get your feet wet and that you're beginning to feel comfortable developing for the iPhone. If you're like us, once you whet your appetite for this platform, you develop a hunger that will keep you motivated. Now take what you have learned and build something fun and exciting! Tell us about your creation at `http://appsamuck.com`. We love to hear from our readers!

4 Building Novelty Apps

The shortest distance between any two points is always a straight line. The shortest distance between you and making your first 99 cents on the App Store is always by making a novelty application. Most iPhone novelty apps tend to be one-trick ponies. For example, you can find applications to allow your iPhone to feature any of the following: strobe light effects, a desk clock, a virtual drink, and much more. And of course, there are the many infamous iPhone farting applications.

We think everyone should try their hand at creating an iPhone novelty application of their own. Even if the application already exists, there is a lot of value in creating an application for yourself. Take a moment to come up with a list of potential iPhone novelty applications of your own. Then compare this list to ours and see if you come up with any more ideas. Great ideas eventually grow up to become great applications.

Here is a list of some of our iPhone novelty application ideas to help get you started thinking of your own:

- **Snow Fall.** Imagine a snow globe on your iPhone. You could let users create virtual wind on the screen by blowing on the microphone. And you could use the accelerometer to have the snow always float back down.

- **Sleep Sound.** Have the iPhone play a white noise audio file in a loop. Maybe allow the user to set an alarm after a certain amount of time or for a certain length of time.

- **Bubbles.** Create an image of a bubble and then randomly display bubbles on the screen for the user to pop. The user's goal is to never let there be more than 10 bubbles on the screen at a time.

- **Hypno.** Hypnotic spinning spirals in different sizes and colors appear all over the screen. The user's goal is to tap all the red ones before it is too late. You might have a time limit to encourage users to hurry.

- **iMood.** Any time the user touches the screen, the entire screen—or just the area of the screen the user touched—changes colors, similar to either a mood ring or a heat-sensitive object.

4 ▶ In This Chapter

Programming: iFlame

Programming: iDrum

Programming: Bonfire

Analyzing business aspects

- **Fractalious.** A living fractal that constantly changes size, shape, and color is displayed on the screen. Maybe the user can pinch the screen to zoom in and out using the iPhone's Multi-Touch capabilities.
- **Fire Wall.** A wall of animated fire is shown on the screen. No matter which way the iPhone is held, the fire always burns in an upward direction.
- **Sound Board.** This app could have lots of buttons with matching sound effects for the user to play as needed. Maybe there would be a nice round of applause or the sound of a jeering crowd, ready on cue.
- **Star Field.** Think of this as a screensaver for your iPhone. Almost any good idea for a screensaver is a good idea for an iPhone novelty application.

CROSS-REFERENCE

Check out Appendix B for details on the 31 iPhone apps we created in one month, including Snow Fall, Sleep Sound, and more.

Programming: iFlame

The application you are going to create is called iFlame, which is a virtual lighter for the iPhone. The idea is to create an application that people can safely use anytime and anywhere instead of having to carry around a separate physical lighter with them. This could be very useful for concerts or karaoke events. See Figure 4.1 for the iTunes listing for iFlame.

When we originally released our iFlame application in August 2008, it was one of the first, if not the first, virtual lighter applications for the iPhone. Today there are probably over a dozen. When you are coming up with your next great iPhone application, it helps if you are one of the first to the market. A good idea can go far; a good original idea can go farther. Even today, almost a year later, we still receive many requests for downloads of our iFlame application on a daily basis.

Another thing you can do to help your application stand out in a crowd is to have unique features. For iFlame we decided to create four unique variations that users can select from. We were also sure to include these details on the App Store. We even renamed the application to "iFlame—Multi Effect Concert Buddy" to make sure we got this key selling point across to potential app purchasers.

Here are the available iFlame effect modes:

- **Normal.** In normal mode, iFlame displays a standard traditional flame that waves and flickers over time.
- **Tiles.** In tiles mode, the flame is much smaller and the video is repeated in a 6 x 6 grid.
- **Cube.** The cube mode shows the flame in a video cube effect. Each face of the cube displays the flame video while the cube rotates.
- **Strobe.** In strobe mode, while the flame video plays the screen fades from the dark video to pure white, creating a strobe effect.

Figure 4.1

iFlame—Multi Effect Concert Buddy

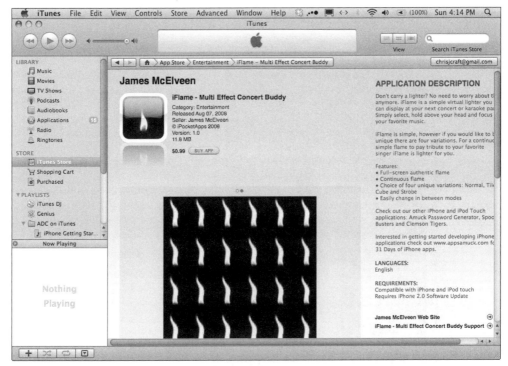

Sometimes magic tricks lose their magic once you understand how a trick works. Take a look at the iFlame application, shown in Figure 4.2. See if you can figure out what the trick is that makes the iFlame application work. Here's a clue: The iFlame application does not generate its images programmatically. Keep reading to learn the secret.

To begin creating a new iPhone application, open Xcode and choose File ⇨ New Project. In the New Project dialog box, under iPhone OS Application, choose the Utility Application template (Figure 4.3).

Name the new project **iFlame** and then click the Save button in the bottom right of the dialog box. You should now have a new Xcode iPhone OS application named iFlame.

NOTE

The secret to how the iFlame application is able to create such a photorealistic flame is that the application is actually playing a video loop of a real lighter's flame. All we did to create the flame video was to take a lighter into a windowless room and record it with a digital video recorder.

Figure 4.2

What's the secret behind the iFlame application?

It was very important for the video of the flame to have a seamless loop. This means that when you watch the flame you never see the flame reset with the video loop repeated from the end of the loop back to the beginning. This is another one of our behind-the-scenes iFlame tricks. Can you guess how we did it? No, we did not record hours and hours of video and find a section of video that just happened to match up over a reasonable interval of time. Here's how we did it: Imagine you have a short video loop that consists of five frames. You could imagine that the following numbers represent those five frames: 1, 2, 3, 4, and 5. Now if you took that video loop and reversed and then pasted it after the original video loop, you would end up with something like this: 1, 2, 3, 4, 5, 5, 4, 3, 2, 1.

Figure 4.3

New Project dialog box

This would technically be a seamless video loop, but it has a couple of problems. The number 5 frame is repeated twice, which will make that frame appear to last twice as long to viewers. And since the first frame is frame 1, and the last frame is frame 1, whenever the video loops back from the end to the beginning, frame 1 will appear to take twice as long as well. This is easy to fix with the following corrections: 1, 2, 3, 4, 5, 4, 3, 2. Notice all we had to do was remove the repeated frames: frames 1 and 5.

While this trick will make any video technically seamless, it is really only useful with video of things that look the same whether the video is being played forward or backward. All it would have taken to ruin this effect for us would have been for the flame to create smoke while it burned. Half the time the smoke would have floated away from the fire, while the other half of the time the smoke would have floated toward the flame. This would have completely destroyed the viewer's suspension of disbelief.

As you can see in Figure 4.4, if you have three frames of video and you want to create a seamless video loop, you will need to take the original three frames and reverse them, and then remove the duplicate first and last frames. Oftentimes with larger amounts of video you will not have to remove these overlapping frames.

Figure 4.4

Simple three-frame seamless video

You can either create your own flame video, which we recommend you try at some point, or use one of ours. There is a lot of video-editing software out there that you can use to create your videos. Start with products like iMovie, since it is free and should already be installed on your machine. You might also want to consider QuickTime Pro, which is affordable (less than $50 at the time of this writing) and powerful. It can open and save video from and to almost any video format, including the iPhone-compatible M4V format. It can even convert videos to sequences of images and vice versa. The iPhone lets only one video play at a time, and it will fill the screen. If you convert your videos to images and then play them as animations, you can have a lot more freedom. The tradeoff is that when videos are converted to images, they usually need more storage space.

For example, this would be a great answer if you had a dozen videos, any one of which the user can play full-screen, but you want the user to be able to see live, independently controlled thumbnails of all the videos at the same time.

You will need to use the `MPMoviePlayerController` class to play video on the iPhone. The `MPMoviePlayerController` is a full-screen movie player. If that does not meet your needs, you will have to find a way to convert your video to a sequence of images and then display them on the iPhone as an animation. You could use QuickTime Pro to convert your videos to image sequences.

Also note that the `MPMoviePlayerController` class can play local movies stored on the iPhone or remote movies from a network-based URL. If you decide to use remote movies, consider saving your movie files in the iPhone Cellular format of 3gp. Again, you can use QuickTime Pro to accomplish this feat. The 3gp format is optimized for the iPhone and for retrieval over cellular connections.

TIP

If your application is larger than 10MB, users will not be able to download it from the App Store using cellular connections. Instead, a Wi-Fi connection will be required. Consider streaming larger videos from remote servers to keep app file size down.

The `MPMoviePlayerController` class allows you to play any movie or audio format that is already supported on the iPhone. This means if it already works on the device, it will work in your application—or more specifically, files with the following extensions will work in your application: MOV, MP4, MPV, and 3gp.

Any time you are working with a new class, it's a good idea to research it first in Xcode's Help menu. Go ahead and take a few minutes to look up MPMoviePlayerController in Xcode's API Reference. One easy way to do this is to type **MPMoviePlayerController** in Xcode and then right-click the text and choose Find Selected Text in API Reference.

Also consider using the Reference Assistant located under Xcode's Help menu. This gives you real-time, context-sensitive help as you work in Xcode. Finally, you can right-click `MPMoviePlayerController` and choose Jump to Definition. This takes you directly to the real code that makes up the `MPMoviePlayerController` class. Not only can you learn more about the `MPMoviePlayerController` class, but this is a great way to learn more about how to program correctly.

You will need to add the MediaPlayer framework to your iFlame Xcode project. To do this, find the Frameworks folder, which is located under the iFlame project in the Groups & Files panel of Xcode, and double-click on the folder to expand it (Figure 4.5).

Right-click on the Frameworks folder and choose the Existing Frameworks option from the Add sub-menu. You will now see a folder listing; find the folder named Frameworks and double-click it to expand it. You will see a listing of a dozen or more framework folders. Once you locate the MediaPlayer.framework folder, select it and then click the Add button in the bottom right.

Note that depending upon a number of factors, such as the current SDK version installed and whether the Developer Tools were already installed, you may not be placed in the correct Framework folder by default when trying to add an existing framework. If this happens to you, you will need to browse up a parent folder or two and find the correct version of the framework. The full location for the MediaPlayer.framework is Developer ➪ Platforms ➪ iPhoneOS.platform ➪ Developer ➪ SDKs ➪ iPhoneOS3.0.sdk ➪ System ➪ Library ➪ Frameworks ➪ MediaPlayer.framework.

Figure 4.5

The Frameworks folder

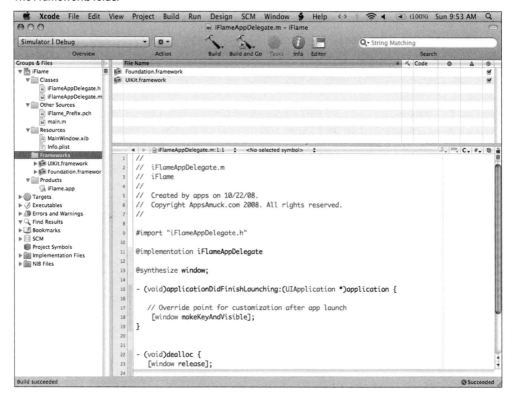

Another screen appears, similar to Figure 4.6. Confirm that Reference Type is set to Default and Text Encoding is set to Unicode (UTF-8). The Add To Targets panel should have iFlame listed with a check box next to it. Click the Add button to proceed. These are the default settings, so you should only have to double-click to confirm them.

You now have added a reference to the MediaPlayer.framework to your iFlame project. The next step is to update your iFlameAppDelegate.h file so that it will use this framework. You can find the iFlameAppDelegate.h file in Xcode under the Classes folder beneath the iFlame root project folder. You can do this by adding a simple import statement to the top of the file:

```
#import <MediaPlayer/MediaPlayer.h>
```

Figure 4.6

Adding a new framework to the iFlame app

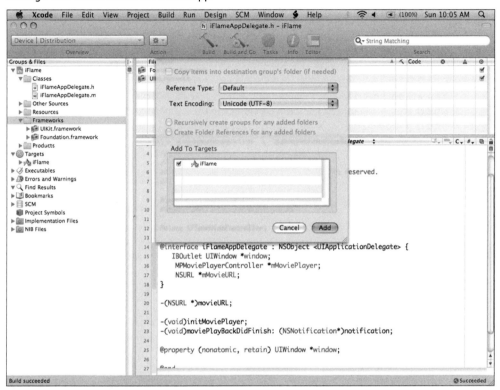

Once you have added this line, your `iFlameAppDelegate.h` file should look like the following:

```
#import <UIKit/UIKit.h>
#import <MediaPlayer/MediaPlayer.h>
@class iFlameViewController;
@interface iFlameAppDelegate : NSObject <UIApplicationDelegate>
{
    IBOutlet UIWindow *window;
}
@property (nonatomic, retain) UIWindow *window;
@end
```

Next, you will need to create the actual `MPMoviePlayerController` object instance. This will go under `IBOutlet` declaration line that is located near the middle of the file. After this you will need to add an `NSURL` object to help keep track of movie URL:

```
MPMoviePlayerController *mMoviePlayer;
NSURL *mMovieURL;
```

NOTE
You can use the `MPMoviePlayerController` to play audio as well as video. The only drawback is the user will be presented with a rather dull screen, with, at most, basic playback controls, while the audio plays.

You will now need to add a couple of notification callback methods so that the movie player object and the iFlame application can load the movie and handle when the movie is done playing. You should add these items right before the `@end` statement:

```
-(NSURL *)movieURL;
-(void)initMoviePlayer;
-(void)moviePlayBackDidFinish: (NSNotification*)notification;
```

Once you have performed these changes, your `iFlameAppDelegate.h` file should look like the following:

```
#import <MediaPlayer/MediaPlayer.h>

@class MainViewController;
@interface iFlameAppDelegate : NSObject <UIApplicationDelegate> {
 UIWindow *window;
   MPMoviePlayerController *mMoviePlayer;
   NSURL *mMovieURL;
}
@property (nonatomic, retain) IBOutlet UIWindow *window;
@property (nonatomic, retain) MainViewController
   *mainViewController;
-(NSURL *)movieURL;
-(void)initMoviePlayer;
-(void)moviePlayBackDidFinish: (NSNotification*)notification;
@end
```

If you look back in the `iFlameAppDelegate.h` file, you will see that the `iFlameAppDelegate` implements the `UIApplicationDelegate`, which, according to the API Reference, means there is an optional `applicationDidFinishLaunching` event that is called when the application has finished launching. You will use this event to start your video.

Now you will move on to updating the corresponding `iFlameAppDelegate.m` file. Start by updating the `applicationDidFinishLaunching` method. Make the changes required so that your `applicationDidFinishLaunching` method matches the following:

```
- (void)applicationDidFinishLaunching:(UIApplication *)
   application {
    [self initMoviePlayer];
    [window makeKeyAndVisible];
}
```

TIP

The media player always does a fade to black whenever a video finishes playing. To avoid this you can copy and paste your video multiple times, even hundreds of times, in QuickTime Pro; while the play time will increase, the file size will not.

Now when the iFlame application finishes loading, it will call your `applicationDidFinishLaunching` method, which is set to then call the `initMoviePlayer` method. You will now add the following `initMoviePlayer` method to your code by modifying the current `initMoviePlayer` method to match this one:

```
-(void)initMoviePlayer
{
mMoviePlayer = [[MPMoviePlayerController alloc]
    initWithContentURL:[self movieURL]];
[[NSNotificationCenter defaultCenter] addObserver:self
    selector:@selector(moviePlayBackDidFinish:)
    name:MPMoviePlayerPlaybackDidFinishNotification
    object:mMoviePlayer];
mMoviePlayer.scalingMode = MPMovieScalingModeAspectFill;
mMoviePlayer.movieControlMode = MPMovieControlModeHidden;
mMoviePlayer.backgroundColor = [UIColor blackColor];
[mMoviePlayer play];
}
```

There's a lot going on in this method, so take a moment to review it now.

The following line of code creates a new `MPMoviePlayerController` object and assigns it to our `mMoviePlayer` object. It also initializes the newly created `MPMoviePlayerController` object with the movie stored at the `movieURL` location:

```
mMoviePlayer = [[MPMoviePlayerController alloc]
    initWithContentURL:[self movieURL]];
```

The purpose of the following line of code is to tell the `MPMoviePlayerController` object that we want to be notified when the movie finishes playback. The name of this notification is `MPMoviePlayerPlaybackDidFinishNotification`, and it is now set to call our `moviePlayBackDidFinish` method once the movie is done:

```
[[NSNotificationCenter defaultCenter] addObserver:self
    selector:@selector(moviePlayBackDidFinish:)
    name:MPMoviePlayerPlaybackDidFinishNotification
    object:mMoviePlayer];
```

There are two other notifications available on the `MPMoviePlayerController`:

- The `MPMoviePlayerContentPreloadDidFinishNotification` event occurs once the movie has been loaded into memory and is ready to play.

- The `MPMoviePlayerScalingModeDidChangeNotification` event occurs if the screen is rotated and so on.

TIP

Consider using `MPMoviePlayerContentPreloadDidFinishNotification` so you can display a loading screen until the movie player is able to load the movie into memory.

Scaling mode determines how any movie that does not exactly fit the screen will be scaled to fill the screen. We went with `MPMovieScalingModeAspectFill` because it was okay if the black around the flame went off the screen and got cropped off.

Here are all the valid scaling modes for displaying movies for `MPMovieScalingMode`:

- **MPMovieScalingModeNone.** Do not scale the movie.
- **MPMovieScalingModeAspectFit.** Scale the movie until one dimension fits on the screen exactly. In the other dimension, the region between the edge of the movie and the edge of the screen is filled with a black bar. The aspect ratio of the movie is preserved.
- **MPMovieScalingModeAspectFill.** Scale the movie until the movie fills the entire screen. Content at the edges of the larger of the two dimensions is clipped so that the other dimension fits the screen exactly. The aspect ratio of the movie is preserved.
- **MPMovieScalingModeFill.** Scale the movie until both dimensions fit the screen exactly. The aspect ratio of the movie is not preserved.

Sometimes it really helps to see the code behind a feature you are working with even if only for reference. So here is the source code for the `MPMovieScalingMode`:

```
typedef enum
{
// No scaling applied at all.
MPMovieScalingModeNone,
// Uniform scale until one dimension fits. One dimension may be
// filled with bars the color of the backgroundColor property.
MPMovieScalingModeAspectFit,
// Uniform scale until the movie fills the visible bounds. One
// dimension may have clipped contents.
MPMovieScalingModeAspectFill,
// Non-uniform scale. Both render dimensions will exactly match
// the visible bounds.
MPMovieScalingModeFill
} MPMovieScalingMode;
```

CAUTION

Be careful when using the `MPMovieScalingModeFill`, as it is the only scaling mode that does not preserve the video's aspect ratio. Using this may cause displayed video to appear distorted.

In this case, you will want to use the `MPMovieControlModeHidden` movie control mode because showing any movie controls will give away the trick to the watcher.

```
mMoviePlayer.movieControlMode = MPMovieControlModeHidden;
```

Here is the source code for the `MPMovieControlMode` enumeration. This should help prove the value of reading through a class's source code to learn more about its inner workings:

```
typedef enum
{
// Standard controls (e.g. play/pause, volume slider, timeline)
   are
// visible
MPMovieControlModeDefault,
// Only the volume control is visible
MPMovieControlModeVolumeOnly,
// No controls are visible
MPMovieControlModeHidden
} MPMovieControlMode;
```

Here are all the valid movie control modes for `MPMovieControlMode`:

- **MPMovieControlModeDefault.** Display the standard controls for controlling playback. This includes play/pause controls, a volume slider, and a timeline control.
- **MPMovieControlModeVolumeOnly.** Display volume controls only.
- **MPMovieControlModeHidden.** Do not display any controls. This mode prevents the user from controlling playback. Use this mode any time you only want the user to be able to see the video. A virtual aquarium video application, for example, would not appear realistic behind a set of playback controls.

The background is used for any area on the `MPMoviePlayerController` that is not filled by the video due to choices made for `MPMovieScalingMode` and so on. In this case you will want to use black. This way if there is any area not covered by the video it will match the black background used in the video:

```
mMoviePlayer.backgroundColor = [UIColor blackColor];
```

NOTE
The movie player's background color is also the color that the screen will fade to and from whenever the video begins or ends. By default, the movie background color is black.

Finally, the simple play command is passed to the movie player object and the magic begins. You can also call stop at any point to pause the video playback and re-call play to resume playback.

Next, you should add the `moviePlayBackDidFinish` notification method. Since you are using a seamless video loop, whenever the video finishes playback you will simply play it again. Here is the code to make that happen:

```
-(void)moviePlayBackDidFinish: (NSNotification*)notification
{
    MPMoviePlayerController* theMovie=[notification object];
    [theMovie play];
}
```

The `notification` object that is passed to the `moviePlayBackDidFinish` method is the `MPMoviePlayerController` object we assigned to be notified on finishing movie playback. You just need to convert it back to an `MPMoviePlayerController` object and call the object's play method.

We now have most of the plumbing we need for our iFlame project. One thing that is missing is a way for the application to determine what video it should play. Add the following code, which does that, and then review it yourself before proceeding:

```
// return a URL for the movie file in our bundle
-(NSURL *)movieURL
{
    if (mMovieURL == nil)
    {
        NSBundle *bundle = [NSBundle mainBundle];
        if (bundle)
        {
NSString *moviePath = [bundle pathForResource:@"movie"
    ofType:@"m4v"];
            if (moviePath)
            {
                mMovieURL = [NSURL fileURLWithPath:moviePath];
                [mMovieURL retain];
            }
        }
    }

    return mMovieURL;
}
```

First, you check to see if `mMovieURL` has already been set. If it is `nil`, this is the first time this method has been called and you will need to assign a value to `mMovieURL`. Next, check that the iFlame project has an `NSBundle`. It will as long as you remember to add a video to the iFlame project. The `NSBundle` object is a powerful class that helps developers to not rely on hard coded paths. This class will find your application's location on the device file system so you can easily access files and resources.

Use the `pathForResource` method to obtain the movie.M4V file's path. If the path exists, assign it to the `mMovieURL` string. The last thing is to simply return it back to the calling method.

CAUTION

Always be sure to test that variables are valid before calling any related methods. A simple if variable != nil is sometimes all it takes to avoid a crashing application.

When the application is done running, it will call `dealloc`, so be sure to clean up any variables you created there. Since you allocated the memory for the `mMoviePlayer` and `mMovieURL` objects, you will need to make sure you deallocate the memory before the application is done. Here is the basic code that is required to do that:

```
- (void)dealloc
{
    [mMoviePlayer release];
    [mMovieURL release];
    [window release];
    [super dealloc];
}
```

There is one important task remaining before you can try out this application. You have to add the movie.mv4 to the project's resources. From Xcode, find the Resources folder under the iFlame project in the Groups & Files panel. Right-click on the folder and choose Add ⇨ Existing Items.

Locate the video you wish to use and select it, then click the Add button. You can use one we have provided in this chapter's sample code, or use one of your own. In the next dialog box, be sure to check the Copy items into the destination group's folder check box. Confirm that Reference Type is set to Default and Text Encoding is set to Unicode (UTF-8). Then click the Add button.

Be sure to set Xcode to Simulator | Distribution and then click the Build and Go button. The application should now load up in the Simulator and run. You should see the iFlame application as shown in Figure 4.7.

Any time you finish an application you should take a step back and perform a quick mental post-mortem. What went right? What went wrong? What could you have done better? What will you do differently next time? Also take some time and think about where you will go from here. We recommend taking the iFlame application you have and creating some new effects of your own. For example, you could create a campfire application or a fireplace application for the iPhone. Maybe you could blow out the fire in the fireplace by blowing on the iPhone's microphone. Users would enjoy this because it would remind them of the famous *Three Little Pigs* children's story.

Figure 4.7

The final iFlame application running in the Simulator

Since you now have a solid template for playing videos in your applications, another enhance-ment idea you can consider for the application, and for others you may create, is to create a video splash screen that you play when the user first runs your application. People have come to expect this high level of professionalism from movies, but it is still rare in iPhone applications. Instead of boring text that tells users about your other products, have you considered creating exciting 10-second video commercials? You would only need to add a new screen, then have some thumbnails to allow viewers to pick which of your applications they are interested in.

Programming: iDrum

Let's now take a look at creating another novelty application. This time you will create a virtual drum for the iPhone. The iDrum features a great graphic and sound effect of a drum. You can use the ones we provide or ones of your own. When you are done, you should end up with an application that looks something like the one in Figure 4.8.

To create a virtual drum for the iPhone, follow these steps:

1. Open Xcode and choose File ⇨ New Project.

2. You will use the Utility Application project template that can be found under the iPhone OS application. Select the Utility Application project template and click the Choose button at the bottom right.

3. Save the new project in a location to your liking and name it **iDrum**.

4. Locate the Default.png file that is included with the chapter's materials.

5. Expand the Resources folder that is located in the Groups & Files panel on the left side of Xcode. Right-click on this folder and choose Add ⇨ Existing Files. Browse until you locate the Default.png file that you located earlier and select it, then click the Add button at the bottom right of the dialog box.

6. Locate the drumbeat.caf file that should also be included in this chapter's materials where you found the Default.png. This is the sound that the iDrum makes when the user taps it. Repeat the same process as before to add the drumbeat.caf to your iDrum project's resources.

7. Do the same for the drum.png and the drumIcon.png files.

You should always include a Default.png in all of your applications. The iPhone displays the Default.png during the time it takes to load the application. This keeps the user from seeing a blank black screen and wondering if the application is locked up. You can either use the Default.png as an application splash screen as we have done (Figure 4.9), or you can use it to make the application appear to load faster.

You can see a good example of this effect in Apple's iPhone applications; in particular, the Clock application. When you first start the iPhone's Clock application, for the first second or two what you see is actually an image that is being used as the Clock's Default.png on application startup. You can see this image in Figure 4.10. It might not look like much, but this screen is very similar to what the iPhone's Clock application looks like when it is running. Basically all of the background elements for the Clock application are drawn to the screen so it is almost ready even before the application starts.

Figure 4.8

The iDrum application

Figure 4.9

The iDrum's Default.png

Once the Clock application has finished loading, it takes over screen output and you finally see the actual Clock application running on your device, similar to Figure 4.11. This is a great effect, and from the user's point of the view, the iPhone seems to be opening most applications almost instantly.

The native audio format that Apple uses for sounds on the iPhone is the CAF audio format. You can convert your existing MP3, WAV, AAC, AIFF, and other audio files to the CAF format using iTunes.

Figure 4.10

The iPhone Clock application's Default.png

Figure 4.11

The iPhone Clock application

To convert to CAF, follow these steps:

1. **Set your Import Settings in iTunes to Import Using: AIFF Encoder.** Open iTunes Preferences and choose Under General Settings ⇨ When you insert a CD: click the Import Settings button.

2. **Convert the audio file you want to AIFF.** Select the song in iTunes, and choose ⇨ Advanced ⇨ Create AIFF version.

3. **Rename the audio file to CAF.** Drag the newly created song to your desktop and rename the AIFF extension to CAF.

A large part of effectively using the iPhone SDK is learning about all the frameworks that are available for you to take advantage of. Instead of you having to create something from scratch, in many cases these frameworks can do the work for you. The following device framework listing summarizes all the device frameworks that are available:

- **AddressBook.framework.** Contains functions for accessing the user's contacts database directly.
- **AddressBookUI.framework.** Contains classes for displaying the system-defined people picker and editor interfaces.
- **AudioToolbox.framework.** Contains the interfaces for handling audio stream data and for playing and recording audio.
- **AudioUnit.framework.** Contains the interfaces for loading and using audio units.
- **CFNetwork.framework.** Contains interfaces for accessing the network via the Wi-Fi and cellular radios.
- **CoreAudio.framework.** Provides the data types used throughout Core Audio.
- **CoreFoundation.framework.** Provides fundamental software services, including abstractions for common data types, string utilities, collection utilities, resource management, and preferences.
- **CoreGraphics.framework.** Contains the interfaces for Quartz 2-D.
- **CoreLocation.framework.** Contains the interfaces for determining the user's location.
- **Foundation.framework.** Contains the classes and methods for the Cocoa Foundation layer.
- **CoreLocation.framework.** Contains the interfaces for determining the user's location.
- **IOKit.framework.** Contains interfaces used by the device. Do not include this framework directly.
- **MediaPlayer.framework.** Contains interfaces for playing full-screen video.
- **OpenAL.framework.** Contains the interfaces for OpenAL, a cross-platform positional audio library.
- **OpenGLES.framework.** Contains the interfaces for OpenGL ES, an embedded version of the OpenGL cross-platform 2-D and 3-D graphics-rendering library.
- **QuartzCore.framework.** Contains the Core Animation interfaces.
- **Security.framework.** Contains interfaces for managing certificates, public and private keys, and trust policies.
- **SystemConfiguration.framework.** Contains interfaces for determining the network configuration of a device.
- **UIKit.framework.** Contains classes and methods for the iPhone application user-interface layer.

iDrum is a good example of an application that uses many existing frameworks to do the work for it. You will need to add the following frameworks to your iDrum project:

- AudioToolbox
- CoreAudio
- OpenAL
- Foundation

The Frameworks folder can be found under the iDrum project in the Groups & Files panel of Xcode. Right-click on the folder to locate the Existing Frameworks menu item, which is found under the Add menu. Click the Existing Frameworks menu item, and then open the selected Frameworks folder. The full location for these frameworks is Developer ⇨ Platforms ⇨ iPhoneOS. platform ⇨ Developer ⇨ SDKs ⇨ iPhoneOS3.0.sdk ⇨ System ⇨ Library ⇨ Frameworks.

With the Frameworks folder open, you can begin adding the required frameworks. You'll need to add these one at a time since Xcode does not support multiple selections in this dialog box. After you have added all the required files and frameworks, your project should look like Figure 4.12.

Figure 4.12

iPhone SDK frameworks added to the iDrum application

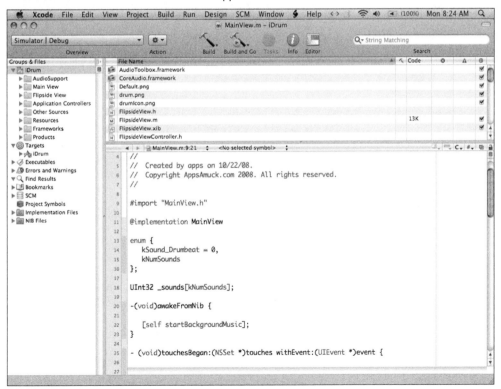

Expand the Main View folder under Groups & Files below the iDrum project. Open the `MainView.h` file in Xcode. You will need to add an import line to include the `SoundEngine.h` file:

```
#import "SoundEngine.h"
```

You will also add a define directive that will declare a constant for setting the listener distance:

```
// Used for creating a realistic sound field
#define kListenerDistance        1.0
```

Next you will need to add an `IBAction` to capture touches on the drum image and a `startBackgroundMusic`:

```
- (IBAction)drum;
- (void) startBackgroundMusic;
```

Once you are done making all of these changes to your `MainView.h` file, it should look something like this:

```
#import <UIKit/UIKit.h>
#import "SoundEngine.h"
// Used for creating a realistic sound field
#define kListenerDistance        1.0
@interface MainView : UIView
{
}
- (IBAction)drum;
- (void) startBackgroundMusic;
@end
```

You should finish building the screen in Interface Builder before beginning work on the matching `MainView.m` file. In the Groups & Files panel, find the Resources folder and expand it. Inside you should be able to locate the `MainView.xib` file. Double-click this file to open it in Interface Builder. Open Interface Builder's Library by choosing Tools ⇨ Library. Find the Image View object located under Library ⇨ Cocoa Touch ⇨ Data Views. Drag the Image View over to the Main View window.

Take the Image View and resize it to fill the entire screen. Now open Interface Builder's Inspector tool by choosing Tools ⇨ Inspector. Make sure the Image View is selected in the Main View's window. Click on the left-most tab at the top of the Inspector window. It should be named Image View Attributes.

Using the pull-down menu, assign the drum.png file to the Image field, and set the Mode to Scale To Fill. This ensures that the image expands to fill all available space. Set Alpha to 1.00 so the image will be completely opaque (Figure 4.13).

Figure 4.13

Main View Attributes dialog box

Now select the Main View window itself. The Inspector window should be titled Main View Attributes. Again, set the Mode to Scale To Fill and Alpha to 1.00. Set the background color to Iron from the color list. Under the Drawing section, check the Opaque check box, and under the Interaction section, check the User Interaction Enabled check box.

At the top of the Inspector window, click on the fourth tab named Main View Identity. Under Class Actions, click the small plus button to add a new Action named drum. Now you will open the `MainView.m` file. First, you need to add a new sound enumeration to the top of this file:

```
enum
{
    kSound_Drumbeat = 0,
    kNumSounds
};
```

The purpose of this enumeration is to simply keep track of how many sounds there are in the application and which one to play at any given time. In this case, the iDrum application has only the drumbeat sound, which is located at index 0. Since the drumbeat sound is set to 1, and kNumSounds is set to 1, everything matches and you have the correct number of sounds available.

Next, you need to add an internal sound variable to track the current playing sound:

```
UInt32 _sounds[kNumSounds];
```

For this application it makes sense to have some background music playing in an infinite loop. This way the user has something playing to add to instead of being responsible for everything. You start the background music when the Main View window is loaded:

```
-(void)awakeFromNib
{
    [self startBackgroundMusic];
}
```

Now when the application is started and it loads the Main View window, this in turn calls the startBackgroundMusic method on the view:

```
- (void) startBackgroundMusic
{
NSBundle* bundle = [NSBundle mainBundle];
// Note that each of the Sound Engine functions defined in
// SoundEngine.h returns an OSStatus value.
// Although the code in this application does not check for
   errors,
// you'll want to add error checking code
// in your own application, particularly during development.
//Setup sound engine. Run it at 44Khz to match the sound files
SoundEngine_Initialize(44100);
// Assume the listener is in the center at the start. The sound
// will pan as the position of the rocket changes.
SoundEngine_SetListenerPosition(0.0, 0.0, kListenerDistance);
// Load each of the four sounds used in the game.
SoundEngine_LoadEffect([[bundle pathForResource:@"background"
    ofType:@"caf"] UTF8String], &_sounds[kSound_Drumbeat]);
//Play start sound
SoundEngine_StartEffect( _sounds[0]);
}
```

Now you add the keystone piece. The touchesBegan method triggers the drumbeat sound any time the Main View is touched:

```
- (void)touchesBegan:(NSSet *)touches withEvent:(UIEvent *)event
{
    SoundEngine_StartEffect( _sounds[kSound_Drumbeat]);
}
```

Be sure to set Xcode to Simulator | Distribution and then click the Build and Go button. The application should now load in the Simulator and run. You should see the iDrum application, as shown in Figure 4.14.

Figure 4.14

The final iDrum application running in the Simulator

The application is mostly done now and just needs some finishing touches. You should create a nice About Us screen for it, and you will need to come up with a great iPhone application icon for users to see both on the App Store and on the iPhone. You might want to consider using the image of the drum itself and then simply resizing it as needed to make your icon.

There are quite a few virtual drum applications on the App Store. What can you do to this application to make it stand out? Well you could add a setting to let people decide what kind of drum they want to play. You could have a standard drum, a Jamaican drum, or a Congo drum for starters.

TIP

The iPhone is a very feature-rich device, and you should always try to use its capabilities to surprise and delight your application's users. If you make your applications high quality and offer great user experiences, people will come back for more. Any time you raise the bar for what people can expect, you have gone from having a customer to having a fan—and you can never have too many of those.

What if when the user tapped the drum the physical iPhone device itself vibrated? In order for an iPhone SDK application to be able to make the device vibrate, the application must include a reference to the AudioToolbox framework. This is not a problem for the iDrum application because it already includes this reference. But you will want to remember this for the next application you write that will support vibration. It will be a real pain if you overlook this detail.

It only takes one line of code to make the iPhone vibrate:

```
AudioServicesPlaySystemSound(kSystemSoundID_Vibrate);
```

Locate the `touchesBegan` method in your `MainView.m` file. It should match the following code:

```
- (void)touchesBegan:(NSSet *)touches withEvent:(UIEvent *)event
{
    SoundEngine_StartEffect( _sounds[kSound_Drumbeat] );
}
```

You will need to update this method so that it calls the vibration code listed earlier, as follows:

```
- (void)touchesBegan:(NSSet *)touches withEvent:(UIEvent *)event
{
    SoundEngine_StartEffect( _sounds[kSound_Drumbeat] );
    AudioServicesPlaySystemSound(kSystemSoundID_Vibrate);
}
```

And there you go—you now have a virtual drum with a force feedback feature, all implemented in one line of code in less than a few minutes' time.

Wouldn't it be great if the drum had a quick animation that played whenever the user tapped it? This would make it much more realistic. What if you create a screen where the user could pick a song and the drum would automatically play it, kind of like how the old player pianos could do? You probably have some ideas of your own as well. What are you waiting for—seize the day!

Programming: Bonfire

The last novelty you are going to create in this chapter is Bonfire. Bonfire is meant to be a virtual campfire that users can carry with them anywhere. And at least with this campfire, nobody has to worry about burning down the forest. When you are finished creating Bonfire, you will end up with an application that looks something like Figure 4.15.

Figure 4.15

The Bonfire application

Once again, open Xcode and create a new project using the iPhone OS Utility Application template. Name this new project **Bonfire**. Go ahead and create a Default.png now and add it to your Bonfire project. To do this, right-click on the Resources folder below the Bonfire project folder in the Groups & Files panel in Xcode. Choose Add ⇨ Existing Files. Find the Default.png file you created, select it, and then click the Add button.

This time we choose to let the Default.png file we created match the first frame of the Bonfire animation. This way the application appears to load faster (almost instantaneously) for the end user. You can see the Default.png file we used in Figure 4.16. You can either use the one we provided or create one of your own if you want something more like a splash screen to show.

Figure 4.16

The Bonfire application's Default.png

It is always best to add a Default.png early on in the iPhone application-making process, even if you only make a temporary Default.png image that has the text "Temporary Default.png" on it, because that way you are less likely to forget to create one in the end. Once you get more involved in the application-making business, it's easy to overlook little details such as including the Default.png image file.

When you created the iFlame application earlier in this chapter, you used the MPMoviePlayerController class to play videos, but we mentioned that you could create animations and play movies that way as long as you had an animation image sequence available of the movie. The Bonfire iPhone application takes this approach to movie playing so you can see how it's done.

The key to making Bonfire is creating the animation image sequence. There are many ways you can create an animation image sequence. One way is to use QuickTime Pro, as we mentioned earlier, to convert an existing video into a sequence of images. You could also take an animated GIF file that you have rights to use and use a program that can pull out each frame of the animation and save it as a separate image.

Of course, you can either have someone create the animation for you or create one of your own. You might think hand-drawn animation would not have the quality required for an iPhone application. But there are many iPhone applications coming out that focus on the fact that they are hand drawn and the characters are stick figures. It has become a genre and style all its own.

Once you have the image sequence you are going to use for Bonfire, you will need to add these images to the Bonfire project. We created an animation sequence consisting of 17 images that, when played in a loop, creates a great animation of a burning campfire. Feel free to use this animation sequence for your own Bonfire application.

You may want to create a new folder to keep all of these animation images in. To add a new folder in Xcode, right-click on the Bonfire project's Resource folder and choose Add ➪ New Group. This creates a New Group folder, which you can promptly rename **Images**. Right-click on the Images folder and choose Add ➪ Existing Files. Find your images, select them, and then click the Add button in the bottom-right side of the dialog box. Once you have added all of your images to your Bonfire project, Xcode should look something like Figure 4.17.

After you have prepared your Bonfire project with all the resources you need to create the Bonfire iPhone application, your main task is to add the code required to make the Bonfire animation play. Open the `MainViewController.m` file in Xcode, located under the Main View folder under the Bonfire project in the Groups & Files panel. Find the `viewDidLoad` method. The `viewDidLoad` method is implemented by all `UIViewController` objects, of which the `MainViewController` class you are in is one. This method is invoked or called when the view is finished loading.

TIP

Don't forget you can use transparency in your animations. You can use images that contain both opaque areas and transparent areas. You can even use images with partial transparency and alpha blended components. This can create some truly stunning effects.

The `viewDidLoad` method should look like the following code:

```
/*
If you need to do additional setup after loading the view,
   override viewDidLoad.
 - (void)viewDidLoad {
 }
*/
```

Figure 4.17

Xcode project with all images added

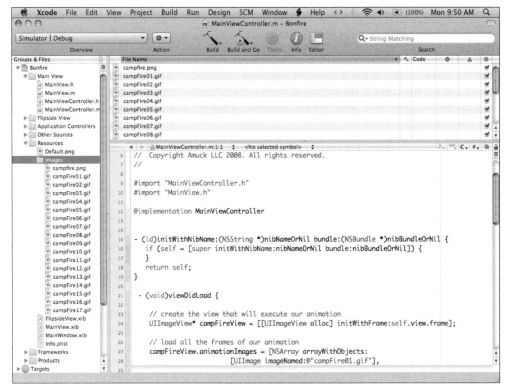

Modify the `viewDidLoad` until it matches the following version:

```
- (void)viewDidLoad
{
// create the view that will execute our animation
UIImageView* campFireView = [[UIImageView alloc]
initWithFrame:self.view.frame];
// load all the frames of our animation
campFireView.animationImages = [NSArray arrayWithObjects:
    [UIImage imageNamed:@"campFire01.gif"],
    [UIImage imageNamed:@"campFire02.gif"],
    [UIImage imageNamed:@"campFire03.gif"],
    [UIImage imageNamed:@"campFire04.gif"],
    [UIImage imageNamed:@"campFire05.gif"],
    [UIImage imageNamed:@"campFire06.gif"],
    [UIImage imageNamed:@"campFire07.gif"],
    [UIImage imageNamed:@"campFire08.gif"],
    [UIImage imageNamed:@"campFire09.gif"],
```

```
        [UIImage imageNamed:@"campFire10.gif"],
        [UIImage imageNamed:@"campFire11.gif"],
        [UIImage imageNamed:@"campFire12.gif"],
        [UIImage imageNamed:@"campFire13.gif"],
        [UIImage imageNamed:@"campFire14.gif"],
        [UIImage imageNamed:@"campFire15.gif"],
        [UIImage imageNamed:@"campFire16.gif"],
        [UIImage imageNamed:@"campFire17.gif"], nil];
    // all frames will execute in 1.75 seconds
    campFireView.animationDuration = 1.75;
    // repeat the annimation forever
    campFireView.animationRepeatCount = 0;
    // start animating
    [campFireView startAnimating];
    // add the animation view to the main window
    [self.view addSubview:campFireView];
    [campFireView release];
    }
```

Now you should review this code and learn more about how it works.

Here you create a `UIImageView` and allocate memory for it. On the next line you assign the Main View's frame to the `campFireView`. The Main View's frame is the view that users see whenever they are on the Main View window. When you modify this view, users automatically see any change you make to it:

```
    // create the view that will execute our animation
    UIImageView* campFireView = [[UIImageView alloc]
    initWithFrame:self.view.frame];
```

The `UIImageView` named `campFireView` is the real workhorse of this application. Be sure to look up the `UIImageView` class in Xcode's API Reference. Take a moment and right-click on the text `UIImageView` and then click Find Selected Text in API Reference and see for yourself. Basically, `UIImageView` is good for displaying a single image or a series of images as an animation. The documentation covers the details on how to perform many tasks with the `UIImageView` class, including initializing a `UIImageView`, animating images with a `UIImageView`, and enabling and disabling user interaction on `UIImageViews`.

In this step you are loading all the animation images from the resource image file you added earlier. The `animationImages` property of `UIImageView` expects an `NSArray` of `UIImage` objects. You must set the last element of the `NSArray` to `nil` so that the array will know when the collection ends:

```
    // load all the frames of our animation
    campFireView.animationImages = [NSArray arrayWithObjects:
        [UIImage imageNamed:@"campFire01.gif"],
        [UIImage imageNamed:@"campFire02.gif"],
        [UIImage imageNamed:@"campFire03.gif"],
        [UIImage imageNamed:@"campFire04.gif"],
        [UIImage imageNamed:@"campFire05.gif"],
```

```
[UIImage imageNamed:@"campFire06.gif"],
[UIImage imageNamed:@"campFire07.gif"],
[UIImage imageNamed:@"campFire08.gif"],
[UIImage imageNamed:@"campFire09.gif"],
[UIImage imageNamed:@"campFire10.gif"],
[UIImage imageNamed:@"campFire11.gif"],
[UIImage imageNamed:@"campFire12.gif"],
[UIImage imageNamed:@"campFire13.gif"],
[UIImage imageNamed:@"campFire14.gif"],
[UIImage imageNamed:@"campFire15.gif"],
[UIImage imageNamed:@"campFire16.gif"],
[UIImage imageNamed:@"campFire17.gif"], nil];
```

In this line you are informing the iPhone SDK how long you want it to take to play the animation you loaded in the previous step. This can be a bit of a trial-and-error process, but it is simple and direct and usually works out very well. Many times you already have numbers you need either from the original video or animated GIF file:

```
// all frames will execute in 1.75 seconds
campFireView.animationDuration = 1.75;
```

TIP

Consider using variables to keep track of your animation durations. This way you can create multipliers that speed up or slow down your animations. On level one all animations take *x* seconds, but on level two all animations take *x* * level modifier seconds. This is an easy way to create slow motion and bullet time effects.

If you do the math, the 17 frames you have are being played in an animation of 1.75 seconds. You are basically getting about 10 frames per second here. That's a little low, but if you watch the animation itself, it seems to work out just fine. A possible enhancement to this application would be to add more frames to the animation, but the tradeoff would be a larger final application size.

In the following code, you will set the animation repeat count, start the animation, and assign it to the application's Main View. This line sets the animation repeat count, which does exactly what you would expect. By setting it to 0 you are telling the iPhone SDK to repeat the animation forever:

```
// repeat the annimation forever
campFireView.animationRepeatCount = 0;
```

The UIImageView's method startAnimating is used to start the animation playing. You can also call stopAnimating if you wish to stop an animation. And there is an isAnimating instance method you can call in case you need to query the run-time to find out if the animation is still running:

```
// start animating
[campFireView startAnimating];
```

Now you need to take the animation you have created and add it to the main window:

```
// add the animation view to the main window
[self.view addSubview:campFireView];
```

Finally, you need to make sure that the iPhone SDK knows you are done using the `campFire-View` so that it will release the memory for it when it finishes playing the animation or the application ends:

```
[campFireView release];
```

TIP

You can create multiple `NSArray` objects with different sets of images for your animations. This way when you create a new blue Bonfire animation, it's a simple matter to change all the animations over to use the new images.

It does not make sense to do so in this application, but keep in mind that you can create `UIImageView` definitions that have animations and that move around the screen. This is a great way to create more advanced game elements to use in other games you may create someday.

Set Xcode to Simulator | Distribution and click the Build and Go button. The application loads up in the Simulator and runs, and you should see the Bonfire application as shown in Figure 4.18.

As always, you want to look back at the path you have taken to get this application to where it is today and decide where you will take it tomorrow. You have a great reusable iPhone animation application template; as long as you can find and come up with great animations, you can keep creating exciting new iPhone applications with minimal effort. It's kind of like once you have a soda factory there is very little stopping you from creating new sodas with different flavors. The hard part is already behind you. Now all you need to do is come up with your own recipe for success.

Screensavers are great sources of inspirations for these types of applications. For example, you could create a little virtual world application that plays an animation of a daytime fantasy world during the daytime and plays a nighttime fantasy world animation at night. Even better would be to have different animations for different weather conditions and play the matching one for the user's location.

Many games have been created by a judicious usage of animations overlaid on one another. Just take animated player characters fighting animated opponents, moving over animated environments in front of animated backgrounds, and you have the makings of a truly great iPhone game.

Almost every application in this book and every application you will create or use could be enhanced and improved by the wise usage of `UIImageView` animation. Make a point of learning and mastering this technique so you can use it in the next iPhone application you create.

Figure 4.18

The final Bonfire application running in the Simulator

Analyzing Business Aspects

Novelty applications tend to be smaller and easier applications than most game, business, or even utility applications. Many developers cut their teeth by making a simple novelty application their first application. It can be a great way to ramp up your knowledge of iPhone SDK programming.

Ideally, when you create a new iPhone novelty application, it should be a truly *new* iPhone application. If your application is really one of a kind and people enjoy the experience of it, it will do much better than if your application is just another face in the crowd. Try to forge new ground and provide people with new experiences whenever possible.

Be sure to add variety to your novelty application whenever you can. Sometimes this can be as simple as creating different skins for your application. For example, for the iDrum you could create a Jamaican drum setting with appropriate matching sound effects. These types of small, easy changes can take an application from mediocre to great.

People love to be surprised, and so they love novelty applications that have surprises in them. Imagine how users would react to finding out that there is an update for the iFlame that allows them to blow out the flame using the microphone. It's a new experience that helps bring their new digital world back into the real world they are familiar with.

Summary

In this chapter you reviewed and created a list of potential iPhone novelty applications that you should now be prepared to begin writing. You reviewed the iFlame application and what you would have to do to re-create this application. You learned to try to always favor original ideas or add a new twist to an existing application idea. You also discovered that it is beneficial to add new features and clever effects to apps. You learned all about seamless video loops and how to create them on your own. You worked with the `MPMoviePlayerController` to create a movie player of your own to play video in your iFlame application, and you learned about the various video player scaling and control modes.

Next, you reviewed the iDrum application and began re-creating it on your own. You made sure to include a Default.png to avoid showing your users a blank screen on application startup. You learned a lot about how to play audio files on the iPhone using the iPhone SDK's sound engine. And you discovered how to convert various audio file types to the CAF format, which is the native audio format of the iPhone. While re-creating the iDrum application, you learned more about the iPhone's sound engine and the Interface Builder. You got to add both graphic resources and audio resources to your iFlame app and the iDrum project. Then you used these resources to add visuals and audios to your application.

You then learned all the details of creating your own animations using the `UIImageView`'s animation capabilities in the Bonfire app. You learned how to create your own animation image sequences and how to add these `UIImages` to the `animationImages` property of the `UIImageView`. Finally, you discovered how to use and set the various options on the `UIImageView` so the animation would run according to your wishes.

Shall We Play a Game?

Producing Action Games

You should now be ready to create your first action game. Remember, the games developed in this chapter can be found on the App Store and the source code can be downloaded from our Web site, `http://appsamuck.com`.

Action games are extremely popular in the game marketplace today. They are challenging and exciting, and most are some kind of test of skill, usually with a time limit. Many people enjoy beating this implied dare. Some players will try to beat a well-done action game almost religiously, playing hours on end and even through the night.

Consider one of the most famous action games ever produced, Pac-Man. *Guinness World Records* officially named Pac-Man as the most successful coin-operated game in history, with nearly 300,000 units of the arcade machine sold from 1980 to 1987. This is just one of many famous examples of great action games. Let's review some of the best. Maybe they will motivate you into creating the next chart-topping action game for the iPhone.

Reviewing Famous Examples

Even though action games come in all shapes and sizes, there are a few common features. Action games tend to involve some type of test of skill; for example, hand-eye coordination or reaction time. Players are usually given a time limit in which to complete a challenge. The challenge might be to save all the villagers before the bomb goes off or to survive the zombie horde long enough for the rescue helicopter to arrive. The developers face a challenge as well: how to make sure their action game is neither too hard, causing players to become frustrated and give up early, nor too easy, causing players to quit the game due to boredom. This is an important part of the formula for creating a great action game, and something to keep in mind as you consider the following successful action games:

- **Pac-Man.** `http://en.wikipedia.org/wiki/Pac-Man`
- **Space Invaders.** `http://en.wikipedia.org/wiki/Space_Invaders`

In This Chapter

- **Asteroids.** http://en.wikipedia.org/wiki/Asteroids_(video_game)
- **Paperboy.** http://en.wikipedia.org/wiki/Paperboy_(video_game)
- **Robotron: 2084.** http://en.wikipedia.org/wiki/Robotron:_2084
- **Doom.** http://en.wikipedia.org/wiki/Doom_(video_game)
- **Frogger.** http://en.wikipedia.org/wiki/Frogger
- **Super Mario Bros.** http://en.wikipedia.org/wiki/Super_Mario_Bros
- **Unreal Tournament.** http://en.wikipedia.org/wiki/Unreal_Tournament

You have probably played at least few of these games before. If not, consider finding some videos on the Internet of people playing a few of these games. You will learn a lot about what makes an action game both fun and exciting for players. If you have played these action games before, consider what made these games great for you. You will want to look back on these games' traits when you start coming up with your own ideas for action games.

Most of these games are considered classics, and one thing true of the classics is that they don't have a lot of clutter. Someone once said that a great song, no matter how fancy, should always be hummable. This is true for any great game as well. It is a lot easier to learn from and reproduce a great game by looking at classic games because they have so very little waste. Again, consider that less is often more when the "less" is of better quality.

TIP
Go back and play some of your favorite classic action games. Take a step back and consider them from a developer's point of view. Have a little fun and you'll probably learn a lot about applying tried-and-true techniques to your games.

Think back to our developer challenge of how to create games that are hard enough but not too hard for players. How have games accomplished this in the past? Many action games have an introductory level or phase that is much easier than the rest of the game; this allows players an opportunity to learn the basics of the game. Sometimes there are fewer enemies for the player to avoid or defeat. For example, the game Asteroids initially starts the player's spaceship in the center of the screen with only a few asteroids located at the very edge of the screen. Over time, more and more asteroids appear, making the player's task of surviving more and more challenging.

Another common approach used in action games is for the early levels to be at a much slower pace. Many of the games from our list take this approach, including Pac-Man, Space Invaders, and Frogger. Unreal Tournament has a feature called spawn protection, which is a period of invulnerability that a player has during only the first 2 to 4 seconds from when his character enters the game.

This gives the player a chance to look around and move around as needed before other players can attack. On the other hand, Doom simply provides the player a menu from which to choose a skill level. All of these approaches allow a wider range of players a chance to enjoy their favorite action games regardless of their current skill level.

Game balance—finding a balance between hard enough but not too hard—is one of the most important aspects of any action game. But it takes more than that to make a truly great action game. Think back to our list of famous action games. What other features do some of the games have in common?

Here are a few ways these games present challenges:

- **Creating time pressure.** When beating the challenge, the player has only a limited amount of time to complete the task.
- **Levels.** The player must complete a series of increasingly challenging levels.
- **Health and lives.** The player's character has either a limited amount of health or a limited number of lives.
- **Score.** It's common for action games to keep track of the player's score. Many of these games even have a high score feature. This presents another goal for players. Players not only want to win, but to be the best.

Action games can be more difficult to create than many other types of games. They tend to require more assets, such as graphics and sounds. They usually need more logic, and logic that is more complex than most puzzle games. Even though they can be more work, many times they are more rewarding to create.

A well-done action game, even a simple one, can become a world unto itself. Some of the most popular action games have gone on to become everything from cartoon shows to television shows to movies. The next time you are in a store with a toy department, look around and see how many toys you can find that are based on one of these types of games.

What have you learned from the examples we have covered to ensure that your game is successful?

Make sure your action game . . .

- Has good game balance—it's neither too easy nor too hard.
- Makes a good first impression and has an attractive overall appearance.
- Is free of any and all bugs and usability issues.
- Engages the gamer in an increasingly challenging series of stages or levels.
- Is addictive enough to keep the gamer coming back and telling his friends about the game.

TIP

Don't lose sight of how important quality is to the overall success of any game, especially action games. Remember, form and function first. If you can make every detail both look and work great, you have the most important ingredients for a successful application.

Understanding Game Design: Excitement and Achievement

One reason people play games is to escape from their everyday ordinary lives. It is a release, a way of letting go of day-to-day pressures. In games we are able to become and do almost anything we can imagine. If, as a child, you wanted to become a famous race car driver, as Apple's recent iPhone commercials say, "There's an app for that." Or maybe you wanted to win an Olympic medal in skiing? Guess what, there's an app for that as well.

If you're thinking that with the tens of thousands of applications already on the App Store, you have missed your chance to be a part of the mobile app revolution, you're wrong. Just as grocery stores do better when they have more products by having more competitors offering more varieties, so does the iPhone App Store.

Enjoying the benefits of competition

Another example is car dealerships. A lone car dealership in an area will actually tend to do worse than a car dealership in another area where there are many dealerships because people will go out of their way to find choice, variety, and options that go along with what the large group of car dealerships offer. Markets with more competition tend to have more opportunities.

You can even consider the iPhone App Store itself to see this effect. By having an App Store on the iPhone, Apple created a single place where there are a huge number of iPhone applications and a lot of competition to create iPhone applications. On many other phones, you either cannot install applications or you have to find each application yourself on the Internet.

When each application is located at something that is similar to the lone car dealership, you can see the difference competition makes. On many phones, fewer than one in ten people have ever added an application to their phone. On the iPhone, we suspect nine out of ten people have installed as many as ten or more applications.

Some of the most popular applications on the iPhone are the ones with the most competition. The more choices people have, the more likely they will find the product that has exactly what they want. When people find a product that is exactly what they want, they usually buy it. And this is exactly what *you* want.

You want competition for your applications for the same reason: It will make your products better, and better products sell better. Obviously, with more competition comes more risks—but also more rewards. Learn from your competition, because they will learn from you.

Creating sprites

When it comes to games, one of the key elements that contributes to excitement and enjoyment of the game is the game's graphics. Figuring out that people want great game graphics is easy, but creating them can be another story. Some people are great programmers and some people are great artists. Very few people are both. Not only that, but programmers tend to be especially challenged at creating quality graphics. Many times game graphics are referred to as game *sprites*. There's even a term for it: "programmer's art."

There is probably no worse insult an artist can receive than to have someone refer to a piece of his work as programmer's art. That said, programmer's art is great for temporary graphics, story-boarding, and prototyping. Unless you are both a programmer as well as an artist, creating great graphics will always be an area you will have to pay extra attention to.

What about the 99 percent of programmers who are not both great programmers and great artists? How do they create great game art? That's a good question. You can, of course, buy game graphics. Either you can pay a designer to create custom graphics for your application, or you can try to find a collection of game graphics already made that you can use. However, paying for custom graphics can be quite expensive. Many new iPhone developers would have a hard time affording this. But finding a collection of ready-to-use game graphics may not be possible.

So you may find yourself thrust upon the horns of a dilemma. You need great graphics. You cannot create them yourself, you cannot afford to have someone else create them for you, and you cannot find a cheap alternative to use instead. Sometimes you have to settle for the next best thing and hope that it is good enough. You are bound to run up against this wall or another just like it when first starting out.

The important thing to remember is that your application is not carved in stone. The second version of your application can be much better than the first version of your application, and so on. A great feature of the iPhone App Store is that iPhone applications can be automatically upgraded. It's important to always do your best to produce a quality piece of work, but perfection may have to wait for another day. Good software released today is always better than perfect software never released, and you never release bad software. Remember, sometimes it takes years to become an "overnight" success.

NOTE
Thomas Edison had to endure as many as 10,000 failures before he perfected a long-lasting light bulb. Hopefully, it will not take you as many tries to create your first successful iPhone application. Don't give up!

The online marketplace

One thing the Internet has done for us is to virtually collapse space and distance between people all around the world. So even though car dealerships have to be physically in the same area to compete with each other, people who create digital goods do not. The Internet has made us all a world of virtual neighbors.

In some ways this is what made the App Store possible, and over time we will see other digital marketplaces appear. We are already starting to see this shift occur. Instead of going to a brick-and-mortar store to buy music, we can buy music online through services like iTunes. While there are many online marketplaces that target the average consumer, there are some that iPhone developers should take note of.

Open Clip Art Library

The Open Clip Art Library (`http://openclipart.org/`) offers an archive of free clip art for any use. There are nearly 10,000 public domain clip art files available on this Web site. There are many ways you can look for the right piece of clip art; for example, you can browse the clip art by tag, by date, or by artist. You can, of course, search the clip art, and there is an advanced search option. There is even a "request a clip art" option that you can use to look for a specific piece of clip art. You can download an archive of many of the library's clip art as a large zip file.

Depending on your game's goals, you may be able to find many of the graphics you need on this single site. Some of the library's most popular categories are animals, cartoons, people, plants, and icons. Sometimes a little creativity will take you a long way. Instead of coming up with the perfect game idea and then trying to find the perfect clip art, consider finding some clip art you really like and then coming up with the perfect game in which to use it. This kind of brainstorming can really open up some new opportunities.

The clip art you see in Figures 5.1 and 5.2 is from an RPG Map collection, which includes over 50 drawings created by Nicu Buculei. We really like the look and feel of all the items in the collection. We also like the fact that you get both a colored version of the buildings and a non-colored blueprint version of the buildings. These would be perfect to create many different games.

Figure 5.1

Fantasy RPG buildings, blueprint style

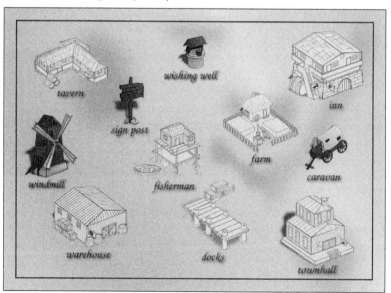

Figure 5.2

Fantasy RPG buildings, standard style

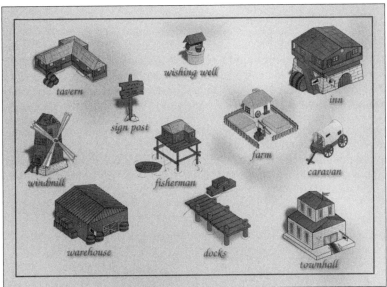

Puzzle game

The player sees a 4 x 6 grid of square cards, facedown. The cards are on a table with a nice wood-texture background. The backs of the cards have a medieval fantasy graphic, perhaps a crossed pair of swords or a knight's shield. The player chooses two cards and the selected cards rotate into view. On the front of each card there is a random image from the RPG Map collection that can be seen when selected. The player's goal is to match all of the pairs of cards in as little time as possible.

The game should have a high score feature based on best time. This could be loaded with a default score for new players. The game should take the best time and display it during play at the top of the screen as a countdown. This way the player can effectively race against the current best player, providing additional challenge and bragging rights. When a player makes a correct match, consider playing a reward sound such as a trumpet fanfare and having the matching cards fade away.

When the player makes an incorrect match, you could play the sound of a crowd jeering and heckling someone. (We discuss creating sounds later in this chapter.) Since there are two sets of RPG buildings, you could have the cards start with the blueprint style and then have the normal style come into full view. This would create a great animation that your players would enjoy. Check out Figure 5.3 to see a mock-up of the user interface.

Real-time strategy game

Real-time strategy games have become extremely popular, and it is reasonable to expect that this type of game would do very well on the App Store. Real-time strategy games are very complex and would likely prove challenging for a single developer to accomplish in a short period of time. But having a good library of appropriate graphics could go a long way toward making this possible.

Here's another idea for a creating one possible version of a real-time strategy game and how it might work on the iPhone. The player sees an open area in the center of the screen that is surrounded by a black fog all the way around the edge of the screen. This fog prevents a player from seeing any area that has not been explored. This matches real life, because until you explore an area you do not know what it contains. This area is just a small part of the entire area that the player can explore.

The game world could be much taller and wider than what the player sees. In the top-right corner of the screen there is a mini-map that shows the player the entire playing area. At the bottom of the screen there are command and production controls that the player can use to create new units and buildings. Take a look at Figure 5.4 to see a prototype of this user interface.

Figure 5.3

Fantasy memory mock-up

Figure 5.4

Fantasy real-time strategy mock-up

TIP

Always do a quick prototype of the application user interface, even if it's on the back of a napkin. This helps to weed out bad ideas early in the design process.

The player is in control of a new village of either humans or possibly elves. But the player is not alone in this world. The land is also occupied by tribes of terrible trolls, or possibly some ornery orcs. Either way, the only thing the other occupants of this land want more than to see the humans leave their land is to have them for dinner. The player's goal is to help his people first survive, and then to thrive in their new homeland. To do this he will need to take steps to defend the human's land, explore surrounding lands, and eventually attack enemies and remove their threat to his people once and for all.

The Lost Garden

The Lost Garden (`http://lostgarden.com`) is an amazing blog devoted to indie game developers. Not only does it have a wealth of great essays on game development, there's also a large number of free game graphics. The site belongs to Daniel Cook, who lists his occupation as Delighter. And we think you'll agree he is good at what he does. Here you can find a great set of game tiles for a 2-D RPG game. This set includes wilderness tiles, building interior tiles, and exterior village building tiles. There are also graphic sets from many games Daniel has worked on in the past, including Tyrian, Sinistar, and Hard Vacuum.

One last graphics set you might want to take note of is PlanetCute. PlanetCute was designed to be useful to the widest range of developers for the widest range of game genres. This graphics set is available as both vectors and bitmaps. Vectors can be resized freely but usually have to be converted before using in a game. Bitmaps can usually be used directly, but editing them can cause a loss of quality.

99 Designs

99 Designs (`http://99designs.com`) bills itself as "a thriving community of nearly 30,000 designers." While most of the listings on 99 Designs are for logos, business cards, and Web sites, that's not all they are designing these days. Many of the icons used by iPhone applications were originally created by a designer found at 99 Designs. And many of these applications even had their user interfaces designed at 99 Designs.

Not surprisingly, if you compare modern Web site design with the iPhone applications being created today, you will find the same kind of quality, variety, and attention to detail in both. Most Web sites are first designed in graphics software and then developers convert them to HTML. A developer can take a similar process to convert graphics to a user interface in Xcode.

99 Designs is not free, but the price is affordable to many. You post on 99 Designs what you need designed. As of this writing there is a fee of $39 to do this. Then you assign a prize to your design contest, generally ranging from $100 to $600 depending on what you're looking for. Designers from around the world then submit designs for you to consider.

Finally, you select the winning design and pay the designer, and your completed design is sent to you along with its copyright. If you need a simple one- or two-screen user interface that looks great, you might want to consider this option.

Creating sounds

Having great visuals for your applications is important, but don't underestimate how important audio is to a great end-user experience. Movie studios invest a huge amount of time, effort, and money into creating the perfect soundtrack for the latest blockbuster movie. You can hear the same attention to detail in many modern video games. After having compelling graphics, one of the best ways to pull the player into your game world is to have first-rate audio. The average developer isn't much better at creating music and sound effects than at creating graphics. Fortunately for us, there are other options:

- **SoundsXtras** (www.soundsxtras.com/). SoundsXtras provides absolutely royalty-free sounds. It's a very large sound library with over 22,000 audio files.
- **PodSafe Audio** (http://podsafeaudio.com/). This is an online community of independent artists who you could work with to use their music in your projects.
- **The Freesound Project** (www.freesound.org/). The Freesound Project is an online community for free and open exchange of sounds. Since all sounds are released under the Creative Commons Sampling Plus License, you are free to create applications using them. The Freesound Project has everything from audio snippets to samples to recordings.
- **Soundsnap** (www.soundsnap.com/). Another online community-driven sound library, Soundsnap maintains an audio library with 100,000 high-quality sound effects and loops. You can get a free account that allows up to five free downloads a month, or get a pro membership. The unlimited annual pro membership fee is currently $149.
- **AudioJungle** (http://audiojungle.net/). AudioJungle is another audio community that has thousands of stock music loops and audio effects. Each audio file has a small fee associated with it, but it's a great place to pick up something special. In many cases a sound effect is around $1, and a song is less than $10.

Programming: AmuckRacer

Gentlemen and ladies, start your engines! You are now ready to take what we have learned in this chapter and create your next exciting iPhone game: AmuckRacer. First, you will need to gather the right graphics for the game. Before you get started writing code, we will go over some design and analysis materials to make sure you are on the right track.

Defining your goals

In AmuckRacer the goal is to create a simple but exciting racing simulation. We are going to use sprites, or game graphics, for our images so the game will be in 2-D. Here are our goals for AmuckRacer:

- The player should be able to steer by tilting the iPhone to the left and right.
- The player should be able to brake by tilting the iPhone backward and accelerate by tilting the iPhone forward.
- The game needs to increase in difficulty as it's played.
- If the player drives off the road, the car should drastically lose speed.
- If the player collides with another car or an oil slick, the car should come to a stop.
- The player must make it to a checkpoint in order to continue playing to the next round.
- The game should include some viral aspect to help increase sales.

Examining your options

It is important to always review your goals and consider your options before you begin actually coding an application. As the saying goes, you want to measure twice and cut once. This way if you ever change your mind you will only have lost design time and not coding time. It is always easier to think of something than it is to code something.

Consider our first two goals: "The player should be able to steer by tilting the iPhone to the left and right" and "The player should be able to brake by tilting the iPhone backward and accelerate by tilting the iPhone forward." Both of these goals can be achieved by using the iPhone's accelerometer. You could take a simple digital reading of true or false for each of the four directions—up, down, left, right. Or you could take a more advanced analog reading with a range from, say, 0 to 1 for each of the four directions—up, down, left, right.

Using a digital reading would be more like playing a racing game on a desktop computer and using the keyboard to drive the car. Either you are pressing one of the left, right, up, or down arrow keys or you are not. Most players feel this is a little awkward and unrealistic. (We doubt anyone would want to drive a real car using only the left, right, up, and down keys to steer!) By using the iPhone's accelerometer, you create a natural range of motion more akin to a real steering wheel. Players can turn a little bit to the left or turn really hard to the left. Happy players make happy developers, so we will cover using the accelerometer for analog driving controls in the AmuckRacer example later in this chapter.

The next goal is "The game needs to increase in difficulty as it's played." This is usually a very easy goal to achieve. You could simply make the car go faster and faster over time. Or you could increase the frequency of road obstacles, such as other vehicles or oil slicks. Another option would be to have the course become more challenging over time. The more the road veers to the left and right, the harder it becomes to stay on the track.

Another goal is "If the player drives off the road, the car should drastically lose speed." You can check the car's position against the road's location, and if the car is off the road, lower the car's speed sufficiently. This will require using the collision detection methods we will cover later in this chapter.

Similarly we have the requirement of "If the player collides with another car or an oil slick, the car should come to a stop." When you check to see if the car is on the road, you can also check to see if the car sprite is touching any other obstacle like another car or an oil slick. If there is a collision, you can bring the car to a stop and require the player to try and make up the lost time.

Consider the goal of "The player must make it to a checkpoint in order to continue playing to the next round." How can we best accomplish this requirement? It would make sense that the player would have to make it to a checkpoint that is a certain distance away in a certain amount of time. Distance is just speed multiplied by time. You can track time very easily using the iPhone SDK's `NSTimer` object. You can track the player's speed with an application variable.

Then, using these two values, you can calculate the distance the player has covered at any given point in the game. Let's plan on having a display that shows the user how much time he has remaining and how much distance he has left to make it to the next checkpoint.

For the goal that "The game should include some viral aspect to help increase sales," let's plan on letting the player send his friends an e-mail anytime he breaks the game's high score. This way we get the word out about our game, and friends can race amongst themselves.

Coding the application

You know the basics of how the game will work, and what it will take to make it all happen. You have reviewed the goals and steps required to accomplish those goals. Now you are ready to start creating this application. Before we open Xcode, it's a good idea to create an application mock-up or storyboard to help visualize what the end application will look like. See Figure 5.5 for one possible idea.

This prototype is intentionally rough, but in a way it helps us simplify the problem and focus on what is really important. We have the latest model red rectangle car, a road, and a lot of area that is not road. That is the meat of the application, and you will probably agree that, at its core, things are pretty straightforward.

Creating the project

We will continue to use the Utility Application template for this application. We will use the Main View for the main game screen, and we will use the information screen for an About Us screen (see Figure 5.6).

Figure 5.5

AmuckRacer prototype

Figure 5.6

The About Us info screen

This About Us screen follows the pattern of previous info screens. Feel free to modify this screen to suit your purposes. We will use this info screen to do the following:

- Show some information and a description for the game.
- Show the player's current high score.
- Provide a button that allows players to brag to their friends about their high score.
- Tell people about this book and show them how to get it.
- Tell people about other games in this book.

Let's write some code. Launch Xcode and choose File ⇨ New Project. From the New Project dialog box, click Application under iPhone OS on the left and then click Utility Application (see Figure 5.7).

Figure 5.7

Creating a new utility application

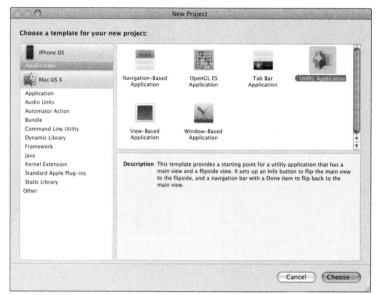

Click the Choose button to create a new utility application. You will want to save the new project to a location on your machine that you will remember. We recommend setting aside a special folder for all of your iPhone applications and giving it a straightforward name such as **Apps**, **Projects**, or **Code**. Once you have picked out your destination folder, save the new project with the name **AmuckRacer**.

You will now see the Xcode Project Explorer (Figure 5.8). On the left you will see a Groups & Files listing, to the right near the top you will see a file details listing, and to the left near the bottom you will see an editor window. You should first import any graphics that will be needed to create AmuckRacer.

In the Groups & Files listing, click the folder named Resources to expand it. Right-click on the Resources folder and choose Add ⇨ Existing Files. Now you will need to navigate your machine and find the AmuckRacer images that you downloaded earlier. Select each of these files and then click the Add button at the bottom right of the screen.

Figure 5.8

Xcode Project Explorer

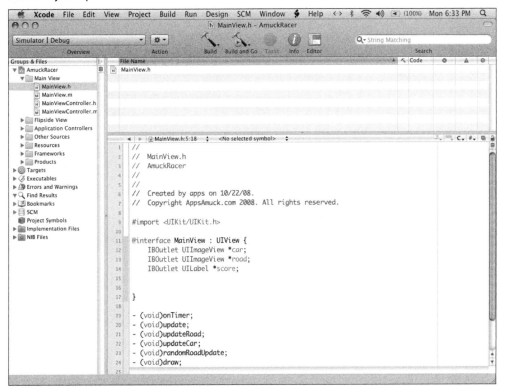

You should now see a small dialog box with options for how to add the selected files to your project (see Figure 5.9). Be sure to click in the top check box labeled Copy items into destination group's folder (if needed) to copy the images to your project's location instead of just making a link to the file. This way if you copy the folder containing the project you will have all the related resource files as well. Choose Default for the Reference Type and Unicode (UTF-8) for the Text Encoding. Below this you should see two options, with Recursively create groups for any added folders selected. Finally, under Add To Targets, you should see the AmuckRacer project listed and selected.

Now that you have the required image files imported into the AmuckRacer project, you can begin laying out the images on the screens. You should still have the Resources folder open in Xcode. Double-click on the `MainView.xib` file to open this file in Interface Builder. It is here that you will design the AmuckRacer's user interface.

Figure 5.9

Add existing files dialog box

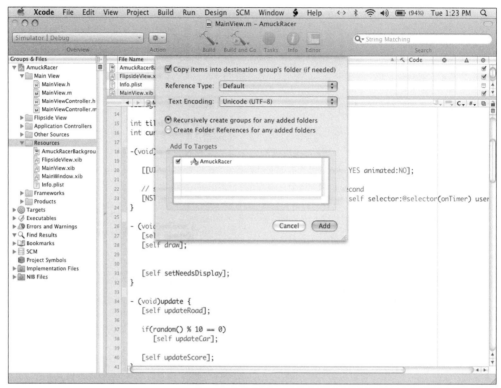

Start by choosing Tools ⇨ Library. Drag an Image View over to the Main View window. It should expand on its own to fill the entire window, as shown in Figure 5.10. This Image View will be the control that displays the game's default background. Drag another Image View over to the Main View window. This time, center the Image View in the bottom of window, as shown in Figure 5.11. As you move the Image View around, blue guidelines should become visible once you have the Image View near the bottom and in the center of the window. This Image View will become the player's car once you have assigned the correct images and written the right code for it.

To do this you need to assign the AmuckRacerBackground.png to your first Image View. Click on the original Image View to select it. From Xcode's Tools menu, choose Inspector. Be sure to select the left-most toolbar item named Image View Attributes. The AmuckRacerBackground.png is 320 pixels wide by 480 pixels tall, which matches the iPhone's screen size. Set the Image combo box to AmuckRacerBackground.png.

Figure 5.10

Adding the road's Image View to AmuckRacer

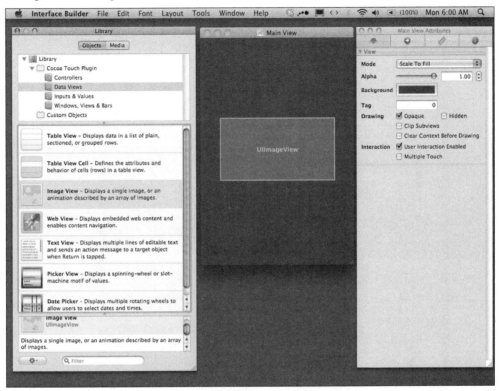

Next, you will assign the car.png to the second Image View. Click on the second smaller Image View that is located near the bottom of the screen in the center. From Xcode's Tools menu, choose Inspector. On the Image View Attributes toolbar tab, set the Image field to car.png. From the Inspector's Image View Size tab, resize the car's Image View to 48 pixels by 102 pixels. The W field is for width; set this to 48. The H field is for height; set this to 102. You'll probably have to reposition the car's Image View after making these changes. This time you can decide where to place the car; just be sure to have it on the road. If you run the code in Xcode now, you should see something like Figure 5.12.

Figure 5.11

Adding the car's Image View to AmuckRacer

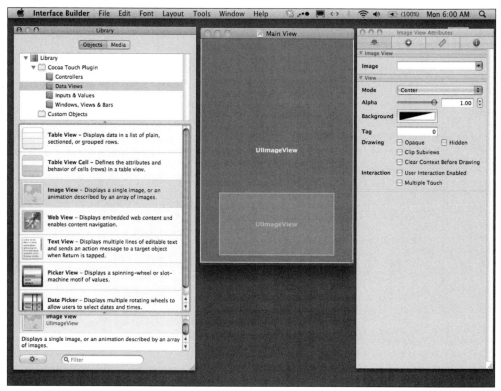

Wiring up the user interface

You will now use Interface Builder to wire up the user interface. Drag the road image over a little to the left so you can see the Main View's gray background. Click the Main View's background. Then choose Tools ⇨ Inspector. On the last tab, named Main View Identity, locate the Class Outlets area. Click the small button with a plus sign on it to add two new class outlets; name the first **car** and the other **road**. Double-click under Type and to the right of the car class outlet and set the Type to UIImageView. Do the same for the road.

Right-click on the car image and drag the small circle to the right of the New Referencing Outlet label and release it above the Main View's gray background. You should see a list with the car and road class outlets you created previously; be sure to choose the car option. Now do the same for the road image, and assign it to the road option.

Figure 5.12

The AmuckRacer car on the road

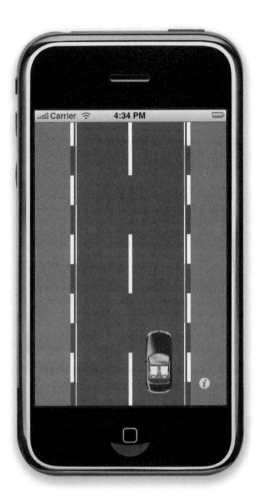

You can now take advantage of Interface Builder's Write Class Files feature. To do this, first move the road image back to where it fills the entire screen. Make sure the Main View window now has the focus by clicking the title bar at the top of the window. Go to the Interface Builder's File menu and choose Write Class Files. You should see a dialog box with the text of MainView set for the Save As field. Click the Save button to have Xcode save its changes to the generated class files. You should see a dialog box that states that `MainView.m` and `MainView.h` already exist. You are asked whether you want to replace these files. Click Merge to combine the newly generated code for the car and road Image Views with the preexisting code for the Main View form. Click Save to save your changes and then click Close to exit Interface Builder.

Removing the Status Bar

You probably noticed that the iPhone Status Bar is still at the top of the screen. While this will not hurt the functionality of the application, many players find this unrelated user interface distracting. For a game to be truly immersive, players must be able to suspend their disbelief. Some will find this difficult if they are being reminded of remaining battery life, current time, and signal strength changes. By removing the iPhone Status Bar you can give the player a full-screen experience without any nongame distractions.

TIP

Remember, it's the attention to details that separates a good game from a great game!

To remove the Status Bar from the top of the screen, you need to add one line of code:

```
-(void)awakeFromNib {

    [[UIApplication sharedApplication] setStatusBarHidden:YES animated:NO];
}
```

This line of code needs to be added to the `MainView.m` file, which is located in Xcode's Groups & Files. Choose AmuckRacer ⇨ Main View ⇨ MainView.m. Once you have found the `MainView.m` file, you will need to add the code from the previous `awakeFromNib` function to it. Once you have finished, your `MainView.h` file should match Listing 5.1.

CROSS-REFERENCE

To download all of the code listings in this chapter, go to `www.wileydevreference.com` and click the Downloads link.

Listing 5.1

AmuckRacer MainView Listing

```
#import "MainView.h"
@implementation MainView
-(void)awakeFromNib {

    [[UIApplication sharedApplication] setStatusBarHidden:YES
    animated:NO];

}
```

```
- (id)initWithFrame:(CGRect)frame {
    if (self = [super initWithFrame:frame]) {
        // Initialization code
    }
    return self;
}
(void)drawRect:(CGRect)rect {
    // Drawing code
}
- (void)dealloc {
    [super dealloc];
}
@end
```

The basics of collision detection

Action games and collision detection go hand-in-hand. It is the rare action game that does not need some form of collision detection, and AmuckRacer is no exception. *Collision detection* is how games are able to tell when one game sprite makes contact with another game sprite. Many famous action games, from Asteroids to Pac-Man, use this concept.

You will need to add collision detection to AmuckRacer for several important pieces of game functionality:

- If the player's car stops touching the road and begins touching the off-road area, the car will respond by decreasing speed.
- If the car collides with another vehicle or an oil slick area, the car will respond by coming to a complete stop.
- If the player makes it to a checkpoint finish line, the player's remaining time will be increased.

The Road Ahead

The road will be the player's primary focus, so it should be one of yours. Consider what the road needs to do:

- Make the player feel that the car is in motion, and give the player the ability to accelerate and decelerate, even allowing the car to come to a complete stop.
- Appear to move to the left and right over distance (very few roads are straight for too long).
- Have checkpoints located along its path and end with a finish line.

Modern programming guidance recommends being agile. While agile software development practices are the topic of whole books by themselves, one of the most important principles is to create software by making small changes in many iterative steps. So, instead of trying to add code to do all three of the preceding goals at once, you should consider and code each goal separately. The wisdom of this principle is evident every time you climb a set of stairs to reach the next floor, versus climbing the exterior wall to the next floor. You might have to walk a longer distance overall, but it's much easier than to take the more direct route straight up. This is true in software development as well. It might appear to be more effort to take many small steps, but in the end it will almost always be less work.

Our first goal is to create the appearance of motion in the road. This creates the illusion that the car is in motion. This is kind of like when you are riding in a car, the car appears motionless relative to you and everything else appears to be moving instead. There are several ways to create a moving road. Let's consider a few:

- 3-D generated world with a road bitmap applied as a texture to large scrolling surface
- 2-D overhead scrolling world with road tiles added from edges of screen
- Full-screen animation of road that is translated horizontally and vertically
- Long bands of road images fall vertically from top of screen and move horizontally

One advantage to a 3-D generated world is the extreme flexibility it would allow. You could zoom in and zoom out, and even rotate the camera all the way around the player. But creating a professional-quality, 3-D generated world is both difficult and challenging. Of all the options, this is the hardest, the riskiest, and the most expensive to do. For the beginning iPhone developer, this is probably not the best choice.

CAUTION

For every 25 percent increase in problem complexity, there is a 100 percent increase in complexity of the software solution. The ultimate success of many software projects often comes down to successfully minimizing complexity.

Another option is to create a 2-D overhead scrolling game board. Since the iPhone is 480 pixels by 320 pixels, the screen could be divided into a grid of 15 squares by 10 squares, with each square 32 pixels by 32 pixels. Each of these squares, more commonly known as *tiles*, would then be used to draw the game board.

Then we move the game board in response to the player's actions. As tiles move off the screen, we remove them and add new ones where needed to replace them. This is a common technique that has been used in countless games over the years.

This technique is much easier than creating a 3-D generated world, but it can still be challenging to pull off without the right graphics. One interesting advantage to the 2-D option is that multiple tile sets can be created and used interchangeably. You could have a snow level, desert level, and jungle level very easily. Once you have one level working, all you really need for a new level is the graphics. Even though this technique is easier, it's an option that is best left until you have a few iPhone applications under your belt.

The next technique is pretty clever and very easy to do. You have probably seen an animated GIF image on the Internet. Imagine that you have an image of a road and that it is almost twice as wide as the iPhone's screen, which is 320 pixels wide. You could then move this image left and right very easily and create the illusion of a moving road.

There are a few questions. Will it be fast enough? Will it be realistic enough? And will it be fun? If not, we will have to find another solution. Another way to think of this technique is to imagine you have a piece of paper with an image of an iPhone printed on it. Now imagine you cut out the iPhone screen from this piece of paper. If you had a somewhat larger image of a road printed on another piece of paper, you would be able to hold it under the iPhone picture and create a simple moving road effect. It's a simple but powerful idea.

The last technique is another brainy solution to our problem. This is an important skill that you should try to learn and apply whenever possible. Instead of working harder and longer, try to find ways to work smarter. Take the problem at hand and look for ways to make it simpler. Sometimes you may find a way that completely collapses the problem into a much smaller and manageable task.

In this case, we have effectively taken the 2-D option and simplified it from having 150 tiles that are 32 pixels by 32 pixels to having 15 bands that are 320 pixels by 32 pixels. Even if we had 480 bands that were 320 pixels by 1 pixel, the code complexity has collapsed. The idea will work, but we will need to test it to see if it is good enough for our players. Another way to think of this method is to imagine you have a piece of paper with an image of an iPhone printed on it. Now imagine you cut out the iPhone screen from this piece of paper. Next, consider if you had a somewhat larger image of a road printed on another piece of paper, and you took this road image and cut it into 15 strips of paper. Now if you took these bands of road and put them under the iPhone picture, you could move the bands left and right independently and create the illusion of a moving, winding road.

As an experiment, let's try making two versions of AmuckRacer, one that uses the full-screen animation and the other that uses the river of image bands, and see which we like better. Sometimes the best way to decide which way is the best is to try them both. Usually you will learn something along the way that will make you glad you went the extra mile.

Full-screen animation

The full-screen animation method can be broken down into two agile development iteration steps: First, have the image move to the left and right over time, and second, have the image animate its motion over time. We could do these steps in any order, but let's add horizontal motion before we add animation to the image since it's a simpler step.

The game loop

One of the most basic game patterns is the concept of the game loop. At its simplest, there is a loop that calls an update method and then a draw method until the game ends. Figure 5.13 shows a basic game loop. A more advanced game loop might do much more and look something like the following code:

```
while( playerHasntExit )
{
    checkForUserInput();
    runAI();
    moveEnemies();
    resolveCollisions();
    drawGraphics();
    playSounds();
}
```

Figure 5.13

A basic game loop

There are two ways you can create a game loop inside your application. The first is to use a looping command like the `while` keyword used in previous code selection. The other is to create a timer that calls your game methods repeatedly. For this example you will use the timer to create your game loop.

Update your `awakeFromNib` method so that it matches the following code:

```
-(void)awakeFromNib {

    [[UIApplication sharedApplication] setStatusBarHidden:YES animated:NO];
    // start a timer that will fire every second
    [NSTimer scheduledTimerWithTimeInterval:(1.0) target:self selector:@
    selector(onTimer) userInfo:nil repeats:YES];
}
```

Now add the following `onTimer` method right below the `awakeFromNib` method. We will update this method as we progress through the creation of AmuckRacer:

```
- (void)onTimer {
}
```

You'll notice when you are working with Xcode that it always creates a pair of files for you to write code in. The first is an h file, which is a header file; and the second is the m file, which is the main file. By default, Xcode expects you to implement your code as an interface. This means you will list your methods inside your header file as a contract, and then you will implement your methods fully in your main file. Let's update our header file to list our new functions so Xcode will be able to understand our class:

```
#import <UIKit/UIKit.h>
@interface MainView : UIView {
    IBOutlet UIImageView *car;
    IBOutlet UIImageView *road;
}
- (void)onTimer;
@end
```

You use `NSTimer` objects to create timers in Xcode. In this case we are using the `scheduled-TimerWithTimeInterval` to specify we want the timer to call the `onTimer` method every 1 second. This will give us an effective frame rate of about one frame per second. That's not very fast by today's gaming standards, but don't worry, we'll decrease our time interval as we move forward.

Note that you cannot simply change the time interval from 1.0 to 0.001 to get 1,000 frames per second unless the hardware is fast enough to allow it. If the hardware is not fast enough to perform 1,000 frames per second, it will either drop requests or potentially cause the system to become unresponsive and possibly unstable. Think about how elevators work. More people pressing the same call elevator button does not necessarily make the elevator come more quickly. The elevator has a hardware-limited maximum speed, and so does the iPhone.

Something else you should be aware of is that all devices are not created equal. The iPhone Simulator on your computer is likely to have access to more powerful hardware overall than an actual iPhone device. This is why it is important to performance test with an actual iPhone device. It's fine to do most of your development on the iPhone Simulator, just be sure to do periodic testing on a real device to ensure both performance and quality. Since the iPhone Simulator is not a true emulator, it is possible to have bugs on a real device that you do not see on the Simulator. Also, be aware that newer devices like the iPhone 3GS can be significantly faster than earlier devices.

CAUTION

While you can write software for the iPhone using only the Simulator, you risk releasing a product that will not run when installed on an actual device. Always test software on a real device before submitting it to the App Store.

You should now update your `onTimer` method to include calls to new update and draw methods that you will add next. Update your `MainView.m` file to match Listing 5.2.

Listing 5.2

Adding the onTimer Method to the MainView.h File

```objc
#import "MainView.h"
@implementation MainView
-(void)awakeFromNib {

    [[UIApplication sharedApplication] setStatusBarHidden:YES
    animated:NO];

    // start a timer that will fire every second
    [NSTimer scheduledTimerWithTimeInterval:(1.0) target:self selector:@
    selector(onTimer) userInfo:nil repeats:YES];
}
- (void)onTimer {
    update();
    draw();
}
- (void)update {


}
- (void)draw {


}
- (id)initWithFrame:(CGRect)frame {
    if (self = [super initWithFrame:frame]) {
        // Initialization code
    }
    return self;
}

- (void)drawRect:(CGRect)rect {
    // Drawing code
}

- (void)dealloc {
    [super dealloc];
}

@end
```

In the update method you will add an `updateRoad` method. While breaking each part out like this does make the code a little wordier, by keeping things separated we increase organization and decrease complexity, which is basically a win-win situation. Modify your `MainView.m` to include and call the `updateRoad` method. When you are done, your update method and `updateRoad` method should look like the following code listing:

```
- (void)update {
   updateRoad();
}
- (void)updateRoad {

}
```

You will also need to update your `MainView.h` header file so Xcode will be able to match your class interface. Make sure your header file matches the following code listing:

```
#import <UIKit/UIKit.h>
@interface MainView : UIView {
    IBOutlet UIImageView *car;
    IBOutlet UIImageView *road;
}
- (void)onTimer;
- (void)update;
- (void)updateRoad;
- (void)randomRoadUpdate;
- (void)draw;
@end
```

We now have the basic scaffolding in place for the application. The code you are going to add now will be the real muscles of the program. This code will move the road image to the left and to the right to create a more realistic winding road effect. There are a lot of ways this effect could work, but let's consider two:

- The road could move a random amount to the left or right.
- The road could move a random amount but always toward one direction until it reached the edge of the screen, then it could reverse direction and repeat the effect.

This first pattern could be the random road update pattern. The second pattern could go by the more exciting name of the sidewinder road update pattern. We will cover how to create both of these road update effects and then you can decide which to use in your version of AmuckRacer.

Consider the following method:

```
- (void)randomRoadUpdate {
   CGPoint oldPosition = road.center;
   road.center = CGPointMake(oldPosition.x, oldPosition.y + 10);
}
```

The first thing this code does is save the road's center position to a variable named oldPosi-tion. Then it creates a new center position that is 10 pixels further down from the old position. The first line inside the method creates a variable of type CGPoint named oldPosition. A CGPoint object is a structure that contains a point in a two-dimensional coordinate system. It has two fields: One is named x and holds the x-coordinate of the point, and the other is named y and holds the y-coordinate of the point.

Add this method to your version of your AmuckRacer's MainView.m file under the existing updateRoad method. Be sure to update your MainView.h file as well. You will also need to update your updateRoad method to call the new randomRoadUpdate function. You can do this by adding the following line of code to the updateRoad method:

```
[self randomRoadUpdate];
```

When you are done making all of these changes, your MainView.m file should match Listing 5.3.

Listing 5.3

Adding the randomRoadUpdate Method to the MainView.h File

```
#import "MainView.h"
@implementation MainView
-(void)awakeFromNib {
   [[UIApplication sharedApplication] setStatusBarHidden:YES
   animated:NO];
   // start a timer that will fire every second
   [NSTimer scheduledTimerWithTimeInterval:(1.0) target:self selector:@
   selector(onTimer) userInfo:nil repeats:YES];
}
- (void)onTimer {
   [self update];
}
- (void)update {
   [self updateRoad];
}
- (void)updateRoad {
   [self randomRoadUpdate];
}
- (void)randomRoadUpdate {
   CGPoint oldPosition = road.center;
   road.center = CGPointMake(oldPosition.x, oldPosition.y + 10);
}
- (void)draw {

}
- (id)initWithFrame:(CGRect)frame {
```

```
    if (self = [super initWithFrame:frame]) {
        // Initialization code
    }
    return self;
}

- (void)drawRect:(CGRect)rect {
    // Drawing code
}

- (void)dealloc {
    [super dealloc];
}

@end
```

Now save and run your changes by clicking the Build and Go button in Xcode. You should see the road image moving down the screen by 10 pixels every second—very nice! You are on your way to creating your first iPhone action game. Instead of moving the road down 10 pixels every second, try moving the road down a pixel every tenth of a second. To do this, you will need to first update the NSTimer code to fire 10 times a second by making the following change:

```
// start a timer that will fire every tenth of a second
[NSTimer scheduledTimerWithTimeInterval:(0.1) target:self
    selector:@selector(onTimer) userInfo:nil repeats:YES];
```

Next, update the randomRoadUpdate function to only move 1 pixel instead of 10 by making the following modification:

```
- (void)randomRoadUpdate {
    CGPoint oldPosition = road.center;
    road.center = CGPointMake(oldPosition.x, oldPosition.y + 1);
}
```

Save and run your update code. You should experience a much smoother animation now. Feel free to modify the code yourself and experiment with different settings to see what outcome they produce. There is more than one way to do just about anything. If you are always looking for a better way to do something, you will learn so much more and your programs will be all the better for it. Not to mention, it's fun to play the role of the mad scientist and see what happens!

Random numbers

Our original goal was to have the road move left and right by a random amount. To do this correctly, we will have to use the random() method. Here is the code to pick a random number from 0 to 9:

```
int randomNumber = random() % 10;
```

TIP
Random numbers are responsible for a lot of the magic in many games, especially action games. Look for ways you can use random values to create variety and surprises in your games for players.

The percent (%) sign is used to denote the modulus operator. This means divide the first number by the second number and return the remainder. It is a clever math trick to perform a useful operation. Here's an example. Pick any ten-digit number; let's say 3141592653. So, 10 can be divided into 3141592653, a total of 314159265 times with a remainder of 3. This is effectively how we are using the `random()` method to create random numbers. The `random()` method picks a huge random number and we scale this down to the range we need by using the modulus operator.

What if we needed a number from –5 to 5? How could we use the random function to achieve this? One way is to use the following line of code. Since –5 to 5 includes 11 numbers, we change the 10 to an 11. Then we subtract 5 from the result to make the range from 0 to 10 to the range of –5 to 5:

```
int distance = (random() % 11) - 5;
```

Modify the `randomRoadUpdate` method to take advantage of what you learned in the preceding section. Instead of moving the road vertically, change the code to move the road horizontally. When you have finished making your changes, your `randomRoadUpdate` method should look similar to the following code:

```
- (void)randomRoadUpdate {
    int distance = (random() % 11) - 5;
    CGPoint oldPosition = road.center;
    road.center = CGPointMake(oldPosition.x + distance, oldPosition.y);
}
```

Again, feel free to make any changes of your own to the code. It's a great way to learn more. You now have a road object that can move to the left and to the right. This means the player is going to have to pay attention or risk running off the road. There is one potential snag in the road's behavior that could be cause for concern. It is possible for the road to move in one direction more than the other, even to the point of moving off the screen. You want to limit this behavior. If a player has to keep his car on the road, the least you can do is keep the road on the screen. It's only fair.

You need to test the road position and check if moving it will move it outside of a certain allowed range. If so, you want to block this move. Start out by only allowing the road to move 20 percent of the screen's width to the left or to the right of the center of the iPhone's screen. Since the iPhone is 320 pixels wide, its center is at 160 pixels from the left. Ten percent of 320 is 32; therefore, 20 percent is 64, and 160 minus 64 is 96, and 160 plus 64 is 224. This gives you an allowed range of 96 to 224. If moving the road by a random distance is within the range of 96 to 224, you should allow it; if not, you should block it. You will have to use an if statement to perform this test.

Animating the road

We can now focus on how to best animate the road to create the illusion of traveling down the road in a car. There are many ways we could do this. Consider the following options:

- Scroll new road images down from the top of the screen as needed.
- Cut the road image up into horizontal pieces and when one falls off the bottom, move it back to the top of the screen.
- Take advantage of the iPhone SDK's ability to tile an image on the screen for you.

The first option is fairly easy, but it would mean you would have to keep track of multiple road objects. This introduces additional complexity that you should try to avoid. The next option goes back to the idea of cutting up the road into many pieces and working with them as a group. This option is related to the first option, except instead of using a second option it reuses itself—not an ideal solution, since it is actually a little harder than the first solution. The best solution is the third idea, which is to let the iPhone SDK figure it out for you.

Tiling an image

The iPhone SDK has a great method called `CGContextDrawTiledImage` that will tile an image for you. Its job is to repeatedly draw an image, scaled to the provided rectangle, to fill the current clip region. The `CGContextDrawTiledImage` method does all the heavy lifting, but it does expect a few parameters from you:

- **Context.** The graphics context in which to draw the image. Basically this is any object that knows how to display an image.
- **Rect.** A rectangle that specifies the tile size and offset. You can increase or decrease the image size.
- **Image.** The image to draw.

You already know the image you want to display. It is the road.png file. And you already know the size you want to display this image. You want it to match the iPhone screen size of 320 pixels wide by 480 pixels high. You want to use the Main View's background to show the road image so you know what the context is.

One thing you may not know is what the offset values are for. They allow you to start reading the image from a location other than the top-left corner. For example, by default Quartz draws an image to the screen by reading from the (0, 0) position in the image file (see Figure 5.14).

But if you tell Quartz to start at another location—say (160, 0)—Quartz will slide the image over 160 pixels to the left, and any pixels that got moved off of the screen to the left will be wrapped around the right of the screen. Consider what Quartz would do if you used an offset of (160, 240). Figure 5.15 shows an example of the output that would be produced.

One way to imagine this would be to take a piece of paper that is 320 mm wide and 480 mm tall and cut it in half at the 160 mm wide mark. Now take the left piece of the paper and move it to the right side of the other piece of paper. You could do a similar action for the top and bottom 240 mm parts of the paper. This would represent a vertical offset of 240 pixels.

The important thing to realize is this creates the effect you want to achieve. When any of the road falls off the bottom of the screen, you want it to reappear at the top of the screen. This way the road could go on forever if you needed it to. You will have to do a little work to get the `CGContextDrawTiledImage` function to work as needed.

You will need to add a class level variable named `currentImage` to keep an instance of the road image in memory to avoid reading from the device memory each time. Many developers think of programming as the art of caching data. If you can read an cached image ten times faster than reading it from a file, you can make that part of your application ten times faster simply by taking advantage of caching. Add a variable named `tileOffset` to keep up with the road's current vertical offset. Then you will need to assign the road.png image to the `currentImage` inside the `awakeFromNib` method. It's best if the road has its own timer that can be increased or decreased separately from the main game loop. When this loop fires you will need to increase the `tileOffset` by 1 pixel and refresh the screen. Last but certainly not least, you will need to update the road image in the Main View's `drawRect` method. All of these changes have been made in Listing 5.4, with the changes you need to make shown in bold.

Figure 5.14

Tiled image with offset of (0, 0)

Figure 5.15

Tiled image with offset of (160, 240)

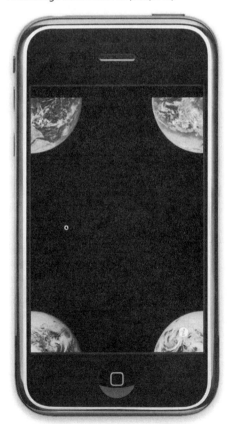

Listing 5.4

Adding a Timer and the CGContextDrawTiledImage Method

```objc
#import "MainView.h"
@implementation MainView
UIImage *currentImage;
int tileOffset = 0;
-(void)awakeFromNib {
    [[UIApplication sharedApplication] setStatusBarHidden:YES animated:NO];
    [car setAlpha:0];
    [road setAlpha:0];
    currentImage = [UIImage imageNamed:@"road.png"];
    // start a timer that will fire every second
    [NSTimer scheduledTimerWithTimeInterval:(1.0) target:self selector:@
    selector(onTimer) userInfo:nil repeats:YES];
    // start a timer that will fire every hundredth of a second
    [NSTimer scheduledTimerWithTimeInterval:(0.01) target:self selector:@
    selector(onTimerRoad) userInfo:nil repeats:YES];
}
- (void)onTimerRoad
{
    tileIndex += 1;
    [self setNeedsDisplay];
}
- (void)onTimer {
    [self update];
}
- (void)update {
    [self updateRoad];
}
- (void)updateRoad {
    [self  randomRoadUpdate];
}
- (void)randomRoadUpdate {
    int distance = (random() % 11) - 5;
    CGPoint oldPosition = road.center;
    if(oldPosition.x + distance < 96 || oldPosition.x + distance > 224)
        return;
    road.center = CGPointMake(oldPosition.x + distance, oldPosition.y);
}
- (void)draw {

}
- (id)initWithFrame:(CGRect)frame {
    if (self = [super initWithFrame:frame]) {
        // Initialization code
    }
    return self;
}
- (void)drawRect:(CGRect)rect {
```

continued

Listing 5.4 *(continued)*

```
CGImageRef image = CGImageRetain(currentImage.CGImage);
CGRect imageRect;
imageRect.origin = CGPointMake(160, 240);
imageRect.size = CGSizeMake(320.0, 480.0);
CGContextRef uiContext = UIGraphicsGetCurrentContext();
CGContextClipToRect(uiContext, CGRectMake(0.0, 0.0, rect.size.width, rect.
size.height));
CGContextDrawTiledImage(uiContext, imageRect, image);
}

- (void)dealloc {
  [super dealloc];
}

@end
```

Putting the player in charge

Now that the road is functioning properly, you want to make the player's race car zoom down the highway as expected. Your first objective is to allow the player to move the car to the left or right using the iPhone's built-in accelerometer. The iPhone SDK makes this very easy. Let's review the code that you will need to add to make this happen.

You will need to create a share instance of the `UIAccelerometer` and set its update interval to every second. At the top of the form you will need to define a constant that stores the accelerometer's refresh rate. Then you will need to point the `UIAccelerometer`'s delegate at the Main View by setting the delegate using the keyword `self`:

```
// Constant for the number of times per second (Hertz) to sample acceleration.
#define kAccelerometerFrequency 40
// Configure and start the accelerometer
[[UIAccelerometer sharedAccelerometer] setUpdateInterval:(1.0 /
   kAccelerometerFrequency)];
[[UIAccelerometer sharedAccelerometer] setDelegate:self];
```

This will inform the iPhone OS that your application would like to be notified of accelerometer changes every second. The following method is the delegate that the iPhone accelerometer will call when the device accelerates:

```
// UIAccelerometerDelegate method, called when the device accelerates.
- (void)accelerometer:(UIAccelerometer *)accelerometer
  didAccelerate:(UIAcceleration *)acceleration {
  [self updateCar:-acceleration.x* 30];
}
```

The delegate will call our worker function, and this function will update the screen as needed to match the player's input:

```
- (void)updateCar:(CGFloat)positionInDegrees {
    int distance = positionInDegrees;
    CGPoint oldPosition = car.center;
    car.center = CGPointMake(oldPosition.x + distance, oldPosition.y - 1);
}
```

Remember to always update your header file to match any changes you make in your main files. Here's the correct header file for the changes we have made so far:

```
#import <UIKit/UIKit.h>
@interface MainViewController : UIViewController <UIAccelerometerDelegate> {
}
- (void)updateCar:(CGFloat)positionInDegrees;
@end
```

Updating the player's score

You want to reward the player's success by adding points to his score. If the player does well, he gets a bonus; if the player makes a mistake, consider imposing a penalty such as taking away points.

TIP

Some people may hate statistics, but players love knowing theirs. Consider tracking your player's accomplishments during a game; for example, by total number of zombies slain or total amount of treasure found. Many players will replay a game to fully "complete" a level or game.

Let's start by creating a very simple scoring system and then allowing you to customize it as you see fit from there. Open the `MainView.xib` file in Interface Builder. Start in the Groups & Files listing in Xcode. Find the AmuckRacer folder and then locate the Resources folder; inside it you should find the `MainView.xib` file. Double-click it to have Interface Builder open it. Open the Library that is found inside the Interface Builder's Tools menu. Make sure you have the Options tab selected instead of the Media tab. Expand the Library folder, then the Cocoa Touch Plugin folder, and finally choose the Inputs & Values folder. Drag a Label control onto the Main View window. Set the label's text to Score: 0. Move the label to the location of your liking (consider placing it at the top in the middle of the screen).

We need to create mappings from Interface Builder's user interface to Xcode classes so that the two can talk with each other. From the Interface Builder's Tools menu, choose Inspector. Make sure that the Inspector window is focused on the Main View by click the Main View's window title. Once you have the Main View selected, you will see Main View appear in the title bar of the Inspector window.

Go to the fourth tab in the Inspector window, named Main View Identity. You should see the two class outlets you created earlier named **car** and **road**. Add another one called **score** by clicking the button that has a plus sign on it. Be sure to set its Type to UILabel. Your screen should now look like the one shown in Figure 5.16.

As before, you will now use Interface Builder's Write Class Files feature to update your Main View's class files with the new control. Make sure you have the Main View window selected before running the Write Class Files command. You should see a screen like Figure 5.17.

Figure 5.16

Adding a score counter to AmuckRacer

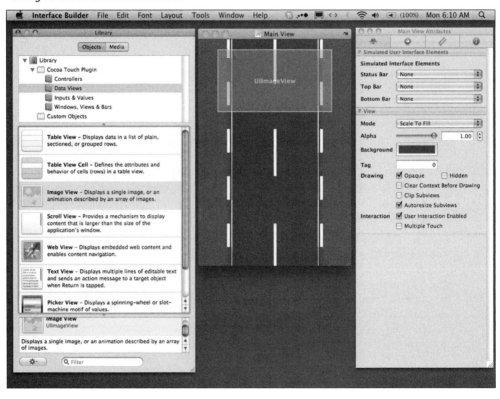

Figure 5.17

The Save dialog box of the Write Class Files feature

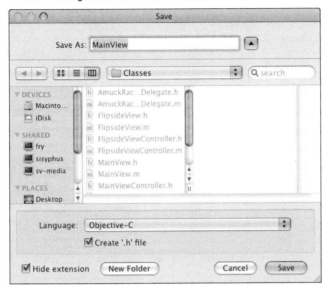

You can find this menu item under Interface Builder's File menu. Next, you will see a merge or replace prompt, as shown in Figure 5.18. Be certain you choose the Merge option; if you choose the Replace option, Interface Builder will replace your edited files with empty new ones. This is a painful lesson to learn!

You have now created the user interface for the player's score. You need to add the code that will update the UI. To do this, you will need a new variable named **score** that will keep up with the player's score for the duration of the game. By default we will add to the player's score upon updating of the game loop. Here are the code changes needed to update the player's score.

First, you will need to initialize the score variable:

```
int score = 0;
```

You will also need to modify the update method as follows:

```
- (void)update {
    [self updateRoad];
    score += 1;
}
```

Figure 5.18

Merge or Replace prompt

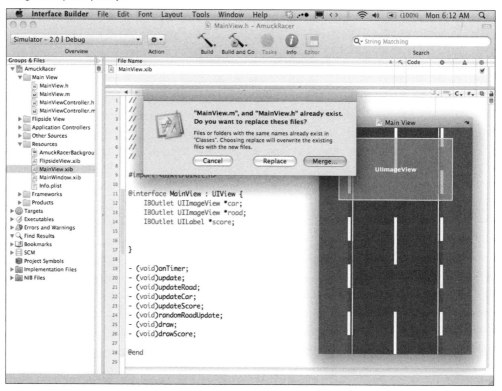

And finally, you should update the draw method to set the label's text to the player's score:

```
- (void)draw {
    score.text = [NSString stringWithFormat: @"Score: d%", currentScore];
}
```

Now when you run AmuckRacer, you should see the player's score at the top of the screen, as shown in Figure 5.19.

Staying alive

It's always important in an action game to decide how the player wins and loses. In this game you will have the player lose if the car ever reaches the bottom of the screen, using a simple form of collision detection. You will make this possible by causing the player's car to slow down if it drives off the road. You can always find the road's position and the player's car position. Using this and what you know about the road, you can calculate whether the player is on the road.

Figure 5.19

AmuckRacer high score

Here is an overview of the math. You know the iPhone screen is 320 pixels wide, and the road is the same size. You know or you can check that the car image width is 42 pixels wide. Even though the road.png image is 320 pixels wide, the road in the image is really only 200 pixels wide. But that is not all you need to determine whether the player is keeping the car on the road. You will need to perform two checks: one to see if the car has driven off the left-hand side of the road, and the other to see if the car has driven off the right-hand side of the road.

To check if the car has driven off the left-hand side of the road, use the road image's center to find the center of the actual road, and subtract 100 to find the road's left-most edge. Compare this to the car's left-most edge to determine if the car remains on the actual road. To calculate the car's left-most edge, you use the car's center and subtract 24. You use the numbers 100 and 21 because these values are half of the widths of the road and car images, respectively. And the center of an image is at the halfway point from the left-most and right-most edges.

Now that you understand the concept, here is the code to make it happen:

```
- (void)updateCar {
    CGPoint roadPosition = road.center;
    int roadLeftPosition = roadPosition.x - 100;
    int roadRightPosition = roadPosition.x + 100;
    CGPoint carPosition = car.center;
    int carLeftPosition = carPosition.x - 21;
    int carRightPosition = carPosition.x + 21;
    if(carLeftPosition < roadLeftPosition)
        car.center = CGPointMake(carPosition.x, carPosition.y + 1);
    if(carRightPosition > roadRightPosition)
        car.center = CGPointMake(carPosition.x, carPosition.y + 1);
    if(carLeftPosition > roadLeftPosition && carRightPosition <
    roadRightPosition)
        car.center = CGPointMake(carPosition.x, carPosition.y - 1);
}
```

Make sure you add this call to your main update method:

```
- (void)update {
    [self updateRoad];
    [self updateCar];
}
```

Don't forget to update your `MainView.h` header file with the new method name:

```
#import <UIKit/UIKit.h>
@interface MainView : UIView {
    IBOutlet UIImageView *car;
    IBOutlet UIImageView *road;
    IBOutlet UILabel *score;
}
- (void)onTimer;
- (void)update;
- (void)updateRoad;
- (void)updateCar;
- (void)randomRoadUpdate;
- (void)draw;
- (void)drawScore;
@end
```

What's Next?

You have been exposed to a lot of ideas and material in this chapter. You are probably already thinking of a few ideas of your own. Everything we have covered in this chapter is great material to take and build upon to create even bigger and better ideas. Here are a few for your consideration:

- Convert the road into water and the car into a boat. Only the center of the water is deep enough for the boat to go fast.
- Convert the road into outer space and the car into a spaceship. The edge of the screen is filled with asteroids that cause the spaceship to slow down.
- Convert the road into snow and the car into a skier. Only the center of the snow is free from trees to allow the skier to ski his fastest.
- Add oil slick images to the game and if the car hits an oil slick, it ignores player input for 2 seconds.
- Add additional cars to the game that force the player to drive around them to avoid collisions.
- Have random nitro canister power-ups that the player can acquire to gain a temporary speed boost.
- Create a variable to track how far the player can maintain on-road status. If the player does very well, give a score bonus and an extra speed boost.

Feel free to use these ideas along with any you may have to "power up" a racing game of your own design. We can't wait to see what you come up with!

Analyzing Business Aspects

You have learned a lot about developing action games for the iPhone in this chapter. But there is more to making a successful action game than writing lines of code and designing game sprites. You also need to master the business aspects of making iPhone action games.

While action games can be more costly and difficult to produce than some other types of applications, such as puzzle applications, they can have a greater return on investment. Because a well-made action game can become a world in itself, action games have the ability to generate a lot of attention and excitement. Once you have finished the game engine that your action game will use, you can reuse it either for a follow-up game or for an entirely new action game. If you plan on this early, many times you can design features and functionality that make this reuse even easier.

TIP

Hollywood makes it a point to reuse sets and props. You should consider doing the same with your game's graphic and audio assets, and with any game engines you create. This helps to increase your return on investment and will help your business grow faster.

The action game market is a little less crowded than some of the other game genres. One reason for this is it takes more time, effort, and skills to create a complete action game than it does to create, say, a novelty or puzzle game. Even so, the best action games find a way to stand out in the crowd. The same way players compete to be the best players with the best scores, action games compete with each other to be the best games with the best players. If this sounds like fun to you, consider making an action game for your next iPhone application.

Even though there are fewer action games than some other kinds of applications, there are still tens of thousands of applications on the App Store. That's a lot of apps, and plenty of competition in all categories. You will want to focus on coming up with ideas that help your application rise above the rest.

You will also want to spread the word about your application. Successfully marketing a new iPhone application is almost its own game. To be really good at it, it takes a lot of practice, hard work, and a little luck. It's a little like running for office—nobody is going to vote for you if they don't know who you are, so get the word out there and promote your game. Tell your friends, write a blog post, and contact every iPhone application review site you can find and let them know what they are missing. The better your application is, the easier it will be to spread the word. Have you considered creating a YouTube video for your action game? Action games look great in video, and many people are hesitant to buy an action game without seeing some live video from an actual game.

Don't underestimate the power of social networking sites like Facebook, Twitter, and Digg. These sites have been able to springboard many an app into top-ten status. Facebook is a great place for fans of your application to meet and discuss ideas. Make sure you have some way for users of your application to give you feedback about what they liked and didn't like. This feedback can result in a version 2.0 of your application that is many times better than the 1.0 version.

Summary

At the beginning of this chapter you learned from famous examples of action games. Then you looked at how action games create challenges and excitement by using limited time, levels, health, and score. You also reviewed what makes an action game successful, including game balance, attractiveness, being free of bugs, being challenging, and addictive game play. You learned how competition isn't all bad. Next, you learned various techniques for creating game graphics, from home-brewed programmer's art to third-party, royalty-free clip art to professionally created, custom designs. From there you were introduced to various methods programmers use to produce great audio for their applications.

After this you began work on creating an action game from the ground up. You learned how it is important to define your goals before you do anything else. Then you examined your options for how to best achieve your set goals. Only then did you begin to actually write any code. You used the tools of the trade for creating iPhone applications, including Xcode, Interface Builder, and its Library and Inspector tools. You saw the value of using programmer's art to generate a quick prototype for applications.

Then you rolled up your sleeves and got into some of the more technically challenging aspects of writing iPhone applications. You saw the value of using info screens for an application. You learned how to remove the iPhone Status Bar. You learned some of the basics of collision detection and collision calculations. You used the concept of a game loop to update and draw both the player's character and the player's game world. After reviewing the details of creating random numbers, you created realistic game motion with only minimum effort. You implemented a very clever method of scrolling the road using image tiling. You reviewed the business of iPhone software development, including marketing and return on investment. And to wrap it all up, you tracked the player's score so he would have something to brag about to his friends. We hope you are beginning to see the power and possibilities of iPhone programming. Don't stop now; we are just getting warmed up!

Building Community with Facebook

It's not enough to have the best graphics, the best sounds, and the best game play. Today's gamers expect the total package. They want it all. They expect high scores, badges, and achievement systems. They want to be able to compete against their friends and share their game experiences wherever they are. Building community is becoming an important part of making a successful top-notch iPhone game.

Today people are more connected than ever. While you can still use the iPhone to keep in touch with friends through phone calls, there are many new and exciting ways to stay in touch. The iPhone allows developers to take advantage of these technologies. With everything from e-mail to text messaging and instant messaging, it is almost like you are carrying your friends with you wherever you go.

How could you be any closer? What about if you could pull all of your friends in from Facebook and interact with them in apps on your iPhone? With Facebook Connect, you can do just that. In this chapter we'll show you how.

Getting to Know Facebook

Facebook (www.facebook.com) is a social utility that connects people with friends and others who work, study, and live around them. In other words, Facebook helps you connect and share with the people in your life. Considering Facebook has over 200 million active users, or users who have returned to the site in the last 30 days, it is very likely you are already familiar with Facebook. If you are not already a member of Facebook, now is the time to join. The more you learn about Facebook today, the more you will be able to use it tomorrow—and Facebook is not going anywhere anytime soon.

We have even created a Facebook fan page ourselves for this book (Figure 6.1).

Figure 6.1

iPhone Game Programming Facebook fan page

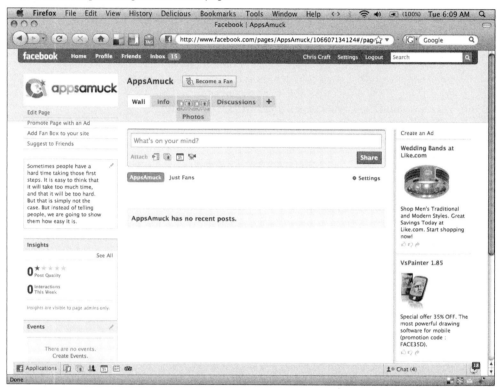

Facebook is made up of pages, and some of the most popular pages for users on Facebook are their Profile, Friends, Networks, and Inbox pages. While a Facebook page can contain user stories, it can also contain Facebook applications. Some of the most popular built-in Facebook applications are Photos, Notes, Groups, Events, and Posted Items.

NOTE

Facebook is one of the most popular Web sites on the Internet today; it is currently the fourth-most popular Web site in the world. It is also one of the most popular development platforms on the Web. According to Facebook, there are more than 52,000 applications currently available in the Facebook Application Directory, and there are more than 660,000 registered developers and entrepreneurs from more than 180 countries using the Facebook platform today.

Connecting to Facebook Accounts

Today you can easily find your Facebook friends on any Facebook Connect–enabled iPhone application. You just log in using your Facebook member account on your iPhone. That iPhone application can then access the same information as on the Facebook site, controlled by your privacy settings. You can even publish stories back to your profile, allowing you to share experiences you have from any Facebook Connect–enabled iPhone application.

Figures 6.2, 6.3, and 6.4 show a few of these applications.

Figure 6.2

Facebook Connect–enabled application: Agency Wars

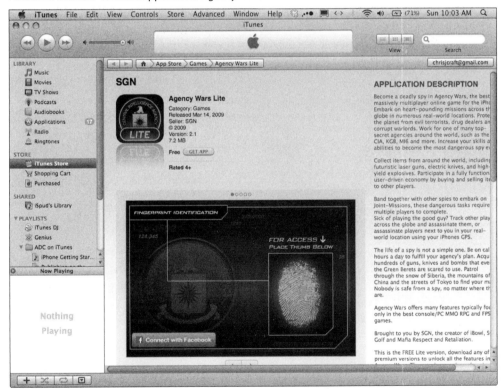

Figure 6.3

Facebook Connect–enabled application: Tap Tap Revenge

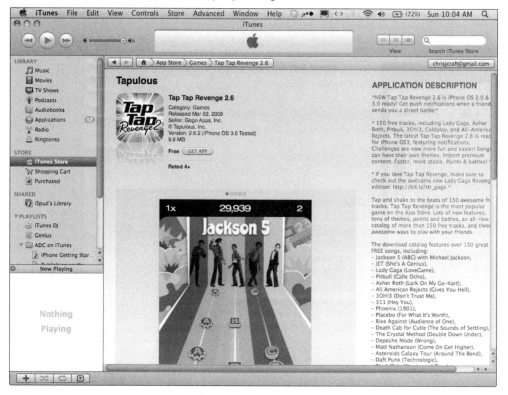

Download the Facebook Connect for iPhone SDK

The first thing you need to do in order to create iPhone applications that can integrate with Facebook is to download the Facebook Connect for iPhone SDK. You should be able to find the zip file you need at the following address:

```
http://svn.facebook.com/svnroot/platform/clients/packages/
    fbconnect-iphone.zip
```

Figure 6.4

Facebook Connect–enabled application: Live Poker

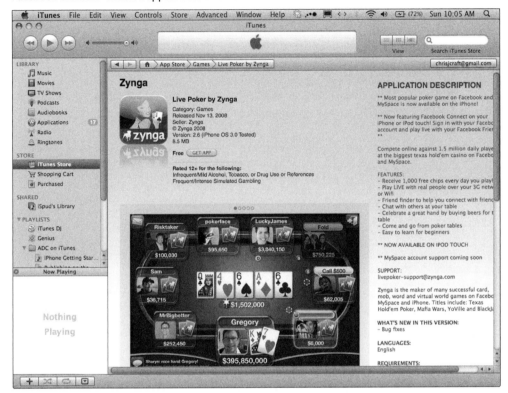

Inside the zip file you will find a samples folder and a source code folder named src (Figure 6.5). First you will explore the Facebook Connect sample project, and then you will go through the steps of creating an iPhone application from scratch to integrate with Facebook Connect.

Figure 6.5

Facebook Connect for iPhone SDK package

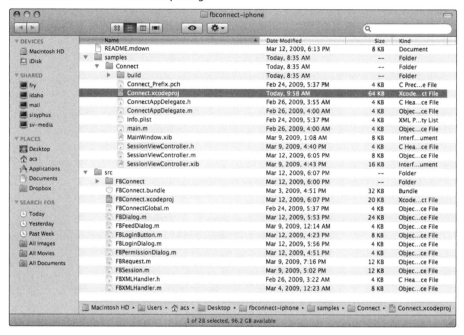

The Facebook Connect sample project

You must open the sample project in Xcode in order to run it. Find the fbconnect-iphone.zip file that you downloaded earlier. Extract the files from the zip file into a folder of your choosing. Open this folder, then open the samples folder, and finally go into the Connect folder. You should now see a file named Connect.xcodeproj. In Figure 6.5, the Connect.xcodeproj file has been selected. Double-click this file to automatically open the project in Xcode.

Now that you have the sample project loaded into Xcode, your screen should look something like Figure 6.6. You can run the sample application by clicking on Build and Go in Xcode. The application should compile and start fine, but you will not be able to connect to Facebook successfully because by default the sample project does not have a correct Facebook API key or application secret. Facebook uses your API key to identify your application. You will need to pass it into any API call you make. The application secret is used by Facebook to authenticate any API calls you make. Effectively these are your applications' user names and passwords, just with fancier names.

Figure 6.6

Facebook Connect sample project loaded into Xcode

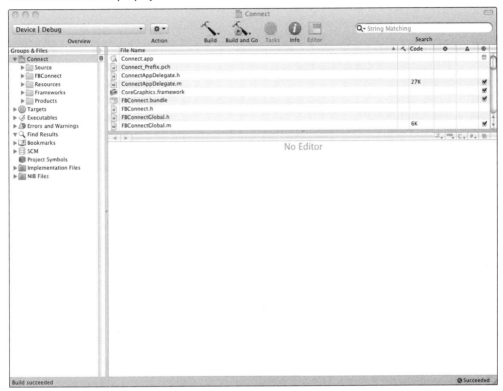

Registering as a Facebook developer

You must do several things before you can get a Facebook API key of your own. First, if you have not already done so, you need to join Facebook and become a member. Just go to www. facebook.com and sign up. It only takes a few minutes to join.

Once you are a member of Facebook, you need to register as a developer on Facebook. Again, this is a very simple process: Go to the Facebook Developers page at http://developer. facebook.com and click the Start Now button. Be sure to take a few minutes and explore the wealth of information Facebook has to offer developers.

On the Facebook Developers page you can find online documentation, forums, events, information on getting started, and more. It's a good idea to bookmark this site and refer to it frequently as you become more and more familiar creating Facebook-enabled iPhone applications.

After you click the Start Now button on the Facebook Developers page, you are redirected to a special "getting started" page where you are asked to install the Facebook Developer App. Click the Allow button to install the Developer App (Figure 6.7).

Figure 6.7

Facebook Developer App prompt

By now you should be a member of Facebook and a registered Facebook developer, and you should have the Facebook Developer App installed on your Facebook account. In order for a Facebook-enabled iPhone application to function correctly, it must have a Facebook application available to connect to on Facebook itself.

Creating a Facebook application

You can get a basic Facebook application up and running in a matter of minutes. In the bottom-left corner of Facebook you should see an Applications button. If you click this and choose the Facebook Developer application, which you added to your profile earlier, you should see a Set Up New Application button in the upper-right corner. Click this button to make your new Facebook application. You are then taken to the Create Application page, where you need to assign your new Facebook application a name, as shown in Figure 6.8. You can use the name **iPhone Test App** or another name of your own choosing. You will have to agree to the Facebook Terms of Service. Once you have entered all of the necessary information, click the Save Changes button to proceed.

You have just created a new Facebook application and are now on the Edit iPhone Test App page (Figure 6.9). Here you can edit and configure your iPhone Test App as needed. At first you might be a little overwhelmed by all the options being presented to you, but there is nothing to be concerned about. You can keep the default settings for most options for this sample project. After you become more familiar with the Facebook API, you can come back and take advantage of some of the more advanced options available here.

Figure 6.8

Create Application page

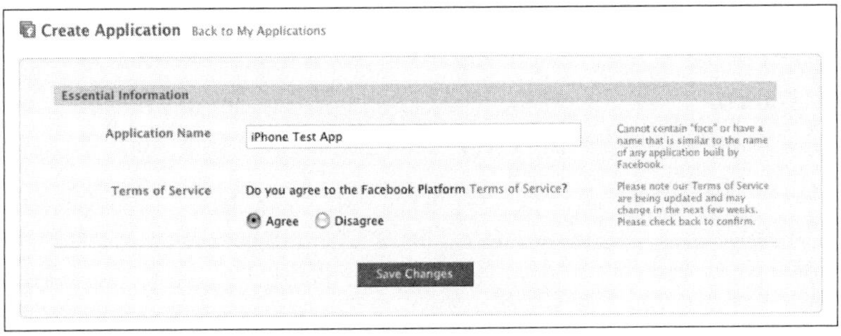

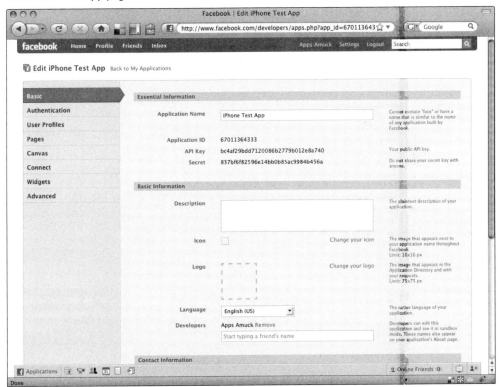

Figure 6.9

Edit iPhone Test App page

Although it is safe to leave most of the iPhone Test App's options on their default settings, it's a good idea to familiarize yourself with what the most important ones are. At the very least, you will want to be aware of the following settings:

- **Application Name.** This is where you assign the name for your Facebook application.
- **Application ID.** This is the unique ID that Facebook assigns to your application.
- **API Key.** This is your public API key. You need to set this in your iPhone application.
- **Secret.** You also need to set your application secret in your iPhone application.
- **Description.** This is the public description for your application.
- **Icon.** This is the 16 x 16 icon that is displayed on Facebook next to your application's name.
- **Logo.** This is the 75 x 75 image that is shown in the Facebook Application Directory.
- **Language.** This is the language that text in your application is in.
- **Developers.** This is a list of Facebook members who have developer access to this application.

Take some time and explore all the additional developer options available to you. These are located in the tabs on the left-hand side of the iPhone Test App page: Basic, Authentication, Profiles, Canvas, Connect, Widgets, and Advanced. One setting of special note is the Sandbox Mode, which can be enabled or disabled from the Advanced Settings section under the Advanced tab. When an application is in Sandbox Mode (Figure 6.10), it is visible only to developers.

Once you have finished updating your Facebook application's settings, click the Save Changes button on the bottom of the screen.

TIP

Facebook allows you to set up accounts to use for testing purposes. You can learn more about Facebook test accounts at `http://wiki.developers.facebook.com/index.php?title=Test_Accounts`.

Figure 6.10

The Sandbox Mode option is located on the Advanced tab.

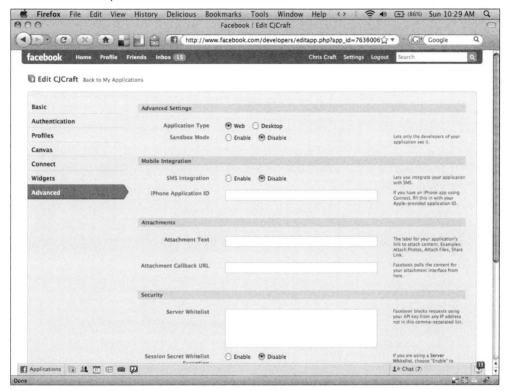

Setting the Facebook API key and application secret

You are now ready to return to the Facebook Connect sample project in Xcode and update the project to use your Facebook API key and application secret. On icon folder to expand it, and then click on the Source folder. Choose the `SessionViewController.m` file, as shown in Figure 6.11.

Figure 6.11

Update Facebook API key and secret

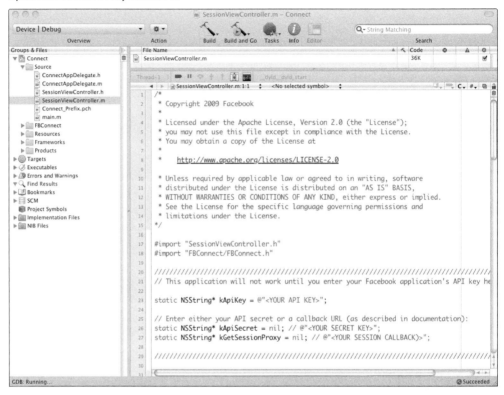

You should see a section of code that matches the following listing:

```
#import "SessionViewController.h"
#import "FBConnect/FBConnect.h"
/////////////////////////////////////////////////////////////
    ///////////////
// This application will not work until you enter your Facebook
    application's API key here:
static NSString* kApiKey = @"<YOUR API KEY>";
```

```
// Enter either your API secret or a callback URL (as described
    in documentation):
static NSString* kApiSecret = nil; // @"<YOUR SECRET KEY>";
static NSString* kGetSessionProxy = nil; // @"<YOUR SESSION
    CALLBACK)>";
//////////////////////////////////////////////////////////////////
    ///////////////////////////////
}
```

You will need to replace the <YOUR API KEY> text with your actual API key, and you will need to update <YOUR SECRET KEY> with your actual secret key. You can find both your API key and your secret key on your iPhone Test App's settings page.

Notice how Facebook allows you to provide either your API secret or a callback URL. Since you want to use your secret key, be sure to uncomment the section of code that assigns your secret key to the kApiSecret variable by removing the two leading forward slashes from that line. When you are done, your code should look similar to the following code listing. The only real difference should be your API key and secret:

```
#import "SessionViewController.h"
#import "FBConnect/FBConnect.h"
//////////////////////////////////////////////////////////////////
    ////////////////
// This application will not work until you enter your Facebook
    application's API key here:
static NSString* kApiKey = @"0123456789abcdefghijklmnopqrstuv";
// Enter either your API secret or a callback URL (as described
    in documentation):
static NSString* kApiSecret =
    @"abcdefghijklmnopqrstuv0123456789";
static NSString* kGetSessionProxy = nil; // @"<YOUR SESSION
    CALLBACK)>";
//////////////////////////////////////////////////////////////////
    ///////////////////////////////
}
```

Now, if you click the Build and Go button in Xcode, you should see a screen appear on your iPhone with a button labeled Connect with Facebook. Click this button to bring up the Connect to Facebook screen, where you can connect your sample iPhone application to your iPhone Test App Facebook application (Figure 6.12).

Figure 6.12

Connect to Facebook

TIP

There is an official free Facebook iPhone application on the App Store. It's a great example of what can be done in an iPhone application. Be sure to check it out.

Once you have logged in to Facebook Connect by entering your Facebook e-mail and password credentials, you will see a screen like the one shown in Figure 6.13. The sample iPhone Facebook Connect application has a few options available for you to test. Even though it is very basic, it really delivers the key features and functionality you will need to implement in your iPhone applications, so feel free to explore its details.

Figure 6.13

Logged in to Facebook Connect

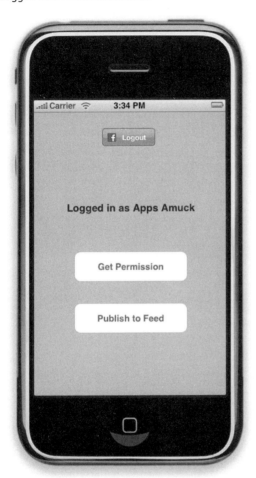

You should see a label in the center of the screen that indentifies who you are logged in as. At the top of the screen is the Facebook Logout button, and in the bottom half of the screen are two large buttons: Get Permission and Publish to Feed.

Creating a feed template

Before you can fully experience all the features of the sample iPhone Facebook Connect application, you still have a little more work left to complete. In order for the Publish to Feed button to work, you need to create at least one feed template for your Facebook application. Go back to the Facebook Developers page located at `www.facebook.com/developers/`. Open your iPhone Test App on Facebook and go back to Edit Settings. From here click on the Connect tab on the left-hand side of the page. If you scroll down the page, you should locate the Template Bundles section, as shown in Figure 6.14.

Figure 6.14

Template Bundles section

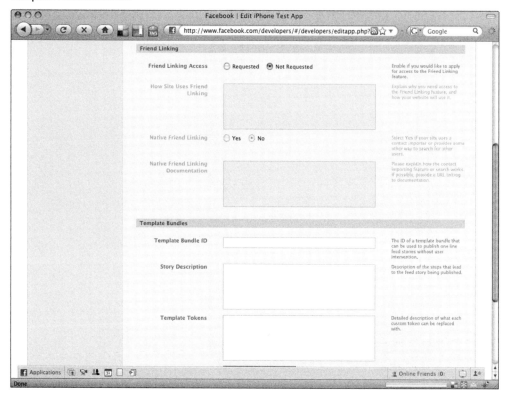

You can also create feed templates using the Feed Template Console tool. To find this useful tool, go to `http://developers.facebook.com`, click the Tools button at the top of the screen, and then click on the Feed Template Console tab. Or you can access the tool directly by going to `http://developers.facebook.com/tools.php?feed`.

TIP

Learn all the details of creating template feeds on the Facebook Developer wiki at `http://wiki.developers.facebook.com/index.php/Template_Data`.

Start by creating a One Line Story template with the Feed Template Console. In the text box under the label One Line Story, enter the following example feed template:

```
{*actor*} just earned {*score*} points, and has achieved the rank of {*rank*} in
    Rochambeau.
```

This example feed template contains three template tokens: `{*actor*}`, `{*score*}`, and `{*rank*}`. The `{*actor*}` token is a special reserved Facebook template token. Facebook automatically replaces the `{*actor*}` token with the name of the currently logged-in Facebook user. You can see the final registered template bundle in Figure 6.15.

Figure 6.15

Registered template bundle on Facebook

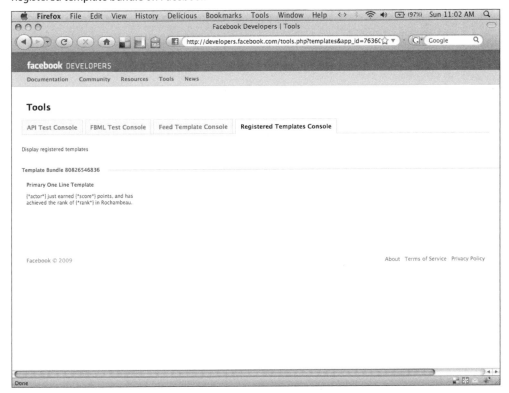

The other tokens are replaced with the values provided from your application, as you will see later in this chapter. But you can supply the Feed Template Console with sample data. Enter the following text into the Sample Template Data field:

```
{"score":"53324", "rank": "Captain"}
```

Click the Next button to test-run your feed template (Figure 6.16). When you are done testing your feed template, click the Next button again to proceed. You are given the option to Create a Short Story template. Short Story templates have a few more options than One Line Story templates. For one thing, you can use Facebook Markup Language (FBML) inside them. But for now you only need to use the One Line Story template, so click the Skip button.

TIP

Facebook Markup Language (FBML) enables you to build Facebook applications that deeply integrate into a user's Facebook experience. Learn more at `http://wiki.developers.facebook.com/index.php/FBML`.

Figure 6.16

The Feed Template Console's Template preview

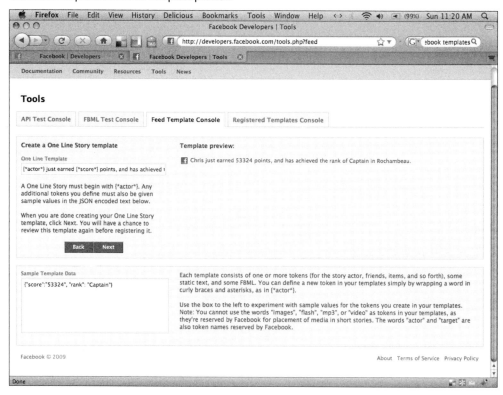

You now have the option of creating an action link—a short string of text that accompanies a Feed story and invites the user to take some action related to that story. An action link is actually a hyperlink to a URL on Facebook, your Web site, or another third-party Web site. You can either skip this option or create an action link pointing to a URL of your choosing. For example, you might decide to create an action link that allows users to click their score and see a more complete high-score board with scores and ranks of other players.

When you're ready to review and register your feed template, click the Register Template Bundle button. You should now see a Template Bundle Registration Succeeded dialog box that presents you with your new template bundle ID.

You will need to update your `publishFeed` to use your new template bundle ID. Once you have done this, click the Build and Go button. You should then be able to navigate to the Publish Story screen (Figure 6.17). After you agree to allow the application to update your profile, you should see a new item on your Facebook page, which should look like Figure 6.18.

Figure 6.17

Publish Story screen

Figure 6.18

Facebook Wall update

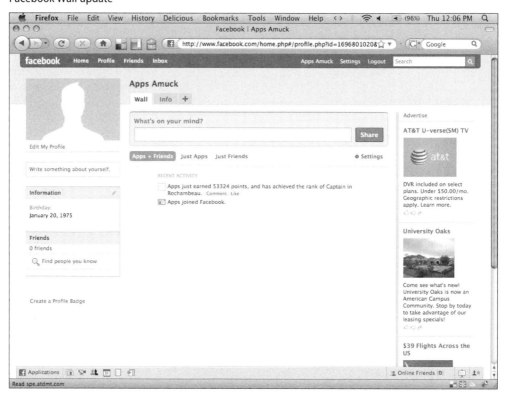

It's your choice whether you use your Facebook application's Template Bundle section or the Feed Template Console Tool, but either one of these techniques lets you create a new feed template, which will be used by Facebook to publish messages from your application to each of your user's feeds. This is done through the `publishFeed` method located in the `SessionViewController.m` file:

```
- (void)publishFeed:(id)target
{
  FBFeedDialog* dialog = [[[FBFeedDialog alloc] init]
   autorelease];
  dialog.delegate = self;
  dialog.templateBundleId = 0123456789;

dialog.templateData = @"{\"score\": \"key1\", \"rank\":
   \"value1\"}";
  [dialog show];
}
```

Imagine if the example feed template had the template bundle ID of 0123456789 in Facebook, which would then match the template bundle ID being used in the `publishFeed` method. The following output would be generated by Facebook to be published on the currently logged-in user's feed. See if you can guess the produced output before reading ahead.

Apps Amuck just earned key1 points, and has achieved the rank of value1 in Rochambeau. Seeing this should help make what is happening click in your mind. You should now update the `publishFeed` method to fill in the example feed template with more appropriate test data. Try setting the points to the value of 53324 and the rank to Captain on your own, and then check the following code listing to see how you did:

```
- (void)publishFeed:(id)target
{
  FBFeedDialog* dialog = [[[FBFeedDialog alloc] init]
   autorelease];
  dialog.delegate = self;
  dialog.templateBundleId = 9876543210;

dialog.templateData = @"{\"score\": \"53324\", \"rank\":
   \"Captain\"}";
  [dialog show];
}
```

Even though feed templates can be a little tricky to understand at first, they become easier to use with practice, and they are incredibly powerful and flexible. You now have a basic understanding of how all the parts of a Facebook feed template work.

Some actions—like updating the user's status, sending the user e-mail, or publishing information to a user's feed—require extended permission from a user before Facebook allows your application to perform them. This is very similar to some features of the iPhone SDK. Even though your application has been approved by Apple to run on any iPhone device, your application must still request explicit permission from the end user to gain access to the device's location data. Even the App Store requires you to reenter your password after a short span of time.

Here's a test you might find interesting. Try clicking the Publish to Feed button without first clicking the Get Permission button. What do you expect will happen? Do you think Facebook will allow you to publish anything to a user's feed without that user's explicit permission? If you said Facebook would prevent this unauthorized access to the user's feed, then you are correct. Facebook Connect protects users from both intentional and accidental threats to their privacy.

TIP

Be sure to check out the video "How To: Implement Facebook Connect on the iPhone in 5 Minutes," located at www.vimeo.com/3616452.

Creating a new Facebook Connect application

Now you will learn how to create a Facebook Connect iPhone application from scratch. Open Xcode and choose File⇨New Project. Be sure that Application is selected under iPhone OS in the left-hand template listing. Choose the Utility Application template and click the Choose button, as shown in Figure 6.19.

Figure 6.19

New Project template dialog box

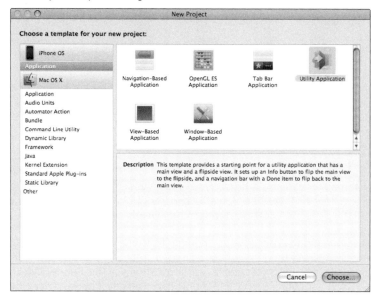

Name the new project **Facebook** or another name of your own choosing, and then click the Save button. Facebook recommends reusing the FBConnect code they provide you in the fbconnect-iphone.zip file, versus trying to re-create this base code every time yourself. That is the approach we will follow here.

Go back to the files you extracted from the fbconnect-iphone.zip and click on the included src folder to open it. Double-click on FBConnect.xcodeproj to open the FBConnect project in Xcode. Find the FBConnect folder that is listed directly under the FBConnect project in the Groups & Files listing on the left-hand side of Xcode (Figure 6.20).

Drag the FBConnect folder from the FBConnect project into the other Facebook project. Be sure to drag it under the Facebook project, and not into another folder already in the Facebook project. After you finish copying the FBConnect folder, Xcode shows an options dialog box. Be sure to uncheck the Copy items into destination group's folder (if needed) check box. Also confirm that the Reference Type field is set to Default and that Text Encoding is set to Unicode (UTF-8). Once you have verified the settings, click the Add button.

Figure 6.20

FBConnect project open in Xcode

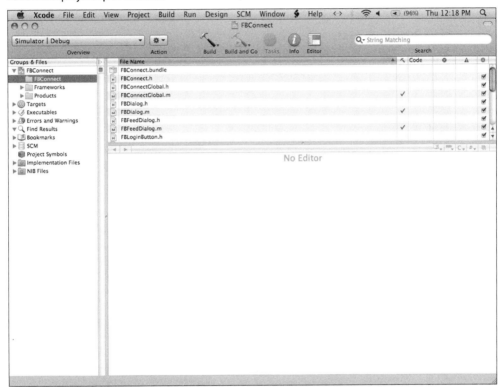

If you try to build the application now, Xcode will return with many errors and warnings. In order for Xcode to successfully compile this project, you will need to add a new framework to this project. Again in the Groups & Files listing, find the Frameworks folder under the FBConnect project. Right-click on the folder and choose Add ➪ Existing Framework. You should see the screen shown in Figure 6.21.

Open the Frameworks folder and select the CoreGraphics.framework folder, then click Add. You will see the add file options dialog box once more, and again be sure to uncheck the Copy items into destination group's folder (if needed) check box. Make certain that the Reference Type field is set to Default and that Text Encoding is set to Unicode (UTF-8). Once you have verified the settings, click the Add button.

Figure 6.21

The select framework folder screen that appears after choosing Add ➪ Existing Framework

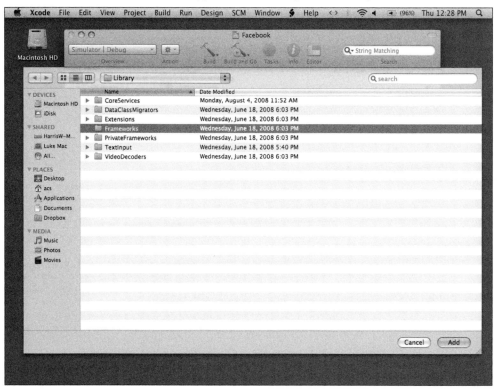

Because some of the source code for the Facebook Connect for iPhone is stored outside of your Facebook application, you will need to add the path for this code to your Facebook project. To do this, choose Project ➪ Edit Project Settings. This brings up the screen shown in Figure 6.22.

Figure 6.22

Project settings screen

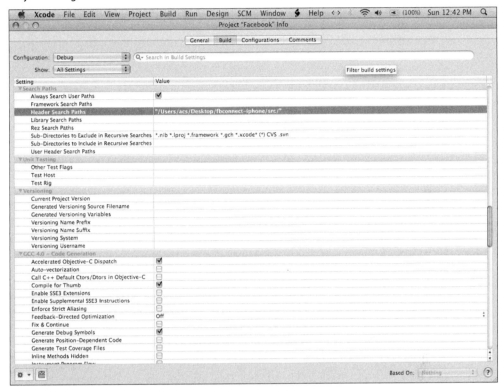

There are lots of project settings, but we are only interested in one of them, Header Search Paths. You could either find this setting yourself through manual searching, or you can enter it in the filter at the top of the screen. Once you locate this setting, double-click in the cell to the right of the field to open the Header Search Paths screen (Figure 6.23). Click the small plus sign located in the bottom-left corner of the form to add a new header search path. Then double-click the cell under the path column to enter the new header search path. If you have spaces in your path, be sure to enclose your path inside double quotes, as we've done in the previous sentence. This will keep Xcode from reading your path as a list of paths separated by spaces.

Figure 6.23

Header Search Paths screen

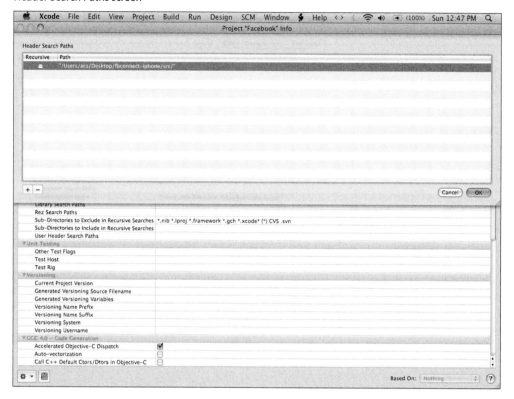

If you build your Facebook application now, you should see the Build succeeded message in the Xcode bottom Status Bar.

Working with sessions

Now you will work on making your Facebook project a more functional application. The `FBSession` object is the key component in the FBConnect API. This object contains a user's authorization and login information. The `FBSession` object requires you to provide your Facebook application's API key and application secret:

```
session = [FBSession sessionForApplication: @"<YOUR API KEY>"
    secret: @"<YOUR SECRET KEY>" delegate:self];
```

Find the `MainViewController.m` file in your Xcode project in the Groups & Files list. It is under the Facebook folder, and then inside the Main View folder. Look in this file for the following code:

```
/*
If you need to do additional setup after loading the view,
   override viewDidLoad.
 - (void)viewDidLoad {
 }
 */
```

You need to uncomment (by removing the leading forward slash) this section of code so that Xcode compiles it into your application and runs any code you add inside of the `viewDid-Load` method. Add the `FBConnect` session line of code you saw in the preceding code listing. Your `viewDidLoad` method should now match this code listing:

```
- (void)viewDidLoad {
session = [FBSession sessionForApplication: @"<YOUR API KEY>" secret: @"<YOUR
   SECRET KEY>" delegate:self];
 }
```

This one piece of code will actually be the plumbing that allows your application and Facebook to communicate with each other. But in order for this plumbing to work smoothly, you still have some work to do. Just like with the Facebook-supplied sample, you need to replace the API key and application secret with yours. You also need to include the `FBConnect.h` header file using the following line of code. Add this import statement at the top of the `MainViewController.m` file under the existing import statements:

```
#import "FBConnect/FBConnect.h"
```

By adding this, Xcode will understand what the `FBSession` object is and does. That enables the `FBSession` object and its `sessionForApplication` method. In the previous block of code, notice at the end of the main line of code that you set the `sessionForApplication`'s delegate to `self`. By doing this you are telling Xcode that this class will be responsible for handling any of the needs of the `sessionForApplication` method.

Learning more about delegates and protocols

Here is a great way to learn what a class will have to implement in order to meet a delegate's requirements. A *delegate* is a way for a class to call out to another class to respond to an event that occurred to it. A simple example might be a button class that tells another class that it has been clicked on. Right-click on the object—in this case it's the `FBSession` object—and choose Jump to Definition. Scroll down the file a bit until you find the `sessionFor Application`. It should look like the following code listing:

```
+ (FBSession*)sessionForApplication:(NSString*)key
   secret:(NSString*)secret
    delegate:(id<FBSessionDelegate>)delegate {
  FBSession* session = [[[FBSession alloc] initWithKey:key
   secret:secret
    getSessionProxy:nil] autorelease];
  [session.delegates addObject:delegate];
  return session;
}
```

If you look on the second line you will see the `FBSessionDelegate` class. Right-click on `FBSessionDelegate` and select Jump to Definition. This opens the `FBSession.h` file and locates the definition of the `FBSessionDelegate` delegate:

```
@protocol FBSessionDelegate <NSObject>
/**
 * Called when a user has successfully logged in and begun a
   session.
 */
- (void)session:(FBSession*)session didLogin:(FBUID)uid;
@optional
/**
 * Called when a session is about to log out.
 */
- (void)session:(FBSession*)session willLogout:(FBUID)uid;
/**
 * Called when a session has logged out.
 */
- (void)sessionDidLogout:(FBSession*)session;
@end
```

A protocol in Objective-C is functionally equivalent to an interface in most other modern programming languages. More specifically, a *protocol* is a list of methods that any class that wishes to adopt the protocol must implement. You can also look at it as a contract that must be met and that the compiler will enforce before allowing the application to compile.

Protocols can have both required and optional methods. By default, methods are required in a protocol. If you read through the `FBSessionDelegate` listing, you will first see the `did-Login` method, followed by the `willLogout` and `sessionDidLogout` methods. Notice the `@optional` keyword; all methods following this keyword are optional. So the `didLogin` method is required, and the `willLogout` and `sessionDidLogout` methods are optional.

TIP

Become a fan of the "iPhone Game Programming Book" on Facebook at `www.facebook.com`. We will be sure to provide updates and announcements here.

If you were to try and build the application now, the compiler would generate the following warning:

```
Warning: class 'MainViewController' does not implement the 'FBSessionDelegate'
    protocol
```

This is because when you wrote the following line of code you assigned the `FBSessionDelegate` to `self` at the end of the line:

```
session = [FBSession sessionForApplication: @"<YOUR API KEY>" secret: @"<YOUR
    SECRET KEY>" delegate:self];
```

Now the compiler is holding you to your end of the bargain. You have learned that the `FBSessionDelegate` protocol has three methods, two of which are optional. You should add the missing required protocol method to the `MainViewController` class. We will leave implementing the optional methods as an exercise for the reader.

There is more to implementing a protocol than simply adding the required methods. You also have to mark the containing class with the name of the protocol. Think about it this way: Just because your class has a `didLogin` method doesn't mean you really intended for it to be used by the `FBSessionDelegate`. Compilers are not designed to trust coincidences.

Here is how to mark your `MainViewController` class so that the compiler will know you wanted to implement the `FBSessionDelegate`. First open the `MainViewController.h` file and find the following section of code inside it:

```
#import <UIKit/UIKit.h>
@interface MainViewController : UIViewController {
}
```

To label the `MainViewController` as implementing the `FBSessionDelegate` protocol, you need to add the name of the protocol to the inside of a pair of angle brackets right before the curly braces:

```
#import <UIKit/UIKit.h>
#import "FBConnect/FBConnect.h"
@interface MainViewController : UIViewController
    <FBSessionDelegate> {
}
```

Also notice how you will need to add a new import statement to the `MainViewController.h` file. This instructs the compiler where to search to learn what makes the `FBSessionDelegate` work.

By adding the `FBSessionDelegate` to your `MainViewController.h` file, you are promising the compiler that it will be able to find any methods required by the `FBSessionDelegate` in your `MainViewController.m` file. That means at a minimum you will need to implement the `didLogin` method of the `FBSessionDelegate` in your `MainViewController.m` file.

Creating alert views

Add the following `didLogin` method to your `MainViewController` class. This code displays an alert view to the user when the application is able to log in to Facebook Connect. The alert view displays the text "Oh Yeah!" and waits for the user to click the OK button to close the dialog box:

```
//////////////////////////////////////////////////////////////////////
// FBSessionDelegate
- (void)session:(FBSession*)session didLogin:(FBUID)uid
```

```
{

    UIAlertView *alert = [[UIAlertView alloc] initWithTitle:nil message:@"Oh
    Yeah!" delegate:self cancelButtonTitle:@"OK" otherButtonTitles:nil];
[alert show];
[alert release];
}
```

Take a moment to examine the code for the UIAlertView. One way to learn more about a class in Xcode is to right-click on it, and chose Find Selected Text in API Reference.

NOTE

You will likely create many alert view dialog boxes in your iPhone applications. They are a great way to present information to users.

Do this now for the UIAlertView. You can now read through the official API Reference documentation, as shown in Figure 6.24. Here you can find much more detailed information about the selected object:

- The Overview section offers a quick synopsis of the object's function and features.
- The Tasks section highlights the most common tasks for that object.
- The Properties section gives you a detailed listing of all properties and methods with full explanations of how each one works.

We recommend referring to the official API Reference frequently. You will learn more about Objective-C and iPhone programming every time you do so.

Did you notice that the UIAlertView has a delegate of its own? This delegate gives you a way to be notified when the user responds to the alert view by clicking one of its buttons. You could learn more about this delegate by choosing Jump to Definition on the UIAlertView, or you could look it up in the API Reference documentation by choosing Find Selected Text in API Reference. Either way, you will learn that the UIAlertView implements the UIAlertViewDelegate, and that all of its methods are marked optional. The default behavior of the alert view is to close the view when the user clicks the Cancel button, but you can optionally implement the alertViewCancel method and respond as needed.

Figure 6.24

API Reference window

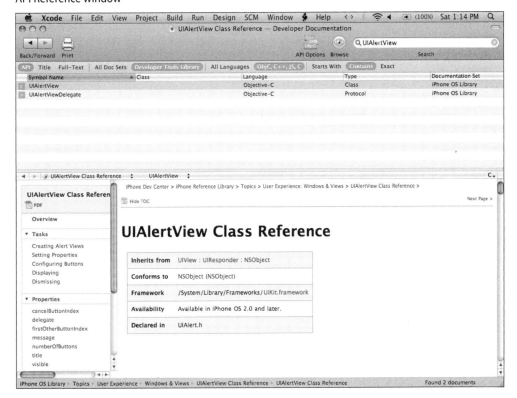

Xcode has another useful tool for finding more information about the code you are writing. It is called the Research Assistant. You can enable the Research Assistant by choosing Help ⇨ Show Research Assistant. You can also use the keyboard shortcut Ctrl+Command+?. You can see the Research Assistant window in Figure 6.25.

The Research Assistant provides real-time, context-sensitive help. This means that as you type, the Research Assistant shows information related to what you have just typed. It contains the following types of related information: a simple abstract, availability of the feature, related APIs, related documents, and even links to sample code. There is no question that the Research Assistant feature of Xcode can help you learn more and do more in less time. And it's easier than trying to learn everything on your own.

Figure 6.25

Research Assistant window

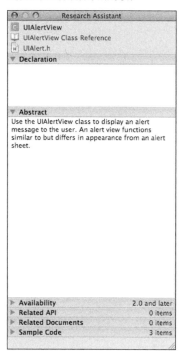

Now you should be able to build your project without any warnings related to `FBSessionDelegate`. But you will get a warning related to using an undeclared variable named session:

```
Error: 'session' undeclared (first use in this function)
```

That is because back when you wrote your line of code to assign the `FBSession` object to your session object, you did not declare the session variable:

```
session = [FBSession sessionForApplication: @"<YOUR API KEY>" secret: @"<YOUR
    SECRET KEY>" delegate:self];
```

The compiler cannot implicitly tell if the session variable is an `FBSession` object, a string, or even an int field. Since the session variable needs to be an `FBSession` object, you should update your project to correct for this:

```
FBSession *session = [FBSession sessionForApplication: @"<YOUR API KEY>" secret:
    @"<YOUR SECRET KEY>" delegate:self];
```

If you try to build your application now, you should be rewarded with a Build succeeded message from Xcode. However, if you run the application, it will not function as expected. You will not see the alert you added to the `didLogin` method. This is because the session variable scope is limited to the `viewDidLoad` method. It is only "alive" during this time.

By the time Facebook has enough of a chance to respond to the application's session request, Xcode has already cleaned up the session variable. You will need to use the `retain` method to tell Xcode to keep this variable until you are done with it. According to Xcode's API Reference, "You send an object a retain message when you want to prevent it from being deallocated without your express permission." And that is exactly what you want to do in this case.

The last thing you need to do to receive the `didLogin` event is to promote a local session variable inside `viewDidLoad` to a property. Open the `MainViewController.h` file and declare a new `FBSession` variable named session. Your `MainViewController.h` file should now match the following code listing:

```
#import <UIKit/UIKit.h>
#import "FBConnect/FBConnect.h"
@interface MainViewController : UIViewController <FBSessionDelegate> {
    FBSession* session;
}
@end
```

You will also need to update the `MainViewController.m` file. Since you have declared the session variable already in the `MainViewController.h` file, you do not need to declare it again in the `MainViewController.m` file. Update your `viewDidLoad` method to match the following:

```
session = [[FBSession sessionForApplication: @"<YOUR API KEY>" secret: @"<YOUR
    SECRET KEY>" delegate:self] retain];
```

Since you have used `retain` to tell Xcode you want to keep the session variable active, you are responsible for telling Xcode when you are done with the session variable. You will want to keep the session variable around for the whole lifetime of the application, basically for as long as it is running. When the application is closed, it will call the `dealloc` method inside the `MainViewController.m` file. You can use the following code to tell Xcode to release the variable session from usage:

```
- (void)dealloc
{
  [session release];
  [super dealloc];
}
```

Logging in

Once you have a session for your application, you can ask the user to log in. The easiest way to do this is to add a standard login button to your application. The following line of code automatically displays the login dialog box when the user touches it:

```
FBLoginButton* button = [[[FBLoginButton alloc] init]
    autorelease];
button.style = FBLoginButtonStyleWide;
[self.view addSubview:button];
```

If you update your `viewDidLoad` method with this code, it should now look something like this:

```
- (void)viewDidLoad
{

    session = [FBSession sessionForApplication: @"<YOUR API KEY>" secret: @"<YOUR
    SECRET KEY>" delegate:self];
FBLoginButton* button = [[[FBLoginButton alloc] init] autorelease];
button.style = FBLoginButtonStyleWide;
[self.view addSubview:button];
}
```

The `FBLoginButtonStyleWide` is an enumeration setting to tell Xcode to use the wider button style when creating the button to show on the screen. You can also try `FBLoginButtonStyleNormal`, which is the default, to see how you like it. Now if you click Build and Go, you should see the Facebook Connect–enabled iPhone application screen shown in Figure 6.26.

One cosmetic feature that is different between your application and the Facebook Connect sample application is the background color. Let's take a moment and learn how to set your application's background to the color of your choosing. In Xcode, find the Groups & Files listing, and then locate the Resources folder under the Facebook project. Click on this folder to expand it and find the `MainView.xib` file.

Figure 6.26

Facebook Connect login

Double-click on this file to open it in Interface Builder. Click in the Main View window, and then choose Tools ⇨ Inspector. Click on the first tab labeled Main View Attributes, and click on the Background color picker. The Colors dialog box appears, as shown in Figure 6.27, and you can choose whichever background color you like. If you want it to match the Facebook Connect sample, set the background color to turquoise.

Figure 6.27

Setting the background color

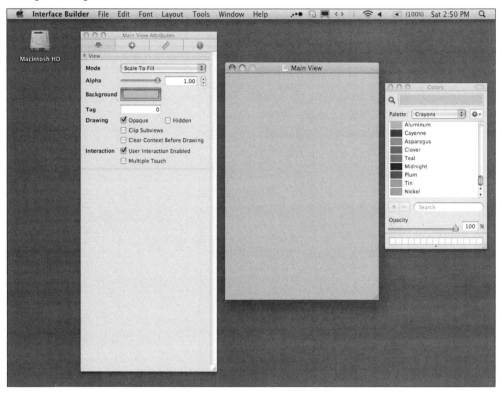

You don't have to use the `FBLoginButton` to allow users to connect to Facebook. You can force the Facebook Connect login dialog box to show manually by calling the following code:

```
FBLoginDialog* dialog = [[[FBLoginDialog alloc] initWithSession:session]
    autorelease];
    [dialog show];
```

The `FBLoginDialog` works very similarly to the `UIAlertView` that you learned about earlier in the chapter. Once the user has successfully logged in, the session object passed to `initWithSession` will have a valid session key from Facebook. One good feature that you get for free by using the `FBLoginButton` is that it automatically becomes a Logout button once the user has logged in.

Whether you allow users to log in to Facebook using the `FBLoginButton` or the `FBLoginDialog` in your Facebook application, once the user has logged in successfully, the `didLogin` method you created is fired and the user sees the screen shown in Figure 6.28.

Figure 6.28

The Oh Yeah! screen

If the user checks the Keep me logged in check box in the Connect to Facebook dialog box, the session never expires. By default, the session object expires after two hours. The FBSession object stores the session information in your application's preferences so that it can be reused later automatically.

The FBSession object has a special method named resume, which you can call to automatically resume a previous session if it is still valid. Update your viewDidLoad method to match the following code listing to enable this functionality:

```
- (void)viewDidLoad
{
    [session resume];
    session = [[FBSession sessionForApplication:@"<YOUR API KEY>" secret:@"
    <YOUR SECRET KEY>" delegate:self] retain];

    FBLoginButton* button = [[[FBLoginButton alloc] init] autorelease];
    button.style = FBLoginButtonStyleWide;
    [self.view addSubview:button];
}
```

The `resume` method returns a YES or a NO, depending on whether it found an active session, which you can use to customize your application to the current situation. The `FBLoginButton` is session aware. If the `resume` method is able to restore an active session, the `FBLoginButton` works as a Logout button; otherwise, it functions as a Login button.

The `FBLoginButton` can automatically handle the details of logging out the user, or you can programmatically do this yourself by calling the following code:

```
[session logout];
```

Getting extended permissions

You are able to access many of the Facebook API calls from your application once you have an active session. But as we mentioned earlier in the chapter, some actions require additional permission before the Facebook Connect API allows your application to perform them. These actions require the user to directly give you explicit permission to perform them. Some examples of tasks that require extended permissions are updating the user's status, sending the user e-mail, or accessing the user's information when the user isn't logged in to your application. To ask your users for extended permission, you need to call `FBPermissionDialog`.

The following code listing shows how to create an `FBPermissionDialog` that requests permission from the user to update his Facebook status, as shown in Figure 6.29:

```
FBPermissionDialog* dialog = [[[FBPermissionDialog alloc] init] autorelease];
dialog.delegate = self;
dialog.permission = @"status_update";
[dialog show];
```

You might have noticed that on the second line you set the `FBPermissionDialog`'s delegate to `self`. That means that the `FBPermissionDialog` has a delegate that you will need to implement in the `MainViewController`, just like you did for the `FBSessionDelegate`.

The `FBPermissionDialog`'s definition is named `FBDialogDelegate`. All of its methods are optional, and it has three methods available for you to take advantage of: `dialogDid-Succeed`, `dialogDidCancel`, and `didFailWithError` methods. Notice that all of the methods have meaningful names. A method has a meaningful name when it is easy for other developers to guess what the function does from reading its name.

Figure 6.29

Extended Permission screen

If you show the user the `FBPermissionDialog` and then the `dialogDidSucceed` method is called, you know the user wanted to grant your application an extended permission and Facebook made it happen. If instead the `dialogDidCancel` method is called, you know the user did not want you to perform the requested action. If the `didFailWithError` function happens, you know something went wrong, and you will have to look at the provided `NSError` object to learn exactly what happened.

CAUTION

Always try to give your methods meaningful names. This not only helps prevent confusion when others read your code, but it also makes it easier for you to remember a function's purpose when you return to it later.

You will use the `status_update` extended permission with the `FBPermissionDialog` to get permission from the user to access his profile information. If the user agrees to give you permission, you will read his user name and display it in an alert view. In order to be able to do this, you need to implement the `FBDialogDelegate`'s optional method `dialogDidSucceed` so that your application will be notified if and when the user agrees to share his profile information. For good measure, you will implement all three of the `FBDialogDelegate`'s optional methods.

First, update your `MainViewController.h` file by adding the `FBDialogDelegate` to the `MainViewController`'s declaration:

```
#import <UIKit/UIKit.h>
#import "FBConnect/FBConnect.h"
@interface MainViewController : UIViewController <FBSessionDelegate,
    FBDialogDelegate> {
        FBSession* session;
}
@end
```

Next, edit your `MainViewController.m` file to add all of the `FBDialogDelegate` methods:

```
//////////////////////////////////////////////////////////////////////
// FBDialogDelegate
- (void)dialogDidSucceed:(FBDialog*)dialog
{
    NSLog(@"dialogDidSucceed Called");
}
- (void)dialogDidCancel:(FBDialog*)dialog
{
    NSLog(@"dialogDidCancel Called");
}
- (void)dialog:(FBDialog*)dialog didFailWithError:(NSError*)error
{
    NSLog([NSString stringWithFormat:@"Error(%d) %@", error.code,
    error.localizedDescription]);
}
```

`NSLog` provides one of the most important debugging tools for your iPhone arsenal. It allows you to write debug output to Xcode's Debugger Console window (see Figure 6.30). The code you wrote to implement the `FBDialogDelegate` uses `NSLog` to record which method was called. And in the case of `didFailWithError`, it records the error code as well.

Figure 6.30

Debugger Console window

As applications become more and more complex over time, `NSLog` allows a developer a back door into the application's workings so that troubleshooting is as little trouble as possible. You can pass variables into `NSLog` as well, as shown in the following code:

```
NSLog(@"Logged in as %@", name);
```

TIP

`NSLog` is an iPhone developer's best friend. Be sure to look up `NSLog` in the Research Assistant, in the API Reference, or online again and again until you learn to fully master its capabilities.

Now you need to update the `dialogDidSucceed` method to display the name of the logged-in user. The following code does just that:

```
- (void)dialogDidSucceed:(FBDialog*)dialog
{
    NSLog(@"dialogDidSucceed Called");
    NSArray* users = result;
    NSDictionary* user = [users objectAtIndex:0];
    NSString* name = [user objectForKey:@"name"];
    UIAlertView *alert =
    [[UIAlertView alloc] initWithTitle:nil message:name delegate:self
    cancelButtonTitle:@"OK" otherButtonTitles:nil];
    [alert show];
    [alert release];
}
```

There are currently ten extended permissions that your application can request. Each extended permission must be authorized by a user individually. In other words, you cannot request more than one extended permission at a time without showing the `FBPermissionDialog` multiple times.

Here is a listing of available extended permissions:

- **email.** Allows an application to send e-mail to the logged in user
- **offline_access.** Allows an application to access a user's data even when the user is not online and does not have an active session
- **status_update.** Grants an application permission to set the user's Facebook status
- **photo_update.** Allows the application to post photos to the user's profile without the user having to approve them
- **create_event.** Grants an app permission to create and modify events for the user
- **rsvp_event.** Allows an application permission to RSVP to an event for the user
- **sms.** Allows an application the ability to send and respond to the user via text messages
- **video_upload.** Allows an app a way to upload videos to post videos to the user's Facebook profile
- **create_note.** Allows the application to write, edit, and delete notes on the user's profile
- **share_item.** Grants an application the right to post links to the profile of the logged-in user

Publishing feed stories

The ability to publish stories to a user's profile is one of the most exciting features you gain by using the Facebook Connect API. The key to publishing your application's story to your user's profile is the `FBFeedDialog` object. You can see the screen that is generated from this code in Figure 6.31:

```
FBFeedDialog* dialog = [[[FBFeedDialog alloc] init]
autorelease];
 dialog.delegate = self;
 dialog.templateBundleId = 30126546835;
 dialog.templateData = @"{\"score\": \"53324\", \"rank\":
\"Captain\"}";
 [dialog show];
```

Figure 6.31

Publishing your application's story to your user's profile.

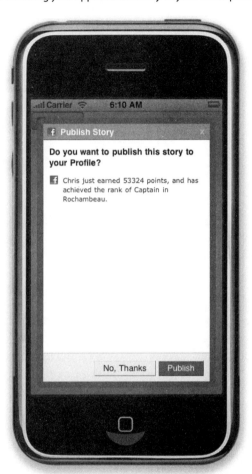

Using the Facebook Platform API

You can use the Facebook Platform API directly from the iPhone or you can use it remotely from servers of your own. The advantage of using it from the iPhone is convenience; the advantage of using your own servers is power and flexibility. If you want to use your own servers, you would send the session key and the session secret to your servers, and have them return the result. The following code shows you how to use the Facebook Connect API to call the Facebook Platform API to get the user's name:

```
- (void)getUserName
{
NSString* fql = @"select name from user where uid == 1234";
NSDictionary* params = [NSDictionary dictionaryWithObject:fql forKey:@"query"];
[[FBRequest requestWithDelegate:self] call:@"facebook.fql.query" params:params];
}
 - (void)request:(FBRequest*)request didLoad:(id)result
{
NSArray* users = result;
NSDictionary* user = [users objectAtIndex:0];
NSString* name = [user objectForKey:@"name"];
NSLog(@"Query returned %@", name);
}
```

The full Facebook Platform API is a much richer, more complete, and more powerful API compared to the Facebook Connect API. Whatever functionality Facebook lets developers have access to can be accomplished through using the Facebook Platform APIs.

TIP

You can learn more about the Facebook Platform APIs at `http://wiki.developers.facebook.com/index.php/API`. This is where the developer's wiki is located with information regarding all of the API methods.

Notice how the Connect to Facebook dialog box uses information from your iPhone Test App's settings. The application name is shown to the user in the text at the top of the screen. Additionally, your application's logo image is displayed in the dialog box. By doing this, Facebook announces your application to users using text and images.

By taking advantage of Facebook Connect for iPhone, you have let Facebook do all the heavy lifting for you. You don't have to build your own community portal for your iPhone application. You can take advantage of one of the largest online communities in the world. Facebook has a great reputation and people trust Facebook with their digital lives.

You are getting to use Facebook's trusted authentication system. Users never give you their Facebook credentials, which protects them and you. Not only do you not have to worry about securing this information, you don't have to worry about supporting the infrastructure required to maintain this system. Facebook pays the bills for all the hardware, electricity, and people needed to make everything work. This saves you both time and money.

Another benefit of using Facebook Connect for iPhone is that users of your applications can make sure of their Facebook identity information. People have already set up their profiles on Facebook, with their real names, photos, and personal information. Instead of having to enter in yet another user for yet another application and duplicate their information once again, they can simply click an Allow button and do it in one simple step through Facebook Connect.

Your application can also be granted access to the user's friends list stored on Facebook. This could be used for in-game chatting, multiplayer games, and more.

Because Facebook uses dynamic privacy, users can allow and disallow access to their personal information as needed and as they see fit. This keeps users in power, and helps them feel safe sharing their personal and confidential information with people who are, in effect, strangers. Users always have the option to not allow an application access to their information. An application can never have permanent access to a user's personal data.

Facebook is all about helping people connect and share with other people in their lives. Because it is built from the ground up to accomplish this one goal, it is a great mechanism to enable social distribution of your application. Many Facebook applications have millions of monthly active users. By tapping into this resource, you open your application up to many new users who may not have heard of your application otherwise.

NOTE
It is up to iPhone developers like you to create tomorrow's great iPhone game experiences. Now take what you have learned and create something amazing. Start from the foundation we have provided you and add something great to it!

Analyzing Business Aspects

You have now learned a great deal about the technical aspects of Facebook Connect on how to integrate and take advantage of this great new technology. It is time to consider the business side of the coin and how you can leverage Facebook Connect into creating more successful iPhone apps.

With all the great capabilities you have seen so far, it might surprise you to know that we have not yet covered one of the best features of the Facebook Connect API: It is completely and entirely free. Not only that, you don't have to pay Facebook anything to register as a Facebook developer. Facebook spends well over one million dollars per month on electricity alone to power all the servers in their datacenters. When you start to add up hardware, bandwidth, and personnel costs, the overhead expense becomes truly large (for them, not you). Any time your application can freely use services provided by and paid for by another party, it is effectively money in the bank for you.

Another great feature of using the Facebook Connect API is that your application can stand out in the crowd of other iPhone applications on the App Store. Now that there are currently more than 35,000 applications on the App Store, it's more important than ever to differentiate your product from your competitors' products. Each user profile update on Facebook from your app is effectively free advertising for your application. Links to a Web page can even be included, which makes this an effective form of viral marketing. Currently there have been more than one billion applications downloaded from the App Store, and users want to see something new and exciting. If two applications have the same basic features and functionality, then one of them is unnecessary—and the market will likely reflect and react to this over time.

Another great feature of using the Facebook Connect API is that you might qualify for seed funding from the fbFund, a fund focused on continuing to create incentives for the development of social and engaging experiences with Facebook Connect. *Seed funding* is when an established company provides funding for another company's idea at a very early stage. The fund started with 10 million dollars in capital, which is given out in investments ranging from $25,000 to $100,000.

TIP

You can learn more about the fbFund at `http://developers.facebook.com/fbFund.php`, or go to `www.facebook.com/fbFund` and become a fan.

Here is a list of the selection criteria from the fbFund home page:

- **Originality of concept.** Have you created something new and original?
- **Market.** Will this application appeal to the masses or just your close friends?
- **Social/useful.** Can this application bring people together? And will users both enjoy it and find it useful?
- **Expressive.** Does this application allow people to better express themselves?
- **Intuitive.** Is the application easy to use and user friendly?
- **Potential.** Will the application make money, and if so, how much and how soon?
- **Team.** Why should people believe that you will succeed?

Facebook Connect represents a win-win situation for both the iPhone application developer and the user. The developer wins because Facebook Connect–enabled applications become a part of the user's social ecosystem. It is the user who will promote her application experience to her friends, request her friends to play against her on her device, and choose to invite your application further into her digital life and her friends' online lives on Facebook.

The user wins because he can bring his friends with him into any Facebook Connect–enabled application. Some games allow you to play against the computer, some games allow you to play against a nearby friend, and some games even allow you to play against others online. But with Facebook Connect, you have the opportunity to play against your friends, wherever they may be, and the results can be posted to the player's profiles for the world to see.

Because Facebook Connect gives your iPhone application access to the full Facebook Platform API, you can look to other traditional Facebook applications for ideas on how you can create the next great iPhone app. Since Facebook applications can have leader boards, chat rooms, and much more, this is a great opportunity to make something truly unique to the App Store.

The decision to use Facebook Connect is almost a marketing strategy in and of itself. Marketing is one of the most compelling reasons why you should use Facebook Connect. Facebook Connect effectively comes with its own built-in viral marketing system that includes over 200 million active users. Your application users are your best salespeople; Facebook Connect makes it easy for them to close the deal.

An idea that has become really powerful in building community in many modern games is creating an achievement system. The idea is to reward the user for accomplishing some game achievement with a badge or status. For example, say you have created a Facebook Connect–enabled iPhone game called Zombie Warrior. If the player makes it through a level without taking on any damage, you offer him an "Untouchable" badge that he can proudly post to his Facebook profile page. Or the player could win a "Zombie Slayer" badge if he makes it through the town and destroys all the zombies in his path.

Be sure to think outside the box when it comes to Facebook. Don't limit yourself to using Facebook Connect for the iPhone. For example, if you create a great iPhone application, consider whether it could be a great Facebook application as well. If so, how about letting Facebook users play against iPhone users? You could even create a special scoreboard to see who the best is.

TIP

Be sure to become a fan of "Apps Amuck" on Facebook at `www.facebook.com/pages/AppsAmuck/106607134124`. We will provide updates and announcements here.

Today many companies and brands are setting up pages on Facebook and elsewhere. If soda companies have fan pages on Facebook for their products, why don't you? Even Facebook does this. For example, not only can you install the Facebook developer application, you can become a fan of it, and you interact with both the Facebook developer application team and other fans. Again, you can do all of this for free, and without having to set up or provide any of the infrastructure.

Summary

Now that Facebook Connect is available for the iPhone, you can integrate the power of the Facebook platform into your iPhone application. Users of your Facebook Connect iPhone applications can share their experiences with their Facebook friends. Users know that their private data is still safe and secure in your application even though they may not know you.

In this chapter you learned how you could build community for your iPhone app creations using the Facebook Connect API. First you covered the basics of what Facebook is and what it offers members and developers. Next you looked at how to get started developing for Facebook and Facebook Connect.

You reviewed the Facebook Connect iPhone sample and then tackled creating a Facebook Connect iPhone application from scratch. You also learned how to create a Facebook application that runs inside of Facebook itself. You used the application to create template bundles for publishing stories to user feeds. You learned the details of the `FBSession` and `FBLoginButton` objects. Then you learned how to directly access the Facebook Platform API from your iPhone application using Facebook Connect.

Users have come to expect to be immersed in great experiences on the iPhone, but now they want to be able to share those experiences with their friends. Facebook has provided a great tool for developers to use to make this happen with Facebook Connect. We have only begun to see what is possible today. Go to `http://appsamuck.com` to send us a note and show us what you've done!

Connecting Players in Real Time

W e could have covered multiplayer apps in a single chapter; however, the technologies exposed in the 3.0 SDK warrant two separate discussions. In this chapter we focus on peer-to-peer (P2P) connectivity. Real-time games are well suited to this technology, so our example game will employ peer-to-peer and head-to-head connections. In Chapter 8 we will cover push notification. Even though push notification was not designed for gaming, it makes a perfect fit for turn-based gaming. It's important to cover peer-to-peer first because you will be able to use what you learn in this chapter to add peer-to-peer connectivity to your turn-based games.

In this chapter, you'll examine multiplayer connectivity in the game AmuckPuck. Air hockey has been a hit on the iPhone, probably because it is such a natural fit for the device. We cover it here partly because of this natural fit and the great illustration it serves for this material; however, it's also one of our personal favorites. We are hoping that you will take this example and build some really cool new versions of air hockey that we can all enjoy.

Finally, since there are already so many versions of air hockey currently available, we will consider how to make a game attractive in a replacement market, adding some value and separation to this app for it to be a success. From a business aspect we will discuss entering a replacement market and review techniques for making your games stand out in the crowd.

Facing the Challenges of Real-Time Multiplayer Games

Simply stated, multiplayer games allow more than one gamer to play in the same game environment at the same time. In this environment a player is no longer limited to competing against algorithms and artificial intelligence. Players can enter a world of social interaction with friends, peers, and even players on the other side of the world.

In This Chapter

Facing the challenges of real-time multiplayer games

Understanding game design: Competition

Choosing your connection options

Hooking up with your peers

Programming: AmuckPuck

Analyzing business aspects

In this world players can do the following:

- Experience dynamic human interaction.
- Play competitively against rivals.
- Play cooperatively with friends.
- Communicate and socialize with other players.
- Form friendships and interact with distant players.

Connectivity is another area of interest and variety. Multiplayer games have changed a lot over the years and new technologies have been introduced that allow gamers to connect in more ways than ever before:

- **Head-to-head.** Players play against each other on the same device with separate or shared controllers.
- **Peer-to-peer.** Players in close proximity can connect with each other with wireless technologies like Bluetooth, with a shared network, or simply by using a cable between two devices.
- **Internet.** Players connect with one or more other players on the World Wide Web.
- **Massive multiplayer.** Players connect to a central server that is responsible for coordinating interaction between players and the game.

A game can be considered real-time if a player's interaction with the game environment is fluid and not suspended by another player's turn or input. In real life a game of air hockey at the arcade would be considered real-time. Playing a round of checkers would be an example of a turn-based game. It is important to understand the distinction between the two types of multiplayer games because the strategies employed to connect the players can be very different.

Connecting players on separate devices has some real challenges. Once connected, packets are continually and rapidly exchanged between participants. These packets contain information about player input, status, and anything else necessary to communicate changes in your virtual world. When exchanging packets, there are two issues that must be reckoned with: network latency and lost packets. Dealing with these issues can be a science of its own; however, for now, you need to at least be aware of the problems.

Network latency

Latency is the time it takes for a packet to travel from one device and to be processed by the connected device. This latency is generally short, but for real-time games it can be enough to render your game unplayable. Most real-time games deal with latency by being predictive, in which you measure the latency and use this information to predict the future move you expect the other player to make. For example, in some scenarios you can use the direction and speed of the remote player to calculate a player's next position, assuming the direction and speed will not change. When the next packet is received, you can correct incorrect predictions by making a smooth transition to the proper location. This generally goes unnoticed by players because they are not looking at the same device as remote players who see their actual location. The downside to this method is that occasionally a player may experience anomalies. For example, a person may walk through a wall or see a bullet appear 20 pixels in front of the cannon whenever a missed prediction is corrected.

Lost packets

Lost packets are easier to deal with than latency. Usually if you lose a packet you can interpolate the missing information. For instance, if you lose packet 2 you can interpolate it from information in packets 1 and 3. In other cases you can ignore lost packets and let your prediction logic for latency compensate for the missing data. This just means the latency will span a larger time interval if a packet is lost. At times you will need to send packets containing data that must be delivered. For example, if you are reporting that a player was destroyed, that message must be received on the other end. If critical messages like this are not received, the integrity of the game state is lost. When messages must be reliable, the recipient needs to issue a return receipt once the critical message arrives. If the sender does not receive the receipt in a timely manner, the original packet should be resent until a return receipt is received.

Understanding Game Design: Competition

It is human nature for people to want to compete. Every day we are faced with a desire to compete. Since the dawn of time we have been in competition for food, water, and mates. Think of all the things you and others compete for:

- Basic needs (food, clothing, and shelter)
- Money and wealth
- Pride and prestige
- Fame and popularity
- Notoriety and attention
- High scores and bragging rights

Competition in gaming is a combat between two or more players. Players want to prove they are better than their rivals. Victory is about pride—we all want bragging rights! Your games should appeal to our instinctive desire to compete.

Practice makes perfect

Competitive games should pave a path that allows players to increase their skill level the more they play the game. This encourages players to play your game longer and harder to get an edge over their opponents. In air hockey, for example, players learn the sweet spots to bounce the puck off of. They learn how to fake out the opponent and make more accurate shots at the goal the more they play. However, the better you become, the better your opponent becomes at defending against you. The stroke of the paddle gives a visual cue to the direction it will send the puck when it strikes. At some point players will learn all the tricks and cues and gain the agility necessary to be an expert at your game. The key to making your game great is to create enough depth that players will not reach that skill level until they have spent many, many hours immersed in your game. If mastery is easily obtained, gamers will grow bored quickly, leave you a bad review, and move on to the next challenge.

Extending the learning curve

Some games, like air hockey, have a natural learning curve. Just mastering the controls and learning the physics take time. In other games you need to build the learning curve in yourself. In order to build new challenges and content that extend the learning curve, we can mimic characters of naturally occurring paths of learning.

In most sports you learn to play both offense and defense. Air hockey is no different—you are on offense if you are in control of the puck and on defense if you are not. For every offensive action there should be a defensive action against it. Each offensive technique should be more difficult to learn and the counter should be equally difficult to learn. Offensive actions should provide cues when they are invoked even if the cue is artificial. If cues are not provided, the defensive player cannot prepare or learn to defend against the move. Just by using this simple technique, you now have a path to systematically add depth and interest to your game.

Let's add some depth to our air hockey example. Many fighting games have special moves that unleash powerful or magical attacks that level the opponent. In many instances these moves are triggered by memorized controller patterns. One way to translate this to the iPhone is to fire off attacks when special gestures are drawn to the touchscreen. For example, when a player draws a "V" shape (Figure 7.1), a stun blast is fired from your puck (Figure 7.2). If the blast strikes the opponent, he is immobilized for a few moments, giving the attacker a free shot at the goal.

Figure 7.1

Mock-up of player drawing a stun blast gesture

Figure 7.2

Mock-up of stun blast being fired

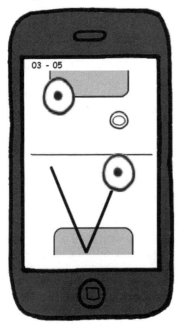

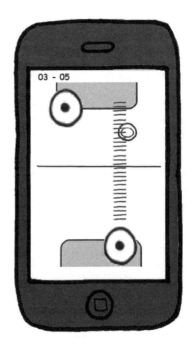

If a player draws a greater than symbol (>) (Figure 7.3), a confusion blast is fired from the puck (Figure 7.4). If this blast strikes the opponent, the puck moves opposite to where the player directs it for a few seconds. Notice that the confusion blast is a more difficult stroke than the stun blast. Also, the confusion blast fans out a little, making it more difficult to avoid.

Figure 7.3

Mock-up of player drawing a
confusion blast gesture

Figure 7.4

Mock-up of confusion blast being fired

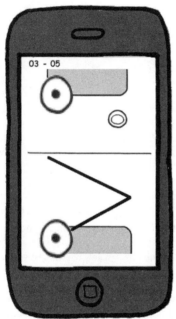

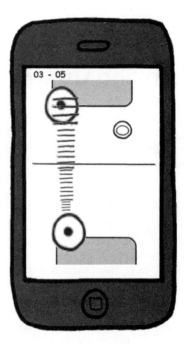

Choosing Your Connection Options

Earlier in the chapter we listed the available connection options:

- Head-to-head
- Peer-to-peer
- Internet
- Massive multiplayer

For our example we are going to support head-to-head and peer-to-peer.

Head-to-head does not really require a connection and therefore is fairly straightforward to implement. However, do not dismiss the importance it carries. Most players will have only one device to play on, so this style may make up the bulk of your market.

At the time of this writing, peer-to-peer is the new kid on the block. Peer-to-peer provides a great gaming experience for those with two compatible devices.

NOTE
Peer-to-peer support requires iPhone OS 3.0 and is only available for the iPod touch second generation, iPhone 3G, and above.

Internet and massive multiplayer connections would be an awesome addition to the game, but the topic is too broad to cover here, especially connecting a real-time game this way.

Hooking Up with Your Peers

Now we are going to walk you through the basics of peer-to-peer connections. In the next section we will take you through the code for AmuckPuck, but for now we need a smaller example that is not cluttered with concerns outside of peer-to-peer. At the time of this writing, a simple example of peer-to-peer was not available from Apple. We have supplied the example "P2P Chat," which you can download from `http://appsamuck.com/gamedevbook/p2pchat`.

Running and reviewing P2P Chat

Peer-to-peer is at the core of the Game Kit framework introduced in the iPhone 3.0 SDK. Apple has provided documentation and getting started videos that outline the features and uses of tools available in Game Kit. Also, Game Kit was new at the time of this writing, so we recommend that you read through the material and watch the videos Apple provides to see what may have been added since this book was written.

Load the project in Xcode and run it in the Simulator so you can get your first experience with the app. To get the full experience, you will need an additional device to connect, but thankfully Apple was kind enough to enable the Simulator to connect with an external device as two physical devices would.

TIP
Remember that the Simulator is just that—a simulator, not an emulator. There is a difference between the two. The Simulator utilizes the processor and other resources directly. An actual device will not perform at the same level. On a physical device, graphics will be rendered more slowly and packets will take longer to arrive. The Simulator is a great way to test, debug, and tune; however, you should always perform testing on a physical device (or two) before you submit your app to the App Store.

Once you have loaded the project, click Build and Go. You will see a simple screen in text view with a Find button, a text field, and a Speak button (Figure 7.5).

Click the Find button to launch the peer picker (Figure 7.6). The peer picker is a nice controller that Apple has provided for you in the SDK. It takes care of all the logic and workflow necessary to connect two players in a peer-to-peer session.

Figure 7.5

The main screen of P2P Chat

Figure 7.6

The peer picker's select connection type screen

The first screen in the peer picker workflow allows the player to select the connection type. Currently, if a user selects Online, the peer picker informs you of this decision and it is up to you to complete the connection. P2P Chat does nothing but close the picker since it is just an example. However, if the user clicks Nearby, this tells the picker that the player wants to connect over Bluetooth using peer-to-peer. If Bluetooth is not enabled, the player will be given an opportunity to turn it on (Figure 7.7).

Figure 7.7

The Bluetooth prompt of the peer picker

If Bluetooth is already on, you will not receive this prompt. If you really want to see it anyway, you can force it to prompt you by going to the Settings application on your device and turning off Bluetooth (Figure 7.8). Then try P2P Chat again, and you will be prompted to turn it on.

Figure 7.8

Turning off Bluetooth in device settings

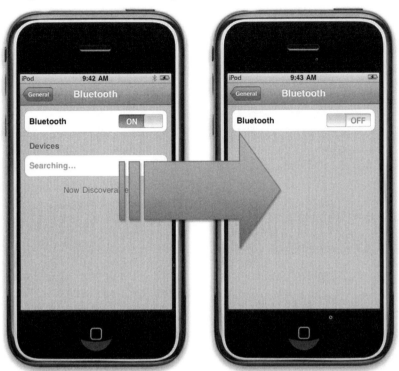

One way or another, you should have Bluetooth on at this point. The next screen in the workflow waits for nearby players to join (Figure 7.9). P2P Chat uniquely identifies itself with a session ID so only nearby devices that have P2P Chat loaded will show up.

As soon as another player is found, the name of that player's device appears in a list (Figure 7.10). One player can then select the other player he wishes to connect with and wait for that player to click Accept on the screen (Figure 7.11).

Once connected, the devices can send messages to each other (Figure 7.12). Okay, sending text messages to someone only a foot or two away isn't exactly revolutionary. However, this illustrates a straightforward implementation of the peer-to-peer connection process.

Figure 7.9

You see this screen when peer picker is waiting on nearby instances of P2P Chat to advertise their session.

Figure 7.10

The peer picker list of nearby sessions

Dissecting the code behind P2P Chat

Now that you are more familiar with P2P Chat, let's look at the code and see what makes it tick. P2P Chat utilizes features of the Game Kit frameworks to connect devices. Game Kit introduces features that allow different devices to connect. At the time of this writing, Game Kit includes two technologies:

- **Peer-to-peer connectivity.** This enables you to create a Bluetooth network between two devices. Even though it was designed for games, Apple encourages its use for any application that can benefit from an ad hoc network between two devices.

NOTE

As of the iPhone 3.0 OS, peer-to-peer has a two-device limit.

- **In game voice.** This provides voice communication between multiple devices over any network. This can be layered on top of a Bluetooth connection or a wireless Internet connection.

In P2P Chat we used the peer-to-peer connectivity currently available in Game Kit. When utilizing this feature you need to utilize two new classes introduced in the frameworks:

- **`GKPeerPickerController`.** This controller manages the peer picker we looked at earlier. You will need to activate an instance of the class as well as implement a delegate that it provides to receive and respond to the messages it sends.

- **`GKSession`.** This is the class that implements the Bluetooth network between two devices. Use an instance of this class to configure and manage the connection between the two devices. `GKSession` also supplies a delegate that is literally used to receive messages.

Figure 7.11

The peer picker "accept connection" prompt

Figure 7.12

P2P Chat is connected and communicating.

Introducing the GKPeerPickerController

Before working with a session, we need to connect to another device. Thankfully, Apple has provided the `GKPeerPickerController` that does just that. The peer picker comes complete with its own user interface for locating and accepting connections.

Here are the steps needed to add peer picker to the P2P Chat example:

1. Whenever the Find button is clicked, create an instance to the class `GKPeerPickerController` if one did not already exist:

```
GKPeerPickerController *picker =
[[GKPeerPickerController alloc] init];
```

2. Attach the delegate:

```
picker.delegate = self;
```

3. Configure the network types that you would like to allow:

```
picker.connectionTypesMask = GKPeerPickerConnectionTypeNearby |
GKPeerPickerConnectionTypeOnline;
```

NOTE

`GKPeerPickerConnectionTypeOnline` is included for demonstration purposes. If you leave it out, nearby connections will be used by default and there will be one less step in the connection process. To leave it out, replace the code for Step 3 with this:

```
picker.connectionTypesMask =
    GKPeerPickerConnectionTypeNearby;
```

4. Set the instance property and release the locale reference:

```
self.peerPicker = picker;
[picker release];
```

5. Finally, disable the Find button to keep the user from clicking it again, and then call `show` to launch the Peer Picker dialog box:

```
findButton.enabled = false;
[self.peerPicker show];
```

These additions will get the peer picker to show on the screen, but you still need to implement the delegate in order to do anything with the session the peer picker configures for you. In order to do this, your class must implement `GKPeerPickerControllerDelegate`:

```
@protocol GKPeerPickerControllerDelegate <NSObject>
    @optional
    - (void)peerPickerController:(GKPeerPickerController *)picker
        didSelectConnectionType:(GKPeerPickerConnectionType)type;
```

```
- (GKSession *)peerPickerController:(GKPeerPickerController *)picker
    sessionForConnectionType:(GKPeerPickerConnectionType)type;
- (void)peerPickerController:(GKPeerPickerController *)picker
    didConnectPeer:(NSString *)peerID toSession:(GKSession *)session;
- (void)peerPickerControllerDidCancel:(GKPeerPickerController *)picker;
@end
```

Here are the details of how the `GKPeerPickerControllerDelegate` is implemented in P2PChat:

1. `peerPickerController:didSelectConnectionType:`

This event notifies the delegate that the user chose a connection type. Online connections are not implementing in this example; for this reason, the Peer Picker dialog box is now closed by calling `dismiss`. Next, a message is displayed to the user explaining why nothing happened. Finally, the Find button is re-enabled so the user can start the process all over again:

```
- (void)peerPickerController:(GKPeerPickerController*)
    picker
    didSelectConnectionType:(GKPeerPickerConnectionType)
    type {
    if (type == GKPeerPickerConnectionTypeOnline) {
        [picker dismiss];
        UIAlertView *alertView = [[UIAlertView alloc]
            initWithTitle:@"Information"
            message:@"Online connections are not supported."
            delegate:nil cancelButtonTitle:@"Close"
            otherButtonTitles:nil];
        [alertView show];
        [alertView release];
        findButton.enabled = true;
    }
}
```

2. `peerPickerController:sessionForConnectionType:`

This event notifies the delegate that the connection type is requesting a `GKSession` object. You should return a valid `GKSession` object for use by the picker. If this method is not implemented or returns `nil`, a default `GKSession` will be created for you:

```
-(GKSession*)peerPickerController:
    (GKPeerPickerController*)picker
    sessionForConnectionType:(GKPeerPickerConnectionType)
    type {
    if(!gameSession) {
        gameSession = [[GKSession alloc]
            initWithSessionID:@"com.appsamuck.p2pchat"
```

```
        displayName:nil sessionMode:GKSessionModePeer];
      gameSession.delegate = self;
      [gameSession setDataReceiveHandler:self withContext:nil];
   }
   return gameSession;
}
```

We will look at the creation of `GKSession` in more depth in the next section.

3. **peerPickerController:didConnectPeer:toSession:**

This event notifies the delegate that the peer was connected to a `GKSession`. Once this is fired, we know we can start communicating on our connection. In P2P Chat, we enable the Speak button when this event fires:

```
- (void)peerPickerController:(GKPeerPickerController*)
  picker
  didConnectToPeer:(NSString*)peerId {
  speakButton.enabled = true;
}
```

4. **peerPickerControllerDidCancel:**

This event notifies the delegate that the user cancelled the picker. Use this event if you need to perform an action when the player cancels the connection process: You need to re-enable the Find button here also:

```
- (void)peerPickerControllerDidCancel:
  (GKPeerPickerController*)picker {
  findButton.enabled = true;
}
```

Introducing GKSession

Now that you have a peer picker set up, you can implement the `GKSession` object that you will use to send and receive messages between devices. In P2P Chat, the `GKSession` object is initialized in the `peerPickerController:sessionForConnectionType:` method implementation for the protocol `GKPeerPickerControllerDelegate`:

```
-(GKSession*)peerPickerController:(GKPeerPickerController*)picker
  sessionForConnectionType:(GKPeerPickerConnectionType)type {
  if(!gameSession) {
    gameSession = [[GKSession alloc]
      initWithSessionID:@"com.appsamuck.p2pchat"
      displayName:nil sessionMode:GKSessionModePeer];
    gameSession.delegate = self;
  }
  return gameSession;
}
```

This line creates and initializes the session:

```
gameSession = [[GKSession alloc] initWithSessionID:@"com.appsamuck.p2pchat"
    displayName:nil sessionMode:GKSessionModePeer];
```

The parameters needed for initializing a session are:

- **sessionID.** A unique string that identifies your application.
- **name.** A string identifying the user to display to other peers.
- **mode.** The mode the session should run in.

In P2P Chat, the `displayName` parameter is set to `nil`. Setting `displayName` to `nil` instructs the picker to use the device name as the `displayName`. We set the mode to `GKSessionModePeer`, which tells the session to act as both server and client. This results in the best user experience.

Once you have created the `GKSession` you begin to send messages. To send a message, you will need to call the method `sendDataToAllPeers:withDataMode:error:`. This method is used in P2P Chat whenever the Speak button is clicked:

```
- (IBAction)speakButtonClicked:(id)sender {
    if (!isConnected) return;
    NSString *message = textField.text;
    NSData *data = [message dataUsingEncoding:NSASCIIStringEncoding];
    [gameSession sendDataToAllPeers:data withDataMode:GKSendDataReliable
    error:nil];
}
```

Take care to notice the parameter data mode. There are two ways to send messages:

- **GKSendDataReliable.** Reliable continues to send the data until it is successfully transmitted. However, it may stall if network congestion occurs. Use this method when you need to guarantee delivery.
- **GKSendDataUnreliable.** Unreliable is the fastest way to send your data. Data is sent one time and does not retry if an error occurs. Data transmitted this way can be received out of order. Use this method for sending small packets of data that must arrive quickly.

The last thing left to do is to implement pertinent methods defined by the protocol `GKSessionDelegate`:

```
@protocol GKSessionDelegate <NSObject>
@optional
    - (void)session:(GKSession *)session peer:(NSString *)peerID
      didChangeState:(GKPeerConnectionState)state;
    - (void)session:(GKSession *)session
      connectionWithPeerFailed:(NSString *)peerID withError:(NSError *)error;
    - (void)session:(GKSession *)session didFailWithError:(NSError *)error;
@end
```

Only one method in this protocol is necessary for P2P Chat. The app needs to know whenever the state of a peer changes relative to the session. For this, the app needs to implement the method `session:peer:didChangeState`. In this method the app needs to react whenever a peer connects or disconnects. The peer picker will handle all other state changes of concern for us:

```
- (void)session:(GKSession *)session peer:(NSString *)peerID
    didChangeState:(GKPeerConnectionState)state {
    NSString* stateName = nil;
    switch (state) {
        case GKPeerStateConnected:
            [session setDataReceiveHandler: self withContext: nil];
            self.isConnected = true;
            self.gameSession = session;
            [peerPicker dismiss];
            break;
        case GKPeerStateDisconnected:
            self.isConnected = false;
            break;
    }
}
```

Note these two lines of code from above:

```
[session setDataReceiveHandler: self withContext: nil];
```

and

```
[peerPicker dismiss];
```

Calling `dismiss` on the peer picker simply closes the peer picker. However, remember to make the call to get the peer picker off the screen. The call to `setDataReceiveHandler:withContext` warrants a little more discussion. Setting the `DataReceiveHandler` tells the `GKSession` which object to send data to as it arrives from the remote peer. The class receiving the data must implement the following method as P2P Chat has done:

```
- (void) receiveData:(NSData *)data fromPeer:(NSString *)peer
    inSession:(GKSession *)session context:(void *)context {
    NSString *message = [[NSString alloc] initWithData:data
        encoding:NSASCIIStringEncoding];
    textView.text = [textView.text stringByAppendingString:
        [NSString stringWithFormat:@"%@\n", message]];
}
```

As illustrated above, whenever data is received from a peer, you can intercept the data in this method and use it in your app as prescribed by your requirements.

Researching performance

Earlier in the chapter we discussed that network games at times have to deal with lost packets and latency. These are the types of issues that can trip us up in the later stages of the development process and lead to an expensive overhaul. As long as we are sending packets quickly and repeatedly, a lost packet here or there will not cause huge hiccups. However, latency could be an issue here. We need a good idea of how much latency to expect in a normal peer-to-peer connection. The best thing to do is to try and measure it so we know what we are dealing with. In order to see what we were up against, we wrote a small app that sends a packet of data back and forth between two peers to constantly record the current time on the device. This allows us to measure how long it takes a packet to round-trip, or get back to the device that it originated from.

NOTE

With Bluetooth, real-world conditions may affect actual performance. Conditions such as the proximity of the two devices and the use of other Bluetooth hardware (headsets, wireless mice/keyboards, etc.) in close proximity will impact latency and packet loss. Also, some devices will perform better than others as "host" devices. An iPod touch does not have to manage extra background processes such as cell phone communications. Also, the 2G iPod touch and the iPhone 3GS have a faster CPU.

We created a small app based on P2P Chat to perform the test. Here is a short breakdown of the key pieces of the application and how it works so you will understand how we arrived at our results. First, we need a packet to round-trip for the test:

```
typedef struct {
    int player;
    int count;
    double time;
} Packet;
```

Once the `GKSession` is established, a message can be sent to the peer. The following code is used to send the message:

```
localPacket.player = playerNumber;
localPacket.count = ++currentCount;
localPacket.time = CFAbsoluteTimeGetCurrent();
localData = [localData initWithBytes:&localPacket length:sizeof(Packet)];
[self.gameSession sendDataToAllPeers:localData
    withDataMode:GKSendDataUnreliable error:&sendError];
```

When the peer receives a packet from a peer, it returns the package back to the sender. When the peer receives a packet that it created, measurements can be recorded. Listing 7.1 shows how this was accomplished.

CROSS-REFERENCE

To download all of the code listings in this chapter, go to `www.wileydevreference.com` and click the Downloads link.

Listing 7.1

The Method receiveData Will Be Called Any Time Data Is Received from a Peer

```
#pragma mark GKSessionDelegate
- (void) receiveData:(NSData *)data fromPeer:(NSString *)peer
   inSession:(GKSession *)session context:(void *)context {
   Packet packetData;
   [data getBytes:& packetData length:sizeof(Packet)];

   if (packetData.player == playerNumber) {
      // This packet originated here
      if (lastCount+1 != packetData.count) {
         // This throws out missed or late packets
         packetData++;
         double elapsedTime = CFAbsoluteTimeGetCurrent() - packetData.time;
         totalElapsedTime += elapsedTime;
         NSString *remoteStatus remoteStatus = [NSString stringWithFormat:
            @"Average time: %f", totalElapsedTime / packetCount];
         textView.text = remoteStatus;
         lastCount = packetData.count;
      }
   }
   else {
      // This packet originated on the peer we need to return it
      remotePacket = received;
      remoteData = [remoteData initWithBytes:&remotePacket
         length:sizeof(Packet)];
      [self.gameSession sendDataToAllPeers:remoteData
         withDataMode:GKSendDataUnreliable error:nil];
   }
}
```

TIP

In peer-to-peer you are writing one app that needs to behave slightly differently on each device. It is not obvious at first how to choose the device to be the host versus the client. We use the `session: didReceiveConnectionRequestFromPeer` method to make that determination for us. This message is sent to only one of the two devices, which helps you decide which device does what:

```
- (void)session:(GKSession *)session
   didReceiveConnectionRequestFromPeer:(NSString *)peerID {
   // This method will only be called on one device
   playerNumber = 2;
}
```

After running the test, we discovered that in peer-to-peer the time it takes to round-trip is as follows:

- Average time: 0.038 seconds
- Worst time: 0.180 seconds
- Best time: 0.012 seconds

Also realize this is a round trip, so we can assume that a single packet will be roughly half of this time. Also, if your packet is larger, it will take longer to send. So what does this tell us? If we keep small packets, we can expect to be able to receive about 50 per second; worst case, we will receive 10 per second. That's not too shabby. What happens if we switch the same example to reliable messaging? You can do this by changing GKSendDataUnreliable to GKSendDataReliable throughout the code.

For example, change this:

```
[self.gameSession sendDataToAllPeers:remoteData
    withDataMode:GKSendDataUnreliable error:nil];
```

to this:

```
[self.gameSession sendDataToAllPeers:remoteData
    withDataMode:GKSendDataReliable error:nil];
```

When this was done in our test, we yielded the following results with reliable messaging:

- Average time: 0.043 seconds
- Worst time: 0.246 seconds
- Best time: 0.015 seconds

As expected, reliable is a bit slower, but still fairly good. Choose whether to use reliable messaging or unreliable messaging according to the needs of your game. For the AmuckPuck game, we will need to use a little of both. For puck and paddle movements, we will use unreliable for speed. For major game events like scoring, we will use reliable messaging. Also, based on the numbers above, we will be able to move forward without prediction or interpolation.

Programming: AmuckPuck

Earlier in this chapter you looked at some ideas and mock-ups for the game AmuckPuck. Now, we will walk you through the critical steps necessary to bring this idea to life (Figure 7.13). AmuckPuck is an exciting application to work on. Peer-to-peer really brings a whole new level to the game that the head-to-head versions of air hockey on the App Store completely lack. This game was really fun to build and test. We had a hard time putting it down every time we fired it up to play it. We hope you enjoy it as much as we have.

Figure 7.13

This chapter guides you through the critical steps needed to transform the game AmuckPuck from an idea to an application.

Making a good first impression

Along with the technical details of a game, remember that appearances are important. When it comes to the App Store today, it is safe to go further and say appearances are of paramount concern. We spent some extra time and effort to make sure that graphics in AmuckPuck make a good first impression.

The first graphic a potential buyer will see in iTunes is your icon. At a glance, your icon should strive to accurately describe your application and capture the eye of someone browsing through the App Store. Figure 7.14 illustrates the icon we settled on for AmuckPuck.

Figure 7.14

Potential buyers see this icon when they come across AmuckPuck on the App Store.

TIP

By default, the iPhone will round the corners of your icon and apply a glossy shine to it. However, notice that the icon used for AmuckPuck already has rounded corners and a shine effect applied to it. You can prevent the iPhone from adding this effect on top of yours by adding the value `UIPrerenderedIcon` to your application's info.plist and setting the value to true.

Once you get potential buyers to take the bait, they will click on your app icon and you'll have an opportunity to wow them a bit more. On the application details screen, you can show up to five screen shots to your potential buyers. This is another opportunity to put your best foot forward. On the details page, AmuckPuck uses a couple of in-game shots, such as the one shown in Figure 7.15. It also shows a splash screen (Figure 7.16), the menu screen (Figure 7.17), and the About Us screen (Figure 7.18).

Figure 7.15

The final version of a screen shot from AmuckPuck

Figure 7.16

The completed splash screen from AmuckPuck.

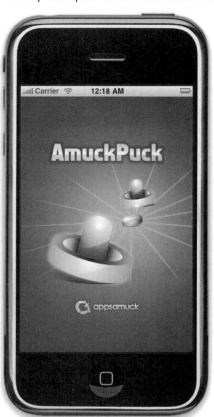

TIP

You can supply a loading screen to your application by adding an image to the resource bundle and naming it Default. png. This image will load the second a user clicks on your application icon and will remain visible until the application fully loads. However, Apple does not want you to use Default.png as a splash screen; they want it to look like the first real screen your users will encounter when they open your app. To get around this, you can load your splash screen first and use an animation to fade it away after a one- or two-second delay. This way you can use your splash screen for Default.png because it is the first screen users encounter.

Now let's take time to look at the application in detail. The full source code for AmuckPuck can be found at `http://appsamuck.com/gamedevbook/airhockey`.

Figure 7.17

The completed menu screen for AmuckPuck

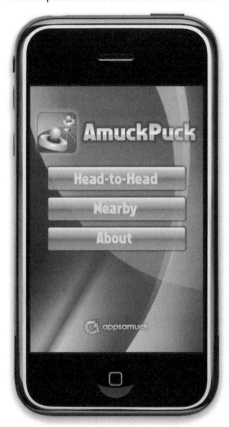

Figure 7.18

The completed About Us screen for AmuckPuck

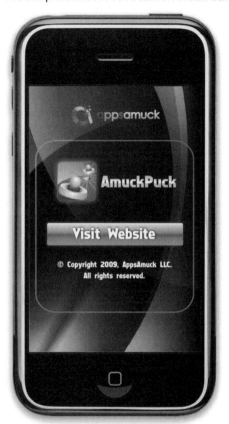

In AmuckPuck we are going to focus on the key class and structures that bring it to life. There are several other files in the application, but these are the standard menu and support files you should already be familiar with. The three items we will focus on are:

- **StateData and EventData.** These are structures defined in `HockeyData.h`. They are used to store the state of the hockey table and are sent as `GKSession` messages between the host and the client.

- **HockeyTableView.** This is the most important file in the application. It renders the paddles based on touch. It handles the physics necessary to animate the puck. It changes the way it behaves depending on how you connect.

- **HockeyViewController.** This is the controller that plays host to the `HockeyViewTable`. This controller is responsible for standing up the `HockeyTableView`, managing, and delegating peer-to-peer duties.

Understanding the data

`StateData` and `EventData` are used to store and communicate data. `StateData` stores the current state of one of the paddles and the puck. The `HockeyTableView` uses two of these structures—one for each of the paddles it hosts. This is also sent between the client and host as a `GKSession` message:

```
#import <Foundation/Foundation.h>
Typedef struct {
    int packetType;
    int player;
    int step;
    bool intersect;
    CGPoint paddleLocation;
    CGPoint paddleVelocity;
    CGPoint puckLocation;
    CGPoint puckVelocity;
    double puckRotation;
    double puckAngle;
} StateData;
```

`EventData` is used only to communicate major system events. When a goal is scored, this message is sent from the host to the client to communicate the event:

```
typedef struct {
    int packetType;
    int eventType;
    int clientScore;
    int hostScore;
} EventData;
```

What is needed to draw the hockey table

Next is the first piece of the `HockeyTableView` header—this is the big one. The following definitions supply several knobs to turn so you can fine-tune the behavior and physics of the hockey table:

```
#define ANIMATION_INTERVAL 1.0 / 60.0
#define MAX_TOP_PLAYER_Y 200
#define MIN_BOTTOM_PLAYER_Y 280
#define MAX_PADDLE_STRIKE 15.0
#define MIN_PADDLE_STRIKE 2.5
#define PADDLE_STRIKE 1.5
#define PUCK_DECAY_RATE 0.10
#define PUCK_SPIN_DECAY_RATE 0.05
#define PUCK_DIAMETER 40
#define PUCK_RADIUS 20
#define PADDLE_DIAMETER 80
#define PADDLE_RADIUS 40
#define GOAL_START 80
#define GOAL_END 240
```

The following enumerations are used to define and communicate the different states that the table can assume:

```
typedef enum {
    NO_CONNECTION = 0,
    HEADTOHEAD_CONNECTION,
    HOST_CONNECTION,
    CLIENT_CONNECTION
} ConnectionType;
typedef enum {
    BOTTOM_PLAYER = 0,
    TOP_PLAYER
} PlayerCode;
typedef enum {
    SCORE_MESSAGE = 0,
    WIN_MESSAGE
} MessageCode;
```

`HockeyTableViewDelegate` is a protocol that is used to send an alert when a goal has been scored. This protocol is needed by the `HockeyViewController` so it can send out a message when a goal is scored:

```
@protocol HockeyTableViewDelegate <NSObject>
@optional
- (void)hockeyTableDidScore:(PlayerCode)playerCode;
@end
```

Next is the remaining "public" definition for the `HockeyTableView` interface:

```
@interface HockeyTableView : UIView {

    id<HockeyTableViewDelegate> delegate;

    ConnectionType connectionType;
    CALayer *bottomPaddleLayer;
    CALayer *topPaddleLayer;
    CALayer *puckLayer;
    StateData bottomPaddleData;
    StateData topPaddleData;

    UIImage *goalImage;
    UIImage *blueWinsImage;
    UIImage *redWinsImage;

    int topScore;
    int bottomScore;

    double messageRotation;

    NSTimer *animationTimer;
```

```
        UILabel *scoreLabel;
        UIImageView *messageView;
}
@property (nonatomic,assign) id /*<HockeyTableViewDelegate>*/
    delegate;
@property (nonatomic) StateData bottomPaddleData;
@property (nonatomic) StateData topPaddleData;
@property (nonatomic) ConnectionType connectionType;
- (void)startAnimation;
- (void)stopAnimation;
- (void)updatePuckData:(StateData)puckData;
- (void)displayMessage:(MessageCode)messageCode
    forPlayer:(PlayerCode)playerCode;
@end
```

At the beginning of the implementation of `HockeyTableView` you will see a short list of private methods. It is helpful to separate fields and attributes of the interface this way, especially when a class becomes as large as this one:

```
//  HockeyTableView.m
#import "HockeyTableView.h"
// private methods
@interface HockeyTableView ()
@property (nonatomic, assign) NSTimer *animationTimer;
- (void)initializeContents;
- (void)drawView;
- (void)updateView;
- (void)updatePuck;
- (void)didScore:(PlayerCode)playerCode;
@end
```

In addition to the private section, we have included a handful of helper methods. These methods do not need to access any class members and could be moved out to another global library. The helper methods have been implemented in C instead of Objective-C to illustrate how you can seamlessly blend the two syntaxes in a single project in Xcode:

```
// helper methods
CGPoint normalVector(double x1, double x2, double y1, double y2);
double distance(double x1, double x2, double y1, double y2);
double paddleSpeed(StateData stateData);
void correctTouchPoint(CGPoint *touchPoint);
```

What is needed to communicate and control the hockey table

`HockeyViewController` manages and hosts the `HockeyTableView`. All peer-to-peer communication that occurs between the two devices is managed right here in this class. This has been extremely beneficial in this project because we can come to one place for all of our communication maintenance:

```objc
// HockeyViewController.h
#import <GameKit/GameKit.h>
#import "FlipsideViewController.h"
#import "MainView.h"
#import "HockeyData.h"
#import "MenuViewController.h"
#import "RootViewController.h"
@interface HockeyViewController : UIViewController
    <GKPeerPickerControllerDelegate, GKSessionDelegate, HockeyTableViewDelegate>
    {
    RootViewController *rootViewController;
    MainView *mainView;
    GKPeerPickerController *picker;
    GKSession *session;
    ConnectionType connectionType;
}
@property (nonatomic, retain) GKSession *session;
@property (nonatomic, retain) GKPeerPickerController *picker;
@property (nonatomic, assign) RootViewController *rootViewController;
- (IBAction)showInfo;
- (IBAction)showMenu;
- (void)sendData;
- (void)showPeerPicker;
- (void)startNearby;
- (void)startHeadToHead;
@end
```

Focusing on the details

Hopefully, the bird's-eye-view tour you just took of the class headers has helped you to see the big picture more clearly. For the rest of the code analysis, we will take you to ground level and review the details of the code. Please realize that not every method that makes `HockeyTable View` and `HockeyViewController` has been listed here. Several methods in these classes are the same run-of-the-mill methods you deal with every day in iPhone development. Remember, you can always download the entire project from `http://appsamuck.com/gamedevbook/airhockey` to see all the mundane details.

First we are going to look at method implementations for the class `HockeyTableView`, then we'll look at the ones for the class `HockeyViewController`.

Setting up a hockey table

The method `initializeComponents` of `HockeyTableView` is called during the construction of the class. This method is responsible for the following:

- Constructing and initializing `CALayer` instances for the two paddles and the puck.
- Loading images for the paddles and puck.
- Loading a background image for our table.

- Setting the initial position of the paddles and puck. The "actual" position of the paddles and puck are recorded in `StateData` structures `bottomPaddleData` and `topPaddleData`. This allows the application to easily grab this information and move it around. This is a requirement for our `GKSession` used in `HockeyViewController`.
- Constructing a `UILabel` to display the score.
- Preloading the `UIImage` objects `goalImage`, `blueWinsImage`, and `redWins Image`. These images are used in the method `displayMessage` listed further down in Listing 7.2.

Listing 7.2

Initializing All of the Game Components

```
- (void)initializeContents {

    self.multipleTouchEnabled = true;

    CGImageRef puckImg = [[UIImage imageWithContentsOfFile:[[NSBundle mainBundle]
        pathForResource:@"AmuckPuck" ofType:@"png"]] CGImage];
    puckLayer = [CALayer layer];
    puckLayer.frame = CGRectMake(0.0, 0.0, CGImageGetWidth(puckImg),
        CGImageGetHeight(puckImg));
    puckLayer.contents = (id)puckImg;
    puckLayer.anchorPoint = CGPointMake(0.5, 0.5);

    CGImageRef paddle1Img = [[UIImage imageWithContentsOfFile:[[NSBundle
        mainBundle] pathForResource:@"RedPaddle" ofType:@"png"]] CGImage];
    bottomPaddleLayer = [CALayer layer];
    bottomPaddleLayer.frame = CGRectMake(0.0, 0.0, CGImageGetWidth(paddle1Img),
        CGImageGetHeight(paddle1Img));
    bottomPaddleLayer.contents = (id)paddle1Img;
    bottomPaddleLayer.anchorPoint = CGPointMake(0.5, 0.57);

    CGImageRef paddle2Img = [[UIImage imageWithContentsOfFile:[[NSBundle
        mainBundle] pathForResource:@"BluePaddle" ofType:@"png"]] CGImage];
    topPaddleLayer = [CALayer layer];
    topPaddleLayer.frame = CGRectMake(0.0, 0.0, CGImageGetWidth(paddle2Img),
        CGImageGetHeight(paddle2Img));
    topPaddleLayer.contents = (id)paddle2Img;
    topPaddleLayer.anchorPoint = CGPointMake(0.5, 0.57);

    bottomPaddleData.paddleLocation = CGPointMake(160, 380);
    topPaddleData.paddleLocation = CGPointMake(160, 100);
    bottomPaddleData.puckLocation = CGPointMake(160, 250);
    bottomPaddleData.puckVelocity = CGPointMake(0, 0);

    // Set the background image
```

```
CGImageRef bgImg = [[UIImage imageWithContentsOfFile:[[NSBundle mainBundle]
   pathForResource:@"stagebg" ofType:@"png"]] CGImage];
self.layer.contents = (id)bgImg;

// Add our sublayers
[self.layer insertSublayer:puckLayer above:self.layer];
[self.layer insertSublayer:bottomPaddleLayer above:self.layer];
[self.layer insertSublayer:topPaddleLayer above:self.layer];

// Prevent things from drawing outside our layer bounds
self.layer.masksToBounds = YES;

// add a label to display the score
scoreLabel = [[UILabel alloc] initWithFrame:CGRectMake(10.0, 10.0, 150.0,
   25.0)];
scoreLabel.textColor = [UIColor whiteColor];
scoreLabel.backgroundColor = [UIColor clearColor];
scoreLabel.font = [UIFont fontWithName:@"Arial" size:18];
scoreLabel.alpha = 0.5;
[self addSubview:scoreLabel];
[self bringSubviewToFront:scoreLabel];

// load images for messages
goalImage = [UIImage imageNamed:@"Goal.png"];
blueWinsImage = [UIImage imageNamed:@"BlueWins.png"];
redWinsImage = [UIImage imageNamed:@"RedWins.png"];

}
```

Using Core Animation

Today it is fairly common for 2-D games to be powered by 3-D graphics. Graphics accelerators are equipped with powerful capabilities. They can blend, rotate, translate, and more without taxing the processor. Therefore, it makes more sense to use the 3-D accelerator to draw in 2-D than it does to try and manage the pixels by hand. In fact, all the views and animations we have used so far are built on top of an underlying 3-D engine.

Until now we have been using UIViews for all of our graphics needs. We could do the same for this game, but this is a great opportunity to pull back the layers a little and work directly with Core Animation. Core Animation is built directly on top of OpenGL ES, so we get the benefits of 3-D acceleration but without the full complexity of a 3-D environment.

If you have done game programming in the past, you may have used a game loop. It really makes sense for AmuckPuck to update the position of items in a game loop, especially the puck. In order to make this happen, we dropped down a level so we could work directly with

CALayer objects. The methods startAnimation and stopAnimation manage an NSTimer object, which is the basis for our game loop. On each pulse of the timer, animate View is called, which in turn calls updateView and drawView:

```
- (void)startAnimation {
    animationTimer = [NSTimer scheduledTimerWithTimeInterval:ANIMATION_INTERVAL
        target:self selector:@selector(animateView) userInfo:nil repeats:YES];
}
- (void)stopAnimation {
    animationTimer = nil;
}
#pragma mark Animate Layers
- (void) animateView {
    [self updateView];
    [self drawView];
}
```

Separation of game logic into updateView and drawView was the goal of using CALayer objects and the NSTimer. This allows the application to manage positional data and game physics in the method updateView. Then we can code rendering and drawing separately in the method drawView.

Now inside the method drawView we can manually change the position of each CALayer. Remember that position, velocity, and rotation puck and paddles are managed in structures that are not part of the CALayer. In the updateView method, we update the position inside of the structures independent of the layers. When this is complete and drawView is called, we render the view by updating the CALayer objects with data from these structures inside of a CATransaction:

```
- (void)drawView {
    // Wrap these layer changes in a transaction and set the animation
    // duration to 0 so we don't get implicit animation
    [CATransaction begin];
    [CATransaction setValue:[NSNumber numberWithDouble:0.]
        forKey:kCATransactionAnimationDuration];

    // Position the paddle
    bottomPaddleLayer.position = bottomPaddleData.paddleLocation;
    topPaddleLayer.position = topPaddleData.paddleLocation;
    puckLayer.position = bottomPaddleData.puckLocation;
    puckLayer.transform = CATransform3DMakeRotation(bottomPaddleData.puckAngle,
        0., 0., 1.);

    if (messageView) {
        messageView.layer.transform = CATransform3DMakeRotation(messageRotation,
            0., 0., 1.);
    }

    [CATransaction commit];
}
```

Notice that in `drawView` we are updating the internal `CALayer` of the `UIView message View`. This is an example of how the `UIView` and `CALayer` can work together. This is being implemented in this manner because it gives us a smooth rotation of the `messageView` that will continue over the course of two separate animations. We will show the rest of the message animation a little later in the chapter.

Calculating believable physics

For a game like this, physics are necessary to emulate a realistic experience. Calculating believable physics can be a real challenge. The following methods are full of calculations, algorithms, and math, working hard to produce believable physics of the puck bouncing around on the hockey table:

```
- (void) updateView {

    if (connectionType != CLIENT_CONNECTION) {
        [self updatePuck];
    }

    // update the message rotation; this is only used if messageView
    // is visible;
    if (messageView) {
        messageRotation += 0.05;
        if (messageRotation > 100*3.24)
            messageRotation = messageRotation - (100*3.24);
    }
}
```

In the `updateView` method above, you see a call out to `updatePuck`. This method is really the meat of the physics engine. The function of each line in this method is not as easily discoverable as most of the others. To compensate, `updatePuck` is decorated with comments much more heavily than the norm (Listing 7.3).

Listing 7.3

Calculating the Next Position of the Puck

```
- (void)updatePuck {

    // handle the puck hitting the paddle
    // Calculate the distance between the centers of the puck and the paddle
    double dist = distance(bottomPaddleData.puckLocation.x,
        bottomPaddleData.paddleLocation.x, bottomPaddleData.puckLocation.y,
        bottomPaddleData.paddleLocation.y);
    if (!bottomPaddleData.intersect & dist < (PADDLE_RADIUS + PUCK_RADIUS)) {
        // calculate a normal vector from the paddle to the puck
        CGPoint vector = normalVector(bottomPaddleData.puckLocation.x,
            bottomPaddleData.paddleLocation.x, bottomPaddleData.puckLocation.y,
```

continued

Listing 7.3 *(continued)*

```
      bottomPaddleData.paddleLocation.y);
    double speed = paddleSpeed(bottomPaddleData);
    vector.x = vector.x * speed;
    vector.y = vector.y * speed;
    // update the velocity of the puck
    bottomPaddleData.puckVelocity.x = vector.x;
    bottomPaddleData.puckVelocity.y = vector.y;
    bottomPaddleData.intersect = true;
}
else
    bottomPaddleData.intersect = false;

dist = distance(bottomPaddleData.puckLocation.x,
    topPaddleData.paddleLocation.x, bottomPaddleData.puckLocation.y,
    topPaddleData.paddleLocation.y);
if (!topPaddleData.intersect & dist < (PADDLE_RADIUS + PUCK_RADIUS)) {
    // calculate a normal vector from the paddle to the puck
    CGPoint vector = normalVector(bottomPaddleData.puckLocation.x,
        topPaddleData.paddleLocation.x, bottomPaddleData.puckLocation.y,
        topPaddleData.paddleLocation.y);
    double speed = paddleSpeed(topPaddleData);
    vector.x = vector.x * speed;
    vector.y = vector.y * speed;
    // update the velodity of the puck
    bottomPaddleData.puckVelocity.x = vector.x;
    bottomPaddleData.puckVelocity.y = vector.y;
    bottomPaddleData.intersect = true;
}
else
    bottomPaddleData.intersect = false;


// decay the velocity of the puck
if (bottomPaddleData.puckVelocity.x > 0.3)
    bottomPaddleData.puckVelocity.x += -PUCK_DECAY_RATE;
else if (bottomPaddleData.puckVelocity.x < -0.3)
    bottomPaddleData.puckVelocity.x += PUCK_DECAY_RATE;

if (bottomPaddleData.puckVelocity.y > 0.3)
    bottomPaddleData.puckVelocity.y += -PUCK_DECAY_RATE;
else if (bottomPaddleData.puckVelocity.y < -0.3)
    bottomPaddleData.puckVelocity.y += PUCK_DECAY_RATE;

// apply terminal velocity.
// the puck should not be traveling so fast that it can pass
// through the paddle without intersecting with it
if (bottomPaddleData.puckVelocity.x > PADDLE_RADIUS)
    bottomPaddleData.puckVelocity.x = PADDLE_RADIUS;
else if (bottomPaddleData.puckVelocity.x < -PADDLE_RADIUS)
    bottomPaddleData.puckVelocity.x = PADDLE_RADIUS;
```

```
if (bottomPaddleData.puckVelocity.y > PADDLE_RADIUS)
   bottomPaddleData.puckVelocity.y = PADDLE_RADIUS;
else if (bottomPaddleData.puckVelocity.y < -PADDLE_RADIUS)
   bottomPaddleData.puckVelocity.y = PADDLE_RADIUS;


// decay the rotation of the puck
if (bottomPaddleData.puckRotation > 0.001)
   bottomPaddleData.puckRotation += -PUCK_SPIN_DECAY_RATE;
else if (bottomPaddleData.puckRotation < -0.001)
   bottomPaddleData.puckRotation += PUCK_SPIN_DECAY_RATE;

// move the puck as prescribed by the rotation
bottomPaddleData.puckAngle += bottomPaddleData.puckRotation;
if (bottomPaddleData.puckAngle > 360.0)
   bottomPaddleData.puckAngle = bottomPaddleData.puckAngle - 360.0;

// move the puck as prescribed by the velocity
bottomPaddleData.puckLocation.x += bottomPaddleData.puckVelocity.x;
bottomPaddleData.puckLocation.y += bottomPaddleData.puckVelocity.y;

// bounce the puck off left and right walls
if ((bottomPaddleData.puckLocation.x + PUCK_RADIUS) > 320) {
   // invert the velocity
   bottomPaddleData.puckVelocity.x = -bottomPaddleData.puckVelocity.x;
   // move the puck back inbounds before it is drawn
   bottomPaddleData.puckLocation.x = 320 - PUCK_RADIUS;
   // change the rotation of the puck according to the angle and speed
   // that it strikes the wall
   bottomPaddleData.puckRotation +=
      -(bottomPaddleData.puckVelocity.y * 0.005);
}
if ((bottomPaddleData.puckLocation.x - PUCK_RADIUS) < 0) {
   bottomPaddleData.puckVelocity.x = -bottomPaddleData.puckVelocity.x;
   bottomPaddleData.puckLocation.x = PUCK_RADIUS;
   bottomPaddleData.puckRotation +=
      (bottomPaddleData.puckVelocity.y * 0.005);
}

// bounce the puck off the top and bottom walls
if (!messageView) {
   if ((bottomPaddleData.puckLocation.y + PUCK_RADIUS) > 480) {
      // let the puck go if it is headed through the goal
      if ((bottomPaddleData.puckLocation.x < GOAL_START)
         | (bottomPaddleData.puckLocation.x > GOAL_END)) {
         bottomPaddleData.puckVelocity.y = -bottomPaddleData.puckVelocity.y;
         bottomPaddleData.puckLocation.y = 480 -PUCK_RADIUS;
         bottomPaddleData.puckRotation +=
            (bottomPaddleData.puckVelocity.x * 0.005);
      }
      else {
```

continued

Listing 7.3 *(continued)*

```
            [self didScore:BOTTOM_PLAYER];
        }
    }
    if ((bottomPaddleData.puckLocation.y - PUCK_RADIUS) < 0) {
        if ((bottomPaddleData.puckLocation.x < GOAL_START)
            | (bottomPaddleData.puckLocation.x > GOAL_END)) {
            bottomPaddleData.puckVelocity.y = -bottomPaddleData.puckVelocity.y;
            bottomPaddleData.puckLocation.y = PUCK_RADIUS;
            bottomPaddleData.puckRotation +=
                -(bottomPaddleData.puckVelocity.x * 0.005);
        }
        else {
            [self didScore:TOP_PLAYER];
        }
    }
}
}
```

Separating logic for host, client, and head-to-head

You may have noticed the `connectionType` flag in some of the previous code listings. This is used to indicate the connection type of the application. In its current version, the application can be connected as follows:

- Head-to-head
- Peer-to-peer host
- Peer-to-peer client

In a head-to-head connection, updates to the puck and paddles are all handled and maintained on a single device. Also, Multi-Touch has to be enabled since two touches (one for each paddle) are observed at the same time. The top player is only updated *locally* in head-to-head connections (Listing 7.4).

Listing 7.4

Change the Position of the Paddles Based on the Last Touch Location

```
- (void)updatePaddlesWithTouches:(NSSet *)touches {
    NSArray *allTouches = [touches allObjects];
    int count = [allTouches count];
    if (count > 0) {
        for (int i=0; i<count;i++) {
            UITouch *touch = [allTouches objectAtIndex:i];
```

```
        CGPoint touchPoint = [touch locationInView:self];

        // if the touchPoint is out of bounds we need to correct it
        correctTouchPoint(&touchPoint);

        if (connectionType == HEADTOHEAD_CONNECTION &
            touchPoint.y < MAX_TOP_PLAYER_Y) {
            topPaddleData.paddleVelocity.x =
                touchPoint.x - topPaddleData.paddleLocation.x ;
            topPaddleData.paddleVelocity.y =
                touchPoint.y - topPaddleData.paddleLocation.y;
            topPaddleData.paddleLocation.x = touchPoint.x;
            topPaddleData.paddleLocation.y = touchPoint.y;
        }
        else if (touchPoint.y > MIN_BOTTOM_PLAYER_Y) {
            bottomPaddleData.paddleVelocity.x =
                touchPoint.x - bottomPaddleData.paddleLocation.x;
            bottomPaddleData.paddleVelocity.y =
                touchPoint.y - bottomPaddleData.paddleLocation.y;
            bottomPaddleData.paddleLocation.x = touchPoint.x;
            bottomPaddleData.paddleLocation.y = touchPoint.y;
        }
        }
    }
}
- (void)touchesBegan:(NSSet *)touches withEvent:(UIEvent *)event {
    [self updatePaddlesWithTouches:touches];
}

- (void)touchesMoved:(NSSet *)touches withEvent:(UIEvent *)event {
    [self updatePaddlesWithTouches:touches];
}

- (void)touchesEnded:(NSSet *)touches withEvent:(UIEvent *)event {
    [self updatePaddlesWithTouches:touches];
}
```

Another important thing to notice in the method `updateView` (repeated below) is that `updatePuck` is not called for client connections:

```
- (void) updateView {

    if (connectionType != CLIENT_CONNECTION) {
        [self updatePuck];
    }
    ...
}
```

In a peer-to-peer client connection, the top player is updated whenever data is received remotely from the method `updatePuckData`:

```
- (void)updatePuckData:(StateData)puckData {
    bottomPaddleData.puckLocation.x = 320 - puckData.puckLocation.x;
    bottomPaddleData.puckLocation.y = 480 - puckData.puckLocation.y;
    bottomPaddleData.puckRotation = puckData.puckRotation;
    bottomPaddleData.puckVelocity.x = 320 - puckData.puckVelocity.x;
    bottomPaddleData.puckVelocity.y = 480 - puckData.puckVelocity.y;
}
```

The previous method ultimately receives its data from a message sent from a peer-to-peer host. This way puck physics are calculated only on one of the two devices. The `sendData` and `receiveData` methods from `HockeyViewController` implement this functionality (Listing 7.5).

Listing 7.5

Using Game Kit Methods to Send and Receive Data Between Two Devices

```
- (void)sendData {
  if (mainView.connectionType == HEADTOHEAD_CONNECTION) return;

  StateData paddleData = mainView.bottomPaddleData;
  NSData *data = [[NSData alloc] initWithBytes:&paddleData
     length:sizeof(StateData)];
  [session sendDataToAllPeers :data withDataMode:GKSendDataUnreliable
     error:nil];
}
- (void) receiveData:(NSData *)remoteData fromPeer:(NSString *)peer
   inSession: (GKSession *)session context:(void *)context {


  int messageType;
  [remoteData getBytes:&messageType length:sizeof(int)];
  if (messageType == 0) {
     StateData paddleData;
     [remoteData getBytes:&paddleData length:sizeof(StateData)];

     // Remote player should display on top so we need
     // to invert the values
     paddleData.paddleLocation.x = 320 - paddleData.paddleLocation.x;
     paddleData.paddleLocation.y = 480 - paddleData.paddleLocation.y;

     mainView.topPaddleData = paddleData;

     // if we are a client we need to copy puck data sent from the host
     if (mainView.connectionType == CLIENT_CONNECTION ) {
        [mainView updatePuckData:paddleData];
```

```
    }

    [self sendData];
}
else {
    EventData eventData;
    [remoteData getBytes:&eventData length:sizeof(EventData)];
    [mainView displayMessage:SCORE_MESSAGE forPlayer:TOP_PLAYER];
}
}
```

Note that `receiveData` inverts the paddle and puck positions that are received from the peer. This way, in peer-to-peer connections, each player controls the paddle on the bottom of the screen.

Back in the `HockeyTableView` class, the method `didScore` is called whenever a player scores a goal. We list this method here to highlight the fact that it calls out to the delegate method `hockeyTableDidScore` conditionally, depending on connection type:

```
- (void)didScore:(PlayerCode)playerCode {

    if (messageView) return;

    if ((bottomPaddleData.puckLocation.y > 480 + PUCK_DIAMETER)
        | (bottomPaddleData.puckLocation.y < -PUCK_DIAMETER)) {
        bottomPaddleData.puckVelocity.x = 0;
        bottomPaddleData.puckVelocity.y = 0;
        [self displayMessage:SCORE_MESSAGE forPlayer:playerCode];
        if (connectionType == HOST_CONNECTION) {
            [delegate hockeyTableDidScore:playerCode];
        }
    }
}
```

This method is needed because all puck movements are calculated on the host in peer-to-peer and the client never knows when the player scores. Calling out to this delegate sends the appropriate message to the client, as seen in the following method `hockeyTableDidScore` from `HockeyViewController`:

```
- (void)hockeyTableDidScore:(PlayerCode)playerCode {
    EventData eventData;
    eventData.packetType = 1;
    NSData *dataPacket = [[NSData alloc] initWithBytes:&eventData
        length:sizeof(EventData)];
    [session sendDataToAllPeers:dataPacket
    withDataMode:GKSendDataReliable
        error:nil];
}
```

Adding a splash of glitz

Earlier in the chapter we discussed how each client is notified when a goal is made. When a player does score, we added a circular "Goal" message that zooms in and out of view while rotating (Figure 7.19).

Figure 7.19

An animated message is displayed after a goal is scored.

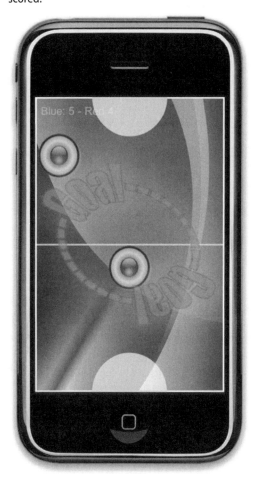

A call to `displayMessage` starts this animation and plays it all the way through. If you run the app you will see that the message zooms out from the center and then pauses for a second. After the pause, the message expands and fades until it is no longer visible:

```
- (void)displayMessage:(MessageCode)messageCode forPlayer:(PlayerCode)playerCode
  {

    UIImage *messageImage = goalImage;
    if (messageCode == WIN_MESSAGE) {
        if (messageCode == BOTTOM_PLAYER)
            messageImage = connectionType =
                CLIENT_CONNECTION ? redWinsImage : blueWinsImage;
        else if (messageCode == TOP_PLAYER)
            messageImage = connectionType =
                CLIENT_CONNECTION ? blueWinsImage : redWinsImage;
    }

    messageView = [[UIImageView alloc] initWithImage:messageImage];
    [goalImage release];
    messageView.alpha = 0.0;
    messageView.frame = CGRectMake(self.center.x, self.center.y, 0.0, 0.0);

    [self addSubview:messageView];
    [self bringSubviewToFront:messageView];

    [UIView beginAnimations:nil context:messageView];
    [UIView setAnimationDuration:0.75];
    [UIView setAnimationCurve:UIViewAnimationCurveLinear];
    [messageView setAlpha:0.5];
    messageView.frame = CGRectMake(self.center.x-150.0, self.center.y-150.0,
        300.0, 300.0);
    messageView.tag = 0;
    [UIView setAnimationDelegate:self];
    [UIView setAnimationDidStopSelector:
        @selector(animateMessageDidStop:finished:context:) ];
    [UIView commitAnimations];
  }
```

By having one animation begin after another ends, we create a nice effect for the game. This is accomplished by assigning `animateMessageDidStop` as the selector in the call to the `setAnimationDidStopSelector` method above. Notice that `animateMessageDidStop` also points its selector back to itself, which provides a nice place to do some cleanup:

```
- (void)animateMessageDidStop:(NSString *)animationID finished:
    (NSNumber *)finished context:(void *)context {
    if (messageView.tag == 1) {
        bottomPaddleData.puckLocation = CGPointMake(160, 250);
        bottomPaddleData.puckVelocity = CGPointMake(0, 0);
        [messageView release];
        messageView = nil;
        return;
    }
    [UIView beginAnimations:nil context:messageView];
    [UIView setAnimationDelay:2.0];
```

```
[UIView setAnimationDuration:0.75];
[UIView setAnimationCurve:UIViewAnimationCurveLinear];
[messageView setAlpha:0.0];
messageView.frame = CGRectMake(self.center.x-750.0, self.center.y-750.0,
    1500.0, 1500.0);
messageView.tag = 1;
[UIView setAnimationDelegate:self];
[UIView setAnimationDidStopSelector:
    @selector(animateMessageDidStop:finished:context:) ];
[UIView commitAnimations];
}
```

During the entire animation, the message is rotated. The rotation is applied to the `CALayer` of the `UIImageView` in the `drawMethod` you saw earlier:

```
if (messageView) {
    messageView.layer.transform = CATransform3DMakeRotation(messageRotation,
        0., 0., 1.);
}
```

Reviewing the last pieces

A handful of helper methods are used to abstract out some of the common logic needed throughout the previous code listings. They are listed here to help connect the last dots of the code in `HockeyTableView`. Listing 7.6 returns a normal vector between x1, y1, and x2; y2 is used to represent direction. It then returns the distance between two points, calculates the speed of the paddle, and prevents the paddle from sliding past its boundary.

Listing 7.6

Helper Methods Used in AmuckPuck

```
CGPoint normalVector(double x1, double x2, double y1, double y2) {
    double run = x1 - x2;
    double rise = y1 - y2;
    double total = abs(rise) + abs(run);
    CGPoint vector;
    vector.x = run / total;
    vector.y = rise / total;
    return vector;
}
double distance(double x1, double x2, double y1, double y2) {
    return sqrt(pow(x1 -x2, 2) + pow(y1 - y2, 2));
}
double paddleSpeed(StateData stateData) {
    double speed = sqrt(pow(stateData.paddleVelocity.x, 2)
        + pow(stateData.paddleVelocity.y, 2));
    speed = abs(speed * PADDLE_STRIKE);
    if (speed > MAX_PADDLE_STRIKE)
        return MAX_PADDLE_STRIKE;
```

```
    if (speed < MIN_PADDLE_STRIKE)
        return MIN_PADDLE_STRIKE;
    return speed;
}
void correctTouchPoint(CGPoint *touchPoint) {
    if ((*touchPoint).x - PADDLE_RADIUS < 0)
        (*touchPoint).x = PADDLE_RADIUS;
    if ((*touchPoint).x + PADDLE_RADIUS > 320)
        (*touchPoint).x = 320 - PADDLE_RADIUS;
    if ((*touchPoint).y - PADDLE_RADIUS < 0)
        (*touchPoint).y = PADDLE_RADIUS;
    if ((*touchPoint).y + PADDLE_RADIUS > 480)
        (*touchPoint).y = 480 - PADDLE_RADIUS;
}
@end
```

Connecting to players with peer-to-peer

The `HockeyViewController` is the final class we will be discussing. This class is responsible for managing our `GKSession` and `GKPeerPickerController` objects. The process is the same as it was in P2P Chat, so you should find the code familiar.

Sending and receiving messages

The methods `connectionType` and `startNearby` are straightforward but noteworthy. When a player selects a game type from the menu, these methods are called to record `connectionType` internally. Peer-to-peer connections start as a host connection and then one peer switches to the client during the connection process:

```
- (void)startNearby {
    connectionType = HOST_CONNECTION;
}
- (void)startHeadToHead {
    connectionType = HEADTOHEAD_CONNECTION;
}
```

The `receiveData` method is called by your `GKSession` whenever data is received from a peer. This method was listed in the preceding code to demonstrate how paddle data is sent to the client in a peer-to-peer connection. When looking at it this time, notice how you can discover the message type by partially reading into the data stream. This is very useful since the message containing `StateData` is sent unreliably and the message containing `MessageData` is sent reliably:

```
- (void) receiveData:(NSData *)remoteData fromPeer:(NSString *)peer
    inSession: (GKSession *)session context:(void *)context {

    int messageType;
    [remoteData getBytes:&messageType length:sizeof(int)];
    if (messageType == 0) {
        StateData paddleData;
```

```
      [remoteData getBytes:&paddleData length:sizeof(StateData)];

      // Remote player should display on top so we need
      // to invert the values
      paddleData.paddleLocation.x = 320 - paddleData.paddleLocation.x;
      paddleData.paddleLocation.y = 480 - paddleData.paddleLocation.y;

      mainView.topPaddleData = paddleData;

      // if we are a client we need to copy puck data sent from the host
      if (mainView.connectionType == CLIENT_CONNECTION ) {
         [mainView updatePuckData:paddleData];
      }

      [self sendData];
   }
   else {
      EventData eventData;
      [remoteData getBytes:&eventData length:sizeof(EventData)];
      [mainView displayMessage:SCORE_MESSAGE forPlayer:TOP_PLAYER];
   }
}
```

Calling `hockeyTableDidScore` and `showPeerPicker` sends out the data we just saw being received in the method `receiveData` from the preceeding code:

```
- (void)hockeyTableDidScore:(PlayerCode)playerCode {
   EventData eventData;
   eventData.packetType = 1;
   NSData *dataPacket = [[NSData alloc] initWithBytes:&eventData
      length:sizeof(EventData)];
   [session sendDataToAllPeers:dataPacket withDataMode:GKSendDataReliable
      error:nil];
}
- (void)sendData {
   if (mainView.connectionType == HEADTOHEAD_CONNECTION) return;

   StateData paddleData = mainView.bottomPaddleData;
   NSData *data = [[NSData alloc] initWithBytes:&paddleData
      length:sizeof(StateData)];
   [session sendDataToAllPeers :data withDataMode:GKSendDataUnreliable
      error:nil];
}
```

Establishing a connection between peers

The following code to connect peers is almost identical to that in P2P Chat. However, one very important step stands out. The method `session: didReceiveConnectionRequest-FromPeer` is used to make the distinction that we are the client if it is called (Listing 7.7).

Listing 7.7

Using the Peer Picker to Establish a Connection Between Peers

```
- (void)showPeerPicker {
    // allocate and setup the peer picker controller
    picker  = [[GKPeerPickerController alloc] init];
    picker.delegate = self;
    picker.connectionTypesMask = GKPeerPickerConnectionTypeNearby;
    [picker show];
}
- (void)peerPickerController:(GKPeerPickerController *)picker
        didSelectConnectionType:(GKPeerPickerConnectionType)type {
    if(type == GKPeerPickerConnectionTypeOnline) {
    }
}
- (GKSession *) peerPickerController:(GKPeerPickerController *)picker
    sessionForConnectionType:(GKPeerPickerConnectionType)type {
    session = [[GKSession alloc] initWithSessionID:
        @"com.yourwebsite.yourapplicationname" displayName:nil
        sessionMode:GKSessionModePeer];
    session.delegate = self;
    return session;
}
- (void)peerPickerController:(GKPeerPickerController *)picker
    didConnectToPeer:(NSString *)peerID {
    [self.picker dismiss];
}
- (void)peerPickerControllerDidCancel:(GKPeerPickerController *)picker {
    [self.picker dismiss];
    [self.rootViewController showMenu];
}
- (void)session:(GKSession *)session
    didReceiveConnectionRequestFromPeer:(NSString *)peerID {
    connectionType = CLIENT_CONNECTION;
    mainView.connectionType = CLIENT_CONNECTION;
}
- (void)session:(GKSession *)session peer:(NSString *)peerID
    didChangeState:(GKPeerConnectionState)state {
    switch (state) {
        case GKPeerStateConnected:
            [self.session setDataReceiveHandler :self withContext:nil];
            [self.picker dismiss];
            [self sendData];
            break;
        case GKPeerStateDisconnected:
            break;
    }
}
@end
```

Analyzing Business Aspects

Building an application like AmuckPuck can be a rewarding venture, but it comes with a cost. Bringing together the many technologies can lead to a lot of research, which can spiral out of control if not managed properly. Development costs can increase in terms of both time and money when you consider all the research and trial and error that come into play when pulling it together. Here are a few things to keep in mind while managing a project like this:

- Physics engines require a lot of trial and error. Be sure to abstract out all of your control variables so you can tweak without refactoring.

- Peer-to-peer can be difficult to debug. With one application that behaves differently as client or host, you end up with lots of conditional logic. When making changes, you will need to redeploy over and over on two separate devices and then establish a connection between them to test. This can take a few minutes to test out a single change.

CAUTION

When developing sophisticated peer-to-peer applications, you should not rely on the iPhone Simulator. At least two devices are required for proper testing and debugging. The performance differences between device models means that the serious P2P developer should have at least one of each model of device. For instance, the 2G iPod touch has a faster CPU and fewer background processes and connections to manage than the iPhone 3G.

Summary

AmuckPuck is an application that we love to play ourselves. In fact, some of our beta testers, our kids, enjoyed it so much we had to fight with them to get the devices back. In many cases, your experiences with an application can translate to how well your clients will like it.

In this chapter you learned about the challenges presented when developing multiplayer games and a few techniques for dealing with those challenges. You learned how to use Game Kit to establish a peer-to-peer connection between two devices using Bluetooth. Also, as a bonus, you learned a little about implementing game physics and how important it is to create a believable and immersive experience for your players.

AmuckPuck turned out to be well suited to a peer-to-peer connection. The game play is natural and responsive. This is very encouraging; especially since peer-to-peer is a new technology and will hopefully only get better in future versions. Be prepared for the wave of peer-to-peer applications that will flood the shelves on the App Store.

Taking Turns with Other Players

N ow that you have been exposed to connecting players in real time, the transition to turn-based game play should be relatively straightforward. Turn-based games do not carry the technical obstacles you face in real-time game development. The game state in a turn-based game is much more portable and the players' moves are not as time sensitive. With fewer obstacles, you can connect players in many more ways.

Of course, you can (and should) still use peer-to-peer and head-to-head connections, but now you can easily connect players who are miles away with the assistance of a Web server. In this chapter we'll guide you through the process of creating the client side of an app that calls Web services to share messages between players. This by itself is powerful, but then you are going to throw fuel on the fire by adding push notification. With push notification you can give a player the power to initiate a game with a friend who may not even have your application up and running. Push notification can update a badge, display an alert, and play a sound. When the opponent accepts the challenge from the alert, the game can launch as soon as his friend is ready.

We have chosen to discuss these topics in the context of our version of the classic game tic-tac-toe, which we are calling it Amuck-Tac-Toe. Most turn-based games closely follow the same pattern as a board game. This version of Amuck-Tac-Toe is no different. There are turns, moves, and a common game state for the server to manage and the client to display.

You have probably heard about the value of viral sales time and again. From a business perspective, viral sales should be your overriding goal in turn-based games. For example, assume you want to play Amuck-Tac-Toe with a friend and you know he has an iPhone; however, you don't know if he has the app installed. You could supply your friend's e-mail address and then make your first move, which can send an e-mail to your friend asking her to play. The e-mail she receives contains an iTunes App Store link to install your application. You can expect more and more sales to come from word of mouth as friends ask other friends to compete.

 In This Chapter

Examining turn-based game play

Understanding game design: Strategy

Choosing your connection options

Finding friends to compete against

Programming: Amuck-Tac-Toe

Analyzing business aspects

Examining Turn-Based Game Play

We mentioned that turn-based games present fewer technical obstacles to developers than real-time games do. While packet latency is still present, it does not adversely affect game play, and that makes a huge difference in implementation. In a turn-based game, the client generally only needs to send updates to the other player at the close of each turn. Since latency usually falls in the sub-second range, the other player won't even notice the small delay. In fact, the players spend most of their time waiting on the other player to make a move not on the network.

CROSS-REFERENCE

For more on packet loss and packet latency, see Chapter 7.

Let's examine the flow of the classic tic-tac-toe game to understand the fundamentals of the process. In tic-tac-toe, players take turns placing Xs or Os on a three-by-three grid until one player places three in a row or the game is declared a draw (Figure 8.1).

Figure 8.1

The classic game of tic-tac-toe

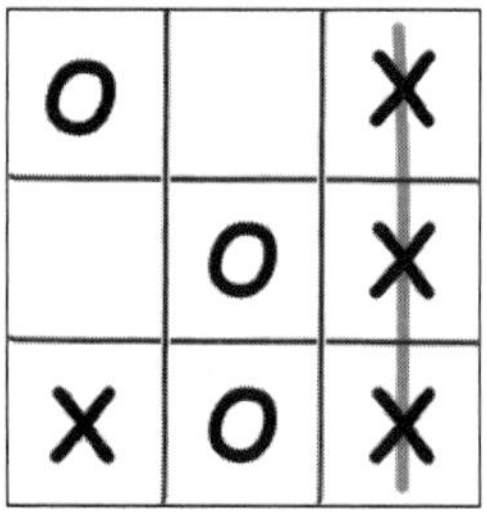

Reviewing the game flow

Now let's break down a full game into all of the moves and steps necessary to carry the play from beginning to end. This will help in understanding how a system could be designed to emulate the same behavior. For this example, we examine the moves when Bob and Laurie play a game of tic-tac-toe (Figure 8.2):

1. Bob moves first, placing an X in the top-right square.

2. Laurie places an O in the middle square.

3. Bob places an X in the bottom-left square.

4. Laurie places an O in the top-left square.

5. Bob places an X in the bottom-right square.

6. Laurie places an O in the bottom-middle square.

7. Bob places an X in the right-middle square, giving him three Xs in a row and winning the game.

Figure 8.2

Bob and Laurie's game of tic-tac-toe

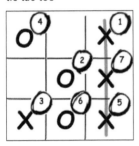

This is simple enough, especially when it is carried out with pencil and paper. Our challenge is to understand the process so we can translate it to game logic.

Understanding the stages

Reflecting on what you just saw in the game, you can extract the different stages and the actions necessary to move through the process. With this information you can construct a diagram that defines and illustrates the relationship between your states and actions (Figure 8.3).

Figure 8.3

A turn-based game diagram helps define the relationship between states and actions.

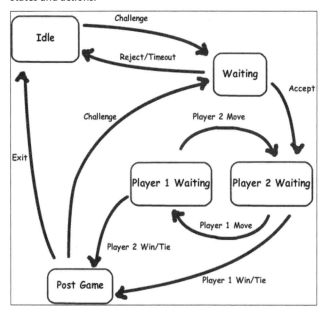

Your application should carry the players through each of these stages. Along the way make sure to keep track of the following game attributes:

- Record information on each player. Make sure you can reconnect later if the connection is lost or if the game play is suspended. Use this same information to quickly start up new matches.
- Record the state at each step in the process. Make sure the game can pick up where it left off.
- Record the game board after each move. For example, in tic-tac-toe you would record the value of every cell in the three-by-three grid.
- As a bonus, keep track of win/loss results between players to foster competiveness.

In the real-time game world we did not try to store the state as it progressed. That would not have been feasible, but it is also much less valuable in a head-to-head or peer-to-peer game. It's important to save the game state so that your players can pause and resume the game at their leisure. This feature of turn-based games can be a huge draw. Games that players would normally never have time to engage in become feasible. A player can spend a few moments making a move, then stick his iPhone back in his pocket until he is alerted that his opponent has made a countermove. In this way games can last for hours or even days.

Understanding Game Design: Strategy

Some turn-based games carry an element of luck, but the best ones are all about strategy. For example, as you saw in Chapter 3, chess is a turn-based game where strategy rules. In chess, players are equally yoked and one does not have an advantage over the other, nor does luck really play a part. Players' moves are based on strategic decisions and not by the roll of the dice or the luck of the draw. The element of strategy is probably one of the reasons this game has stood the test of time. Even though there are only half a dozen different pieces on the board, players develop thousands of different strategies for playing the game.

TIP

A game that requires strategy will hold your players' interest much longer than a game based on luck. Make it your goal to create a game that encourages players to develop and devise strategies. A rich set of rules, boundaries, and options will equip players with the tools necessary to develop personalized strategies they can use to defeat their opponents.

While there is some strategy involved, it's not a strong point of classic tic-tac-toe, because players soon discover what the optimal move is in every situation. If two players know the strategy, their game will always end in a tie. If players had more options, they could mix it up a little and begin to develop more than one strategy to throw at their opponent. This allows players to surprise each other by changing their angle of attack. The lesson here is to make sure your game has enough depth. Challenge your players, help them develop strategy, and you'll keep them coming back for more.

If you look at the current version of Amuck-Tac-Toe, you will see that it is not your typical version of tic-tac-toe (Figure 8.4).

In the design process of the Amuck-Tac-Toe game, we chose to follow the advice we are offering here. Amuck-Tac-Toe is a spiced-up version of classic tic-tac-toe. This was done in an effort to create the additional opportunity for players to develop strategy. We expanded the board to four-by-four. If a player gets three Xs or Os in a row, she scores a point instead of winning. When the board has been filled, the player with the most points wins.

Figure 8.4

As you can see, Amuck-Tac-Toe is not your typical version of tic-tac-toe.

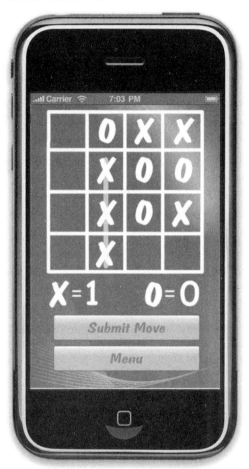

After some test runs on paper, it became obvious that the player who moves first always has the upper hand in the game and can always win. In order to balance the game more, a special cancel move was added. This move can be used by each player once during the game. Here's how the cancel move works. When a player decides to use the cancel move, she chooses a square that the opposing player occupies. For example, if your opponent is using Xs, the cancel move must be placed on a square that already has an X in it. When the cancel move is placed, the X square is converted to the cancel symbol (a circle with a slash through it, shown in Figure 8.5). Now that square will be ignored for the remainder of the game. Neither player can use that square again.

Figure 8.5

Amuck-Tac-Toe after a player uses the special cancel
move to cancel one of the opponent's squares

Simple changes like these are often enough to add a little extra dimension to a classic pastime.
See if you can devise your own strategies to add even more variety and depth to the game.

Choosing Your Connection Options

Turn-based games afford you a great deal of flexibility when it comes to connectivity options.
Most of the time the information necessary to represent a game can be transported and stored
with ease. When developing turn-based games, the game state carries a smaller footprint, the

latency becomes negligible, and reliable messaging becomes the norm. Here are just a few of your many different connection options:

- Head-to-head
- Peer-to-peer
- Web services
- Push notification

Head-to-head

Head-to-head is not just for real-time games. Old-school tic-tac-toe played on paper is a perfect demonstration of a head-to-head game in one of its oldest forms. Usually it does not take a lot of additional effort to incorporate this connection style into your game if it makes sense.

Here are some pros and cons of supporting head-to-head:

Pros

- Two players can play against each other with just a single device.
- It does not require an Internet connection.
- It is usually an easy addition to an existing game.
- Players do not have to deal with establishing a connection to another player.

Cons

- It is difficult for players to conceal moves from each other.
- It does not contribute to viral sales as much as other connection options.
- It does not fit all turn-based game scenarios, especially long-running games.

Peer-to-peer

In Chapter 7 we discussed establishing peer-to-peer connections. Most of the same lessons apply to turn-based games. All you need to do is follow the same steps as you did in the last chapter to establish a connection. The good news is that when you send messages, you don't need to deal with unreliable messages.

Here are some pros and cons of supporting peer-to-peer:

Pros

- It's the easiest way to connect two devices.
- It does not require an Internet connection.
- It does not require a Web server to manage connections.
- It provides more than enough throughput for just about any turn-based game.

Cons

- It's not supported on first-generation iPhones or first-generation iPod touches.
- It requires players to be in close proximity to each other.
- As of this writing, it supports only connecting devices.

Web services

Another option is to connect your players through a central server using Web services. To do this you will need to construct a centralized server that can relay messages between players who are connected. For turn-based games, this can be accomplished with an HTTP server that can serve dynamic content. This should be a straightforward task for anyone who is familiar with hosting dynamic Web pages. To service the needs of a turn-based game, you could use a server side language like PHP, Perl, Java, .NET. . . and the list goes on and on. Whichever technology you pick, you will need to expose services that your application can consume. We'll go into more depth on this topic later in this chapter.

Here are some pros and cons of using Web services:

Pros

- Players can connect to anyone in the world who can connect to the Internet.
- It has a strong potential for viral sales.
- It can connect with all models of iPhones and iPod touches that are connected to the Internet.
- The game state can be stored, so a single game could be played with intermittent interaction over the course of several days.

Cons

- It requires an active Internet connection.
- It requires that the application is running for it to receive messages from the other player.
- You must host your services on a central Web server. This requires monthly fees and ongoing maintenance.
- You have to implement a system for players to advertise, discover, and connect game sessions with players who are miles apart.

Push notification

Push notification is the newest option you have in your bag of tricks. Using push notification in your game will yield results that are very similar to using Web services. The biggest difference is that you have the ability to send messages to players who do not have your application running. As with Web services, we will cover push notification in more detail when we examine the application later in this chapter.

Here are some pros and cons of using push notification:

Pros

- Players can connect to anyone else in world who can connect to the Internet.
- The application is not required to be running for it to receive notifications from other players.
- It has a strong potential for viral sales.
- It can work in conjunction with a game using Web services to connect.
- The game state can be stored, so a single game could be played with intermittent interaction over the course of several days.

Cons

- It requires an active Internet connection.
- It requires that you host your services on a central Web server, which requires monthly fees and ongoing maintenance.
- It requires that you implement a system for players to advertise, discover, and connect game sessions with players who are miles apart.
- It require users to be running on iPhone OS 3.0 version. Not all users necessarily upgrade to the latest firmware, particularly in the case of iPod touch users, where the firmware carries an additional expense.

Finding Friends to Compete Against

If you choose to play with a head-to-head connection, your opponent is obviously sitting right next to you since you are playing on a single device. Likewise, if you choose to play with a peer-to-peer connection, you're playing with a known opponent who is in close proximity. However, when connecting with a friend using Web services, finding an opponent or friend to play with can be a challenge.

When looking at the pros and cons of connecting with Web services, we mentioned that there are some challenges involved in getting players connected. This is an opportunity for you to be creative; however, implementing a system to connect players in a fun and engaging way can be very time consuming. Be sure to carve out sufficient time in your schedule to make it happen, or you might end up with a great game that does not encourage players to connect. On the other side of the coin, if you do a good job here you can increase sales virally.

When finding friends to connect with, you have many options to consider. There are several user stories you can follow that lead to two players becoming connected. It all depends on how much time you want to put into it. Here are a few questions a player should ask about connecting to other players:

- Can I challenge a friend if he has not registered with the game server?
- Can I challenge a friend if she does not have the application running?
- Can I challenge a friend if he does not have the application installed?
- Can I store game results on a leader board?
- Can I connect with random players who are looking for a challenge?

Connecting players with Web services

In order to establish a connection, you will need a server to relay the messages between the two players. The messaging required by a turn-based game can be managed with a standard HTTP server. HTTP servers are commonplace these days and you can program them to manage the game on the server side. You can develop this server logic using a host of different languages. Developing a Web server is outside the scope of this book, but we'll focus on the client side code necessary to connect to such a server. For more information on server side services, go to our Web site, `www.appsamuck.com/gameservices/`. There we have links to resources that will help you build and host your own server side services.

Connecting players with the application installed

Once you have access to a server with the services you need, you can start your connection process. If both of the connecting players have the application installed, establishing a connection is a much smoother process than when it is not installed. There are many ways to approach this process, but the way we have chosen to proceed works much like an e-mail server. In fact, we have chosen the e-mail address to be the value that uniquely identifies players. Here are the basics of the process (see Figure 8.6):

- If the application has been launched and no e-mail address has been supplied, prompt the user for his e-mail address. Preferably you would confirm that the e-mail address actually belongs to the user.
- If the e-mail address is available, search the game server with the e-mail for friends who are challenging the user.
- If the user chooses, he can enter the e-mail address of a friend he wishes to play against. When friends search, they'll see that a buddy is asking to play against them.

You should start with this basic process, but you can (and should) expand on this system to make the process more engaging. For example, you could keep track of a friend list for the user and constantly poll to see if the friends are online. Then the user can just click the name of an online friend and ask him to play.

CAUTION

It is paramount that you make it easy for players to connect or your game will fail. If the connection process is difficult, many players will get frustrated, delete your app, and give you a bad rating.

Figure 8.6

The workflow of two players with the application already installed

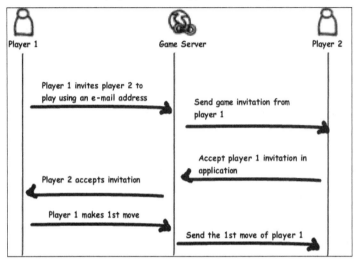

Connecting players without the application installed

Connecting players without the application installed is a slightly bigger challenge. However, this is your opportunity to increase your sales virally. It was no accident that we chose to use the e-mail address as the unique identifier. Not only is it unique and verifiable, but we can also use it to communicate with players outside of the constraints of our application. If a player does not have the application installed, we can simply send an e-mail and ask him to install it. Here is an expanded version of the workflow you just looked at, but now we are sending out an e-mail to player 2 if he does not already have the application installed (Figure 8.7).

Adding push notification to the process

Push notification is an exciting feature added to the iPhone SDK beginning with version 3.0. Without push notification, you are limited to receiving game requests via e-mail, via SMS, or when your game is open. When you add push notification, you can alert players whenever a friend challenges them to a new game or even when they make a new move. With push notification, you can issue the following alert types:

- **Alert box.** An alert box is a standard alert box similar to the one you see when you receive an SMS text message without the application open.

- **Sound.** A sound alert is exactly what you would expect: a sound that plays when the notification is received. The sound that is played must be in your application bundle.

Figure 8.7

The workflow of two players connecting if one does not have the application installed

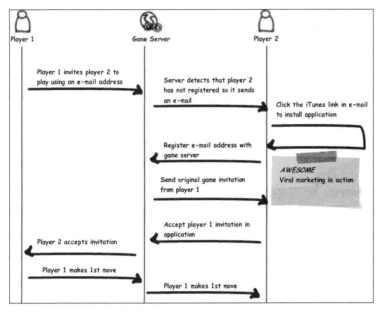

● **Badge.** A badge is a counter that appears in the corner of your application's Home screen. This is the same badge that you see on other applications such as Mail. For example, when you receive e-mails without the e-mail client open, the number in the e-mail badge will be incremented. You can use badges in your application; however, push notification allows you to set the badge value without opening your application.

Adding push notification to your process definitely enriches the user experience. Implementing push notification is a little more of a challenge than setting up a simple Web server. Your server must maintain a connection to the Apple Push Notification server in order to send push notifications. Figure 8.8 shows a modified version of the workflow you saw earlier, but with the Apple Push Notification server included.

Notice in this workflow that player 2 is interrupted with a phone call. Push notification helps you continue the game flow with a user-friendly experience. Again, building the server side of push notification is outside the scope of this book, but there is good documentation on the Apple Developer Connection site, and example implementations of the server can be found in the user forums for several different server side languages. This information is changing daily; for more information, see Appendix A or check our site, `www.appsamuck.com/gameservices/`.

Figure 8.8

The workflow of the game, including the Apple Push Notification server

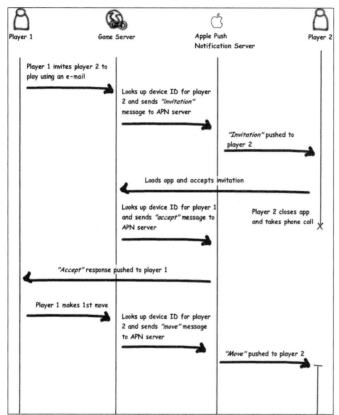

Programming: Amuck-Tac-Toe

If you have followed all of the examples we've presented so far in this book, you already know what is necessary to create iPhone games. The example we explain next will add a few more skills to your repertoire. Amuck-Tac-Toe has a very simple game board and set of rules. We like this because we do not want you to have to spend all of your time learning the details of what makes the game tick. Instead, we want you to focus your attention on the new technologies needed to develop this application. After touching on its design and concepts, you will dig into the details of the app and learn to build turn-based applications of your own.

Designing the application

Any application begins with a good design. Always take time to write down your ideas, even if you just use a napkin. The game screen for Amuck-Tac-Toe is easy enough to envision. We just need a normal tic-tac-toe board with four cells instead of three (Figure 8.9).

Figure 8.9

Amuck-Tac-Toe game screen mock-up

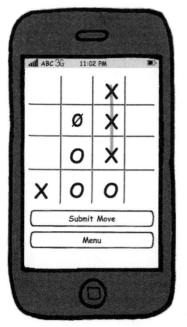

We like Balsamiq Mockups (`www.balsamiq.com`). Using this tool, it is almost as easy to make the mock-ups as if you were sketching them by hand. We used Balsamiq to mock up the game screen. This game has a lot of menu options, so it was handy to mock up the menus before committing a design to code.

The following figures show the menu screens that we mocked up. The first one is the main menu screen—this is the screen that you see when the application first loads (Figure 8.10).

Figure 8.10

Amuck-Tac-Toe main menu screen mock-up

This screen organizes all the options the user needs to be presented to begin playing a game:

- **Head-to-Head.** Choose this option if a player wishes to play a friend sitting next to him using the same device.
- **Nearby.** Choose this option if a player wishes to play a friend nearby on a second device.
- **Internet.** Choose this option if a player wishes to play a friend remotely over the Internet.
- **Continue.** Choose this option if a player wishes to continue a previous game that has not been completed. This allows for a game to be played over the course of days or weeks.
- **Internet Settings.** This option allows the player to change his e-mail address used for identification.

● **About.** This option loads a standard About screen with information about the creators of the game.

In this chapter we're focusing on Internet connections, so we will continue with the mock-ups for these screens. Whenever you click New Internet, the player is given the opportunity to invite or challenge another player to play. When this screen loads, it should look like the one shown in Figure 8.11.

Figure 8.11

Amuck-Tac-Toe screen mock-up to invite a friend to play

This is the screen that collects the e-mail address necessary to initiate a game with a friend. Once he clicks the Invite button, the player who initiated the game must wait until the player he challenged accepts the challenge. In the event that the initiator closes the Amuck-Tac-Toe application before the friend accepts the challenge, the game is not aborted. The initiator can click Continue at any time to see if the opponent has accepted the challenge (Figure 8.12).

NOTE

If you are clever in your implementation, you can allow your players to manage several games at once with different friends. This is a great advantage of turn-based games that may not always be feasible in real-time games. When you add push notification to your game, the process gets really powerful. Now, when your friend accepts the challenge, the notification can display as an alert even when the Amuck-Tac-Toe application is closed.

Figure 8.12

Amuck-Tac-Toe Continue Game
screen mock-up

Abstracting for separation and reuse

In Amuck-Tac-Toe, we allow players to connect using three different methods. Each of the three methods of connectivity follows a different paradigm. However, the game follows the same rules and workflow regardless of the connection method. For this reason we should abstract the connection details away from the game controller. One way to handle this is to put all of our connectivity logic in a black box that implements the same properties and methods for each of our connectivity types.

To achieve this type of abstraction, a factory pattern works well. You need a factory that instantiates each of your connection types and returns each of them on demand as a common interface. Following is the definition for the base interface and supporting types used in the example:

```
#import <Foundation/Foundation.h>
typedef enum {
    GameConnectionMessageError = 0,
    GameConnectionMessageConnect,
    GameConnectionMessageDisconnect,
```

```
    GameConnectionMessageSessionId,
    GameConnectionMessageData,
    GameConnectionMessageCustom
} GameConnectionMessageType;
@protocol GameConnectionDelegate <NSObject>
@optional
- (void) receiveMessage:(NSString*)message
      ofType:(GameConnectionMessageType)messageType;
@end
@interface GameConnection: NSObject {
    id <GameConnectionDelegate> _delegate;
}
@property(nonatomic,assign) id /*<GameConnectionDelegate>*/ delegate;
- (void) connectWithPlayerName: (NSString*)playerName;
- (void) connectWithSessionId:(NSString*)sessionId;
- (void) sendMessage:(NSString*)message
      asType:(GameConnectionMessageType)messageType;
+ (GameConnection*) createWithName:(NSString*)gameConnectionClassName
    delegate:(id)gameConnectionDelegate;
@end
```

There is very little in the implementation of this interface. This class defines how a game connection should send and receive messages in a common fashion. Now the implementation can be deferred to overloading classes. This gives you the ability to extend your application by adding new implementations of the GameConnection class. Each implementation can introduce a new type of connection without changing the actual code for the Game View.

This class can also create the overloading class by passing in the name of the game connection class you want to create to the method createWithName: delegate:. Here are the details of this powerful method:

```
+ (GameConnection*) createWithName:(NSString*)gameConnectionClassName
    delegate:(id)gameConnectionDelegate {
    id obj = [[NSClassFromString(gameConnectionClassName) alloc] init];
    if (obj == nil) {
       [NSException raise:@"Invalid game connection class name" format:
          @"The game connection class '%@' was not found and cannot be created",
          gameConnectionClassName];
    }
    GameConnection *gameConnection = (GameConnection*)obj;
    gameConnection.delegate = gameConnectionDelegate;
    return gameConnection;
}
```

This method uses NSClassFromString to instantiate a GameConnection class from its name. If the class cannot be constructed, the method throws an exception. This method is very nice because now the class GameConnection can be completely oblivious to the implementation of any other GameConnection derivative classes.

Examining the details

Now that you have an understanding of how to separate your connection concerns, you can look at the details of this example that differ from the applications you have reviewed up until now. There are a lot of details to this application, but most should be quite familiar to you by now. You can download the full application source to the completed version (Figure 8.13) of Amuck-Tac-Toe from `http://appsamuck.com/gamedevbook/amktactoe`.

Figure 8.13

Amuck-Tac-Toe is an example of a multiplayer turn-based game.

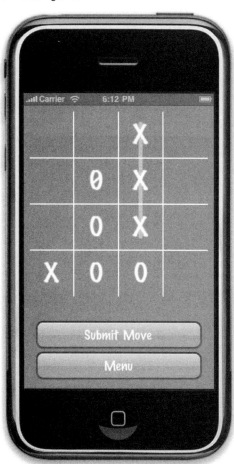

Here are a few items that you may not be familiar with:

- Displaying data in a `UITableView`
- Calling Web services using `NSURLConnection`
- Receiving notifications from Apple Push Notification

These items are fairly straightforward to grasp, and they add a tremendous amount of power to your application. We will start by examining the table view.

Presenting options with a table view

Even though we have not covered it, you should be familiar with the appearance of a table view. The `UITableView` is a very common element in iPhone development. You see it in many of the native apps, such as Settings, Contacts, and Phone. The `UITableView` is an ideal choice for you to use in your game menus, as shown in Figure 8.14.

In most cases, the `UITableView` works in close relation to a `UINavigationBar`. Together these two components create the slide in and out navigation you have become accustomed to on the iPhone. To create this effect, you need to implement the `UITableViewDelegate` method and push and pop view controllers to the navigation stack. The following listing comes from the main menu screen of Amuck-Tac-Toe, which does just that.

The method `viewDidLoad` is used to set up a background color that is tiled. This is done by creating a pattern image color:

```
- (void)viewDidLoad {
    [super viewDidLoad];
    // The title of the main view controller will be used as the title of the
    // navigation bar.
    // This is actually a nice feature of the MVC architecture because if you
    // decide to use a tab view instead it will use the same title.
    self.title = @"Amuck-Tac-Toe Menu";
    UIImage *backgroundImage = [UIImage imageNamed:@"chalkGreen.png"];
    self.view.backgroundColor = [[UIColor alloc]
        initWithPatternImage:backgroundImage];
    self.tableView.sectionHeaderHeight = 30.0f;
    [backgroundImage release];
}
```

Figure 8.14

Select how to connect to other players in the Amuck-Tac-Toe main menu.

The method `numberOfSectionsInTableView:` returns the number of sections in a given table view. In our table view we have two. The first is Connection Types and the second is About and Options:

```
#pragma mark Table view methods
- (NSInteger)numberOfSectionsInTableView:(UITableView *)tableView {
    return 2;
}
```

Next, we need to implement the method `tableView:numberOfRowsInSection`. In this method we inform the `UITableView` how many rows to render per section.

```
// Customize the number of rows in the table view.
- (NSInteger)tableView:(UITableView *)tableView
  numberOfRowsInSection:(NSInteger)section {
    if (section == 0) {
        return 4;
    }
    else {
        return 2;
    }
}
```

The method `tableView:cellForRowAtIndexPath:` (Listing 8.1) is more involved, but you will get the hang of it soon enough. In this method you must return a properly initialized cell view for every row that is requested. You are given the section and row that are requested in the form of an `NSIndexPath`. Also notice that the cell views are being cached. This is very beneficial for performance. Constructing an object for every row takes time and consumes resources. Be sure to use the cache available to speed up your views.

 CROSS-REFERENCE

To download Listing 8.1, go to `www.wileydevreference.com` and click the Downloads link.

Listing 8.1

Supplying Cell Data When the tableView:cellForRowAtIndexPath Method Is Called

```
// Customize the appearance of table view cells.
- (UITableViewCell *)tableView:(UITableView *)tableView
  cellForRowAtIndexPath:(NSIndexPath *)indexPath {
  static NSString *CellIdentifier = @"Cell";
  static NSString *SubtitleCellIdentifier = @"SubtitleCell";
  UITableViewCell *cell = [tableView
    dequeueReusableCellWithIdentifier:CellIdentifier];
  UITableViewCell *subtitleCell = [tableView
    dequeueReusableCellWithIdentifier:SubtitleCellIdentifier];
  if (cell == nil) {
  cell = [[[UITableViewCell alloc]
    initWithStyle:UITableViewCellStyleDefault reuseIdentifier:CellIdentifier]
    autorelease];
   }
  if (subtitleCell == nil) {
    subtitleCell = [[[UITableViewCell alloc]
```

continued

Listing 8.1 *(continued)*

```
        initWithStyle:UITableViewCellStyleSubtitle
        reuseIdentifier:SubtitleCellIdentifier] autorelease];
}

if (indexPath.section == 0) {
    switch (indexPath.row) {
        case 0:
            cell.textLabel.text = @"Head-to-Head";
            cell.accessoryType = UITableViewCellAccessoryDetailDisclosureButton;
            return cell;
        case 1:
            cell.textLabel.text = @"Nearby";
            cell.accessoryType = UITableViewCellAccessoryDetailDisclosureButton;
            return cell;
        case 2:
            cell.textLabel.text = @"New Internet";
            cell.accessoryType = UITableViewCellAccessoryDisclosureIndicator;
            return cell;
        default:
            if (self.activeGameCount > 0) {
                subtitleCell.textLabel.text = @"Continue";
                NSString *gameText =
                    self.activeGameCount > 1 ? @"games" : @"game";
                subtitleCell.detailTextLabel.text = [NSString
                    stringWithFormat:@"%d %@ currently active",
                    self.activeGameCount, gameText];
                subtitleCell.accessoryType =
                    UITableViewCellAccessoryDisclosureIndicator;
                return subtitleCell;
            }
            cell.textLabel.text = @"Continue";
            cell.accessoryType = UITableViewCellAccessoryDisclosureIndicator;
            return cell;
    }
}
else {
    switch (indexPath.row) {
        case 0:
            cell.textLabel.text = @"Internet Settings";
            cell.detailTextLabel.text = @"Change your connection options";
            cell.accessoryType = UITableViewCellAccessoryDisclosureIndicator;
            return cell;
        default:
            cell.textLabel.text = @"About";
            cell.accessoryType = UITableViewCellAccessoryDisclosureIndicator;
            return cell;
    }
}
}
```

The method `tableView:viewForHeaderInSection:` has been used to customize the appearance of the head on each of our sections. All we need to do is supply a `UIView` for each header callback:

```
- (UIView *)tableView: (UITableView *)tableView viewForHeaderInSection:
    (NSInteger)section {
    UIView *headerView = [[UIView alloc] initWithFrame:CGRectMake(0, 0,
        self.tableView.bounds.size.width, 30)];
    UILabel *headerLabel = [[UILabel alloc] initWithFrame:CGRectMake(10, 0,
        headerView.bounds.size.width, 30)];
    headerLabel.backgroundColor = [UIColor clearColor];
    headerLabel.font = [UIFont boldSystemFontOfSize:18];
    headerLabel.textColor = [UIColor whiteColor];

    if (section == 0)
        headerLabel.text = @"Game";
    else
        headerLabel.text = @"Preferences";

    [headerView addSubview:headerLabel];
    return headerView;
}
```

There are a handful of methods that push a view on the `UINavigationBar`. The one here serves as a sample of how to accomplish this. The push occurs when `pushViewController:animated:` is called:

```
- (void) startNewInternetGame {
    NewInternetGameMenuViewController *newInternetGameMenuViewController =
        [[NewInternetGameMenuViewController alloc]
            initWithNibName:@"NewInternetGameMenuViewController" bundle:nil];
    [self.navigationController
        pushViewController:newInternetGameMenuViewController animated:YES];
    [newInternetGameMenuViewController release];
}
```

A little deeper in the code, the Game View is loaded. Following is an example of how this is done. This is where the abstraction we talked about earlier in the chapter comes into play. The `GameViewController` is created and a game connection is injected into it. This injection type is based on the game class name we pass to `GameConnection:createWithName:delegate:` as follows:

```
GameViewController *gameViewController = [[GameViewController alloc] initWithNib
    Name:@"GameViewController" bundle:nil];
gameViewController.gameConnection = [GameConnection
    createWithName:@"InternetGameConnection" delegate:gameViewController];

gameViewController.modalTransitionStyle = UIModalTransitionStyleFlipHorizontal;
self presentModalViewController:gameViewController animated:YES
    [gameViewController release];
```

Finally, the method `tableView:didSelectRowAtIndexPath:` is implemented to fire the appropriate response to the main menu selection:

```
- (void)tableView:(UITableView *)tableView didSelectRowAtIndexPath:
  (NSIndexPath *)indexPath {
  if (indexPath.section == 0) {
     switch (indexPath.row) {
        case 0:
           [self startNewHeadToHeadGame];
           break;
        case 1:
           [self startNewNearbyGame];
           break;
        case 2:
           [self startNewInternetGame];
           break;
        case 3:
           [self continueGame];
           break;
     }
  }
  else {
     switch (indexPath.row) {
        case 0:
           [self showSettings];
           break;
        case 1:
           [self showAbout];
           break;
     }
  }
}
```

Making calls to Web services

At this point you can handle many of the basics of game development. A new challenge is connecting to other players who are connected to the Internet. We discussed this feature earlier, and fortunately, it is actually a very straightforward process to code on the client.

Earlier you reviewed the `GameConnection` class and how it is used to abstract the connection details away from the game. We are now going to focus on the class `InternetGameConnection` that extends the class `GameConnection` and handles Internet-based connections:

```
#import <Foundation/Foundation.h>
#import "GameConnection.h"
#define SERVICE_END_POINT @"http://services.appsamuck.com/turnbased/"
@interface InternetGameConnection : GameConnection {
```

```
        NSString *serviceEndPoint;
        NSString *responseData;
        NSURLConnection *urlConnection;
}
@property (nonatomic, retain) NSString *responseData;
- (void) apiConnectWithSessionId: (NSString*)sessionId;
- (void) apiConnectWithPlayerName: (NSString*)playerName;
- (void) apiSendMessage:(NSString*)message
        asType:(GameConnectionMessageType)messageType;
@end
```

In `GameConnection`, the method `connectWithPlayerName:` is called when a player wants to initiate a new game with a friend. This method is actually implemented in the class `InternetGameConnection`. Walking through this call shows you how Internet connectivity is achieved. This method is simply a pass-through with a sentinel. The parameter `playerName` is checked with the sentinel and the pass-through call to `apiConnectWithPlayerName` is issued:

```
- (void) connectWithPlayerName:(NSString*)playerName {
    [super connectWithPlayerName:playerName];
    if ([playerName length] == 0)
        [NSException raise:@"Parameter required"
            format:@"Parameter playerName cannot be null or empty"];
    [self apiConnectWithPlayerName:playerName];
}
```

The method `apiConnectWithPlayerName` issues a request to the Internet server, which begins the Web request process. This is the same process that is followed when you start a Google search in your browser.

NOTE

We have chosen to issue our request as an HTTP POST. With a POST, the parameters can be bundled as in the body of the request. This has two advantages: First, it's easy to extract the parameters in your server implementation; and second, you can switch to SSL, which encrypts the parameters that are embedded in the request body.

The method builds an `NSMutableURLRequest` and uses an `NSURLConnection` to issue the request with a call to `connectionWithRequest`. The call to `connectionWith Request` is followed by a call to `start`, which starts the request process. The important thing to observe is that this is only the beginning of the process. `InternetGameConnection` implements the `NSURLConnectionDelegate` methods necessary to receive the server response:

```
- (void) apiConnectWithPlayerName: (NSString*)playerName {
    NSString* content = [NSString stringWithFormat:@"playerName:%@", playerName];
    NSMutableURLRequest *request = [NSMutableURLRequest requestWithURL:
        [NSURL URLWithString: [SERVICE_END_POINT stringByAppendingString:
        @"connectWithPlayerName"]]];
    [request setHTTPMethod: @"POST"];
    [request setHTTPBody:[content dataUsingEncoding: NSASCIIStringEncoding]];
```

```
        self.responseData = [NSString stringWithString:@""];
        urlConnection = [NSURLConnection connectionWithRequest:request
            delegate:self];
        [urlConnection start];
    }
```

After the request has been sent, `NSURLConnection` receives a response either in the form of data or an error (hopefully it's data). If you do receive data, it arrives as a call to the delegate method connection `didReceiveData:`. It is also possible—and likely—that the response will be too large to arrive in one piece. If this happens, the data is broken up and arrives in chunks. This results in multiple calls to `connection:didReceiveData:`. Each call appends the received chunk to the property `responseData`. Finally, `connectionDidFinishLoading` is fired, which informs you that all the pieces of the response are received and the complete reconstituted data can be retrieved from the property `responseData`:

```
    #pragma mark NSURLConnection delegate methods
    - (void)connection:(NSURLConnection *)connection didReceiveData:(NSData *)data {
        NSString *stringReply = [[NSString alloc] initWithData:data
            encoding:NSUTF8StringEncoding];
        self.responseData = [self.responseData stringByAppendingString:stringReply];
    }
```

The data you receive from the server is entirely up to you and depends on how you wish to communicate with your Web server. If you are looking for a standard, REST (representational state transfer) is a good choice for iPhone development because making calls to REST is very straightforward. The class `URLConnection` is all you need on the client. There is a lot to implementing a Web server, a discussion that is outside the scope of this book. Check out `www.appsamuck.com/gameservices/` for more information.

REST is not the only protocol available; Web services come in many different flavors. For example, SOAP (originally defined as Simple Object Access Protocol) is a mature protocol that has been around for a while. However, there is currently no native support for SOAP in the iPhone SDK. You could spend countless hours building a SOAP client from scratch. Fortunately, there are tools available that have already done the work for you. For example, RemObjects Software (`www.remobjects.com/iphone`) has a SOAP Web service framework that fills this gap. They also offer a free tool for quickly setting up a push notification server. Third-party tools do come with a price, but they can be huge timesavers and the cost is almost always less than what it would cost you to take the time to do it yourself.

As we've mentioned, `connectionDidFinishLoading` is called whenever the complete response has been received from the server. When this happens, you call `receiveMessage:ofType:`, which sends the complete message to the delegate `GameControllerDelegate`:

```
    - (void)connectionDidFinishLoading:(NSURLConnection *)connection {
        GameConnectionMessageType messageType = GameConnectionMessageData;
        [self.delegate receiveMessage:self.responseData ofType:messageType];
    }
```

When an error is encountered, `connection:didFailWithError:` is called. You retrieve the message description and again call `receiveMessage:ofType:`, which sends the complete error message to the delegate `GameControllerDelegate`:

```
- (void)connection:(NSURLConnection *)connection
    didFailWithError:(NSError *)error {
    GameConnectionMessageType messageType = GameConnectionMessageError;
    NSString *message = [error localizedDescription];
    [self.delegate receiveMessage:message ofType:messageType];
}
```

Accepting messages from Apple Push Notification

You can completely implement an Internet-ready game without push notification. However, push notification adds that extra piece that allows your game to behave as if it were always running. You should still use the methods we just discussed to send, receive, and manage game messages. It is better to use push notification to accomplish tasks that enrich your game that only push notification can achieve.

Sending a message with push notification must be done from a server connected to the Apple Push Notification server. This means that for your app to send a push notification to another device, it must do so through a server that you build. Since this is the case, you can choose any method you like to send the message to your server.

Coding your application to receive push notifications is another matter. Before you can receive a message, you must first register your app to receive notifications. You can register your app for notifications by calling the method `registerForRemoteNotificationTypes:`. Apple recommends that you call this in the method `applicationDidFinishLaunching` as follows:

```
- (void)applicationDidFinishLaunching:(UIApplication *)app {
    [[UIApplication sharedApplication]
        registerForRemoteNotificationTypes:(UIRemoteNotificationTypeBadge |
        UIRemoteNotificationTypeSound | UIRemoteNotificationTypeAlert)];
}
```

If the registration is successful, you will receive notification via the delegate method `didRegisterForRemoteNotificationsWithDeviceToken`. When you receive this message you'll know that you have successfully registered for push notification. After this, the `GameConnection` can send the device token and the user's e-mail address to your server as needed for this example:

```
- (void)application:(UIApplication *)app
    didRegisterForRemoteNotificationsWithDeviceToken:(NSData *)devToken {
    self.devTokenBytes = [devToken bytes];
    self.registered = YES;
}
```

If the registration fails, you will receive a call to the following method. Be sure to alert the user and, if necessary, disable any options that depend totally on push notification:

```
- (void)application:(UIApplication *)app
   didFailToRegisterForRemoteNotificationsWithError:(NSError *)err {
   NSString *message = [NSString stringWithFormat:@" Error in registration.
      Error: %@", err];
   UIAlertView *alert = [[UIAlertView alloc] initWithTitle:@"Error"
      message:message delegate:nil cancelButtonTitle:@"OK"
      otherButtonTitles:nil];
   [alert show];
   [alert release];
}
```

In this case, you can simply poll your server for messages when your application fires up. Once the app is registered for push notification, your app could be loaded as a result of a user simply clicking Accept on a push notification alert. If your app is loaded in this manner, the method `application:didFinishLaunchingWithOptions` will be called. You can use this event to trigger your app to load with a game already in progress if the situation warrants it.

Analyzing Business Aspects

The major business aspect of turn-based games connected over the Internet is the opportunity for viral sales. This is key—if your game is fun and engaging, then friends will want to play other friends, which will lead to more sales. Play up this feature by allowing players to invite friends through means other than e-mail. Use Facebook, Twitter, and other social media avenues. Post game results to social news stories and leader boards. Create an environment that fosters competition. The more competition and rivalry, the more friends will want to connect and interact, which leads to better sales.

Turn-based games allow for a game to be played over the course of days instead of at a single sit-down. This can attract a different audience to your game. Some people have families and small kids, which may make it difficult to find time to sit down and play a long, drawn-out game. However, if you can start a game and continue to take turns when you can steal five minutes to make a move here and there, it becomes possible to cobble time together over the course of a day or week to complete a full game. This is an attractive feature to potential buyers. In your application description, tell the story of busy family guys and gals and how this game is designed with them in mind.

Summary

Turn-based games are well suited for the iPhone. Since the iPhone is an on-the-go device, it is especially well suited for games that you can play during the day. You can start a turn-based game, make a few moves, head to work, make a few more moves at lunch, and finally finish up when you get home. Turn-based games complement the on-the-go lifestyle, which embodies the culture of iPhone owners.

In this chapter you learned technologies useful for implementing turn-based games. You learned that the best and most entertaining games require more strategy than luck to master. You reviewed tic-tac-toe and saw how it lacks strategy, and from there you saw some changes we made in an effort to introduce more strategy to this classic game. You reviewed new ways to connect players that work well for turn-based games. Locating friends to play against is an integral part of a successful multiplayer game. For this reason, you need to allow sufficient time in your development cycle to design and develop a system for connecting friends. Finally, you reviewed the technical details of the turn-based game, Amuck-Tac-Toe.

Games connected over the Internet are positioned to be king in viral sales, especially small games with a small price. It is worth a dollar or two to play even a single round of a game with an old college buddy. Also, remember when you get two or more people to play, your profit is multiplied. As always, make your game fun and engaging, but invest the time into making it simple and straightforward. The social interaction with friends should be effortless, fun, and competitive. Your game can build and strengthen relationships between players. This will keep them coming back.

Advanced Technical and Business Programming Concepts

Grasping Advanced Programming Topics

I n this chapter we cover some of the advanced topics you have not been exposed to in the preceding chapters. The discussion in some sections may not always feel directly relevant to game development. However, you will find that almost any technology can be incorporated into your applications if you are creative. Sometimes these creative combinations can offer an exciting experience that is new and attractive to potential buyers.

Each section in this chapter is focused on different and unrelated advanced topics. At times we reference examples from `http://appsamuck.com` that cover the topic. Some sections use examples from the iPhone Reference Library—Sample Code, at `http://developer.apple.com/iphone/library/navigation/SampleCode.html` (login required). Finally, in some instances you will find the specific code you need listed in the section.

Exploring the Camera

The camera is a technology that does not generally come to mind when one thinks of gaming. But ten years ago you may have asked how a guitar can be used in gaming. Today's Guitar Hero and Rock Band are really cashing in on guitar games. You could consider using the camera to snap photos of items in a scavenger hunt; there's one idea. We will leave the creative planning up to you and give you a short tour on how you can integrate the camera into your applications.

We are going to look at some code snippets from the example PhotoFrame, an `appsamuck.com` original from day 27. The code for PhotoFrame can be found at `http://appsamuck.com/day27.html`.

In This Chapter

Exploring the camera

Getting oriented with the compass

Turning up the audio

Looking into video

Discovering geolocation

Stepping into the third dimension

CROSS-REFERENCE
See Appendix B for all of our 31 days of iPhone apps.

This example lets you select a photo and display it inside of a frame, giving your iPhone the appearance of a framed photo. On the options screen, you select a photo by clicking one of the following two buttons (Figure 9.1):

- Select Existing Photo From Library
- Take New Photo With Camera

Figure 9.1

In the PhotoFrame application, you can choose a photo from your Photo Library or take a new photo with the camera.

If you tap Select Existing Photo From Library, the message `selectPhotoFromLibrary Clicked` is fired:

```
- (IBAction)selectPhotoFromLibraryClicked {
    PhotoPickerController *photoPicker =
        [[PhotoPickerController alloc] initWithSourceType:
        UIImagePickerControllerSourceTypePhotoLibrary];
    [self presentModalViewController:photoPicker animated:TRUE];
    [photoPicker release];
}
```

This message creates an instance of the `PhotoPickerController`, which is what you want to use to access the Photo Library on your device. Notice that `UIImagePickerControllerSourceTypePhotoLibrary` is passed in as the source type. This is what tells the `PhotoPickerController` to read from the Photo Library. Inside of the `PhotoPickerController` an instance of `UIImagePickerController` is created, which, when configured with a source type of `UIImagePickerControllerSourceTypePhotoLibrary`, launches the picker starting in the Photo Library. Users are guided through a series of screens that assist them in selecting and editing their photo (Figures 9.2, 9.3, and 9.4).

Figure 9.2

When launched with a source type of `UIImage` `PickerControllerSourceTypePhoto` `Library`, the user is given the opportunity to select a Photo Album.

Figure 9.3

After selecting a Photo Album, the user can select a specific photo from the album.

Figure 9.4

Finally, the user can scale and/or resize the selected photo.

If you tap Take New Photo With Camera, the message `takePhotoWithCameraClicked` is fired:

```
- (IBAction)takePhotoWithCameraClicked {
    PhotoPickerController *photoPicker =
        [[PhotoPickerController alloc]
        initWithSourceType:UIImagePickerControllerSourceTypeCam
    era];
    [self presentModalViewController:photoPicker animated:TRUE];
    [photoPicker release];
}
```

The only difference here is that the source type has been set to `UIImagePickerController SourceTypeCamera`. This small change tells the `PhotoPickerController` to launch the camera instead of an old photo that is already saved (Figure 9.5).

Figure 9.5

Capturing a new image with the camera without leaving your application

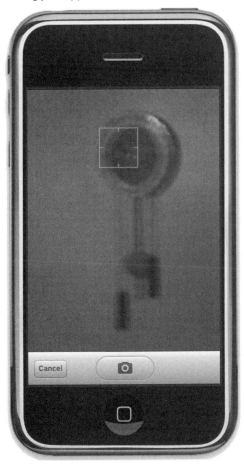

The actual listing for the header of `PhotoPicker` can be found in the source in the file `PhotoPickerController.h`. As you've seen, the `PhotoPickerController` is a convenient wrapper that minimizes the code needed to select photos in your application:

```
#import <UIKit/UIKit.h>
@interface PhotoPickerController : UIImagePickerController
    <UIImagePickerControllerDelegate, UINavigationControllerDelegate>
    - (id) initWithSourceType:(UIImagePickerControllerSourceType)sourceType;
    - (void)imagePickerControllerDidCancel:(UIImagePickerController *)picker;
    - (void)imagePickerController:(UIImagePickerController *)picker
      didFinishPickingImage:(UIImage *)image editingInfo:(NSDictionary *)
      editingInfo;
    - (void)navigationController:(UINavigationController *)navigationController
         willShowViewController:(UIViewController *)viewController
            animated:(BOOL)animated;
    - (void)navigationController:(UINavigationController *)navigationController
            didShowViewController:(UIViewController *)viewController
         animated:(BOOL)animated;
@end
```

The implementation for this class can, of course, be found in the same source, in the file
`PhotoPickerController.m`. There you see `UIImagePickerController` and how it is
used to capture the image data. Notice the `sourceType` that is passed in and notice the delegate has been set to `self`:

```
#import "PhotoPickerController.h"
#import "MainViewController.h"
@implementation PhotoPickerController
- (id) initWithSourceType:(UIImagePickerControllerSourceType)sourceType {
    if (self = [super init]) {
        if ([UIImagePickerController: isSourceTypeAvailable:
            UIImagePickerControllerSourceTypePhotoLibrary])
        self.sourceType = sourceType;
        self.delegate = self;
        self.allowsImageEditing = TRUE;
        self.navigationBar.barStyle = UIBarStyleBlackTranslucent;
    }
    return self;
}
```

Since we assigned `self` as the delegate above, the message `imagePickerController` is
sent to the same class whenever a picture has been selected. This message returns the selected
image, and in this implementation we store the image to disk:

```
- (void)imagePickerController:(UIImagePickerController *)picker
    didFinishPickingImage:(UIImage *)image
    editingInfo:(NSDictionary *)editingInfo {
        NSString *uniquePath = [[NSHomeDirectory
            stringByAppendingPathComponent:@"Documents"]
        stringByAppendingPathComponent:@"selectedImage.png"];
        [UIImagePNGRepresentation(image) writeToFile: uniquePath atomically:YES];

    [self.parentViewController dismissModalViewControllerAnimated:YES];
    [[MainViewController getInstance] loadImage];
}
```

NOTE

In the previous code, the word `atomically` in the method `UIImagePNGRepresentation:writeTo File:uniquePath atomically:` may look like a typo, but it's not. If you set this value to YES, you are guaranteed that the path, if it exists at all, won't be corrupted even if your device should crash during writing.

Later, when you return to the main screen, this image is loaded from disk and displayed in the photo frame (Figure 9.6).

Figure 9.6

After the user selects a photo, it is presented in a simulated photo frame.

Finally, the message `imagePickerControllerDidCancel` is sent in the event that the user clicks Cancel in the image picker and does not select a picture. Put code in this method when you wish to take special action in this situation:

```
- (void)imagePickerControllerDidCancel:(UIImagePickerController *)picker {
    [self.parentViewController dismissModalViewControllerAnimated:YES];
}
```

Getting Oriented with the Compass

The iPhone 3GS originally came equipped with a compass (Figure 9.7) containing heading information on magnetic north, true north, and accuracy. You can also take advantage of a 3-D vector that reports the device's deviation from the magnetic lines the compass is tracking.

Figure 9.7

The compass application was first introduced
with the release of the iPhone 3GS.

The compass is bundled in Core Location as part of the `CLLocationManager` class. If you are not new to Core Location and you have used the `CLLocationManager` before, using the compass is simple. If you have not used the `CLLocationManager` before, don't worry; that's easy, too. In your controller class you will want to add `CLLocationManagerDelegate` to your class definition:

```
#import "FlipsideViewController.h"
#import <CoreLocation/CoreLocation.h>
@interface MainViewController : UIViewController
   <FlipsideViewControllerDelegate, CLLocationManagerDelegate> {
   IBOutlet UILabel *infoLabel;
}
- (IBAction)showInfo;
@end
```

Now, in the implementation of your class, you need to create an instance of a `CLLocationManager`. After creating the class you need to set the delegate to `self` and send the message `startUpdatingHeading`. This tells the location manager to activate and start sending heading information to the assigned delegate:

```
- (void)viewDidLoad {
   [super viewDidLoad];
   CLLocationManager *locationManager = [[CLLocationManager alloc] init];
   locationManager.delegate = self;
   [locationManager startUpdatingHeading];
}
```

Heading information comes in regular intervals in the form of the message `locationManager:didUpdateHeading:`. In this message you pass a `CLHeading` object, which contains properties that report on all the heading data available:

```
- (void)locationManager:(CLLocationManager *)manager
   didUpdateHeading:(CLHeading *)newHeading {
   NSString *heading = [NSString stringWithFormat:
      @"x:%f\ny:%f\nz:%f\ntrueHeading:%f\n
         magneticHeading:%f\nheadingAccuracy:%f",
      newHeading.x, newHeading.y, newHeading.z,
      newHeading.trueHeading,
      newHeading.magneticHeading,
      newHeading.headingAccuracy];
   infoLabel.text = heading;
}
```

This simple example is just a new application created from the utility template with the code listed here added. A label was also used to display the raw compass information that is updated every time the message above is fired (Figure 9.8).

Figure 9.8

A display of the raw compass heading data supplied by CLLocationManager

When tracking compass data, you'll also want to implement the method locationManager-ShouldDisplayHeadingCalibration:. If you are not planning to supply calibration instructions that are termed to match your application, you can return YES in this message to have the device display the default message (Figure 9.9):

```
- (BOOL)locationManagerShouldDisplayHeadingCalibration:(CLLocationManager *)
  manager {
  return YES;
}
```

Figure 9.9

If you do not wish to provide a custom calibration message, you can fall back on the default calibration display as rendered by the device.

If you return NO, you will need to supply your own message as the native compass application does in Figure 9.10.

Figure 9.10

If you do not wish to use the default display, you can use your own, as shown here in the native compass application.

Turning Up the Audio

What is a game without sound? Of course, you can still have a game that does not play any sounds and you may even get away with it in some puzzle games. But even the most benign puzzle game can gain new life if you add a little sound to it.

When scheduling your game project, don't underestimate the time it will take you to incorporate sound. There's more to it than compiling your sound files into the application bundle. First you have to get your files in the correct format. We have had the best experience using MPEG-4 files for music and CAFF files for sound effects.

You can convert your music files to MPEG-4 with a licensed version of QuickTime Pro. This is by far the easiest way to do the conversion. When saving the file we recommend sticking with mono because it is lighter on the CPU and it generates smaller files. The only added value to using anything other than mono is when a player uses headphones to experience stereo-quality sound. However, most of the time players will just use the speaker on the device, so any gain is lost.

You will want to use CAFF files for all of your whizzes, bangs, and booms. For this one, Apple has provided us with the tool `afconvert`. This command line tool can read one audio file and write it to another format. Simply put your audio in a location where it can be seen, set your options, and run the tool. For example, let's say you have a file boom.wav and you need to convert it to boom.caf. To do so, put it in an appropriate folder and run afconvert, like so:

```
afconvert -f caff -d LE16 boom.wav boom.caf
```

Sound code tends to get mixed and meshed in with all the other things going on in a game, which makes it tough to see the full picture. In the following sections we show you two different ways to fire up sounds in your applications without all the rest of the noise that drowns out the sound code.

Playing simple sounds with AudioToolkit

If you are writing a simple puzzle game or you are just looking to add some sounds to a user interface, you will probably be happy with the services provided by AudioToolkit. The following listing manages to play a sound and pull it off with only four lines of code:

```
SystemSoundID soundId;
CFURLRef fileURL = (CFURLRef)[[NSURL fileURLWithPath:[[NSBundle mainBundle]
    pathForResource:@"sound" ofType:@"caf"]] retain];
AudioServicesCreateSystemSoundID (fileURL, &soundId);
AudioServicesPlaySystemSound (soundId);
```

It doesn't get much easier than this. In your actual implementation you'll want to keep an array of sound IDs so that you can load several sounds at once on startup and then play them back in an instant as needed.

CAUTION

The ease of AudioToolkit does come at a cost: It is rarely powerful enough for intense games.

Making some "real" noise with OpenAL

OpenAL is a whole other beast compared to AudioToolkit. The quality, flexibility, and power of OpenAL is far superior to other options. However, there is a cost for this power: OpenAL has a much steeper learning curve. Here, we are going to show you the basic steps of firing up the OpenAL engine and playing a simple sound. OpenAL is akin to OpenGL in its state machine style of management. Most of your code will be busy setting up state and then you can finally sit back and make short calls to play your sounds.

oalTouch is an example application you can download from the iPhone Dev Center (Figure 9.11). The steps here are as close as possible to the example, except that you are not jumping from method to method to see them. We also took advantage of the class `MyOpenALSupport` included in the example. This is a big help and it is perfectly acceptable for you to do the same in your applications.

Figure 9.11

The main screen from iPhone Dev Center's example oalTouch. For this example, put on your headphones and move the speaker and the listener around. The position and volume of the sound will change with respect to the position of the elements on the screen.

N O T E
Apple allows anyone to use their examples in their testing and even production applications. In fact, most if not all of the example applications have been compiled and published to the App Store by developers with no changes. (Well, they added their names as the authors.)

Here are the steps to initializing and playing a sound with OpenAL. Your first step is creating an audio session. The following code first initializes the session, then it configures the session, and finally, it activates the session:

```
// initialize the session
OSStatus status = AudioSessionInitialize(NULL, NULL,
   interruptionListener1, self);
if (status)
   return false;
// configure the session
UInt32 category = kAudioSessionCategory_AmbientSound;
status = AudioSessionSetProperty(
   kAudioSessionProperty_AudioCategory,
   sizeof(category), &category);
if (status)
   return false;
// activate the session
status = AudioSessionSetActive(true);
if (status)
   return false;
```

After creating an audio session we need to retrieve a reference to the default output device. We can get this by calling `alcOpenDevice` with no parameters:

```
ALenum error;
ALCcontext *newContext = NULL;
ALCdevice *newDevice = NULL;
newDevice = alcOpenDevice(NULL);
if (newDevice == NULL)
   return false;
```

Now we need a context that we can use to render to the device we just opened. Once we get the context, we need to tell OpenAL to use it by calling `alcMakeContextCurrent`:

```
newContext = alcCreateContext(newDevice, 0);
if (newContext == NULL)
   return false;
alcMakeContextCurrent(newContext);
```

Now we need a buffer object to host our sounds and we need a source object to reference our sounds:

```
ALuint buffer;
alGenBuffers(1, &buffer);
if((error = alGetError()) != AL_NO_ERROR)
   return false;
alGenSources(1, &source);
if(alGetError() != AL_NO_ERROR)
   return false;
```

With buffer and source objects initialized, we need to load our sounds from the resource bundle into the buffer:

```
// clear out existing errors
alGetError();
error = AL_NO_ERROR;
ALenum format;
ALsizei size;
ALsizei freq;
void *data;
// reference the main bundle
NSBundle *bundle = [NSBundle mainBundle];
// load the audio from a resource file
CFURLRef fileURL = (CFURLRef)[[NSURL fileURLWithPath:[bundle
   pathForResource:@"sound" ofType:@"caf"]] retain];
if (fileURL) {
    data = MyGetOpenALAudioData(fileURL, &size, &format, &freq);
    CFRelease(fileURL);

    if((error = alGetError()) != AL_NO_ERROR)
       return false;

    // use the static buffer data API
    alBufferDataStaticProc(buffer, format, data, size, freq);

    if((error = alGetError()) != AL_NO_ERROR)
    return false;
}
else {
    data = NULL;
    return false
}
```

The file is loaded into the buffer and now you can set engine options, the position for the sound source, and the distance from the listener:

```
error = AL_NO_ERROR;
alGetError();
// turn on looping
alSourcei(source, AL_LOOPING, AL_TRUE);
```

```
// set source location
float sourcePosAL[] = {0.5f, 0.5f, kDefaultDistance};
alSourcefv(source, AL_POSITION, sourcePosAL);
// set distance from listener
alSourcef(source, AL_REFERENCE_DISTANCE, 50.0f);
```

Finally, you need to bind the source to the buffer. The source is what will be referenced to play the sound when needed:

```
// attach source to the buffer
alSourcei(source, AL_BUFFER, buffer);
if((error = alGetError()) != AL_NO_ERROR)
    return false;
```

You are done setting up OpenAL; now all you need to do is fire off your sounds when you need them. Thankfully, this only takes one line of code—well, a few more if you count the fact that you should check for errors—but nothing like the number of lines it took to get here.

To play the sound, you need to call `alSourcePlay` with a source reference:

```
alSourcePlay(source);
ALenum error;
if((error = alGetError()) != AL_NO_ERROR) {
    // handle error
}
```

To stop a sound from playing, you call `alSourceStop`:

```
alSourceStop(source);
ALenum error;
if((error = alGetError()) != AL_NO_ERROR) {
    // handle error
}
```

That's it—you are all set to add OpenAL and great sound to your games!

Looking into Video

As your applications begin to grow and mature, you may need to add video, cut scenes, or display an opening story before a user plays the game for the first time. Fortunately, your iPhone was designed from the beginning to display video, and the code to do this is really straightforward.

LavaFlow is another one of our examples from `http://appsamuck.com`. Download LavaFlow and you will find an example of playing a short video that turns your iPhone into a virtual lava lamp (Figure 9.12).

Figure 9.12

LavaFlow illustrates how to play video files on the iPhone.

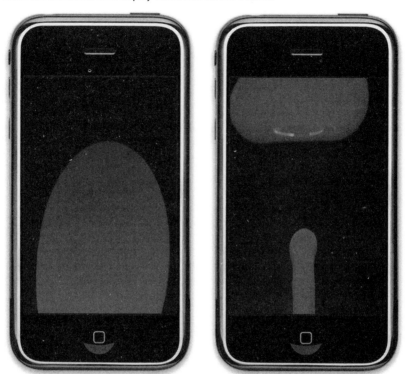

In the `awakeFromNib` message of LavaFlow, you see all of the code that initializes and plays the movie. The actual movie is embedded in the application. The first step is to retrieve the movie from the resource bundle, so you call the `NSURL` needed to pass to the movie player you will start next:

```
NSBundle *bundle = [NSBundle mainBundle];
NSString *moviePath = [bundle pathForResource:@"lavaFlow" ofType:@"m4v"];
NSURL *movieURL;
if (moviePath) {
   movieURL = [NSURL fileURLWithPath:moviePath];
}
if (movieURL == nil)
   return;
```

If the URL is retrieved successfully, the application can proceed to the next step. An `MPMoviePlayerController` is instantiated with the URL we just discussed:

```
moviePlayer = [[MPMoviePlayerController alloc] initWithContentURL:movieURL];
```

Next, bind the event `moviePlayBackDidFinish` to the movie player event `MPMoviePlayerPlaybackDidFinishNotification`. This ensures that when the movie finishes playing you will receive notification and can take appropriate action:

```
[[NSNotificationCenter defaultCenter] addObserver:self
    selector:@selector(moviePlayBackDidFinish:)
    name:MPMoviePlayerPlaybackDidFinishNotification
    object:moviePlayer];
```

Finally, set some movie player options and send the message `play`. The movie takes over the screen and begins to play:

```
moviePlayer.scalingMode = MPMovieScalingModeAspectFill;
moviePlayer.movieControlMode = MPMovieControlModeHidden;
moviePlayer.backgroundColor = [UIColor blackColor];
[moviePlayer play];
```

As a final note, we will look at the `moviePlayBackDidFinish` message. This is the message we bound to the movie player event `MPMoviePlayerPlaybackDidFinishNotification`. In this novelty example we simply play the movie again, but in your games you will probably want to clean up any movie-related objects and resume your game:

```
-(void)moviePlayBackDidFinish: (NSNotification*)notification{
    moviePlayer = [notification object];
    [moviePlayer play];
}
```

CROSS-REFERENCE

For more on using the movie player, see Chapter 4.

Discovering Geolocation

Geolocation data can be collected through Core Location services if the device has support for it. You saw this earlier in the compass section, but this time we are going to look at the location data itself and not the heading.

Altimeter is an example that uses Core Location to discover the altitude of your current location. Download Altimeter from `http://appsamuck.com/day19.html` and fire it up to discover the altitude where you are (Figure 9.13).

Figure 9.13

The Altimeter example illustrates how to use Core
Location to determine altitude.

All in all, Altimeter has hardly any code. It is simply regurgitating the information returned from
Core Location. The code that is executed on application startup should look very familiar to the
code you saw in the earlier compass example:

```
locmanager = [[CLLocationManager alloc] init];
[locmanager setDelegate:self];
[locmanager setDesiredAccuracy:kCLLocationAccuracyBest];
[locmanager startUpdatingLocation];
```

This time we implemented `locationManager:didUpdateToLocation:`, which is called when location data is reported to your application. The parameter `newLocation` contains the altitude information we are looking for in this app, but don't worry, you can get the latitude and longitude from the same place:

```
- (void)locationManager:(CLLocationManager *)manager
    didUpdateToLocation:(CLLocation *)newLocation
    fromLocation:(CLLocation *)oldLocation {
    altitude.text =
        [NSString stringWithFormat: @"%.2f m", newLocation.altitude];
}
```

In the event that location information could not be retrieved, we respond to `location Manager:didFailWithError:` to clear the display:

```
- (void)locationManager:(CLLocationManager *)manager
    didFailWithError:(NSError *)error {
    altitude.text = @"0.00 m";
}
```

NOTE

Altitude data is only available on devices that have a GPS chip, and is only available where there is a GPS fix (for example, outdoors with a clear view). Wi-Fi-based location services, such as those found on the original iPhone and the iPod touch, cannot obtain altitude information.

Stepping into the Third Dimension

As you probably know, the iPhone supports OpenGL ES for 3-D graphics. Just that fact alone speaks volumes about the capability of the device. OpenGL is a huge topic that could fill many books in an effort to cover all the details and nuances introduced with this powerful API. While you are not going to learn all the details of OpenGL in this section, we have provided you with this primer to help introduce you to programming in 3-D on the iPhone.

Analyzing the OpenGL ES template

To get started on this journey, you will not have to go far. Xcode provides you with an incredible template to help you get started programming in OpenGL. You will analyze this template in this section to get a better understanding of what has already been done for you.

Here is what you need to do to get started:

1. Launch Xcode.

2. Choose File ➪ New Project.

3. Inside the New Project dialog box in the iPhone OS section, choose Application ➪ OpenGL ES Application.

4. Name the project and click Save. We recommend you name yours **GLSquare** to stay consistent with the naming in this study.

5. Click Build and Go to execute your new project in the iPhone Simulator (Figure 9.14).

Figure 9.14

This is the result you will see without adding any lines of code to the OpenGL ES Application Template.

Looking at OpenGL code for the first time can feel pretty alien to first-timers. When you dig into the details, do you know what is going on here? Look back at the GLSquare project and open the Classes folder to view its contents, as shown in Figure 9.15.

Figure 9.15

All of the noteworthy code generated by the OpenGL ES Application Template can be found in the Classes folder.

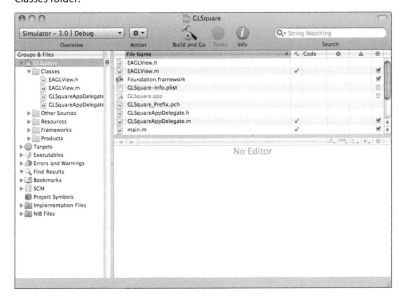

In the Classes folder, you will find the following files:

- **EAGLView.h.** This is the header file for the class `EAGLView`. This is our major class of interest as it is responsible for rendering the 3-D scene.

- **EAGLView.m.** This is the implementation file for the class `EAGLView`. This is the class that implements the `drawView` method that renders the scene.

- **GLSquareAppDelegate.h.** This is the header file for the class `GLSquareAppDelegate`. This header file defines properties for the `UIWindow` and the `EAGLView`.

- **GLSquareAppDelegate.m.** This is the implementation file for the class `GLSquareAppDelegate`. This class responds to `UIApplicationDelegate` events in order to set the `animationInterval` of the `EAGLView`.

Open up the file `EAGLView.m` and take a minute to read through the code. You might see a lot of talk about buffers and other technical jargon that you may be unfamiliar with. It's important to understand at least a little about these items before the rest of it will begin to make sense to you.

Here's a short list of definitions that may help as you dig deeper into this template:

- **Frame buffer.** The frame buffer is the last stop in the graphics pipeline. This is the buffer that everything will be rendered in.

- **Depth buffer.** Enabling the depth buffer triggers drawing operations to check the buffer before placing pixels onto the screen. The buffer stores Z order information with each pixel to ensure the correct pixels rise to the top.

- **Color buffer.** The color buffer is what you see on the screen. It stores a color value for each pixel on the screen.

- **Render buffer.** A render buffer is a buffer used for off-screen rendering.

- **Rasterization.** This is the process of converting shapes from a vector graphics format into pixels for screen display.

Now look into `EAGLView.m` again. You will see the following methods that are responsible for setting up and rendering the 3-D scene:

- **initWithCoder.** You have probably seen or will see `initWithCoder` several times in your work as an iPhone developer. This method is called whenever the view is created indirectly as part of an Interface Builder XIB file, as in this case. In this particular class, `initWithCoder` is responsible for opening the OpenGL context (`EAGLContext`).

- **layoutSubviews.** The method `layoutSubViews` is called whenever something occurs on the device that requires that subviews recalculate their positioning. This can happen when views are moved around on the screen. When `layoutSubviews` is triggered, it will call `destroyFramebuffer`, `createFrameBuffer`, and `drawView`, respectively.

- **createFramebuffer.** As its name implies, the method `createFrameBuffer` creates the frame buffer. In addition, a render buffer is created and the new width and height of the render buffer are calculated.

- **destroyFramebuffer.** This method deletes the frame buffer and the render buffer.

- **drawView.** The method `drawView` is responsible for the action you see on the screen. It positions the cube and renders the screen.

The `drawView` method is the most important method in this class. You will learn more about the details in the following breakdown of the method. Listing 9.1 shows the complete code.

CROSS-REFERENCE

To download Listing 9.1, go to `www.wileydevreference.com` and click the Downloads link.

Listing 9.1

The drawView Method Is Responsible for Rendering the Scene

```
- (void)drawView {

    // Replace the implementation of this method to do your own custom drawing

    const GLfloat squareVertices[] = {
```

```
        -0.5f,  -0.5f,
         0.5f,  -0.5f,
        -0.5f,   0.5f,
         0.5f,   0.5f,
};
const GLubyte squareColors[] = {
    255, 255,   0, 255,
    0,   255, 255, 255,
    0,     0,   0,   0,
    255,   0, 255, 255,
};

[EAGLContext setCurrentContext:context];

glBindFramebufferOES(GL_FRAMEBUFFER_OES, viewFramebuffer);
glViewport(0, 0, backingWidth, backingHeight);

glMatrixMode(GL_PROJECTION);
glLoadIdentity();
glOrthof(-1.0f, 1.0f, -1.5f, 1.5f, -1.0f, 1.0f);
glMatrixMode(GL_MODELVIEW);
glRotatef(3.0f, 0.0f, 0.0f, 1.0f);

glClearColor(0.5f, 0.5f, 0.5f, 1.0f);
glClear(GL_COLOR_BUFFER_BIT);

glVertexPointer(2, GL_FLOAT, 0, squareVertices);
glEnableClientState(GL_VERTEX_ARRAY);
glColorPointer(4, GL_UNSIGNED_BYTE, 0, squareColors);
glEnableClientState(GL_COLOR_ARRAY);

glDrawArrays(GL_TRIANGLE_STRIP, 0, 4);

glBindRenderbufferOES(GL_RENDERBUFFER_OES, viewRenderbuffer);
[context presentRenderbuffer:GL_RENDERBUFFER_OES];
}
```

The first item in the method `drawView` is a declaration for the array `squareVertices`. The following array defines the vertices and, indirectly, the face for your square. In an effort to maintain cross-platform compatibility, OpenGL uses a simple one-dimensional array to represent this data. This array defines the X and Y coordinates of four vertices. You can interpret the following array as follows: { x1, y2, x2, y2, . . . }.

```
const GLfloat squareVertices[] = {
        -0.5f,  -0.5f,
         0.5f,  -0.5f,
        -0.5f,   0.5f,
         0.5f,   0.5f,
    };
```

OpenGL ES cannot directly render a square, so you must define your square as two triangles. The order in which you define the vertices is very important. OpenGL uses the order in which you specify the vertices to determine which side of the triangle is the front and which is the back. By default, the face that is wrapped by vertices in a counterclockwise order is the front face (Figure 9.16). The face that is wrapped by vertices in a clockwise order is the back face. It's important to know which side is the front because that plays an important role in the way the shape is drawn.

TIP

Another way to determine the front face is to use the right-hand rule: First use your right hand to wrap the vertices with your fingers pointing in the direction that the vertices are ordered. Then extend your thumb and it will be pointing in the direction of the front-facing side.

Figure 9.16

If the order of the defining vertices wraps the first triangle in a counterclockwise direction, that will be the front-facing side.

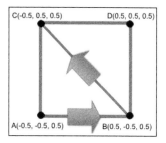

The next array in the code defines the colors you see on the screen. As with the previous array, OpenGL expects a one-dimensional array to define the color values using an expected order instead of a strong type. The repeating order used to define the colors is as follows: { red1, green1, blue1, alpha1, red2, green2, blue2, alpha2, . . . }. The following array is how you will see it in the code:

```
const GLubyte squareColors[] = {
    255, 255,   0, 255,
    0,   255, 255, 255,
    0,     0,   0,   0,
    255,   0, 255, 255,
};
```

Each color entry in the previous array matches the corresponding vertices in the previous matrix by order. You'll notice when you run the example that the colors are blended from the corners. This effect is achieved by defining the color of each of the vertices.

The following lines bind the frame buffer to the view containing the OpenGL context. In short, this creates the binding that ultimately results in the square shape rasterizing to the `UIView` where you expect to see it:

```
[EAGLContext setCurrentContext:context];
    glBindFramebufferOES(GL_FRAMEBUFFER_OES, viewFramebuffer);
    glViewport(0, 0, backingWidth, backingHeight);
```

The following lines clear all transforms that may have been applied to the projection matrix:

```
    glMatrixMode(GL_PROJECTION);
    glLoadIdentity();
```

Next, you need to define a viewport. A viewport is not a camera, but a camera is probably the easiest way to think of it. A viewport is your window into the 3-D world. There are two types of viewports in OpenGL ES: You can define an *orthogonal* viewport or a *frustum* viewport. For this example, we use the orthogonal viewport. The following line of code defines the dimensions of the orthogonal viewport that we used for our viewing area.

An orthogonal viewport is the shape of a rectangle. This is not ideal for most 3-D environments because it does not produce a real-world perspective when rendered. However, this type of viewport works well for this example and for close-up views where perspective does not matter. If you need to render a larger area with objects deep in the background, you would want to switch to a frustum viewport. A frustum viewport is not shaped like an orthogonal viewport and it does produce real-world perspective when rendered.

The following line defines the orthogonal viewport:

```
    glOrthof(-1.0f, 1.0f, -1.5f, 1.5f, -1.0f, 1.0f);
```

The following two lines switch to our model matrix mode and rotate:

```
    glMatrixMode(GL_MODELVIEW);
    glRotatef(3.0f, 0.0f, 0.0f, 1.0f);
```

The following lines replace all the pixels on the screen with gray:

```
    glClearColor(0.5f, 0.5f, 0.5f, 1.0f);
    glClear(GL_COLOR_BUFFER_BIT);
```

The following lines load the vertices of our square. The first parameter tells OpenGL that we are using two dimensions assumed to cycle through X and Y, respectively:

```
    glVertexPointer(2, GL_FLOAT, 0, squareVertices);
    glEnableClientState(GL_VERTEX_ARRAY);
```

The next lines load the vertices' color definitions. The first parameter tells OpenGL that we are using four values per color assumed to cycle through red, green, blue, and alpha, respectively:

```
glColorPointer(4, GL_UNSIGNED_BYTE, 0, squareColors);
glEnableClientState(GL_COLOR_ARRAY);
```

The next line draws the square with four vertices starting at index 0. The square is drawn to the render buffer:

```
glDrawArrays(GL_TRIANGLE_STRIP, 0, 4);
```

The following lines tell the render buffer to bind to the context and in turn the frame buffer. This step triggers the objects in the render buffer to begin rasterizing. When complete, you will see your square on the screen:

```
glBindRenderbufferOES(GL_RENDERBUFFER_OES, viewRenderbuffer);
[context presentRenderbuffer:GL_RENDERBUFFER_OES];
```

Drawing a cube with volume

The next step is converting your OpenGL ES Application Template into an example that displays a 3-D cube with depth, color, and volume, as shown in Figure 9.17. You can download the full source for this example from `http://appsamuck.com/gamedevbook/opengl`.

In the previous example, notice that the square is defined by defining the vertices that outline it. It's kind of like playing connect the dots. Defining a cube is the same as defining a square, with a couple of exceptions. First, you have to define six squares, one for each side. Second, you have to include X, Y, and Z coordinates instead of just X and Y. In the square example, you defined the array as follows:

```
const GLfloat squareVertices[] = {
    -0.5f, -0.5f,
     0.5f, -0.5f,
    -0.5f,  0.5f,
     0.5f,  0.5f,
};
```

Figure 9.17

A view of the 3-D cube rendered in this example with a different color on each face

Now the new definition that includes six sides and the additional Z coordinate looks like this:

```
const GLfloat cubeVertices[] = {
    // Front Face
    -0.5f, -0.5f,  0.5f,
     0.5f, -0.5f,  0.5f,
    -0.5f,  0.5f,  0.5f,
     0.5f,  0.5f,  0.5f,
    // Back Face
    -0.5f, -0.5f, -0.5f,
    -0.5f,  0.5f, -0.5f,
     0.5f, -0.5f, -0.5f,
     0.5f,  0.5f, -0.5f,
    // Top Face
    -0.5f,  0.5f,  0.5f,
     0.5f,  0.5f,  0.5f,
    -0.5f,  0.5f, -0.5f,
     0.5f,  0.5f, -0.5f,
    // Bottom Face
    -0.5f, -0.5f,  0.5f,
    -0.5f, -0.5f, -0.5f,
     0.5f, -0.5f,  0.5f,
     0.5f, -0.5f, -0.5f,
    // Left Face
    -0.5f, -0.5f,  0.5f,
    -0.5f,  0.5f,  0.5f,
    -0.5f, -0.5f, -0.5f,
    -0.5f,  0.5f, -0.5f,
    // Right Face
     0.5f, -0.5f, -0.5f,
     0.5f,  0.5f, -0.5f,
     0.5f, -0.5f,  0.5f,
     0.5f,  0.5f,  0.5f,
};
```

As you see, there are a good many more items in the array, but this is necessary to define all the vertices in the cube. There are different ways to define the faces, but for this example we wanted to stick with the same method for clarity.

Now from the previous example you will need to change the following line:

```
glVertexPointer(2, GL_FLOAT, 0, squareVertices);
```

Change the first parameter from a 2 to a 3 to indicate that the array of vertices contains X, Y, and Z coordinates instead of just X and Y, as seen in the following line of code:

```
glVertexPointer(3, GL_FLOAT, 0, squareVertices);
```

The next change is more significant. First, the array of vertex colors from the previous example is removed in favor of face colors. In the following code snippet, you see a call to `glColor4f` before the call to `glDrawArrays`. The `glColor4f` method defines the color of the next face that will be drawn. And of course, instead of having one call to `glDrawArrays`, you now have six calls, one for each face. Notice how the second parameter increases by a factor of 4 on each call. Since the vertexes are in one big array, this tells the method what index to start with:

```
glColor4f(1.0f, 0.0f, 0.0f, 1.0f); // red
glDrawArrays(GL_TRIANGLE_STRIP, 0, 4);
glColor4f(0.0f, 1.0f, 0.0f, 1.0f); // green
glDrawArrays(GL_TRIANGLE_STRIP, 4, 4);
glColor4f(0.0f, 0.0f, 1.0f, 1.0f); // blue
glDrawArrays(GL_TRIANGLE_STRIP, 8, 4);
glColor4f(1.0f, 1.0f, 0.0f, 1.0f); // yellow
glDrawArrays(GL_TRIANGLE_STRIP, 12, 4);
glColor4f(0.0f, 1.0f, 1.0f, 1.0f); // cyan
glDrawArrays(GL_TRIANGLE_STRIP, 16, 4);
glColor4f(1.0f, 0.0f, 1.0f, 1.0f); // magenta
glDrawArrays(GL_TRIANGLE_STRIP, 20, 4);
```

If you have been making the changes manually, you can click Build and Run to see the output. You will notice that the cube has a strange effect as it rotates. This is caused by the back face of each of the squares showing in front of some of the front faces. To eliminate this problem, you need to enable back-face culling. Simply stated, back-face culling removes the back face of each of the squares, which results in the desired output. To enable this feature, you need to add the following lines of code after the method call `glMatrixMode(GL_PROJECTION)`:

```
glMatrixMode(GL_PROJECTION);
glCullFace(GL_BACK);
glEnable(GL_CULL_FACE);
```

Finally, just for fun, we can start tracking finger swipes to rotate the cube. This is more interesting than just simply spinning the cube around a single axis. This is more of a challenge than you may realize because the orientation of the axis of the render buffer changes when it is rotated. Simply rotating around a static X or Y axis will not work. If you do this, the cube will spin in wild, unpredictable patterns. To achieve the desired result, you can use the following pattern.

First, make a copy of the current transform matrix of the render buffer. Next, reset the render buffer by loading the identity matrix. Now the axis is correct and you can perform your rotation. Finally, apply the transform matrix you saved in the first step to merge the results. Now you can see the cube react to your finger motions as expected. The following code illustrates this process:

```
glMatrixMode(GL_MODELVIEW);
// save model transform matrix
GLfloat currentModelMatrix[16];
glGetFloatv(GL_MODELVIEW_MATRIX, currentModelMatrix);
// clear the model transform matrix
glLoadIdentity();
```

```
// rotate the x and y axes of the model transform matrix
glRotatef(rotateX, 1.0f, 0.0f, 0.0f);
glRotatef(rotateY, 0.0f, 1.0f, 0.0f);
// slow down the spinning if it is spinning
[self decayRotation];
// reapply the previous transforms
glMultMatrixf(currentModelMatrix);
```

Now you can move the cube around and see all the faces with the flick of a finger (Figure 9.18).

Figure 9.18

Swipe the cube with your finger to change its orientation.

Summary

This chapter discussed a few technologies that our examples did not cover. There are many more technologies to learn about in the iPhone SDK that may appear to be completely outside the realm of games. However, technologies that are uncommon in games can sometimes be incorporated in creative ways to produce unique and appealing games. If you can pull this off, you might just invent the next great genre in the gaming industry.

In this chapter you learned how to capture images with the camera and select images from the camera roll and Photo Library. You also learned how to read data from the compass so you'll know which direction your device is headed. The details of incorporating sound into your applications were also covered in this chapter. You first looked at AudioToolkit, which can be used to add simple sounds and alerts. You then got a more in-depth look at the powerful sound library OpenAL. Adding video to your applications can incorporate an element of excitement, and you had a chance to see how using the movie player accomplishes this. You also learned how to track positional data so you will know the precise location of your device if it has the correct hardware.

We ended the chapter with a short but exciting 3-D primer. You broke down the details of the OpenGL ES Application Template. After that you got to create an example of a 3-D cube with volume that you can spin with your finger.

We hope you find these additional technologies useful in the applications you build. There are many more technologies you can leverage for the iPhone and more are being added with new hardware and software releases. Continue to watch the news feeds in iPhone Dev Center and at `http://appsamuck.com`. Stay on top of new developments and be the first to write a game that leverages the latest and greatest new feature of the iPhone!

Understanding the Business of Software

There is more to writing a successful application than simply creating a great application. Even if you have a great idea and great code to go with it, there are still literally thousands of other applications that can say the same thing. It is possible for you to have the best app in a given category and still not have the app that everyone is purchasing.

Like anything else, sometimes life is just not fair. But there are many things you can do to help stack the odds in your favor. This chapter provides you with an in-depth foundation of what it takes to ride an application all the way to the top.

Consider the following quote (with apologies to William Shakespeare): "Be not afraid of greatness. Some apps are created great, some achieve greatness, and some have greatness thrust upon them." With almost no effort, great apps rise to the top and dominate the charts. Many times this occurs when a company with an already successful application creates an iPhone version of their software.

Other times an application is simply lucky and has greatness thrust upon it. The application is just in the right place at the right time. A good example of a lucky application is when someone decided to create that first farting application. Apple rejected this app for being crude. The developer then gained massive media attention and people worldwide wondered why Apple rejected this harmless novelty application.

Eventually the developer got Apple to accept the farting application due to public outcry. The media immediately did a follow-up story on how an underdog developer was able to overcome great challenges and obstacles and finally get his farting application on the App Store. Thousands of users downloaded the farting application to find out for themselves what all the controversy was about. Finally, the developer bought a small island in the tropics and retired at the ripe old age of 23 (at least that's what we might imagine!).

In This Chapter

Learning marketing strategies

Making the best apps

Exploring App Store concepts

Customer reviews

Using App Store search secrets

Marketing yourself

Epilogue: Looking ahead

Learning Marketing Strategies

You can have the greatest product in the world, but if nobody knows about it you are never going to make that first sale. People have to find and know about your applications before they can buy them. Not only do you want them to know that your applications exist, but you want them to know what your applications are all about. This burden rests on your shoulders and not on the consumers'. You also need to know information about how well your application is doing in the market and what buyers think about your products. Let's take a look as some ways you can achieve these goals.

App Store reports

Which came first, the chicken or the egg? You have probably heard of this riddle before. Here is another one for you: Which came first, business or reports? It's hard to say for sure, but today the two tend to go hand-in-hand. From day one, the App Store has had reports, and likewise, you should take advantage of these reports from the first day your applications are listed on the App Store. Here is what you need to know to be able to do that.

Financial reports

Apple provides developers with financial reports every month (Figure 10.1). These reports will prove invaluable to you over time because they are the authoritative source for how well your applications are doing on the App Store. Unlike the sales/trend reports, financial reports are not purged and are currently available indefinitely. However, it is still wise to download backups of all reports for your records.

The financial reports are available as tab delimited text files. This means you can open them directly and read them yourself, or even better, you can open them in programs like Numbers or Excel and do more advanced analysis and research.

As an application developer, you will receive up to seven regional financial reports every month. Reports are generated monthly for any regions in which you have had sales. Table 10.1 lists the seven possible financial report regions.

Table 10.1 Financial Report Regions	
Region	*App Store Currency*
United States	USD
Canada	CAD
Europe	EUR
United Kingdom	GBP
Japan	JPY
Australia	AUS
Rest of world (Middle East, Africa, and European and Asian Pacific countries)	USD

Figure 10.1

Financial reports for iTunes Connect

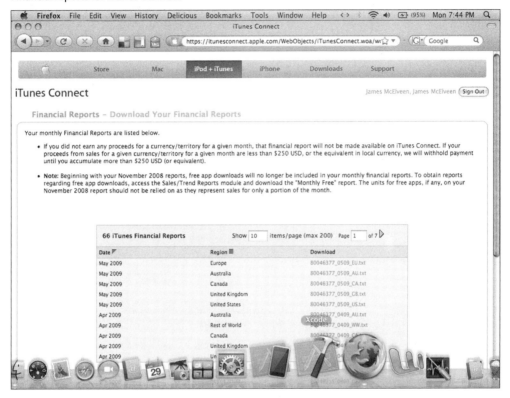

If you open a financial report in an editor of your choice, you will see that the report has over 20 fields. This is indeed a wealth of useful data. Table 10.2 details the information available in a financial report.

Table 10.2 Financial Report Fields

Field	Purpose	Format
Begin Date/Start Date	Date of beginning of report.	MM/DD/YYYY
End Date	Date of end of report.	MM/DD/YYYY
UPC (Universal Product Code)	You can assign a UPC to your application when you add it to the App Store. It then appears in your financial reports.	20 characters maximum

continued

Table 10.2 Continued

Field	Purpose	Format
ISRC (International Standard Recording Code)	The ISRC is the international identification system for sound recordings and music video recordings. It is meant to be used by iTunes content providers, not so much by application developers.	20 characters maximum
Vendor Identifier	This is a vendor identifier that is provided by you when you add your application to the App Store. If your company has multiple departments or subcontractors, this field may be more useful to you.	20 characters maximum
Units/Quantity	This is the total number of units sold.	Integer/whole number
Partner Share	*Partner* refers to you, and *share* refers to the percentage of the sale that is yours. It is the percentage of the proceeds you will receive per unit. For application developers, this is fixed at 70 percent.	Currency field
Extended Partner Share	This is a calculated field. Its value is always *quantity* times *partner share*.	Currency field
Partner Share Currency	This is the currency that will be used to pay you.	3 characters
Sales or Return	You will always see either an S (for sale) or an R (for return) here.	1 character, either an S or an R
Apple Identifier	This is the unique identifier that Apple assigns your application on the App Store.	18 characters maximum
Artist/Show/Developer	In this case, you should see the developer name you used to join the developer program.	4,000 characters maximum
Title	This shows your application's title.	5,000 characters maximum
Label/Studio/Network/Developer	If you registered as a company instead of as an individual, you see your company name here.	1,000 characters maximum
Grid	This is a product identifier.	30 characters maximum
Product Type Identifier	This field defines the type of product that was purchased (song, application, etc.). If it's an application purchase for an iPhone or an iPod touch, it is always a 1. If it's an application update, it is a 7.	5 characters maximum
ISAN (International Standard Audiovisual Number)/Other Identifier	An ISAN is a voluntary numbering system and metadata schema enabling the identification of any kind of audiovisual works, such as films, shorts, documentaries, television programs, sports events, and advertising, as well as their related versions.	50 characters maximum
Country of Sale	ISO country code that indicates what iTunes Store front the purchase occurred in.	2 characters

Field	Purpose	Format
Preorder	Currently preorder is applicable only to music and related media purchases, not applications. When an item is a preorder fulfillment, a P is present in this field; otherwise, this field is empty.	1 character
Promo Code	This is another field that is currently only for music and related media purchases.	10 characters maximum
Customer Price	This is the price the customer paid.	Currency field
Customer Currency	This code indicates the currency the customer paid in.	3 characters

Consider working with your favorite spreadsheet application to take your monthly financial reports and create some useful formulas and charts to help you keep your finger on the pulse of your application sales.

Sales/trend reports

Apple provides developers with many App Store resources, including sales and trend reports. You can find these reports on the iTunes Connect site at `https://itunesconnect.apple.com/`.

Even though the sales/trend reports have only the summary report type available, you do have three reporting period options: monthly free, weekly, and daily. Be aware that Apple removes any daily reports older than 7 days and any weekly reports older than 13 weeks, so be sure to keep local backups of these files. Once they are purged there is no way to go back and get previous reporting data.

CAUTION

Sales/trend reports are for directional purposes only. You should not use them for financial statement purposes; instead, use the financial reports for that purpose.

You can download your sales/trend reports or preview them online (Figure 10.2). If you preview them online, be aware that you can only see the top 50 rows from each report. The reports are sorted in descending order by the number of sales.

These reports show data for each sale, refund, and update of any application you have for any of the currently available 77 iTunes Store fronts. Even something as simple as changing the price of an application causes additional rows to be created. In other words, it is very easy for you to outgrow the sales/trend reporting preview feature. It's okay to spot-check things using the preview feature, but for any serious sales analysis you should skip the preview and work directly off downloaded files, which contain all the data.

The daily, weekly, and monthly free summary reports all have the same fields. Many of the fields in these reports are very similar to the ones in the financial reports, but in most cases the field's position has been changed or the field's name has been modified. There are also some new fields. Table 10.3 gives you more information about these changes.

Figure 10.2

Sales/trend report for iTunes Connect

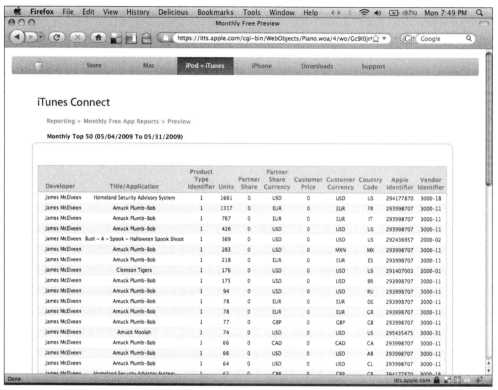

Table 10.3 Summary Report Fields

Field	Purpose	Format
Provider	This field always contains the text APPLE.	50 characters maximum
Provider Country	This field always contains the text US.	50 characters maximum
Vendor Identifier	This is a vendor identification that is provided by you when you add your application to the App Store. If your company has multiple departments or subcontractors, this field may be more useful to you.	20 characters maximum
UPC (Universal Product Code)	You can assign a UPC to your application when you add it to the App Store. It then appears in your financial reports.	20 characters maximum
ISRC (International Standard Recording Code)	The ISRC is the international identification system for sound recordings and music video recordings. It is meant to be used by iTunes content providers.	20 characters maximum

Field	Purpose	Format
Artist/Show	In this case, you should see the developer name you used to join the developer program.	4,000 characters maximum
Title/Episode/Season	This shows your application's title.	5,000 characters maximum
Label/Studio/Network	If you registered as a company instead of as an individual, you see your company name here.	1,000 characters maximum
Product Type Identifier	This field defines the type of product that was purchased (e.g., song, application, etc). If it's an application purchase for an iPhone or an iPod touch, it is always a 1. If it's an application update, it is a 7.	5 characters maximum
Units/Quantity	This is the aggregated number of units sold.	Integer/whole number
Royalty Price	This is the royalty price for the item.	Currency field
Begin Date/Start Date	Date of beginning of report.	MM/DD/YYYY
End Date	Date of end of report.	MM/DD/YYYY
Customer Currency	Code that indicates the currency the customer paid in.	3 characters
Country Code	ISO country code that indicates what iTunes Store front the purchase occurred in.	2 characters
Royalty Currency	This is the royalty currency.	3 characters
Preorder	Currently preorder is applicable only to music and related media purchases, not to applications. When an item is a preorder fulfillment, a P is present in this field; otherwise, this field is empty.	1 character
Season Pass	This field is currently only for music and related media purchases.	20 characters maximum
ISAN (International Standard Audiovisual Number)	An ISAN is a voluntary numbering system and metadata schema enabling the identification of any kind of audiovisual works, such as films, shorts, documentaries, television programs, sports events, and advertising, as well as their related versions.	50 characters maximum
Apple Identifier	This is the unique identifier that Apple assigns your application on the App Store.	18 characters maximum
Customer Price	This is the price the customer paid.	Currency field
CMA	This field is currently only for music and related media purchases.	10 characters maximum
Asset/Content Flavor	The field is currently only applicable to video content.	20 characters maximum
Vendor Offer Code	This is a product identifier.	30 characters maximum
Grid	This is a product identifier.	30 characters maximum
Promo Code	If the transaction was a part of a promotion, this field contains a value.	10 characters maximum
Parent Identifier	This field is currently only for music and related media purchases.	100 characters maximum

App Store statistics

A doctor learns more about a patient's health by looking at that person's vital statistics. Similarly, an iPhone developer has his application's sales/trend reports to learn more about his application's health. The sales/trend reports provide you with an early detection system that you can use anytime to monitor all of your applications.

Consider a scenario where you have been getting many sales each day, but then suddenly you are not getting any sales for one of your applications in particular. That may be a sign that the application has been removed from the App Store due to a content issue. This could be an expensive oversight if you did not find out about it until you saw the much smaller royalty check that followed. Remember, royalty checks are monthly, but always for the previous month's sales. That's a long time for an issue to go unhandled.

Application size

The App Store allows you to upload a new application as large as 2GB. But be aware that if your application is larger than 10MB, it will not be available to download directly to a device unless it is connected to a wireless network. Users who are out and about and only connected via a cellular connection will not be able to download the application directly. It's best to try and fit your application in a space of less than 10MB.

Application price

You have a lot of freedom when deciding how to best price your application. You can decide to make your application totally free; in other words, it is free to download and it contains no ads. Or you could make your application free to download but there are ads displayed in the app. The next option is to sell your application on the App Store for a set price. The average price of an application on the App Store is around $2.50. One of the most common prices that developers charge for their application is $0.99.

The monetization strategy that you choose for your application is one of the largest factors in how much revenue your application generates once on the App Store. And now you find yourself in a dilemma: If you charge too much, users may decide not to purchase your application, thereby lowering your profit. But if you charge too little, you may not get enough return on your investment to generate as much profit as you could have otherwise.

What should you do? Unfortunately, you are going to have to figure out the best answer to that question on your own. Our recommendation is to keep detailed records and measurements so you can experiment and try new things frequently. This way you can adapt and change as needed and learn and grow over time to help maximize both your success and profits.

Originally, the App Store allowed developers to set the price of their applications from $0.99 to $999.99, but later Apple lowered the maximum application price. Currently, it appears you can once again set your application price to $999.99. When you add your application to the App Store, you must apply a pricing tier to your application. There are 85 pricing tiers.

Pricing tier 1 means your application costs $0.99; tier 2 means your application costs $1.99; and so on, up to pricing tier 50, in which your application sells for $49.99. After that things start to get a little more complicated, with the price increasing exponentially all the way to $999.99 at pricing tier 85.

- Tier 1: $0.99
- Tier 2: $1.99
- Tier 3: $2.99
- ...
- Tier 47: $46.99
- Tier 48: $47.99
- Tier 49: $48.99
- Tier 50: $49.99
- Tier 51: $54.99
- Tier 52: $59.99
- Tier 53: $64.99
- Tier 54: $69.99
- Tier 55: $74.99
- Tier 56: $79.99
- Tier 57: $84.99
- Tier 58: $89.99
- Tier 59: $94.99
- Tier 60: $99.99
- Tier 61: $109.99
- Tier 62: $119.99
- Tier 63: $129.99
- Tier 64: $139.99
- Tier 65: $149.99
- Tier 66: $159.99
- Tier 67: $169.99
- Tier 68: $179.99
- Tier 69: $189.99
- Tier 70: $199.99
- Tier 71: $209.99
- Tier 72: $219.99
- Tier 73: $229.99
- Tier 74: $239.99
- Tier 75: $249.99
- Tier 76: $299.99
- Tier 77: $349.99
- Tier 78: $399.99
- Tier 79: $449.99
- Tier 80: $499.99
- Tier 81: $599.99
- Tier 82: $699.99
- Tier 83: $799.99
- Tier 84: $899.99
- Tier 85: $999.99

CAUTION

You should feel free to set the price of your application as you see fit, but be aware that there are not too many iPhone owners who are willing to pay $999.99 for an application. Be careful not to price your application out of existence.

Refunds

Refunds on the App Store are uncommon. The App Store refund policy is "All sales are final." But Apple will provide a customer a refund in the case of application quality issues. Apple recommends monitoring the rate of refunds for applications, since it is a strong indication of quality issues that you may be able to correct with a simple application update.

Parental controls

The iPhone and App Store support parental controls and age-based restriction settings. If you want your application to appeal to a broad audience, be sure to keep your application strictly PG. When you add your application to the App Store, you will have to choose how frequently your application exposes users to various types of content. The levels of content frequency are none, infrequent/mild, and frequent/intense. The various types of content Apple reviews are as follows:

- Realistic violence
- Sexual content or nudity
- Profanity or crude humor
- Alcohol, tobacco, or drug use, or references
- Mature/suggestive themes
- Simulated gambling
- Horror/fear themes
- Prolonged graphic or sadistic realistic violence

App ratings

Based on your choices for frequency of reviewed content, your application will be given an app rating. Apple's app ratings state the age appropriateness for your application. An app rating of 4+ means your application is appropriate for anyone four years and older. But note that regardless of rating, applications must not contain any obscene, pornographic, offensive, or defamatory content or materials of any kind (text, graphics, images, photographs, etc.), or other content or materials that in Apple's reasonable judgment may be found objectionable. There is a correlation between ESRB (Entertainment Software Rating Board), PEGI (Pan-European Game Information), and Apple's App Rating, as shown in Table 10.4.

Table 10.4 App Ratings			
Apple's App Rating	*ESRB Equivalent*	*PEGI Equivalent*	*What It Means*
4+	EC	3+	Applications contain no objectionable materials.
9+	E10+	None	Applications may contain mild or infrequent occurrences of cartoon, fantasy, or realistic violence; and infrequent or mild mature, suggestive, or horror-themed content, which may not be suitable for children under the age of 9.
12+	T	12+	Applications may also contain infrequent mild language; frequent or intense cartoon, fantasy, or realistic violence; mild or infrequent mature or suggestive themes; and simulated gambling, which may not be suitable for children under the age of 12.
17+	Mature	16+	Applications may also contain frequent and intense offensive language; frequent and intense cartoon, fantasy, or realistic violence; and frequent and intense mature, horror, and suggestive themes; plus sexual content; nudity; and references to alcohol, tobacco, and drugs, which may not be suitable for children under the age of 17.

Restriction settings

Device owners can enable restriction settings on their device in Parental Controls to filter applications that can be installed on the device (Figure 10.3). The restriction setting levels match the app ratings that Apple assigns to applications on the App Store: Don't Allow Apps, 4+, 9+, 12+, 17+, and Allow All Apps.

Quality control

You can measure your application quality by analyzing your sales/trend reports. According to Apple, the typical ratio of refunds to overall sales should not exceed 0.5 percent. If you are seeing refunds in excess of that amount for a given application, it means that application's quality is likely subpar. Not only are you losing revenue due to refunds, but unhappy customers are likely to leave negative reviews and turn other potential customers away from your applications.

Figure 10.3

Restriction settings

Making the Best Apps

Another way you can surprise and delight users is by including hidden features and functionality in your applications. These hidden features are sometimes known as *Easter eggs*. Figure 10.4 shows an example of one possible Easter egg.

Figure 10.4

Possible iPhone OS Easter egg: Emoji icons

Imagine that you have a fantasy role-playing game, and as the characters explore the land there is one screen where they can see an animated waterfall. It appears to be a part of the background imagery, but if a character tries to walk behind the waterfall, he is taken to a secret room that has some magical items that will aid him on his mission.

Using sound

What would movies be without music, soundtracks, and special effects? The same vacuum is made when you create an application without sound. An application without sound is only a little better than an application without graphics. Sound gives you yet another chance to surprise and delight your users, and you should never miss a chance to do this.

While you should always make an effort to include sound in your applications, you should also always include an easy way for your users to disable any audio you have in your app. While audio is a great feature for your applications to have, sometimes users don't want the extra attention it brings, or they may find it distracting. Make sure to always keep your application's user in charge.

You should be very excited to know that developers now have the ability to use music and playlists from the device iPod library in iPhone OS 3.0. This is a huge and largely untapped feature that would be a great advantage for your next game.

OpenGL ES

OpenGL ES (OpenGL for Embedded Systems) is a subset of the OpenGL 3D graphics API. All versions of the iPhone support OpenGL ES, but only the iPhone 3GS supports the latest version, OpenGL ES 2.0. This new version runs two to four times faster than OpenGL ES 1.1 on the previous models of the iPhone.

You can see the sample OpenGL ES application that Apple makes available in Figure 10.5. It may appear to be a simple shape, but many computer-generated images, especially in games, are built up from simple shapes like triangles. Like most things in math, once you master the basics you can do so much more.

Once again you may find yourself facing a dilemma. If you are considering doing any 3-D development for the iPhone using OpenGL ES and you want to support all devices, your application should target OpenGL ES 1.1. If you need the new texture and shading features of OpenGL ES 2.0 or the increased performance it allows, you will have to limit your application to the iPhone 3GS.

Transitions

One simple thing you can do to make all of your applications better is to take advantage of transitions. You'll notice that in almost all of the built-in iPhone applications, any time you go from one screen in an application to another, some sort of transition is fired. Maybe the next screen slides in from the right, or the screen curls up to reveal the screen behind it, as shown in Figure 10.6. But generally there is some eye candy to keep the user's attention and focus. You should want the same for your application's users.

Figure 10.5

Apple's OpenGL ES demo application

The `UIViewAnimation Transitions` that are available in the iPhone SDK include the following:

- `UIViewAnimationTransitionNone`
  This skips showing a transition and immediately shows the next screen instead.

- `UIViewAnimationTransitionFlipFromLeft`
  This transition flips the screen from left to right vertically.

- `UIViewAnimationTransitionFlipFromRight`
  This transition flips the screen from right to left vertically.

- `UIViewAnimationTransitionCurlUp`
  This transition curls the view up from the right.

- `UIViewAnimationTransitionCurlDown`
  This transition curls the view down from the top.

Figure 10.6

`UIViewAnimationTransitionCurlUp` being used to curl up view to reveal screen underneath

Xcode tools

Even the best carpenter in the world would have a hard time without the right tools. Make sure to take advantage of all the great tools you have available to you as an iPhone application developer. Here are some of the most important ones:

- **Xcode.** Xcode (Figure 10.7) is the development environment for iPhone applications.
- **Interface Builder.** Interface Builder is a visual design tool you use to create the user interfaces of your iPhone applications.

- **Dashcode.** This allows for the creation of Web pages that are optimized for Safari on the iPhone.

- **Organizer.** You use the Organizer to add Provisioning Profiles to your development device.

- **Debugger.** The Xcode Debugger window offers a traditional but rich GUI debugging experience.

- **Console.** This allows you to interact with the Debugger on the command line.

- **Research Assistant.** The Research Assistant shows the selected symbol's declaration or availability information. You can also find sample code and related documents.

- **Shark.** Shark is a tool for understanding and optimizing application performance.

- **Instruments.** Instruments is an application for dynamically tracing and profiling iPhone application code. It includes the following useful templates: activity monitors, CPU sampler, file activity, leaks, object allocations, and UI recorder.

Figure 10.7

Xcode integrated development environment

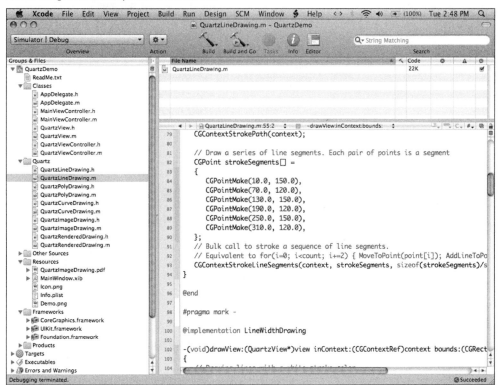

Development Provisioning Assistant

You can use the Development Provisioning Assistant (Figure 10.8) to create and install a Provisioning Profile and iPhone Development Certificate needed to build and install applications you're developing for iPhone and iPod touch devices.

Figure 10.8

Development Provisioning Assistant

There is a lot of work that must be done to configure your development machines and your development devices so they can work together and allow you to deploy applications you are developing. The Development Provisioning Assistant can do all of the manual steps for you and remove the chore from the process.

NOTE

You can find out more about the Development Provisioning Assistant and download it at
`http://developer.apple.com/iphone/manage/overview/index.action`.

Apple Bug Reporter

Apple provides developers with a tool they can use to submit bug reports and enhancement requests. Developers can then track submitted bugs and enhancements using the Apple Bug Reporter, shown in Figure 10.9. If you do find a bug and it is a problem for you, you can even request a workaround using a technical support incident.

Figure 10.9

Apple Bug Reporter

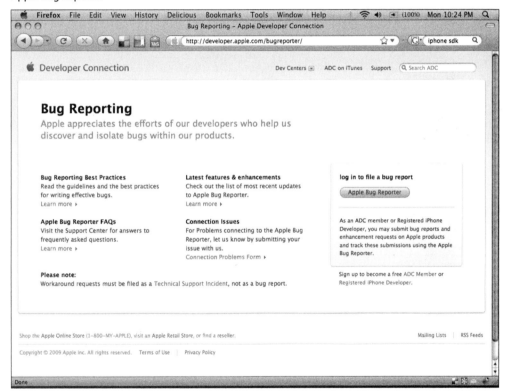

It's great knowing that if you encounter an issue while developing for the iPhone, Apple is there to support you. But what's really great is knowing that if you have an idea for an improvement to the iPhone, you can submit an enhancement request, and just maybe your idea will be a part of the next iPhone.

iPhone 3GS features

Recently Apple released the iPhone 3GS (Figure 10.10), and along with it a new iPhone OS 3.0 and iPhone SDK that allow developers to fully take advantage of this device's new capabilities. Here's an introduction to what has been added and what is new:

Figure 10.10

iPhone 3GS

- **Accessibility.** iPhone 3GS offers accessibility features to assist users who are visually or hearing impaired. These features include the VoiceOver screen reader, a Zoom feature, White on Black display options, Mono Audio, and more.

- **Compass.** Combine a GPS with an accelerometer and now a digital compass and you have the ultimate mobile navigation tool that fits right in your pocket.

- **Open GL ES 2.0.** Open GL ES 2.0 allows applications the ability to feature richer visuals and smoother game play performance. One of the biggest differences between Open GL ES 1.0 and Open GL ES 2.0 is that the latest version includes more advanced shader support.

● **Video recording.** Now you can enjoy the same power and flexibility that the iPhone brings to photos with video. You can record, edit, and share video right on the device.

iPhone OS 3.0 features

The new iPhone OS 3.0 (Figure 10.11) brings a lot of new features and functionality. Not only is their support for new hardware found on the iPhone 3GS, but many of the new iPhone OS 3.0 capabilities work on all devices, including devices before the iPhone 3GS.

Figure 10.11

iPhone OS 3.0

Make sure to always keep up with new OS features so your apps can take full advantage of new opportunities:

● **Automatic Wi-Fi login.** Device automatically logs in to any Wi-Fi hotspot that it has seen before.

- **Cut, copy, and paste.** You can now cut, copy, and paste text from any application. And you can even copy and paste images from Safari.

- **Find My iPhone.** If you lose your phone you can now track its location via Find My iPhone.

- **Internet tethering.** Your laptop can now access your device's Internet connection through either Bluetooth or USB.

- **iTunes Store account.** The on-device App Store now allows users to log in to iTunes with different accounts.

- **Landscape keyboard.** Need more room to type? More applications support the landscape keyboard feature, including Mail, Messages, Notes, and Safari.

- **MMS.** You can now send audio, contact information, and photos using MMS messages.

- **New languages and keyboard layouts.** iPhone now features 30 new languages as well as 40 new keyboard layouts.

- **Parental controls.** You're in charge of deciding what apps, music, and videos your kids have access to.

- **Remote Wipe.** Remote Wipe ensures your personal and private information is always safe.

- **Shake to shuffle.** You can now shuffle to another song with ease by giving your device a quick shake.

- **Spotlight Search.** Search calendar, contacts, e-mail, notes, and media content from one screen using Spotlight Search.

- **Stereo Bluetooth.** Hear your iPhone audio in stereo using any compatible Bluetooth audio hardware device.

- **Sync notes.** Notes now can be synchronized back to desktop using iTunes.

- **Voice memos.** You can record audio memos using the iPhone's microphone or even your headset.

- **YouTube login.** You can log in and access your YouTube account, including bookmarks and favorites.

iPhone SDK 3.0 features

So the iPhone 3GS brings new features, and the iPhone OS 3.0 contains new capabilities, but you'll need to use the iPhone SDK 3.0 (Figure 10.12) in order to fully take advantage of either of these.

It is through the iPhone SDK 3.0 that you will be able to tap into the new framework and libraries:

- **In App Purchase.** The Store Kit framework (`StoreKit.framework`) provides a means for you to make additional content and services available from within your iPhone applications. For example, you could use this feature to allow the user to unlock additional application features. Or, if you are a game developer, you could use it to offer additional game levels.

● **Apple Push Notification service.** The Apple Push Notification service allows you to alert your users to new information, even when your application is not actively running. Using this service, you can push text notifications, trigger audible alerts, or add a numbered badge to your application icon. These messages let users know that they should open your application to receive the related information.

● **Accessories.** The External Accessory framework (`ExternalAccessory.framework`) provides support for communicating with hardware accessories attached to an iPhone or iPod touch device. Accessories can be connected through the 30-pin dock connector of a device or wirelessly using Bluetooth.

Figure 10.12

iPhone SDK 3.0

● **Peer-to-peer connectivity.** The Game Kit framework (`GameKit.framework`) lets you add peer-to-peer network capabilities to your applications. Specifically, this framework provides support for peer-to-peer connectivity and in-game voice features. Although these features are most commonly found in multiplayer network games, you can incorporate them into non-game applications as well.

CROSS-REFERENCE
See Chapter 7 for a full discussion on peer-to-peer connectivity.

- **Maps.** The Map Kit framework (`MapKit.framework`) provides a map interface that you can embed into your own application. Based on the behavior of this interface within the Maps application, it provides a scrollable map view that can be annotated with custom information.

- **iPod library access.** Several new classes and protocols have been added to the Media Player framework (`MediaPlayer.framework`) to allow access to the user's audio library.

- **Cut, copy, and paste.** The UIKit framework provides new classes to support pasteboard operations and also incorporates selection and pasteboard behaviors into some existing UIKit views. You can use the new classes to incorporate cut, copy, and paste behaviors into your application.

- **Audio recording and management.** The AV Foundation framework (`AVFoundation.framework`) includes new classes and protocols for recording audio and managing audio sessions.

- **Core Data.** The Core Data framework (`CoreData.framework`) is a technology for managing the data model of a Model-View-Controller application. Core Data is intended for use in applications where the data model is already highly structured. Instead of defining data structures programmatically, you use the graphical tools in Xcode to build a schema representing your data model.

- **In-app e-mail.** The Message UI framework (`MessageUI.framework`) is a new framework that provides support for composing and queuing e-mail messages in the user's outbox.

- **Streaming video.** There is now support for the playback of live video that is stored on the Web. Streamed content can be played back on an iPhone OS–based device using the `MPMoviePlayerController` class.

- **Safari features.** Safari supports the audio and video HTML elements, which allow you to embed audio and video content into your Web applications. Safari also supports geolocation JavaScript classes, which work with the onboard location services to retrieve the current location of the device.

- **Shared keychain items.** It is now possible for you to share keychain items among multiple applications you create. Sharing items makes it easier for applications in the same suite to interoperate more smoothly. For example, you could use this feature to share user passwords or other elements that might otherwise require you to prompt the user from each application separately.

- **Accessibility support.** Accessibility support makes it easier for people with visual, auditory, or physical disabilities to use iPhone OS–based devices.

- **Compass support.** The Core Location framework now includes support for obtaining heading information from iPhone OS–based devices with a built-in magnetometer. Heading information obtained from such devices can be used to implement a real-time compass or other navigation-related programs.

- **OpenGL ES 2.0.** Applications can now take advantage of the OpenGL ES 2.0 specification on iPhone OS–based devices with appropriate graphics hardware.

Simulator vs. device

The Simulator can do much of what a real device can do, but to completely know how an application will work in the field, you much test it on true devices. Many things such as battery life, performance, and hardware-related APIs are only valid on actual devices.

Simulator limitations include the following:

- Accelerometer supports only shakes and rotation.
- Camera is not supported.
- Location/GPS is hardcoded to one location.
- Multi-Touch events are not supported.
- OpenGL ES is not supported.
- Peer-to-peer (P2P) is not supported.
- Time zone cannot be set on Simulator.

If your application is built around any of these features, you will only be able to fully test your applications on true devices. Again, the Simulator works great for quick and dirty testing, but always run your application on a real device for final testing.

Worldwide Developers Conference

The Apple Worldwide Developers Conference (WWDC) provides developers with in-depth technical information and hands-on learning about the powerful technologies in iPhone OS and Mac OS X from the Apple engineers who created them. The WWDC is a great opportunity for developers to learn more about the iPhone SDK directly from the source. The conference typically lasts five days and has over a thousand Apple engineers who give presentations and are available to answer your questions. The conference always sells out well in advance.

WWDC highlights include the following:

- iPhone OS and Mac OS X developer-focused content
- Technical sessions
- Hands-on labs

- Special events, such as Stump the Experts and the Apple Design Awards
- 5,000 other developers on site

TIP

Find out more about the Worldwide Developers Conference at `http://developer.apple.com/wwdc/`.

Apple Developer Connection (ADC) memberships

You have to join the iPhone Developer Program if you want to be able to create applications that can be installed on real devices from the App Store. But you can also get an Apple Developer Connection (ADC) membership. Membership levels are Premier ($3,499), Select ($499), Student ($99), and Online (free) for a one-year membership. Figure 10.13 shows the ADC membership page.

Figure 10.13

Apple Developer Connection membership page

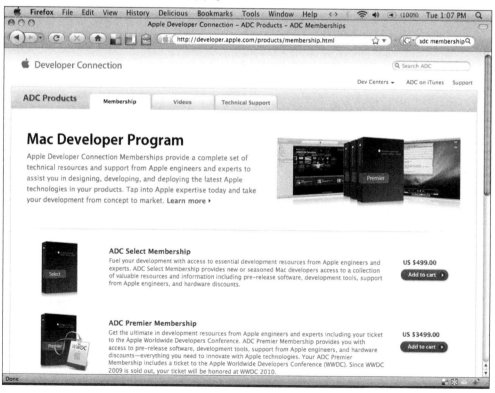

ADC memberships offer many more benefits, including:

- One ticket to the Apple Worldwide Developers Conference (Premier only)
- Software Seeding Program (Premier and Select only)
- Technical Support (eight calls per year for Premier and two calls per year for Select)
- Developer Forums (Premier and Select only)
- ADC on iTunes (Premier and Select include full access; limited otherwise)
- Compatibility Labs (three days per month for Premier and two days per month for Select)
- Hardware Purchase Program (10 systems per year for Premier and 1 system per year for Select)

Apple Developer Forums

Just as no man is an island unto himself, as the saying goes, no developer can figure out everything on his own. You've probably already figured this out for yourself, or you wouldn't have bought this book in the first place. The day will come when you will have a problem and no clue what to try next. When that day arrives, one of the first places we recommend you look is the Apple Developer Forums (Figure 10.14).

The Apple Developer Forums allow developers to discuss iPhone development with other iPhone developers and Apple engineers. It is one of the few places where developers can go and discuss iPhone SDK features that may still be under NDA, or non-disclosure agreement. Apple typically requires developers to not publicly discuss material related to beta releases of either the iPhone OS or iPhone SDK in order to better protect their intellectual property. Once these items are publicly released, developers usually are free to discuss details publicly.

The Apple Developer Forums cover many topics, including Getting Started, Cocoa Touch, Core OS, Graphics and Media, Web Technologies, System and Device Features, Performance, Developer Tools, Distribution, and User Experience. If you are having a problem figuring out a way to accomplish something using the iPhone SDK, then others have probably already had the same issue and maybe even found a solution that they would be willing to share with you.

Figure 10.14

Apple Developer Forums

Apple Push Notification service

With iPhone OS 3.0, developers now have the power to use Apple Push Notification service. Instead of allowing background applications on the iPhone, Apple decided to implement a remote notification system. The goal was to maximize battery life and performance. With push notifications, your application can receive events even when it is not running (Figure 10.15).

Apple Push Notification ideas include:

- Sports game scores
- Instant messaging and chat applications
- Workflow and task management applications
- Game challenges and invites
- Deal-of-the-day applications

Figure 10.15

Example of Apple Push Notification received while
application not running

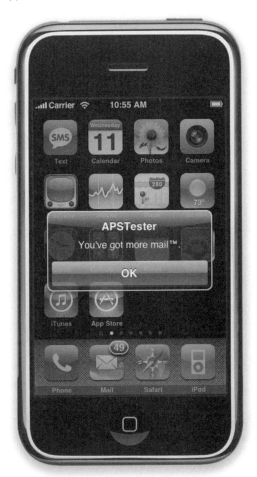

Be aware that when the iPod touch screen is on and has a Wi-Fi connection, push notifications
are received at any time. If the iPod touch screen is asleep, it will check every 15 minutes for a
notification.

Product icons

Product icons make up a large part of the first impression many users have of your application,
as shown in Figure 10.16. Since app icons are 59 x 59 pixels for the device icon and 512 x 512
pixels for the App Store icon, there is potential to include marketing messages on the icon itself.

Take a look at the top apps on the App Store today and you'll find many applications with some kind of marketing text as a banner, badge, or overlay. Some of the more common ones are Sale!, Sales 75%, 99¢, FREE!, and LITE.

Figure 10.16

iFlame's 512-x-512-pixel App Store icon

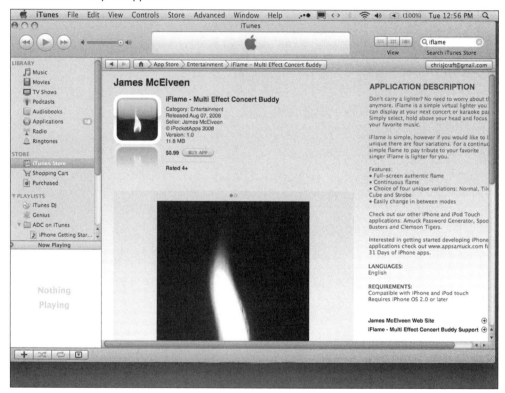

NOTE

You might have noticed that the App Store always has three large application ads at the top of the main page in iTunes. You might be wondering how much it costs to advertise on the App Store yourself. Unfortunately, for the most part, you cannot simply purchase this advertising on the App Store. These are not usually paid ads. You must be approached directly from Apple for your application to be featured here.

Supporting different iPhone OS versions

When Apple was preparing the iPhone OS 3.0 for release, there was a period where developers were required to support multiple versions of the OS. This meant that your application had to work on the current version of the iPhone OS as well as on an upcoming version of the iPhone

OS. It can get expensive purchasing multiple devices to test different iPhone OS versions on. Fortunately, it is possible to downgrade a device's firmware in order to test an application on an earlier OS version. This can be necessary if you begin to get reports from users that your application is having issues on iPhone OS version X.X.X and you're on a newer version.

In order to do this, you have to put your device in Device Firmware Update (DFU) mode. Here are the steps to do that:

1. Open iTunes and connect your device.

2. Press and hold down the Home button and the Sleep/Wake button at the same time.

3. After 5 to 10 seconds, release the Sleep/Wake button. Continue holding down the Home button until iTunes displays a message telling you it has detected an iPhone in recovery mode. Note that your screen should remain blank during this process—if you see the Apple logo or a Restore screen, try again.

4. Right-click the Restore button in iTunes, and you should be able to select any firmware version to load.

Exploring App Store Concepts

Being a developer and working with the App Store is a bit like being a manufacturer and working with Wal-Mart. You are not the one in power in this relationship and there are certain ways of going about things that you have to learn before you can be successful in this marketplace.

Supply and demand

If you have taken any basic economic classes, you are familiar with the concept of supply and demand. Why are people willing to pay more for diamonds than for water, when they need water to survive? It is because diamonds are scarcer than water. If you changed the supply of either water or diamonds enough, you could be sure to change which one people would be willing to pay more for.

Supply and demand applies to the App Store as well. Let's say your application has been getting 10 sales a day, at $4.99 per sale. This works out to about $50.00 per day of revenue for this application. What would happen if you offered a special where you lowered the price to $0.99? If you were to get 100 sales a day at $0.99 per sale, you would be making about $100 per day in revenue. In other words, for no real extra work or cost, you would double your income simply by lowering your price. This is a win-win situation for both you and your users. Notice that by reducing the price of your product you were able to increase the demand for your product.

This can work in reverse as well. Suppose you were selling another application on the App Store for $0.99 and you were getting as many as 100 sales a day. Now you decide to raise the price to $9.99, and find out you lose a majority of your sales, but you still get around 20 sales a day. In this case you went from making around $100 a day to making close to $200 a day on this one application. This time you saw that by increasing the price of your product you were able to better capture the full monetary demand for your product. Your sales/trend reports can help you better find your application's profit-maximizing price point. It is always easier to get more sales simply by lowering the price. But if you want to maximize your application's profit, you need to experiment and use a little trial and error to find your application's profit "sweet spot."

Promo codes

Apple allows developers to request promotional codes that will give users free downloads of applications. You can generate a promo code for any of your applications by going to `https://itunesconnect.apple.com/` and choosing Request Promotional Codes. The request promotional code Web page has a View History feature (Figure 10.17), which allows you to view your requested promo code history for the last 60 days.

NOTE
You are given 50 promotional codes for each version of an application. They will expire after four weeks, and they can only be used in the U.S. iTunes Store.

Why would you want to give away any of your applications for free? What if you wanted to have a contest for one of your applications, and give the winner a free copy of another one of your applications? Promo codes make contests like this quick and easy for everyone involved. You can even make the contest a part of one of your applications. Or you could run the contest on Twitter, Facebook, or another social networking site. By tapping into a social networking site, you have the potential of creating a viral marketing event. Viral marketing is about creating a buzz—for example, creating a video that viewers enjoy so much that they pass it along to their friends. Say you create an app demo video that you manage to get in front of 1,000 people, who each share it with two of their friends, who in turn share it with two of *their* friends, and so on. You can see the snowball effect this creates. Another situation in which you might want to share free promo codes with others is if you have a few beta testers who have been testing your new application and you want to reward them for all their hard work with a free copy of the final product.

In iPhone OS 3.0 it is possible to redeem promo codes right from the App Store application on the phone. Currently it is not possible to send promo codes as links either through text messaging or e-mails, but users can take promo codes that they may have received in an e-mail and copy and paste the code into the redeem section of the new App Store iPhone application. There are even Web sites devoted to giving away iPhone application promo codes. For example, `www.appgiveaway.com/` helps developers generate buzz about their applications by creating promotional giveaways around the app promotional codes. Consider that while only a few people can win the promotional codes for the free applications, many more people see the applications listed on the site. This is a great form of advertising and marketing.

Finally, you may want to allow someone to review your application. There are many sites that focus specifically on reviewing iPhone applications. Many of these sites request that you provide them with a promo code so that they can review your application without having to buy it.

It can get very expensive for a site to review hundreds of iPhone applications if the site has to pay for all of the applications it reviews.

Figure 10.17

Requesting promotional codes

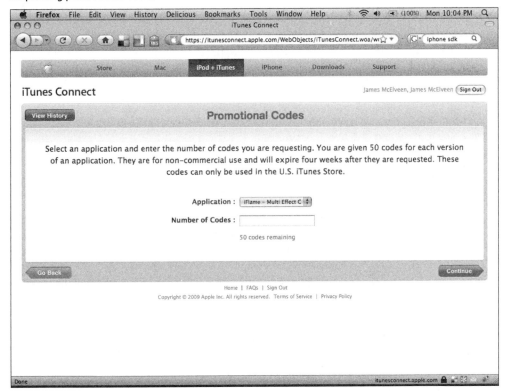

Contests

We mentioned earlier that you could have contests for your application where you give away App Store promo codes to users so they can download your applications for free. But that's not the only way you can take advantage of contests to promote your applications.

Many developers of graphics- and photo-related iPhone applications hold contests for their applications where users can submit content that they have created with their applications. In one case people might compete to draw the best picture, and in the other case users might try to take the best photo.

Other ideas are to create in-game challenges and reward users with prizes accordingly. Usually these contests would be framed around the basic idea of the application. For example, if you created a game with many challenging levels, you could run a contest for the first player to make it through all 13 levels. If you have a puzzle game that is a time-based challenge, you could give a prize for the player with the best score in the next 30 days. The possibilities are endless. You just have to find the right ones to fit your applications.

App Store rejections

One day you are likely to have one of your applications rejected by Apple for the App Store. It happens, and you shouldn't let it affect you personally. In most situations you will be able to address the issue and resubmit your application and have everything work out for the best.

If you have an application rejected, often you can find another application that already exists on the App Store that does exactly what your application was rejected for. It can be quite frustrating, but getting upset will not do anything to help the situation. Just assume that there is another developer looking at one of your other applications already on the App Store and wondering why his got rejected and yours did not.

There are several reasons an app may be rejected:

- **Application bugs.** Your application should be, for the most part, free of any application bugs. Otherwise you run the risk of either the App Store rejecting your application or, even worse, your application users rejecting your application.

- **Data.** Apps that transfer large amounts of data over cellular connections have been another common candidate for rejection. This includes everything from tethering applications to video applications.

- **Duplication.** There is an expression that says if two people are exactly the same then one of them is unnecessary. Apple has this philosophy to applications that duplicate functionality of applications already existing in the iPhone OS. Even if you make a better app, it may be rejected if one just like it already exists. After we created iFlame, we went back and created Camp Fire, which was summarily rejected because it reminded someone too much of iFlame.

- **Graphics.** Be careful when reusing existing graphic elements from the iPhone OS. In many cases, a developer who copies icons, images, or logos from the iPhone OS and uses them in their application will have their application rejected.

- **Icons.** Your 57-x-57-pixel application icon must be the same as your 512-x-512-pixel App Store icon. The only difference allowed is that one is larger than the other. At one point we had some text on the large icon that wasn't on the smaller icon. This caused the entire application to be rejected until we redid the icons to match.

- **Offensive material.** Any offensive material in your application, whether in text or image form, will cause your application to be rejected. You can even run this risk if your application pulls down third-party data streams like Twitter, Facebook, RSS, and so on. Apple says: "Applications must not contain any obscene, pornographic, offensive, or defamatory content or materials of any kind (text, graphics, images, photographs, etc.), or other content or materials that in Apple's reasonable judgment may be found objectionable by iPhone or iPod touch users."

- **Using private frameworks.** You are not allowed to use any of the private frameworks in your applications.

- **Vibration.** Vibration can only be used in limited amounts. Apps that use excessive amounts of vibration tend to be rejected due to concerns about device battery life.

App Store custom backgrounds

You may have noticed that many of the more popular applications on the App Store have a custom background (Figure 10.18) instead of the default blue gradient background. You might be wondering how you can create a custom App Store background for your applications. Unfortunately, you cannot. Apple decides which applications get to have custom backgrounds. If your application becomes popular enough, you might hear from Apple about creating an App Store custom background.

Figure 10.18

Custom background as shown in Apple's Texas Hold 'em

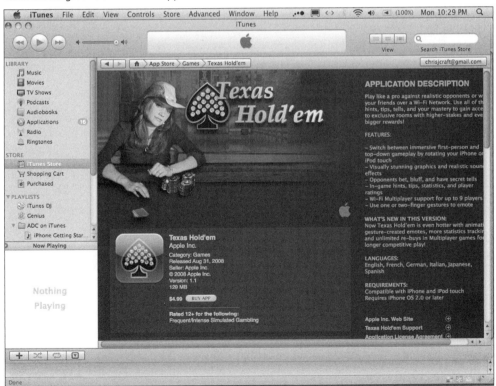

Top free and paid applications

It is common for new developers to wonder how to make their application become one of the top applications on the App Store. The ultimate goal is to be in the top 25 paid applications, as shown in Figure 10.19, or in the top 25 free applications. An easier goal is to be in the top 25 applications for an App Store application category, such as Games or Entertainment. Or better still, you could create a top 25 application in a less popular category, such as Weather or Finance.

Figure 10.19

Some of the top 25 paid applications

The specific details for how application rank is calculated are a secret. But most developers agree that it's based on a sliding scale, using number of sales per day for a small time period (for example, three days). For some of the more popular categories such as Games or Entertainment, your application will need to have hundreds, maybe even thousands, of sales each day to be in the top 25. For other less competitive categories, your application may only need a hundred or so sales a day.

iTunes Deep Links

You can copy an iTunes Store URL from inside iTunes. First, find an application you like on the App Store. Then right-click on either the developer's name or the application's name. You should see a context menu appear named Copy iTunes Store URL. If you click this menu item, you will have a link like the following URL: `http://itunes.apple.com/WebObjects/ MZStore.woa/wa/viewSoftware?id=287545019&mt=8`. This link works great for any hyperlinks on your Web pages or in your e-mails, but it is a bit unwieldy to show to people.

Another issue with this link is that you cannot tell what application it's for just by looking at it. For the most part, only we and Apple know this link is for the AppsAmuck iFlame application. If you want to have friendly URLs, one thing you can do is to use iTunes Deep Links. Creating a deep link is simple; just add the name of your app after `itunes.com/apps/`. Go to `http:// itunes.com/apps/iFlame` to see an example of how much better this method is. We think you will agree that iTunes Deep Links is the way to go.

CROSS-REFERENCE
For a discussion on creating the iFlame application, see Chapter 4.

Worldwide distribution

Currently there are 77 App Store fronts. Each App Store front is targeted for a specific region. Apple does this so the iPhone OS platform can reach as many people as possible. If this book were not written in a language you were familiar with, would you have bought it? The same way this is important for the App Store and for this book, it is important for your applications. You should make an effort to allow your application to support as many of the world's App Store fronts as possible—ideally all of them.

However, note that if your application has country-specific functionality, such as SMS integration with limited carriers, or depends on Web services that aren't available outside of the United States, it should be limited to those countries where it does work. Customers tend to assume that an app available in their country's App Store will actually work in their country.

App Store Logo License Program

By now you have probably seen the Available on the App Store artwork. Developers enrolled in the iPhone Developer Program can join the App Store Logo License Program. Users now recognize the Available on the App Store artwork (Figure 10.20), and they know that when they see it there is an application available for their device on the App Store.

CROSS-REFERENCE
See Chapter 1 for more on the iPhone Developer Program.

Joining the App Store Logo License Program is a simple process. You will need to read the program's App Marketing License Agreement, then complete and mail the agreement to the address provided. Once you have read and complied with the agreement, you can download the Available on the App Store artwork and use it in your advertising, Web sites, and other application marketing items.

Figure 10.20

Available on the App Store artwork

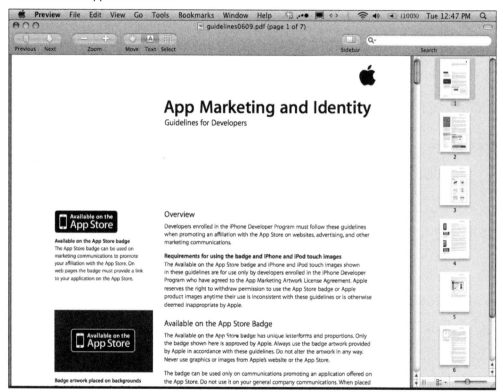

iTunes Affiliates Program

As an iPhone application developer, you earn 70 percent royalties on any application you sell on the App Store. But did you know that iTunes has an affiliates program you can also join that lets you earn commissions on any sales through your generated affiliate links?

The iTunes Affiliates Program, shown in Figure 10.21, covers applications on the App Store, but it also applies to music, TV shows, movies, and audio books. As an iTunes affiliate, you earn a 5 percent commission on all qualifying revenue.

Consider this: You can spend a month creating a great iPhone application and earn 70 percent of the revenue generated for any sale, or you can spend a minute creating an affiliate link and earn 5 percent of the revenue generated for each sale through one of your links. Finally, you can earn up to 75 percent of the revenue for a sale if you created the application and it came from one of your affiliate links.

Figure 10.21

iTunes Affiliates Program

There is a lot of money to be made in creating iPhone applications, but it can be a lot of work. No doubt it is the path we would recommend you take. But there is some wisdom in considering opportunities that are available through affiliate links as well. You should definitely consider creating affiliate versions of any links you control for any of your applications on the App Store. Sometimes 5 percent can be the difference between a successful company and a company that eventually ends up going out of business.

Customer Reviews

Customer reviews, like the ones shown in Figure 10.22, play an important part of an application's success. Not only can customers leave reviews for applications, but users can vote on specific reviews as to whether or not a review was helpful to them. You want to make sure your application is as good as possible to keep the highest voted customer review from being "This app does not work!" You will be much happier if your highest voted customer review is "Well worth the money!" If you put enough effort into the fit and finish of your iPhone application, you should not have anything to worry about.

Figure 10.22

Customer reviews for Bust-A-Spook

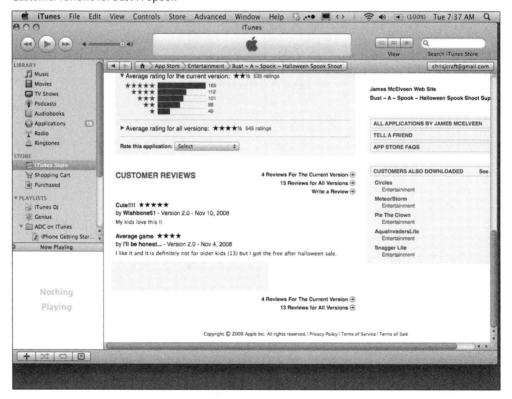

Each customer review is made up of the following information: review title, customer rating, user name, application version review applies to, review date, review details, and the number of customers who found the review helpful or not. Customer reviews are by default sorted by most helpful, but you can sort reviews by most helpful, most favorable, most critical, or most recent.

NOTE

Only customers who have actually purchased your application can leave a review.

Treat your customers well. An upset customer is much more likely to leave a customer review and rating than a happy customer, so you want to do all that you can upfront to avoid giving a customer a reason to be upset with anything about your application. And if one user is having an issue with your application, there is a good chance that others are as well. Respond quickly and decisively to any issues reported.

You can encourage users of your application to leave reviews for your application. Any time someone requests a new feature in one of your applications and you add it, consider asking the person who made the request to leave a review for your application on the App Store. Most users will be thrilled to have an opportunity to do something in return for you.

Feedback

Apple has done a very good job of creating systems to allow application owners to provide feedback to others and developers. You have everything from customer ratings to customer reviews. The App Store also has a Tell a Friend feature. All App Store application listings have a company Web site link and a customer support Web link. You should make certain to monitor and respond to any feedback you receive from your application users.

You should also consider building custom feedback systems into your applications. Customers appreciate being able to find related Web sites and contact information easily and directly from inside the application itself. Even if all you do is create a couple of hyperlinks that either open your company's Web site or send an e-mail to your company's support e-mail address, you will likely earn the gratitude of more than one customer. With iPhone OS 3.0, you can now take advantage of in-app e-mail features, which means users don't have to leave the app to send an e-mail message.

People also like it when companies have community message boards or forums for their products. If a user is having an issue with an application, he may prefer to send you an e-mail, but if he just wants to learn more about your application's possibilities, sometimes forums are a more natural fit.

Review sites and testimonials

Many applications include reviews from famous iPhone app review sites. There are quite a few of these kinds of sites; a simple search provides you with a good list of some to contact about reviewing your application. You can think of these types of reviews as being like professional customer reviews.

As we've mentioned, many of these sites will be glad to review your application for free if you provide them with a promo code allowing them to download your application for free. It's one of those symbiotic relationships, where if you scratch their back they will scratch yours. You are providing them with content to add to their site, and they are providing you and their readers with a professional-quality review.

Here's a list of some great iPhone application review sites:

- **iPhone Application List.** http://iphoneapplicationlist.com
- **iPhone App Reviews.** www.iphoneappreviews.net/
- **Apple iPhone School.** www.appleiphoneschool.com/
- **What's on iPhone.** www.whatsoniphone.com/
- **I use this iPhone software.** http://iphone.iusethis.com/
- **AppVee.** www.appvee.com/
- **App Store Apps.** www.appstoreapps.com/
- **iLounge.com.** www.ilounge.com/

All applications on the App Store can have customer reviews, but there is nothing stopping developers like you from highlighting specific user testimonials in their applications' descriptions. This is a great way for you to show off all the great feedback your applications have received from users.

Customer ratings

Customer ratings are a prominent part of your application's App Store listing. They are important to potential buyers, and they should be important to you. Originally the App Store would allow anyone to leave ratings or reviews for your application, even someone who had never purchased your app. This lead to a great deal of weeping and gnashing of teeth for many developers due to random people—sometimes even competitors—leaving negative reviews for applications they had never even bothered to try. Eventually Apple changed how customer ratings work on the App Store so only users who actually purchase an application can leave ratings or reviews on it.

An application owner can rate an application on a scale of one to five stars, with five stars being the highest rating and one star being the lowest. Once users have left their rating for an application, this information becomes available for other potential buyers to consider. It is imperative that you make every effort on your part for your applications to become five-star applications.

Your application's App Store listing shows customer ratings in various formats. Potential buyers can see the average rating for the current version, which could be something like four and a half stars. Next to this value there is a number that shows how many ratings this average is derived from. Right below that there is a breakdown of how many votes the application received for each score value from one to five stars.

Take a quick look at the customer ratings for the current number-one application on the App Store. You will probably see values similar to the following:

- Average rating for the current version: 4.5 stars (2,843 ratings)
- 5 stars: 2,178 (77 percent)
- 4 stars: 309 (11 percent)
- 3 stars: 105 (4 percent)
- 2 stars: 41 (1 percent)
- 1 star: 210 (7 percent)

It's important to note that over 90 percent of the ratings for this application are three stars or higher. Also notice that even the number-one application on the App Store has a decent number of one-star ratings. That just goes to show you that the App Store is a cruel mistress, and there is very low tolerance of any imperfection.

CAUTION

Since iPhone OS version 2.2, Apple has prompted users to rate an application before it is deleted from the device. Users tend to remove their least-favorite apps first.

You can see the average rating for the current version of the application, but you also get to see the average rating for all versions of the application. And again, you can expand the average rating for all versions so you can see the breakdown of votes for each rating score. This allows potential buyers to see if the quality of an application is getting better or worse over time. Users can even use this as a kind of litmus test to see if they want to install the latest update for an application. If a recent update has a lot of poor ratings, it may be a sign that there are issues with that update.

Using App Store Search Secrets

When you hear the term *search engine optimization*, or SEO, the first thing you probably think of are Web-based search engines such as Google. But in the highly competitive world of iPhone applications, your App Store SEO might be more important than your Google SEO.

The primary factor in your application's App Store SEO is its title. For example, our air hockey game is named Amuck Puck but it is listed as Amuck Puck—Air Hockey. This way our application can get hits for searches on its name and on the term "air hockey." We definitely want our app to come up in searches for "air hockey," since that is what the app really is—an air hockey game.

TIP

Check out your favorite applications and see what they are doing, and discover for yourself what really works. From time to time make a point of reviewing all of the featured and top 25 apps on the App Store for ideas on how to better market your own applications.

Keywords

Be sure to consider important keywords for your application title and description. Some people go so far as to include keywords in their company name, while others have noticed that having company and product names starting with the letter A can improve App Store search rankings and results. Be sure to search for Apps Amuck on the App Store and see our latest releases.

App Store application description

The App Store isn't perfect, but in a lot of ways it levels the playing field for everybody. It doesn't matter who you are; your application description must be 700 characters or less. That is both good and bad. It's good because none of your competition can use more than 700 characters to describe their application, but it's bad because more than likely you would prefer to have more than 700 characters to describe your application.

Not only do you have a limited number of characters that you can use to describe your application, but you can only use plain text for the description. You cannot use HTML or any other markup in your application description—but then again, neither can your competition. That means no HTML, no JavaScript, no AJAX, and no jQuery. How about bold? No. What about italics? No. Surely you can underline your text? No. If it's a text character, then maybe you can use it; otherwise, forget it.

That doesn't mean there aren't any tricks you can take advantage of. For example, it is possible to use some special Unicode characters. This allows you to include more graphic and symbolic characters in your application description. We have seen stars, squares, and so forth. It is common to see hyphens and asterisks being used in a row to create a virtual line out of text. It's true: Sometimes less really is more. So instead of trying to create advanced ASCII art in your application's description, focus on creating a well-formatted, easy-to-read description for your application.

TIP

Because you cannot include a hyperlink directly in your App Store description, consider using a URL-shortening service like `http://bit.ly,` which creates short URLs that redirect users to the much longer original URLs that you provided.

On sale

People love a good sale. Does anything actually sell for the manufacturer's suggested retail price anymore? It seems like products are designed from day one to go on sale. Think about how many people look forward to Black Friday, the day after Thanksgiving, which marks the beginning of the holiday shopping season in the United States. Many people line up hours before stores even open and risk life and limb in the hope of grabbing some doorbuster sale items.

Similarly, many apps on the App Store seem to have a permanent "Limited Time SALE!" of "80% OFF!" Basically these applications are marketing themselves as $4.99 applications that are on sale for $0.99. Who says a limited time sale cannot last for the next 10 years? You should definitely consider having an on-sale promotion period for your applications, but maybe your limited time offers really should be limited time offers.

Videos

The App Store does not allow videos of iPhone applications. You cannot place a video demo of your application in your App Store application description, but you can add a video section to your description and place links to premade application demo videos there. Unfortunately, you cannot add active hyperlinks, but you can add the text for the URL. Consider putting a note to visit your Web site to see a demo right in the description.

There is more value in creating video demos of your applications than just for including links to them in your application description. You should consider including videos, along with screen shots, on your application's Web site as well. The average Web site visitor has a very short attention span. If you are lucky she will see your application video and decide to watch at least one of the demo videos. And from there, she just might decide to purchase the app.

Consider posting your applications' demo videos to video-sharing sites like YouTube, Vimeo, and Google Video. These sites get a lot of traffic. It is possible to create a marketing video that becomes popular enough to go viral and gain widespread Internet fame. Don't forget that many social networking sites, including Facebook, allow you to post pictures as well as videos.

Maximum number of applications

Each page of applications on the iPhone can hold 16 applications, besides the 4 bottom dock icons. Before iPhone OS 3.0, you could have up to 9 pages of applications; with iPhone OS 3.0, you can have up to 11 pages of applications. That gives you 148 apps (9 x 16 + 4) for older operating systems, and 180 apps (11 x 16 + 4) for iPhone OS 3.0. Keep in mind there are almost 20 icons that Apple does not allow end users to remove from their device.

Before the iPhone OS 3.0, if users ran out of slots on their device to install applications, they could not install any new applications. This would prevent a world of applications from being installed (Figure 10.23). But on the iPhone OS 3.0, if there are no remaining application slots, the application can still be installed, but users must use the spotlight search feature to find the application first in order to launch it.

Figure 10.23

148 application icons from various iPhone apps

So it looks like most users probably have room left on their device for your application, which is a good thing. Now all that is left for you to do is convince them that they should fill that empty slot on their device with your application.

App Store application categories

You can publish your application in up to two App Store application categories (Figure 10.24). Just as in retail stores, you have to decide where to put your products. The choice of App Store category can greatly affect the number of downloads your app receives.

App Store application categories include the following:

- Books
- Business
- Education
- Entertainment
- Finance
- Games
- Healthcare & Fitness
- Lifestyle
- Medical
- Music
- Navigation
- News
- Photography
- Productivity
- Reference
- Social Networking
- Sports
- Travel
- Utilities
- Weather

Some categories such as Games or Entertainment have a huge number of applications. And while they're quite popular, it is almost impossible for the average user to browse these large categories. On the other hand, smaller categories such as Weather are easily browsed from the App Store application on the iPhone.

It is possible for your application to rank higher in one category than in another. For example, since there are so many more applications in the Games category than in the Weather category, it is harder for an application to be in the top 25 games than for it to be in the top 25 weather apps. Sales tend to increase exponentially as you move closer to the top of a category, but the more popular categories carry more rewards for being in the top 25 as well. Be mindful of this aspect of App Store marketing.

There is a limit to the number of applications the App Store will return to a user for any given category on the App Store. At most a user can browse 3,500 applications in one App Store category. At 25 applications per page, this works out to allowing users to see 140 pages' worth of apps. But realistically, how many users would be willing to browse through 3,500 apps?

Assume that a certain percentage of people—let's say 100 percent, to keep things simple—is willing to look through the first page of 25 applications in a category, and a smaller percentage is willing to look at each additional page. So, for the applications on the second page of 25 apps, maybe only 90 percent of people are willing to browse this far. And only 80 percent might be willing to go far enough to see the applications in the 51 through 75 rankings. If this is the case, if you can promote your application enough to move from the third page of apps to the first page of apps, you increase the percentage of people who see your application from 80 percent to 100 percent.

Figure 10.24

The App Store categories

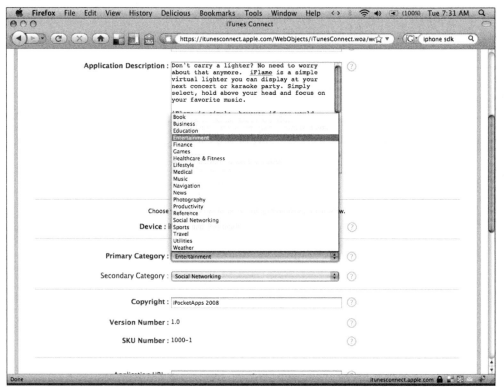

App Store approval wait times

When you submit your first application to the App Store, you will likely be very anxious about it getting approved to be on the App Store. There is no fixed time for how long this approval process takes. It has taken about seven days for one of our typical applications to get approved, sometimes longer. In some cases you may even receive an Extended Approval Time Notice e-mail from Apple informing you that your application is taking longer than typical to review.

Not only will you have to wait for your application to be approved when you first add it to the App Store, but all updates will have to be approved as well. This is true for bug fixes and feature enhancements to applications.

Marketing Yourself

Today's marketplace requires developers to create loyal customers who will purchase tomorrow's applications. Competition is extreme and margins are tight, so you need to stand out in a crowd and be memorable. Here are some ways to further promote yourself so that you stand out against the competition.

Social networking

One of the strongest ways to promote your iPhone applications is to use social networking technologies. Sure, you probably have a Twitter account, but does your company have one? (You can see ours in Figure 10.25.) How about your latest application? There are times when it makes sense to have a company Twitter account, and there are times when it makes sense to have a Twitter account for an individual application, especially if it is a popular app.

Social networking makes it easy to put people in touch with each other. That's also why it's so great for companies and their products. If you have good synergy between your company and your products, you can probably simply use one account for all of them. But if your company has two very different products—say, one is a "death-to-all-zombies" type of game and the other a kids' lullaby application—you might want to create two separate accounts.

This applies to Facebook just as much as Twitter. Again, maybe your company should have a fan page, and maybe your application should have one as well. A Facebook fan page is a great place for you to share pictures and a video about your applications. It gives users a comfortable place to go to give you feedback without having to worry about you using their contact information inappropriately.

In-app marketing and advertising

You know you can have in-app advertising show ads inside your application. But there are other forms of advertising and marketing that you can include in your application as well. For example, many developers include a More Games or More Apps screen in their applications.

Figure 10.25

AppsAmuck on Twitter

This is a great opportunity to upsell your application's customers. If a customer loves one of your applications, he will probably like another one of your applications. Be sure to create a link to either your application's Web site or a direct link to your application's App Store listing (Figure 10.26) so that you can actually complete the sale if the customer is really interested. Links directly to the App Store listings are more valuable, because with an App Store link you can direct users right to the on-device App Store so they can buy and download the app immediately.

Take advantage of the iPhone's capabilities to help pitch your other applications to your clients. You can include screen shots, videos, and HTML descriptions for applications. There is nothing stopping you from even including a limited demo of one application inside another application.

You could let users try one level from your most popular application inside all your other applications. Or you could change what application trial you included in the next update for your application. Fresh content is always appreciated by users. Remember to have fun and always surprise and delight your users.

Figure 10.26

In-app marketing screen for iFlame

Many more people will download a free version of an application than pay for an application. In some cases you can make more money by giving away your application for free and adding in-app advertising to your application. You may wish to experiment with this by having a lite version of your paid app that has in-app advertising.

In-app advertising sites include:

- **AdMob.** www.admob.com/
- **AdWhirl.** www.adwhirl.com/

Competition

Users enjoy competition. You can take an application to a whole new level if you can add a healthy dose of competition to your applications. For example, a game could include a built-in high-score board that all application users can see. You could create an online high-score board as well, so that potential buyers can see the challenge and completion waiting for them once they purchase your app. Obviously, you could include contests and achievements in your application, among other ideas, to further expand its appeal.

CROSS-REFERENCE

See Chapter 7 for more about building competition into your game design.

Testing

Testing is not optional. It is a fundamental and critical requirement for all of your applications. Yes, you can create a new version of your application that fixes any issues in a previous version of your application. And yes, Apple will perform a cursory test and review your application; however, that is no excuse for not performing adequate testing on your own first.

You cannot afford to ship applications that do not function as advertised. Today's users are very vocal and outspoken about any frustrations caused by faulty applications. They will remember the issue, they will tell others, and they will move on to the next product. When applications cost less than a cup of coffee, you can only expect so much loyalty and patience from a customer. Also note that since all updates submitted to Apple must go through the full review cycle as well, this can lead to frustrated users if they have to wait for critical bug fixes.

In App Purchases

With iPhone OS 3.0, it became possible to include In App Purchases, like the one shown in Figure 10.27, in your application. This means that users can now buy new application content from right inside your application. If you have a game, you could include additional levels that users could purchase for $1.99. Or maybe your application has other themes and skins available for it for a small fee. There are an endless number of ideas for how you could use the store kit framework in your applications.

Here are some ideas to get you started:

- Application subscription—for example, monthly access to reverse phone number lookup database
- Additional levels
- Additional characters
- Additional weapons
- Additional character items
- Additional application features—for example, the ability to access local music from the app

Figure 10.27

Application demonstrating In App Purchase

Payments for In App Purchases are handled via iTunes just the same as payments for application purchases. The developer picks the price, and 70 percent of the revenue goes to the developer. There are no credit card fees, and the developer is paid monthly.

Free applications remain free. This means that if your application is free, you cannot have In App Purchases. Apple was concerned that if it allowed In App Purchases in free apps, developers would be tempted to create a bunch of free software that wasn't really free and would not function until users purchased additional content for the application.

Be careful about changing your applications from being free to paid and vice versa when it comes to In App Purchases. Currently it appears that if you change a free app into a paid one you will enable In App Purchases, and you will disable In App Purchases if you do the reverse. The concern has been that developers might make free apps and build up large user bases and then change the app to a paid app and enable In App Purchases. Once users get the latest version, their free app might no longer be free. This could lead to community backlash or direct action from Apple to prevent this scenario.

Blogs

In most cases it makes sense for either you or your company to have a blog, like ours shown in Figure 10.28. It may even be useful for you to create an application-specific blog. In this case there should be a lot of activity going on around the given iPhone application. Most blogs should be updated every two or three days, and certainly at least once a week. Any less and the blog will atrophy and lose its followers over time.

Figure 10.28

Apps Amuck's blog

Lite version

Many of the most popular applications on the App Store have a free version, usually known as a lite version. This is because Apple does not allow applications to have built-in trial capabilities. These lite versions usually only contain one level from the paid version of the application. This allows users to try out applications, like Trism-Lite shown in Figure 10.29. This is very important, since the App Store refund policy is "All sales are final." These lite versions of applications are the only way people interested in your products can test them out to be sure they will like them.

Figure 10.29

Trism-Lite

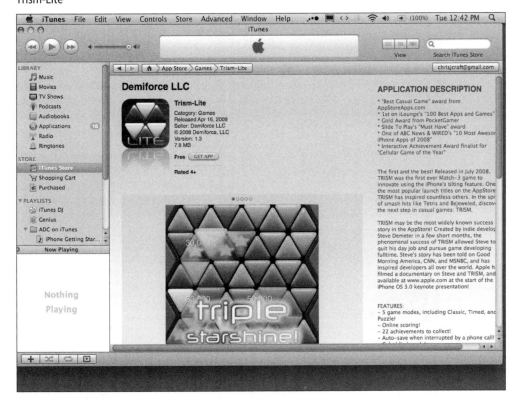

App updates

It's a good idea to update your applications from time to time (Figure 10.30). There are several reasons why you should do this. For one reason, it helps keep your applications visible on the App Store. Updating your applications frequently also keeps your application fresh in the mind of your users.

Figure 10.30

Facebook iPhone application update

Mind share is an important part of an app's ultimate success in the marketplace. Consider if a user has two applications on his device. One of them is yours, and the other is your competitor's. You've been busy lately and have not been good about updating your application. But your competitor has been. This user really liked your application better at first, but when he saw all the new updates coming down for your competitor's application, he couldn't resist giving it another try. And he noticed that with every version the other app was getting better and better, until finally, it was better than your application.

Eventually, he even decided to uninstall your application to make room for something else that caught his eye. Then, as a final loss, later someone asked him for a recommendation for a new application to try, but instead of recommending your app, he recommended the other app. It is almost like a digital war where every device is a small piece of land that your application has to battle for, and every battle counts.

If your application has in-app advertising, you should be sure to update your application frequently as well. Updating your application often tends to encourage users to return to your application regularly to see what is new. The same way you want to water plants and flowers, you want to update your application with new features and improvements.

Consider also that frequent application updates can be a feature of your application that you can market to help propel your application's growth. This is called creating *serial content* for your application. You can let users know in your application's description that every week you will add new capabilities or content to your application. This could take many forms:

- New levels
- New weapons
- New characters
- Bug fixes
- User-suggested ideas
- New application themes and skins
- New features
- New music
- New languages
- New Easter eggs

Ad Hoc beta testing

Apple created Ad Hoc distribution to allow developers to easily beta test their applications. You can create an Ad Hoc distribution for any of your applications, as shown in Figure 10.31, and send it to beta testers to install on their device. Beta testers must first send you their Device ID, and you will have to add it to your currently registered devices.

CAUTION

Be aware that removing a device from the list of currently registered devices will not replenish the current number of devices available. You will not be able to reset your device list until you renew your Apple developer membership.

You can manage your currently registered devices at `http://developer.apple.com/iphone/manage/devices/index.action`. Apple allows you to have a maximum of 100 devices allocated for your development team, which includes beta testers. Once you have added your beta testers' devices, you can create a beta build for your application and send it to them. From there, testers can install the application through iTunes and test on their devices.

Figure 10.31

Ad Hoc beta testing

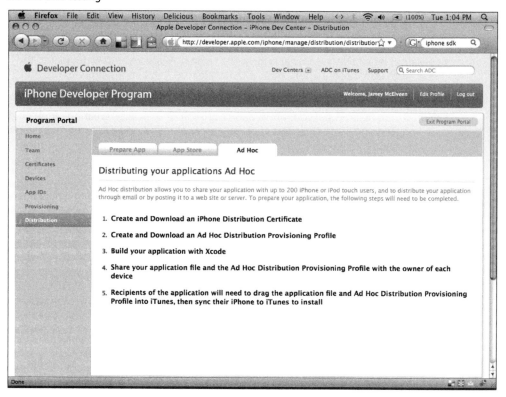

While on one hand you want to make sure to take advantage of all the opportunities Ad Hoc beta testing brings, be sure not to use up all of your device slots too soon. Remember, Apple releases new devices regularly, and if a beta tester upgrades from one device to another, you will lose another slot. You want to make sure you always have some device slots left for yourself.

Application names

Your iPhone application name is very important because it is shown under your application's icon on the actual device. While your App Store application title can be quite long—up to 5,000 characters—your actual application name must be fairly short.

Your app's name cannot contain special characters like UTF-8 characters. The font used for showing application names on the iPhone is not a fixed-width font, so there is no specific number of characters that will not fit. Just be aware that if your application's name is too long, the iPhone OS will insert an ellipsis into the application name and remove any extraneous characters, making the name short enough to fit in the space allocated.

If you try to use a name for your application that is already taken, you will receive the following error message:

The Application Name that you provided has already been used. Please provide a unique Application Name.

CAUTION

Once you assign a name to your application, it can be a bit of a challenge to completely rename it later on. You can rename it easily enough in Xcode, but if you want to rename every file, you will have to invest a little time finding and then replacing each reference.

Application piracy

For the most part, developers don't have to worry too much about application piracy. It does exist, but marketplace forces keep it in check. In order to pirate an iPhone application, you have to be able to afford an iPhone and an iPhone data plan. Most applications are very affordable, many only $0.99. Buying applications from the App Store is so easy and affordable it is hard to imagine a pirated version existing that could compete. Plus pirated applications can only be run on hacked devices, which further reduces the risk.

Screen shots

The App Store allows you to include up to five screen shots of your application, and you should try to include as many of these screen shots as you can. It's one of the quickest and easiest ways users can get a look at your application and get an idea of what the user experience will be.

Screen shots are very useful to include on the App Store, as shown in Figure 10.32, but be sure to include them on your application's Web site as well. One nice thing about including screen shots on your Web site is that you can include more than five of them. Also consider posting screen shots to various social networking sites such as Facebook. Screen shots allow you to market your application to users early in the development process before your application has been listed on the App Store. This allows developers to create buzz for their upcoming releases well in advance, creating momentum and increasing initial sales.

TIP

Sending screen shots along with "press releases" to blogs and sites that cover iPhone-related news is a great way of promoting your app before it's released.

Figure 10.32

Password Generator's primary screen shot on the App Store

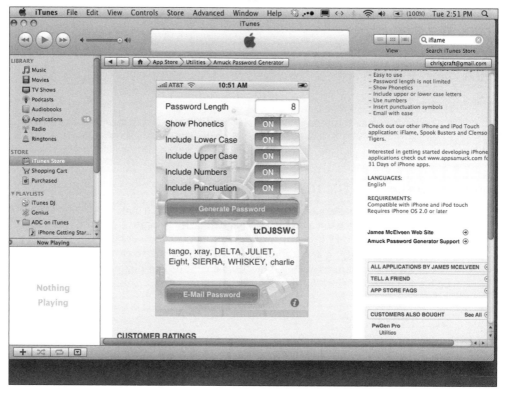

Summary

In this chapter you learned a great deal about the business of software. You should now have a basic understanding of how to take advantage of the information and statistics in your applications' App Store reports. You should also understand more about how application size and price affect your sales. You are aware of how parental controls like app ratings and the device's restriction settings can block your application from being bought, and you realize how important quality control is to the ultimate success of your app.

You have learned how supply and demand control your application's sales. You know where to find help on the Apple developer forums, and you know how to promote your application using promo codes and contests. You've also learned about many of the new features of the iPhone 3GS, iPhone OS 3.0, and iPhone SDK 3.0.

You've become familiar with the important role that keywords play in App Store search engine optimization. You also know how critical a great App Store application description is. You have reviewed how an application that is on sale can be a powerful influence on consumers. And you know how to show off your application using videos. You are aware of App Store application categories and approval times. You should realize users enjoy cinematic experiences on their device and want to be surprised and delighted often.

Finally, you've learned that great marketing is as important as having a great app. You should try to take advantage of every opportunity you have to market your application. This includes social networking, in-app marketing, in-app advertising, screen shots, videos, and blogs. This also includes making sure you have a lite version of your application. You understand how to further grow your application revenue by taking advantage of In App Purchases.

You should now be fully prepared to unleash your ideas on the App Store. Remember, some apps are created great, others have greatness thrust upon them, and the rest have to work for it. There is an expression that describes this perfectly: Most people find it takes years of hard work and perseverance to become an overnight success. But when it does finally happen, it can be extraordinary. Hang in there. It really can happen. Work hard—and then enjoy the benefits!

Epilogue: Looking Ahead

Many consider the iPhone a revolutionary device—and it is, if you look at the whole package. But if you look at each piece individually, you will find that the iPhone is not the first device to attempt to become the "keystone" device—the device that people carry with them everywhere and always look to first. But today it looks like the iPhone is on the track to achieving this goal. The iPhone is the first device that combined a plethora of existing technologies into one device and coupled them with a user experience like no other. This tells you what most people already think. The iPhone is cool, awesome, and all those things that attracted you to it in the first place. However, it also tells you that we can step back and look at the industry to find what lies down the road.

To travel this road at a pace necessary to keep up, you will need to refine your skills. You have to become proficient at iPhone development so you can crank out new products and features as the platform moves forward.

Understand that the platform is always moving forward. Build and layer your solutions in a way that you can quickly and easily change and add features as necessary. You may have a great app today, but if a new app comes along that competes with yours and adds one great new feature, it could sink yours. Be ready to adapt before that happens. Look at other mobile devices and technologies that are popular. There's a good chance that those features will be brought to the iPhone down the road. Build your app in such a way that you can quickly integrate the new feature before it is announced. If you are feeling really confident, build a whole new app around this feature. If you are right and if you are the first to do so, the rewards can be great.

Refining your skills

Practice makes perfect, and that principle applies to iPhone development as it does any form of development. This is called experience, and that is why most jobs require a certain level of experience before you are even considered. As you begin to develop on the iPhone, you will likely become discouraged and frustrated, as we did. But don't worry; it will become more natural as you practice more and more.

Study the snippets in this book. Download the examples from `http://appsamuck.com` and from the Apple sample code library. Study the details of each example and try to learn more than just the specific technology being demonstrated. Look for patterns and practices you can adopt and reuse. Become an expert at finding answers to your questions. Search the Internet for examples that solve problems similar to yours. Search the Apple development forums and ask questions there. If you have a question, chances are that several others have the same question, so ask. Your questions will only help others and the community.

Finally, don't give up. Coming from other languages and disciplines to iPhone development can be tough. However, the best thing about developing for the iPhone is the reward. It is an incredibly satisfying experience. Once your see your creations take life on-screen in the palm of your hand, you will be hooked.

Answering the question: Is there more?

In short, the answer is yes! There is much more to learn and there will continue to be more. The iPhone SDK is a living and breathing project. It can be challenging to keep up with the changes; in fact, we had to change course while writing this book to include 3.0. Also, Apple released the iPhone 3GS, which introduced a whole new API for reading directional data from the internal compass.

The first iPhone was released in 2007; Tables 10.5, 10.6, and 10.7 list what the OS release schedule has been from then until the time of this writing.

Table 10.5 1.x: First Release of the iPhone OS

Version	Release Date
1.0	Jun 2007
1.0.1	Jul 2007
1.0.2	Aug 2007
1.1	Sep 2007
1.1.1	Sep 2007
1.1.2	Nov 2007
1.1.3	Jan 2008
1.1.4	Feb 2008
1.1.5	Jul 2008

(This was the release that introduced the App Store)

Table 10.6 2.x: Second Major Version of iPhone OS Released with the iPhone 3G

Version	Release Date
2.0	Jul 2008
2.0.1	Aug 2008
2.0.2	Aug 2008
2.1	Sep 2008
2.1.1	Sep 2008
2.2	Nov 2008
2.2.1	Jan 2009

Table 10.7 3.x: Third Major Version of iPhone OS Released with the iPhone 3GS

Version	Release Date
3.0 B1	Mar 2009
3.0 B2	Mar 2009
3.0 B3	Apr 2009
3.0 B4	Apr 2009
3.0 B5	May 2009
3.0 GM	Jun 2009
3.0	Jun 2009

As you can see, this is an intense schedule. With every step in the release cycle you must be vigilant and adapt to features and changes that can trip you up or offer opportunity. These changes can render your application obsolete and potentially break your existing code, or they can open the door for you to greatly enhance your game. The point is that you must keep a watchful eye on all changes as they come, or pay the price of falling behind. With the 3.0 release alone, several enhancement features and changes were applied, including the following:

- Spotlight Search
- Cut, copy, paste
- Earth magnetic compass (iPhone 3GS only)
- In-application maps
- MMS functionality (iPhone 3G and up) to send pictures, audio files, and more
- Push notification for third-party applications
- Peer-to-peer connectivity
- Access to the iPod music library
- In-app payment API for paid application add-on features

Apple tends to cluster their most significant changes around major releases. Apple also tends to limit and restrict access for certain releases and certain related features. For example, very few developers had access to push notifications before Apple made the service available to everyone. In some cases, you may have to react very quickly to a new change made in a new OS release. Both the 2.1 and 2.2 releases had this problem, causing many apps to be broken on release day and leaving developers scrambling to catch up.

Where to learn more

As we've mentioned, getting good at finding answers to your questions and solutions to your problems is one of the most important skills you can develop. We learned from the resources Apple offers and from newsgroups. Many of these resources are listed in Appendix A, but here are a couple of good ones to get you started.

Apple resources

`http://developer.apple.com/iphone/`

- Getting started videos
- Getting started documents
- iPhone reference library
- Coding how-to's
- Sample code

Examples, questions, and answers

- `http://appsamuck.com`
- `http://DevForums.Apple.com`
- `http://StackOverflow.com`

Preparing for the future

We have established the fact that you will always learn more and you will need to embrace changes in the SDK to keep current. The challenge is to build an application that employs strategies that minimize the impact of SDK changes.

Building apps with change in mind

You saw in the Amuck-Tac-Toe application in Chapter 8 how we used a factory to instantiate our connection class. This pattern is useful because it allows a single code base to effectively connect with any connection that can implement the protocol. However, this pattern is also useful for insulating the components of our application from changes in the iPhone SDK.

In the new 3.0 releases, a new sound library has been introduced. If you previously implemented a pattern that abstracts your sound actions from your sound engine, you could simply replace your sound engine implementation with a new one. This would effectively swap implementations without recoding every line that calls out to the sound engine.

Predicting the future

Okay, we cannot read minds, and we cannot teach you to read them, either. However, you can watch the industry and plan for obvious changes that you believe will be implemented. Remember that the iPhone is not the first mobile device to hit the market. Several features that are "new" to the iPhone are not new to mobile devices. The following new and exciting features that are now on the iPhone were, in some cases, available much earlier on other devices:

- 3G networking
- P2P over Bluetooth
- GPS

- Compass
- Turn-by-turn directions
- MMS
- Video
- Push notification

This is important, because if you code for a feature that is not available yet, you can be that early bird that gets the worm. On the other side, you may build an app that never gets the feature it needs to run, but eventually you will get lucky. What do you think the future holds for the iPhone? Here is a list of ideas that may or may not come to fruition in the future:

- More space, more memory, faster processors
- Higher-resolution screens
- Bigger iPod version with bigger screen
- Smaller iPod version with smaller screen (new nano?)
- More APIs that are available today in Mac OS
- More accurate GPS
- More carriers
- More languages
- Flash support
- Multitasking/background processes
- Ability to download apps without the App Store

Watch the newsgroups, evaluate the rumors, and you will be able to pick some items you feel confident will happen. Take this knowledge and be the first to build the next cutting-edge app before the competition can even begin to catch you!

Appendixes

Resources

Useful Links

71squared

www.71squared.co.uk/

This is a great Web site that focuses specifically on iPhone game development. It is updated often with new material.

148Apps.biz

http://148apps.biz/

There is a good focus on the business and marketing realities of iPhone application development.

AppsAmuck

http://appsamuck.com/

Famous for the 31 days of iPhone applications, this is the site that many of the apps in this book originated from.

How to make iPhone Apps

http://howtomakeiphoneapps.com/

This site has a wealth of material on how to create iPhone applications and how to market them.

iCodeBlog

http://icodeblog.com/

This blog is focused on iPhone programming and has many detailed iPhone programming tutorials with source code and walk-through screen shots.

iDevGames

www.idevgames.com/

Billing itself as the Mac and iPhone Game Developer Community, this site features articles, interviews, news, reviews, tutorials, and forums.

iLounge

www.iLounge.com/

This is another useful site that you may want to check out. While iLounge is not directly about iPhone development, it offers many game reviews and comparisons in the "iPhone Gems" series that serve as useful references to what's out there.

iPhone Dev Center

http://developer.apple.com/iphone/

The iPhone Dev Center provides access to technical resources and information to assist you in developing with the latest technologies in iPhone OS.

iPhone Dev SDK

www.iphonedevsdk.com/

This site has a large number of moderated forums dedicated to programming with the iPhone SDK.

iPhone SDK Articles

www.iphonesdkarticles.com/

This site contains a series of iPhone SDK tutorials. There are forums and an iPhone programming-related blog as well.

Mobile Orchard

www.mobileorchard.com/

Mobile Orchard is a great iPhone programming blog that has podcasts, tutorials, and more. Be sure to check out the top posts links.

The Unofficial Apple Weblog

www.tuaw.com/

Although not entirely devoted to iPhone programming or even to the iPhone, this site consistently manages to find out the latest news before anyone else.

Wiley's Developer Reference Series

www.wileydevreference.com

Check out this Web site for links to all of the books in Wiley's Developer Reference series. Click on the link for *iPhone Game Development* to see code listings for this book.

Books

Cocoa Touch for iPhone OS 3.0

By Jiva DeVoe

Wiley, 2009

This book covers the Cocoa Touch framework that you need in order to develop for the iPhone, as well as the entire iPhone development process from provisioning to utilizing a complicated database backend in SQLite. It offers easy-to-understand tutorials and discussions to help you create unique user interfaces and powerful applications.

iPhone 3GS Portable Genius

By Paul McFedries

Wiley, 2009

This book is like a mini Genius Bar all wrapped up in an easy-to-use, easy-to-access, eminently portable format. It's the perfect companion for learning how to use your iPhone to the fullest.

iPhone Fully Loaded

By Andy Ihnatko

Wiley, 2009

This one-of-a-kind reference shows iPhone and iPod touch users how to put anything and everything on their Apple iPhones or iPod touches. It is done completely in color and covers everything from basic iPhone instruction to advanced topics to software recommendations.

Certification and Training

Certificate in iPhone and Cocoa Development

www.extension.washington.edu/ext/certificates/iph/iph_gen.asp

The University of Washington offers a certificate in iPhone and Cocoa development. The program is for experienced developers and sets out to show developers how to design, build, and sell their own quality iPhone applications.

Stanford University's iPhone Application Programming Class

http://itunes.stanford.edu/

Stanford University posts their iPhone Application Programming class on iTunes for everyone to listen to for free. Subscribe and you will have some of the best computer science professors in the world teaching you iPhone programming at no charge.

WWDC 2009 Session Videos

http://developer.apple.com/products/videos.html

If you were not able to attend the Apple Worldwide Developers Conference (WWDC) in 2009, you can still purchase all of the session videos from the conference. Even if you were able to attend, this is a great way for you to go back and catch the sessions you missed. There are sessions on iPhone development and Mac OS X development. And for $499, you can purchase all 126 sessions.

31 Days of iPhone Apps

Over the years, we have given many presentations on developing mobile applications. One thing we have heard time and time again is that people have a hard time taking those first steps to write their first iPhone application. It's easy to think that it will take too much time or be too hard, but that is simply not the case. But instead of telling people this, we decided we would show them how easy it really is. And with that, Apps Amuck was born.

One of our first goals was to write 31 iPhone applications in 31 days. By doing so we thought we could prove to everyone that it's not as hard as they might have first thought to create an iPhone app. The month just flew by, and before we knew it, we were done. All 31 apps were completed in record time.

This was a tough challenge, and we really had to push ourselves to accomplish our goal. Along the way we learned a lot, and we know from all the e-mails we've received that many of you have, as well. What follows are the 31 applications that we created. For each app we have included a description, technical details, a source code link, and the splash screen image.

We hope that with all of these applications—and with this book—you will learn even more and go even further in your goals for iPhone game development.

Day 1: Minutes to Midnight

Minutes to Midnight counts down the minutes from the current time until 12 a.m. This simple-to-use application is particularly helpful to anyone who must meet a deadline before the day is over. We created this first application on Friday, October 1, 2008, the very first day that Apple released the NDA that was preventing developers from discussing and sharing code. We have always been proud of being there for iPhone developers since that very first day. For the first app we noticed that the iPhone had a digital-looking font available on it, and decided we could create an iPhone clock around that easily enough. From there we created the clock application. It worked well and gave us a chance to share the code and knowledge with other developers.

Minutes to Midnight covers working with fonts and how to use timers. You can also learn how to access the current date and time on the device.

TIP
You can find the source code for Minutes to Midnight at `http://appsamuck.com/day1.html`.

Day 2: Bonfire

With day 2 we decided to heat things up and created our Bonfire application, which gives you an instant campfire on your phone. The campfire is not just an image, but a video on a loop. The loop allows the flames to be shown as realistically as possible. The loop also keeps the video of the flames from pausing, thus making it appear more realistic. This application has many uses. It is stronger than an ordinary flame when it appears on the screen. Also, its infinite loop allows it to last longer than a regular match or even candles. And finally, it's great for concert-goers who would love to hold up a flame at a concert but don't want to carry matches or a lighter.

This app teaches developers how to create animations and work with lots of images.

TIP
You can find the source code for Bonfire at `http://appsamuck.com/day2.html`.

Day 3: openURL

openURL helps you launch Maps, SMS, Browser, Phone, and other applications. A developer can look at the source code and learn everything he wants to know about opening URLs on the iPhone. openURL's purpose in life is to open other applications for people. It is the butler of applications, if you will. If you need to make a call, it will open the Phone Dialer application. If you need to see a Web site, it will open Safari on the iPhone, and so on.

This is a great application for developers since it shows them how to do common features like make a phone call, send a text message, or send an e-mail. Many applications could be improved easily by adding this kind of functionality to them.

TIP
You can find the source code for openURL at `http://appsamuck.com/day3.html`.

Day 4: What Is My IP?

Have you ever had trouble finding what IP address your phone is using? You may work with a friend or family member and typically you would have them use IPConfig or a Web site to return the IP address. However, it's not that simple on the iPhone. With the What Is My IP? application, you can get an IP address with ease. At some point, many developers find themselves needing to know the IP address of the machine they are working on. We ran into this problem around day 3 and decided to write an application for it.

This is a very focused application that does only one thing, but it does that one thing well: It provides developers with the code needed to get the IP address of the device their application is running on.

TIP
You can find the source code for What Is My IP? at `http://appsamuck.com/day4.html`.

Day 5: Count Me In

Count Me In gives you a new take on an old problem—making sure you don't lose count. This easy-to-use, digital counting application has an uncluttered interface that shows a single window with your count tally. Ergonomically sized tally buttons are a great feature. The green button adds another count while the red button subtracts. This useful app is great for coaching and sports, perfect for doing inventories of all kinds, and handy whenever you need to focus your concentration on more than one thing at a time. It works for quick counts and long-term tallies, so if you really need to make sure all the kids got back on the bus or simply want to keep track of how many pizzas you've ordered out this year, Count Me In is your solution.

Count Me In covers utility applications, `awakeFromNib`, `UIButtons`, `UILabels`, `UIImageViews`, and more.

TIP
You can find the source code for Count Me In at `http://appsamuck.com/day5.html.`

Day 6: Reaction Time

Simple reaction time is usually defined as the time required for an observer to detect the presence of a stimulus. For example, an observer might be asked to press a button as soon as a light turns on or a sound is made. Mean reaction time is approximately 180 to 200 milliseconds to detect visual stimuli. Do you know yours? Reaction Time is a fun little application that attempts to measure your reaction time. It is loosely based around one of the ultimate measures of reaction times: the drag race. There is a traffic light that changes from red to yellow to green, and then it kicks off a timer. As soon as racers see the green they need to press the accelerator pedal.

Reaction Time covers utility applications, `awakeFromNib`, `UIButtons`, `UIImageViews`, and more.

TIP
You can find the source code for Reaction Time at `http://appsamuck.com/day6.html`.

Day 7: Speed Dial

Speed Dial is one of the most useful things you can use on your phone. Instead of having to go through your contacts to find people you call frequently, putting them on speed dial makes it extremely easy to reach them. It makes multitasking easier as well—you simply press a button to dial while you do something else. Speed dial is extremely easy to set up. Most phones come with a 99-number speed dial capacity.

If there is one thing the iPhone is, it's a phone. It even has phone as the main part of its name. That being said, we thought it would be important to cover how to have your application use the iPhone as a phone.

Speed Dial covers creating settings bundles, reading and writing user settings, and more.

TIP
You can find the source code for Speed Dial at `http://appsamuck.com/day7.html`.

Day 8: Flickr KML

Do you have great pictures on your Flickr account that you think should be uploaded to Google Maps? Try Flickr KML, a cool iPhone app that lets you upload the pictures straight to the Google Maps application. For every photo you upload, a pushpin appears on the map to show recently geo-tagged images on Flickr. It's a great feature that you can experience in the Map application on the iPhone. The animation that goes along with each pushpin really takes this feature over the top. KML is underused by the developer community, so we decided to create an app for it.

You can learn how to have code run before your application really begins by using the `awakeFromNib` event. Find out how to use `UIButtons`, `UIImageViews`, and more. Learn more about utility applications for iPhone with Xcode, and find out how you can call Google Maps from your application.

TIP

You can find the source code for Flickr KML at `http://appsamuck.com/day8.html`.

Day 9: Snow Fall

If you're looking for an application that will spread seasonal cheer, Snow Fall is for you. This application uses the image of a single snowflake and repeats it on the screen as multiple flakes falling down the screen. It's a great app if you're experiencing winter-weather withdrawal or if you just love to watch the snow fall. The beautiful white-and-blue design of this app will remind users of winter all year long. We started the 31 days of iPhone applications in October, and while it had not snowed yet, it was starting to get cold, and all the stores were displaying Christmas-related goods. We came up with the idea of creating a virtual snow shower, and from there we created Snow Fall.

You learn how to use Quartz animations in your animations, timers, random number generators, and more. You also learn more about utility applications for iPhone with Xcode.

TIP
You can find the source code for Snow Fall at `http://appsamuck.com/day9.html`.

Day 10: Where Am I?

Are you an avid hiker, backpacker, back-country explorer, or just simply an adventurer? Have you ever been stranded in a remote location and needed to communicate your exact location in order to be rescued? Ever been walking down the street and wondered, "Hmm, I wonder what my exact location is at this very moment?" The Where Am I? application uses the GPS device in your iPhone to pinpoint your latitude, longitude, and even altitude. Some developers tend to seek out the hardware features of their devices. It was not long before we did the same. Both the GPS and the accelerometer are exciting features of the iPhone. We wanted to learn more about them, and by the end of the day we had created the Where Am I? application.

You learn how to use GPS to access longitude, latitude, and altitude. Learn about `UIButtons` and `UIImageViews` and how to access the hardware capabilities of the iPhone in your app.

TIP
You can find the source code for Where Am I? at `http://appsamuck.com/day10.html`.

Day 11: Plumb Bob

The Plumb Bob application helps ensure straightness in carpentry, masonry, and other jobs or projects. The Plumb Bob is a plummet, or weight, that is suspended by a string and used to check that lines are vertical. The application must be turned on and then lined up with the object in question. If the string on the iPhone is straight, it ensures that the object is straight. If the object is not straight, the application shows that. We like that the iPhone has replaced many other common devices that people tend to carry around with them, such as calculators, note-pads, and cameras. But what other tools could we replace with an iPhone application? That's why we created a virtual plumb bob.

This application teaches the basics of working with the accelerometer. The code also uses `UIImages`, `UIImageViews`, rotation transforms, and more.

TIP
You can find the source code for Plumb Bob at `http://appsamuck.com/day11.html`.

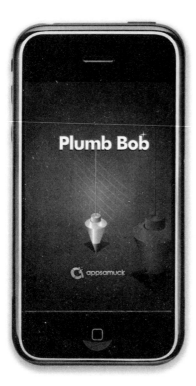

Day 12: U Decide

If you have trouble making decisions or finding the right answers to questions, you'll love the U Decide application. It has an easy-to-use interface, and responses are clearly shown at the top of the iPhone screen. This app handles simple decisions that involve answers of yes/no, true/false, and others; but it's also capable of helping users decide between more complicated options. For example, a user can select that the answer be a number from 1 to 100 or a buy/sell/hold decision. Other options include A/B/C/D responses, left/right/center responses, and more.

The biggest focus of U Decide is creating and working with random numbers. All decisions are made using randomly generated numbers. There are also a lot of `IBActions`, `UIButtons`, `UILabels`, and more.

TIP
You can find the source code for U Decide at `http://appsamuck.com/day12.html`.

Day 13: My Google

Enjoy the Google application on your iPhone without the navigation bar or toolbar. Google can come in handy to help you search for anything you may need to know. The entire purpose of the My Google application is to show developers that their native iPhone applications can hold a Web page inside them without opening a separate instance of Safari. This can be very powerful; because only one application can run at a time on the iPhone, being able to show a Web site or HTML and not close your application is a great win.

This application teaches you how to host Web sites and HTML inside your application. You also learn how to enable user interaction for your application.

TIP
You can find the source code for My Google at `http://appsamuck.com/day13.html`.

Day 14: Sleep Sound

The Sleep Sound application generates calming sounds that gently lull you to sleep. It's also ideal for meditation or for those times when you need to let the stress melt away. One of the best features of the Sleep Sound generator is that it goes everywhere with you—it's as close by as your iPhone. You'll find Sleep Sound simple to use right from the moment it's downloaded. We wanted an application that showcased the audio capabilities of the iPhone. We knew we wanted a sound-effect application of some kind, but we weren't sure about coming up with the sounds in such a short amount of time. Finally we decided on creating a lullaby-type application that would help users sleep, something we were always looking forward to by the end of the day.

The highlight of this application is learning how to loop background sounds. There is also code to work with `UIImageViews` and `UIButtons`.

TIP
You can find the source code for Sleep Sound at `http://appsamuck.com/day14.html`.

Day 15: ZipWeather

Enter a ZIP code, and ZipWeather gives you a weather forecast for that location. The current conditions, the forecast for the following days with highs and lows, and a link to the Yahoo! weather site are all provided. This is a reliable application because all information is provided by the Weather Channel. The fact that forecasts are looked up by ZIP code means you can find weather forecasts for locations before arriving at your destination, giving you more time to prepare for the weather you may face. ZipWeather is sure to be a useful application for almost any iPhone user.

One reason we decided to create a weather-related application was to show people how to pull data off the Internet and interact with it. The key topic featured in this tutorial is the basics of downloading data with `NSURLConnection`. We also cover how to use `UIWebViews`.

TIP
You can find the source code for ZipWeather at `http://appsamuck.com/day15.html`.

Day 16: World Tour

World Tour lets you know exactly when the iPhone Tech Talk World Tour will be in your area. This app keeps you up to date on the tour and allows you to view the stops that the tour will be taking, so you won't miss out. We wanted to create an app about the iPhone Tech Talk World Tour to help spread the word about all the great events Apple does to help developers learn more about programming the iPhone.

We cover lots of good stuff in this tutorial, including opacity with images, using rotation transformations, tiling images, and creating animated wallpapers. We also discuss how to play sounds in a loop.

TIP
You can find the source code for World Tour at `http://appsamuck.com/day16.html`.

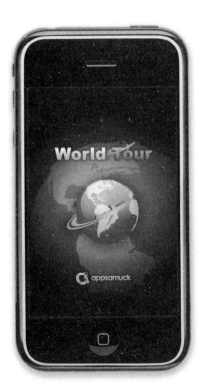

Day 17: Fireball

The Fireball application acts like a screensaver for the iPhone. The screensaver appears as an orange ball of fire floating against a black background, leaving a trail of gray balls in its path. You can use this screensaver to entertain others and show off another neat application. We would have been remiss if we did not cover a bouncing-ball type of demo at some point. But instead of a bouncing ball we did a ricocheting fireball. It's lots of fun, and nobody gets hurt.

This application has a strong focus in using `UIImageViews` and `UIImages`. Again, we took advantage of semitransparent images. This tutorial covers the basics of creating a particle emitter and how to use `setAnimationDidStopSelector` to remove an animation.

TIP
You can find the source code for Fireball at `http://appsamuck.com/day17.html`.

Day 18: Homeland Security

The Homeland Security application acts as an official alert to any Homeland Security advisories. The app appears as a blue screen with the Homeland Security Advisory System heading. Below the heading are five levels of risk of terrorist attacks. The current risk level is highlighted. This application helps you stay aware of any changes in the risk of terrorist attacks, or use it as an interesting conversation starter between family and friends. This is another application that uses information on the Internet to decide what it should show.

Homeland Security is a great application to learn the fundamentals of downloading data using `NSURLConnection`. You can also find out more about `UIImageViews` and working with semitransparent images.

TIP
You can find the source code for Homeland Security at `http://appsamuck.com/day18.html.`

Day 19: Altimeter

If you are a hiker, biker, skier, snowboarder, or climber, you may want to download the Altimeter application. It's important to know your altitude level because it affects oxygen saturation. Anything over 8,000 feet can be dangerous. With this app you can carry your iPhone with you and always know how high up you are. Everyone seemed to be focusing on the latitude and longitude aspects of the iPhone's built-in GPS. But it can also do altitude. We decided we would create an application that did nothing more than find the altitude to try to promote this feature a little more.

Altimeter is a great application to learn more about working with the iPhone's GPS hardware, and it's a great source for finding out more about utility applications.

TIP
You can find the source code for Altimeter at `http://appsamuck.com/day19.html`.

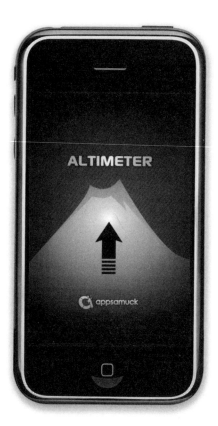

Day 20: Temperature Converter

Memorizing conversion factors is tedious. Even if you memorize the equations to convert degrees, it's difficult to do without a calculator. You may not always have the necessary tools to convert temperatures. With the Temperature Converter application, simply enter the temperature in Fahrenheit, Celsius, or Kelvin degrees. The iPhone then shows you how many degrees that would be in the other systems of measuring degrees. It's a great tool for those interested in weather or traveling abroad and using other measurements of temperature. We noticed that the iPhone had some great hardware features but it didn't have a thermometer. That didn't stop us from creating a thermometer-focused application.

This application explores performing numeric calculations on data and working with UI controls.

TIP

You can find the source code for Temperature Converter at `http://appsamuck.com/day20.html`.

Day 21: iDrum

Do you love music? Do you wish you had a drum but you cannot afford one? This application instantly converts your iPhone into a drum. After purchasing the application, you can play the drums anywhere, anytime. The iDrum application is great for those who want to learn how to play the drums or for those who already know how to. Family and friends will be entertained by the user's musical skills. It's also a fun application to help pass the time! We wanted another audio application and decide to create a virtual drum. It just goes to show you how a simple application can create something special.

This application is about touch and sounds. If you are looking to add either of these to your application, you might want to look into this application.

TIP
You can find the source code for iDrum at `http://appsamuck.com/day21.html`.

Day 22: Pumpkin Face

Kids love pumpkins, Halloween, and iPhones, and the Pumpkin Face application puts all of these together. It's a handy tool to help kids see at night while trick or treating, and it's a wonderful theme for autumn. This app also serves as cool wallpaper for your iPhone. Pumpkin Face helps protect your precious toy in style. The app is fun and friendly and spooky, all at the same time. Your kids will love it, and you will love it. It's inexpensive and family-friendly. We created all of these applications in October, so it's no surprise that a little Halloween fun made its way in.

This application is full of animations, `UIImageViews`, and more.

TIP
You can find the source code for Pumpkin Face at `http://appsamuck.com/day22.html`.

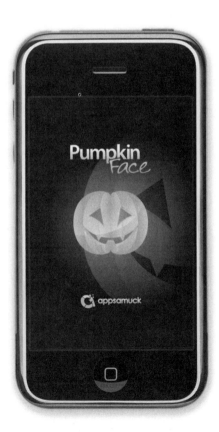

Day 23: Hypno

Hypno is a great optical illusion app that will have you mesmerized by your iPhone in no time. It's a great app to have so you can take it with you wherever you want and show all your friends. Don't get caught looking at Hypno for too long, but make sure you show everyone this great app. It's always fun to play with. This application has a great set of animation spirals that create a mesmerizing optical illusion effect.

Hypno is full of rotating semitransparent images. Each image is randomly sized and placed and each spiral spins at a random speed, creating a fascinating effect.

TIP

You can find the source code for Hypno at `http://appsamuck.com/day23.html`.

Day 24: AmuckColors

If you have ever done any HTML design work, you know how hard it can be to find that perfect color. That's where AmuckColors comes in. We can't think of anything handier than something that fits in your pocket and remembers all of those cryptic HTML color codes for you. It's easy to look up color values on the go, with red, green, and blue values and HTML codes written on every swatch. Our goal was to create an application that hosted an image much larger than the display of the iPhone.

This application shows you how to use the `UIScrollView` to view images larger than the screen. You can also learn more about the `UIToolbar`.

(Special thanks to Bob Stein at `http://visibone.com` for permission to use this image.)

TIP
You can find the source code for AmuckColors at `http://appsamuck.com/day24.html`.

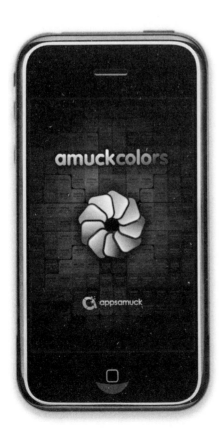

Day 25: Sierpinski

This application allows you to zoom in to one of the most well-known fractals, the Sierpinski triangle. Fractals are infinitely complex sets based on an initial image that is then iterated upon itself, and often presented as two-dimensional. Fractals are always a great way to show off the graphics capabilities of a platform, and the Sierpinski fractal, with its rainbow of colors, is one of the best. The zoom feature uses a mathematical algorithm to continuously redraw the fractal as the levels of magnification intensify. It's a must-have for any fractal, math, art, or programming enthusiast.

This app teaches the user to use `UIImageView`, Quartz graphics, and the basics of fractal geometry.

TIP
You can find the source code for Sierpinski at `http://appsamuck.com/day25.html.`

Day 26: LavaFlow

Remember those "gotta have 'em" things from yesteryear—you know, the disco ball, the bell-bottom jeans, and of course, the lava lamps? Well, we thought we'd mix a little bit of that nostalgia in with today's hottest piece of technology, your iPhone. The result is LavaFlow, the grooviest way to chill out, whether you're in your bedroom at home, on the plane waiting to take off, or just lying in a field smelling the daisies. Kids will love watching those blobs of goo rise and fall over and over again, just like we did with our lava lamps years ago.

This application demonstrates how to play a looping video and shows the basics of working with video files.

TIP

You can find the source code for LavaFlow at `http://appsamuck.com/day26.html`.

Day 27: PhotoFrame

If you don't like the boring, bland framing of the conventional iPhone screen and want to display your photos with the beauty they deserve, you'll want to check out the PhotoFrame application. Using the iPhone screen, PhotoFrame enhances any photo and turns images captured by the iPhone camera into works of art that you can display to your friends and loved ones. PhotoFrame takes the imaging capabilities of the Apple iPhone to the next level. We created this app during the time that everyone was starting to buy digital photo frames for their families for Christmas. We decided we could create an app to do that.

This application takes an image using `UIImagePickerController` and overlays an image of a frame.

TIP
You can find the source code for PhotoFrame at `http://appsamuck.com/day27.html`.

Day 28: DigiClock

DigiClock is a plain-and-simple app that gives you the feel of an old-school alarm clock that you've grown to love over the years. The digital clock is nothing extravagant, just easy to read from any location.

This tutorial covers basic image animation techniques and a touch of transparent images.

TIP
You can find the source code for DigiClock at `http://appsamuck.com/day28.html`.

Day 29: Password Generator

With all the passwords we create today, it's no wonder every developer tries to create the next great password generator. Here is our attempt to do just that. Tell Password Generator whether you want to use numbers, upper- or lowercase letters (or both), and punctuation symbols; specify the length of your desired password; and then touch Generate Password to create a new, completely random password. For extra safety, Password Generator can show the phonetic expansion of your password, reducing the chance that you will mistake a 0 for an o or a number 1 for a lowercase L. Using Password Generator makes it much more difficult for hackers to crack your password-protected account.

In this application you learn about skinning a `UIButton` and working with many of the built-in iPhone UI controls, and there's content on basic animations and random numbers as well.

TIP
You can find the source code for Password Generator at `http://appsamuck.com/day29.html`.

Day 30: DeathCalc

Just in time for Halloween, we created the DeathCalc, which comes with some bad news: It's designed to tell people the statistically most likely date of their demise. It even calculates your time left in seconds so you can watch them ticking away. This is a fun app that is great to show off and impress your friends with. Everyone will want their information to be entered to see when their time will come. Don't be surprised if you start looking at time in a whole different way!

There is a strong focus on working with UI controls and data calculations in this application, and there's some good material on using strings.

TIP

You can find the source code for DeathCalc at `http://appsamuck.com/day30.html`.

Day 31: Moolah

Recession? Depression? Forget about it! Feel better about life with this app that rains money on you. If you've always wanted to swim in money—and who hasn't?—Moolah is just what you need. For our final application we wanted to create something with some nice special effects. We decided on Moolah with its screen full of money. Many of us hope we can strike it big with our mobile apps and have the money just rain on us. Have fun with this entertaining app.

This is a full-featured app that was previously rejected by the App Store. It has been resubmitted with the enhancements that are included in this example.

TIP
You can find the source code for Moolah at `http://appsamuck.com/day31.html`.

Glossary

accelerometer The iPhone responds to motion by using a built-in accelerometer. This is used to detect any changes in orientation, such as when you rotate the device from portrait to landscape. This feedback can be used in applications in many creative ways. For instance, the accelerometer makes it possible to react to shake gestures or to move objects on the screen when the device is tilted.

alpha channel Images that have an alpha channel are images that have transparency information stored in them. Many image formats support alpha channels, and this is a great way to create advanced graphics and user interfaces for your iPhone applications.

animations The `UIImageView` supports using a series of images as an animation. This is a great effect that is very easy to use and always makes an application stand out.

application An application (app for short) is a computer program that executes on a device utilizing the features of the device to perform a task for, serve as a reference for, or entertain a user.

Application Programming Interface (API) An API defines a collection of protocols, interfaces, and delegates that can be used to interact with applications, hardware, and services of the underlying OS.

App Store The App Store is where users can go to easily download iPhone apps. Once you own an application, the App Store automatically notifies you when there's an update. Apple collects a 30 percent royalty and the rest goes to the developers. The App Store can be accessed for the iPhone or from iTunes on the user's desktop.

Bluetooth A communications protocol that is similar to Wi-Fi, except that it is a peer-to-peer technology. It is a local area network connection also known as a personal area network. The iPhone 3.0 SDK offers ad hoc connectivity built on Bonjour-powered data sharing.

Bonjour A general method to discover services on a network. Bonjour can help devices find each other on the same network with ease. With Bonjour, one device can advertise a service, and then other devices can search for that service on the network with the service name alone.

Cocoa Touch Cocoa Touch is the API for creating software applications to run on Apple's iPhone and iPod touch.

Core Animation Most of the UI animation effects you see on the iPhone are created using the Core Animation libraries. For example, when views flip or curl, that's the Core Animation library at work.

Core Data Core Data is a framework that makes working with data far less tedious. Instead of having to manually edit XML, binary, and SQLite objects directly, you can use higher-level entities that represent the same data.

Core Graphics The Core Graphics framework is an API that provides low-level, lightweight 2-D rendering with superb output fidelity. The Quartz 2D API is part of the Core Graphics framework.

Core Location Use the Core Location framework to determine the current latitude and longitude of a device, and to configure and schedule the delivery of location-related events.

firmware This refers to the iPhone operating system. Apple releases updates to the iPhone's firmware regularly. Each firmware is assigned a new version number. To date we have had the following iPhone OS firmware versions: 1.0, 1.1, 2.0, 2.1, 2.2, 3.0, and 3.1.

framework A framework in the iPhone SDK is a software programming library or API. Examples of iPhone SDK frameworks are the Core Location framework and the OpenAL framework.

head-to-head Describes a scenario where two players are playing a game against each other on the same device, usually at the same time.

In App Purchase In App Purchase allows applications to process financial transactions for purchasing content and services from within your application.

Inspector The Inspector is a component of Xcode that allows developers to modify UI control properties. Using the Inspector, you can modify anything from colors to size.

Instruments Instruments is an application for debugging and profiling Mac OS X and iPhone OS code. Instruments helps you understand what is going on behind the scenes of applications.

Interface Builder Interface Builder is an application for designing and testing user interfaces. It is a part of Xcode and allows developers to use a visual editor, instead of code, to create their user interfaces.

iTunes iTunes is Apple's digital media player application. iTunes connects to the iPhone and iPod touch and synchronizes music, video, and apps to the device. It is also used to update the OS firmware on the devices.

localization (i18n) This is also known as internationalization and localization. This feature means applications running on the iPhone can handle different languages and regional differences.

Multi-Touch The technology that allows users to use multiple fingers to control many iPhone OS applications.

NSMutableArray The `NSMutableArray` class creates a modifiable array of objects. This class takes the `NSArray` and adds insertion and deletion options in addition to basic array capabilities.

opacity Refers to how opaque something is. If something is completely opaque, it cannot be seen through. Opaque and transparent are opposites of each other. Many user interface controls in the iPhone SDK have an opacity setting.

OpenAL Short for Open Audio Library, it is an audio API that can process multichannel three-dimensional audio.

OpenGL ES OpenGL for Embedded Systems is a mobile optimized version of the OpenGL 3D graphics API.

OS The iPhone OS stands for the iPhone Operating System. Developers create iPhone applications that are run on top of the iPhone OS. The iPhone OS is made up of many other software libraries, APIs, and applications.

peer-to-peer (P2P) Describes a network situation where two or more systems connect and share responsibilities. Unlike client server connections, a peer in a peer-to-peer configuration will at times act as both client and server. In the iPhone SDK, peer-to-peer is a popular choice for connecting nearby devices over Bluetooth.

PNG A PNG or portable network graphics format file is an image file with an 8-bit transparency alpha channel. It is the native image format of the iPhone SDK.

Quartz When you hear Quartz as it relates to the iPhone, always think graphics. Quartz is the primary 2-D graphics-rendering library for the iPhone—and for Mac OS, for that matter.

SDK The iPhone SDK stands for the iPhone Software Development Kit. Developers can use the iPhone SDK to create applications for the iPhone.

Simulator The iPhone Simulator lets you build and run your iPhone applications on your computer without using a real device. One advantage of the Simulator is that even registered developers can use it. You do not have to be a paid developer to utilize the Simulator.

sprite The general term for an image or graphic object. Sprites are very common in game programming circles.

SQLite SQLite is the database of choice for iPhone applications. It is small, powerful, and free. Support for SQLite is included in Core Data.

Status Bar The iPhone Status Bar contains the icons located at the top of the screen, which give information about the iPhone's current status. Common status information includes Wi-Fi and cellular connectivity. It can also include Bluetooth and remaining battery status.

transparency Transparent objects are clear and can be seen through. Transparent and opaque are opposites of each other. Many objects in the iPhone SDK, such as the `UIImageView`, support transparency.

UDID The UDID is the unique device identifier for an iPhone or iPod touch.

UIAlertView A `UIAlertView` is used to show the user a standardized view containing alert information. It operates as a message box and allows the end user to acknowledge and respond appropriately.

UIButton The `UIButton` class is a `UIControl` that creates a button on the screen. A button can receive and respond to touch events. You can set the title, image, and other properties of the button. You can also assign a separate appearance for each button state.

UIColor A `UIColor` object is used throughout the iPhone SDK to represent color information. It can be used to assign colors to UI elements both at design time and run-time.

UIDevice The `UIDevice` class represents the current device. From this object you can get information about the device, such as unique ID, assigned name, device model, and operating system name and version.

UIImage A `UIImage` object is a high-level way to display image data. You can create images from files, from Quartz image objects, or from raw image data you receive. The UIImage class also offers several options for drawing images to the current graphics context using different blend modes and opacity values.

UIImageView A `UIImageView` object can display either a single image or an animation of a series of images. You can set the frequency and the duration of the animation, and you can start and stop the animation as needed.

UILabel The `UILabel` class creates a read-only text view. You can also use this class to draw either one or multiple lines of text. You have options to modify the appearance of your text as well.

UINavigationBar The `UINavigationBar` is used for navigating up and down through hierarchical content. The `UINavigationBar` is usually shown at the top of the screen. It has options for a back button, a title, and an optional right button. You can apply custom views for any of these.

UIScrollView `UIScrollView` is the base class for any object that needs to display content that is larger than the size of the application's window. It allows the user to scroll and resize the contents.

UITextView The `UITextView` is a user interface control that allows for a scrollable, multiline text region. This control allows display of text using a custom font, color, and alignment, and it also supports text editing. You can use a text view to display multiple lines of text.

UIToolbar The `UIToolbar` class can contain one of many buttons, called toolbar items.

UIView The `UIView` class is a base class that defines structure for drawing and handling events. You can also use a `UIView` class to contain other views.

UIViewController The `UIViewController` class handles the foundation view management for the iPhone. Everything from tab bars to navigation bars and application views are managed by the `UIViewController`. Model views and rotating views are also supported through the `UIViewController`.

UIWebView You use the `UIWebView` class to add Web content control in your application. This control also allows you to move backward and forward in the history of Web pages, and you can set some of the control's options programmatically.

user interface User interface is short for graphical user interface. The user interface can be thought of as the means in which a user interacts with an application. This comprises the buttons and other controls of the app. How does the application get input, and how does it return output? It does this through its user interface.

Wi-Fi Wi-Fi is a shortened form of wireless LAN, or local area network. Wi-Fi is supported by both the iPhone and the iPod touch and many other computing platforms today.

Xcode Xcode is Apple's development environment for creating Mac OS and iPhone OS applications. It is included with every copy of Mac OS X as well.

Index

M

T

Everything You Need to Craft Killer Code for Apple Applications

Whether you are a seasoned developer or just getting into the Apple platform, Wiley's Developer Reference series is perfect for you. Focusing on topics that Apple developers love best, these well-designed books guide you through the most advanced and very latest Apple tools, technologies, and programming techniques. With in-depth coverage and expert guidance from skilled authors who are proven authorities in their fields, the Developer Reference series will quickly become your indispensable Apple development resource.

The Developer Reference series is available wherever books are sold.

Take the Book with You, Everywhere

How to purchase

Go to www.wileydevreference.com and follow the link to purchase the app in iTunes.

Wiley's Developer Reference app is just 99¢ and includes Chapter 21, "Using the Game Kit API" from *Cocoa Touch for iPhone OS 3*. When you're ready for a full Developer Reference book, you can purchase any title from the series directly in the app for $19.99.

Want tips for developing and working on Apple platforms on your iPhone? Wiley's Developer Reference app puts you in touch with the new Wiley Developer Reference series. Through the app you can purchase any title in the series and then read, highlight, search, and bookmark the text and code you need. To get you started, Wiley's Developer Reference app includes Chapter 21 from *Cocoa Touch for iPhone OS 3*, which offers fantastic tips for developing for the iPhone and iPod touch platforms. If you buy a Wiley Developer Reference book through the app, you'll get all the text of that book including a searchable index and live table of contents linked to each chapter and section of the book.

Here's what you can do

- Jump to the section or chapter you need by tapping a link in the Table of Contents
- Click on a keyword in the Index to go directly to a particular section in the book
- Highlight text as you read so that you can mark what's most important to you
- Copy and paste, or email code samples, out of the book so you can use them where and when needed
- Keep track of additional ideas or end results by selecting passages of text and then creating notes and annotations for them
- Save your place effortlessly with automatic bookmarking, which holds your place if you exit or receive a phone call
- Zoom into paragraphs with a "pinch" gesture

Now you know.

Cocoa Touch and iPhone are trademarks or registered trademarks of Apple, In